CW00539841

Nachtjagd

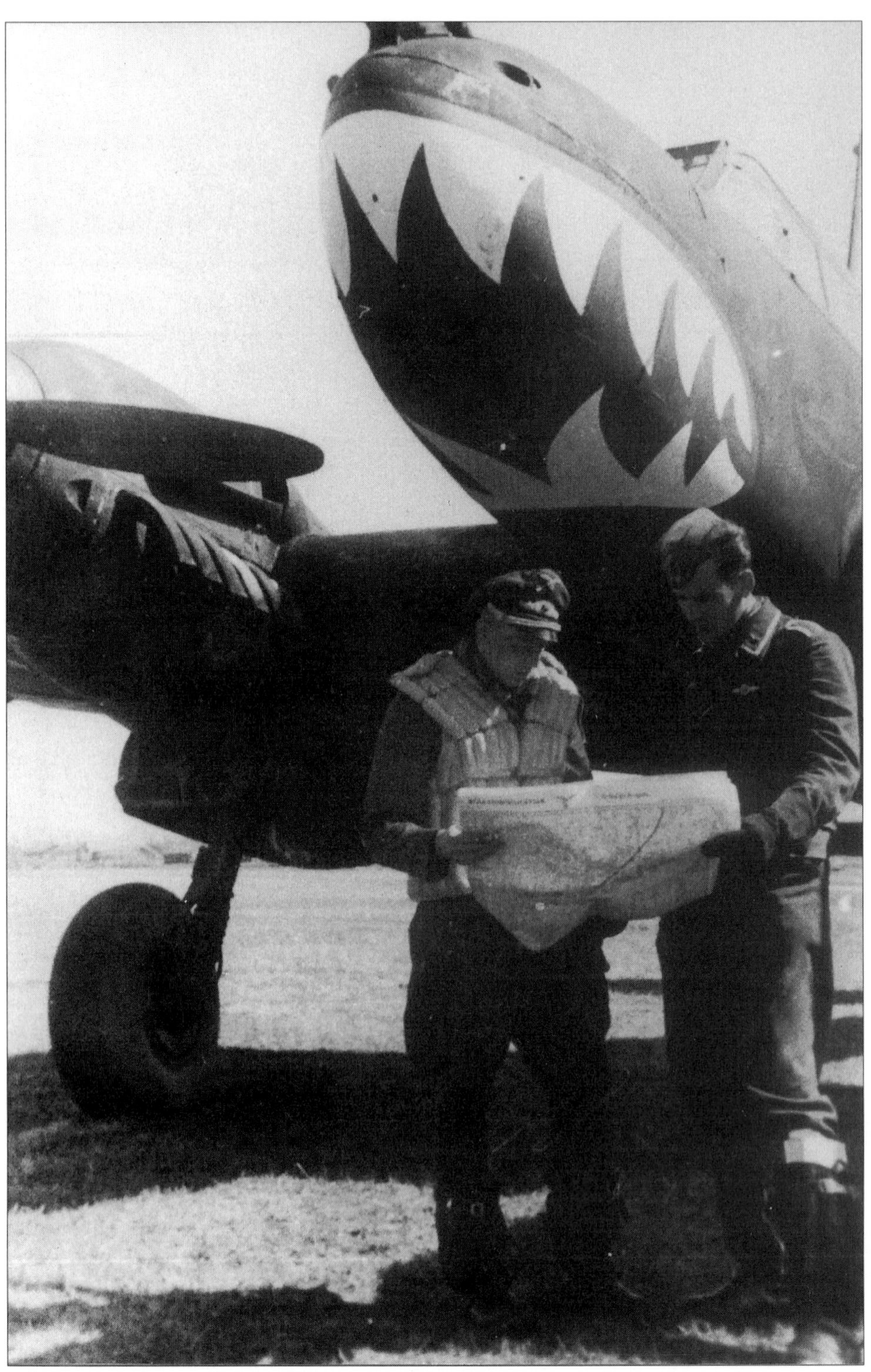

NACHTJAGD

The Night Fighter versus Bomber War over the Third Reich 1939–45

Theo Boiten

The Crowood Press

First published in 1997 by
The Crowood Press Ltd
Ramsbury, Marlborough
Wiltshire SN8 2HR

British Library Cataloguing in Publication Data

A catalogue record for this book is available from the British Library.

ISBN 1 86126 086 5

Front cover painting: oil painting of the destruction of a Lancaster by Ju886 flown by Ofw. Helmut Bunje (4./NJG6) at 19.34 hours on 4/5 December 1944 during a raid on Heilbronn.

Photograph previous page: Lt Martin Drewes with his *Bordfunker* Uffz. Fritz Hrachowina preparing a mission in 4./ZG76 during 1941.

Typeface used: Garamond.

Typeset and designed by
D & N Publishing
Membury Business Park, Lambourn Woodlands
Hungerford, Berkshire.

Printed in Great Britain by The Bath Press.

Contents

Acknowledgements

Many people have helped me over the past seven years in the preparation of this work; fellow researchers and above all dozens of veteran aircrews from both Bomber Command and the Luftwaffe Nachtjagd. I am deeply grateful to them all as without their help it would have been impossible for me to write this book. In the following acknowledgements, I have omitted ranks and decorations of the Allied and Nachtjagd aircrew, which would otherwise overwhelm these pages: John C. Adams (Pilot, 50 Sqn); Gebhard Aders (Historisches Archiv Stadt Köln); Mike Allen (Nav., 141 Sqn); Bruce D. Bancroft (Pilot, 158 Sqn); Ted Baumfield (Special Op., 214 {SD} Sqn); Doug Benbow (WOp., 460 {RAAF} Sqn); Leslie Boot (special Op., 223 {SD} Sqn); Geoffrey Breaden (Nav., 83 {PFF} Sqn); Dick Breedijk; John Brigden (MUG. 149 Sqn); Don Bruce (Obs. 115 Sqn); Helmut Bukowski; Helmut Bunje (pilot III./NJG101 & 4./NJG6); Robert Catt (AG. 466, 640 & 635 Sqns); Hendrik Cazemier; Bob Chester-Master (RG. 514 Sqn); Len Collins (WOp./AG. 149 Sqn); Jim Coman (WOp./AG. 149 & 90 Sqns); Noel 'Paddy' Corry ('A' Flt Cdr 12 Sqn); Ted Cox (WOp./AG. XV Sqn); Hans-Peter Dabrowski; Pieter Davids; Roy Day (Pilot 50 Sqn); Rob de Visser; Horst Diener; Jim Donnan (WOp. 550 Sqn); Arnold Döring (Pilot 2. & 7./JG300, 7./NJG2 & 10./NJG3); Martin Drewes (Pilot III./NJG3 & Gr.Kmdr. III./NJG1); Douwe Drijver; Manfred Eidner (groundcrew & AG. 11./NJG1); Fritz Engau (Pilot & St.Kpt. 5./NJG1); Wolfgang Falck (founding father of Nachtjagd); Kurt Frasch (Bordfunker 6./NJG2); Stanley Freestone (Pilot 142 & 199 Sqns); Otto H. Fries (Pilot II./NJG1); Mrs. Betty George MBE (Blenheim Society); Ken Goodchild (WOp. 51 Sqn); Alex H. Gould (Pilot 61 Sqn); Wyb Jan Groendijk; Fritz Habicht (*Bordfunker* 3./NJG1); Charles Hall (MUG. 207 Sqn); Jack F. Hamilton (MUG. 463 Sqn); Thomas Hampel; Gottfried Hanneck (Pilot 5./NJG1); Chris Harrison (Pilot 515 Sqn); Heinz-Otto Hartmann (NJG1 & NJG2); Engelbert Hasenkamp; Leslie Hay (Pilot 49 Sqn); Gerhard Heilig (Special Op. 101 & 214 {SD} Sqns); Maurice 'Frank' Hemming (FE. 97 Sqn); Peter C. Hinchliffe (Nav. 51 Sqn); Werner Hoffmann (St.Kpt. 5./NJG3 & 4./NJG3, Kmdr I./NJG5); Marcel Hogenhuis; Bill 'Dutchy' Holland (Special Op. 199 {SD} Sqn); Helmut Hörning; Ron James (AG. 90 Sqn, 214 {SD} Sqn); Ab A. Jansen; Dr. Karl-Heinz Jeismann; Alfred Jenner (WOp./AG. 99 Sqn); Wilhelm Johnen (Pilot, St.Kpt. & Kmdr III./NJG6); Graham Jones (Nav. 214 Sqn); Geoffrey Kemp; Charles Kern (Pilot NJG4); Chistian Kirsch; Werner Kock; Fritz E. Krause (Pilot 1./NJGr10); Kurt Lamm (Pilot 5./JG301 & 10./NJG11); Rudy Lang (Special Op. 214 {SD} Sqn); Emil Lechner; Cecil Loughlin (Nav./BA. 149 Sqn); Sectie Luchtmachthistorie Koninklijke Luchtmacht (Den Haag); George Luke (WOp./AG. 106 Sqn); Angus MacAskill (WOp./AG. 40 Sqn); Norman Mackie (Pilot 83 Sqn); Len Manning (AG. 57 Sqn); Dr. Fritz Marktscheffel; Geo Mather (FE. 630 Sqn); Peter Menges; Bernard 'Max' Meyer (Pilot 144 Sqn); Hans Meyer (Pilot 3./NJG3 & St.Kpt. 10./NJG6); Rolf Michelsen (*Bordfunker* 5./NJG2); Mick Mills (AG. 44, 49 & 50 Sqns); Harry Mohin (BA. 425 Sqn); Frank Mouritz (Pilot 61 Sqn); Douglas Mourton (WOp./AG. 102 Sqn); Jan Mulder; John Neville (Nav. 239 Sqn); Peter 'Smoky' Osborne (Nav. 236 Sqn); Bill Pearce (WOp./AG. 100 & 156 Sqns); David Penman (Pilot 44 & 97 Sqns); Alan Penrose (Nav. 157 Sqn); Helmut Persch; Frank Petch (WOp. 550 & 150 Sqns); Peter Petrick; Ken Phelan (AG. 214 {SD} Sqn); Norbert Pietrek (Pilot 2./NJG4 & 10./NJG5); John Price (AG. 150 & 104 Sqns); Frank Pritchard (550 Sqn); Dennis Raby (Pilot 239 Sqn); Robert Ramshaw; Hans Rasper (Pilot 4./NJG1 & NJG101); Willi Reschke (pilot JG301/302); George Reynolds (WOp. 149 Sqn); Albert E. Robinson (Obs. 115 Sqn); Heinz Rökker (Pilot & St.Kpt. 1. & 2./NJG2); Alan F. Scanlan (WOp./AG. 50 Sqn); Kurt Schmidt (AG. 12./NJG1); Walter Schneider (*Bordfunker* II./ NJG1); Ted Smith (AG. 115 & 514 Sqns); Hans-Jakob Schmitz; Gerhard Schubert; Vera Sherring; Peter Spoden (Pilot NJG5 & 6, Gr.Kdr. I./NJG6); Kathryn Squire; Martin Stark; Ted Strange (Nav. 76 Sqn); Karl Strasser; Tom Thackray; Eric Thomason; Gene Thomason (BA. XV & 622 Sqns); Alex Tod (WOp. 460 {RAAF} Sqn); Wout van den Hout; Luit van Kampen; Ad van Lingen; Don E. Webb (Nav./Radar Op. 239 Sqn); Alfred F. Weinke (*Bordfunker* NJG102 & 4./NJG1); Len Whitehead (MUG. 61 Sqn); Len Wood (WOp./AG. 83 Sqn); Robert Woodberry; Jaap Woortman; Franz Zimmermann.

A special word of thanks goes out to my friend and colleague Martin Bowman, who thoroughly proofread the manuscript of this book.

Groningen, September 1996

Preface

'Night fighting! It will never come to that!' The subject was dismissed out of hand when it was raised at a conference of German service chiefs just before the war in 1939. But RAF Bomber Command started attacking German industrial targets in the Ruhr area at night on 15/16 May 1940, followed by further raids during the spring and summer of 1940. Although those early British strategic bombing raids caused little damage, they were a nuisance to the Germans, and clearly demonstrated that anti-aircraft artillery on its own could not provide an efficient defence at night. Thus, on 26 June 1940, Generalfeldmarschall Hermann Göring, C-in-C of the Luftwaffe ordered the creation of Nachtjagd, a night fighting arm. For this purpose, Nachtjagd was equipped with fighter aircraft, searchlights, radar equipment and an extensive ground control organization. With German thoroughness, the new arm swiftly developed into a feared adversary for Bomber Command, and tens of thousands of German men and women were diverted into the night air defence of the Third Reich. But, in spite of the fact that Nachtjagd, both in its defensive and offensive roles, soon succeeded in inflicting mounting losses on its British adversary, it never succeeded in shielding the Reich's industry, towns and cities from the devastating raids which finally transformed the German cities into a wasteland of ruins.

This book aims to create a picture of the development of Nachtjagd in the Reich's aerial defence. It also tries to explain events from the strategic perspective from which the German leaders looked at (air) warfare. In my opinion, this research approach provides the key to the final understanding why Nachtjagd failed to achieve its main goal of providing the Reich with an 'impenetrable roof'.

The evil thing called war is cooked up by elder politicians and military leaders, but it is left to the young generations to fight it out. I have therefore also focused on what it was like to fly in a night bomber aircraft to heavily defended targets in the German Reich, and, on the other hand, on the experiences of the Luftwaffe night fighter crews who hunted the Bomber Command 'heavies'. In order to reach a better understanding of the personal experiences of the tens of thousands of men who flew, fought and often died a violent death in the great night air battles, I have contacted many survivors from both sides. Their personal recollections of those far-off nights, together with the now yellowing photos from their wartime albums, vividly and grippingly illustrate the strategic and tactical developments in the battle for supremacy in the night skies over the Third Reich during World War II.

We hated the bombers, because they destroyed our cities with all their historical treasures. If one, like I personally did, watched beneath our wings how so many German cities were on fire, without being able to do anything appropriate to help, one would probably understand this hatred.

We did not hate the men who flew in these bombers, these men who we characterized as 'comrades from the other side', in whom we saw airmen, who just like ourselves loved to fly, and who in those dark nights with their manifold dangers had to endure the same fears as we had to.

Lt Otto Fries, eighteen night victories in II./NJG1 during 1943–44.

CHAPTER 1

Genesis of a Nightfighter Force

During World War I, the German Air Force experimented with the use of fighter aircraft at night, as did the British and the French. In all, some 25 French and British night bombers were destroyed by German fighter units between early 1917 and the fall of the empire in November 1918. However, the difficulties of intercepting enemy night bombers were so serious that such experience that had been acquired in Germany rapidly sank into oblivion after the end of the war. Moreover, unlike the British, the Germans had failed to develop specialized nightfighter units and a fighter ground control system.

In the fifteen years between 1918 and 1933, the Treaty of Versailles prevented Germany from rearming fully. Yet as soon as the Nazis came to power in January 1933, they set up a large-scale rearmament programme. At the outset, this had to be carried out in secret due to the restrictions of the Versailles treaty. On 16 February 1935, the programme finally lost its undercover character. Reich Chancellor Adolf Hitler declared that Germany was no longer bound by the limitations of the 'dictat' of Versailles and the nation was now able to openly rearm itself.

Hitler had set himself the objective of controlling the Eurasian continent and he was convinced that apart from a strong army and navy, he also needed a powerful air force. First of all, Hitler had to take into account a possible invasion by the surrounding countries, particularly France and Czechoslovakia. These nations could nip the German rearmament programme in the bud. In order to dodge this risk, Germany's Risiko-Luftflotte (Risk Air Fleet), as its new air force was now named, had to be swiftly equipped with bombers as a means of deterring any hostility.

Right at the birth of the Luftwaffe in the mid-thirties, the concept of the Risk Air Fleet ruled out a purely defensive strategy in which a strong fighter force formed the air defence of the homeland. In the event of war, the Luftwaffe was to be used primarily to support a rapid advance of the German Army. According to the German strategic planners, this could be best realized by deploying a huge bomber force against targets in the enemy's hinterland. By cutting off the enemy's front line from his headquarters, communication lines and reserves, German forces should be able to easily knock out their adversary's defences. Thus we see that from the outset, emphasis in Luftwaffe strategy was placed on offence and not on defence. For this purpose, German industry was ordered to concentrate on medium and light (dive) bomber and reconnaissance aircraft and build only a few fighters.

Strategic air defence of the Third Reich by fighter aircraft was considered to be of secondary importance by the Luftwaffe High Command; the Air Force's offensive principles suppressed

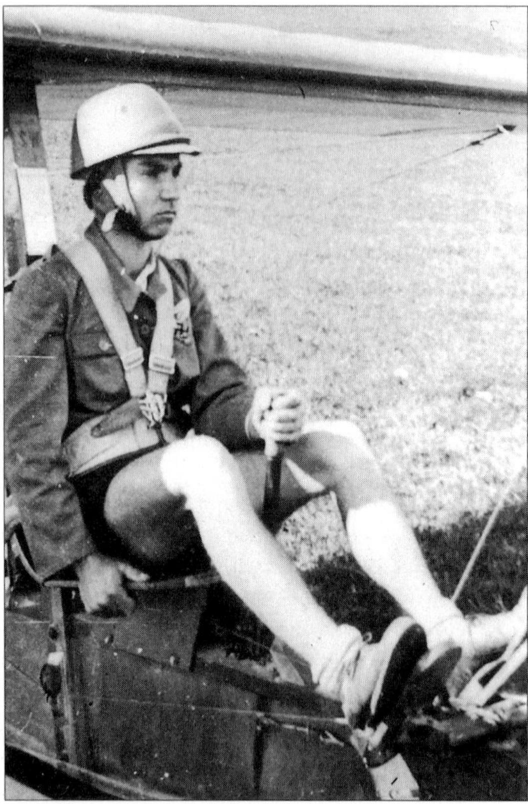

This is how it started for thousands of young men who later served in the Luftwaffe. Here Hitler Youth Alfred Weinke gets his first taste of flying in a glider during 1940. Weinke went on to be trained as a Bordfunker *and served in NJG102 and 4./NJG1 during 1944–45.* Coll. Alfred F. Weinke.

considerations of a more defensive nature. The Wehrmacht was preparing to wage war in a few swift and victorious *Blitzkriege* and in this mode of thought there was hardly any room for defensive contemplations. Moreover, when making preparations for war, the German supreme command disregarded almost completely any possibilities of Allied night bombing developing on a heavy scale.

Only a small-scale organization for the fighter defence of Germany had been set up before the war, but it was still under construction until well into 1940. During the 'Phoney War' this radar-equipped defence line sufficed by day. At night, it was a different story altogether and the fighters proved almost impotent against the few British aircraft that dared to penetrate German airspace.

The major burden of defence against enemy bombers, both by day and by night, was borne by anti-aircraft artillery (flak) units. Flak had produced the best results against night bombers during World War I and in the Spanish Civil War. Although shortly after the outbreak of war in 1939, flak proved to be rather ineffective at night and against high altitude targets, the Germans continued to place strong emphasis on flak throughout the war. It was not until 1944 that the Flak arm was to gain substantial results against bomber formations, mainly against the Americans in daylight.

The only night defence of vital war industries was established in the Ruhr Valley as the Germans considered this area to be the most logical target for British and French night bombers. By the end of 1939, a series of searchlight and Flak batteries stretching from Münster to Stuttgart had been completed and was baptized the 'Luftverteidigungszone West' (Aerial Defence Zone West). These Flak regiments were considered to be the Luftwaffe's crack units and their vitally important role in warding off any enemy aircraft was inflated by German propaganda. And undeservedly so, as would become painfully apparent in the ensuing war years. After inspecting one of these Flak units on 9 August 1939, Generalfeldmarschall Göring was even tempted to make his famous statement that no enemy aircraft would reach the Ruhr. Should this ever happen, the German people could call him Meyer (Meyer being a common name among German Jews).

During 1938 and the spring of 1939, experimental 'Nachtjagd Staffeln' (Nightfighter Flights) were established in several day fighter Geschwader (Wings) to ward off eventual future Czech, French or British night bombing raids. Equipped with the single-engined Messerschmitt Bf109 day fighter however, these 'Mondlicht Staffeln' (Moonlight Flights) were hardly able to carry out night sorties. The Bf109, which could not be flown blind, was unsuitable for the role of combating enemy aircraft at night. But for two Staffeln, these units returned to daytime operations shortly before the invasion of Poland and the outbreak of war. Thus, on the eve of W.W.II., only two 'Versuchsnachtjagd Staffeln' (Experimental Nightfighter Flights) were operational in the German Air Force.

Just like the Luftwaffe, the RAF had concentrated on the development of a bomber force during the interwar period. Chief of the Air Staff in the 1920s, Sir Hugh Trenchard, had made a decisive impact on the thinking about the role of the bomber. The RAF relied on its bombers to find and destroy any target in the enemy's hinterland whilst flying in close and self-defending formation. 'The bomber always gets through' was the core of the thinking of the day in Great Britain. It was even thought that air power alone would be able to bomb the enemy into submission by breaking the morale of his workforce.

During the 1920s and 1930s, the RAF was organized along regional lines in the Air Defence of Great Britain (ADGB). Due to the rapid expansion of the Air Force, this was changed during 1936 when the RAF was split up into Bomber, Fighter, Training and Coastal Commands. Bomber Command units were mainly based at aerodromes in East Anglia, as from these counties the bombers had the shortest flight to Germany. The coming strategic bomber offensive was to be waged from this 'Bomber Country'.

Once war had been declared in September 1939, the RAF tentatively dispatched the first night sorties to the Reich's territory, although official British strategy prohibited the bombing of German territory for fear of Luftwaffe reprisals against cities in the United Kingdom. As a result the RAF only flew sporadically into German airspace, and with the sole purpose of dropping propaganda leaflets. These nocturnal intruders could not induce the Luftwaffe High Command into creating a nightfighter force. When the subject of night fighting was raised at a conference of German service chiefs just before the war, according to General Kammhuber it was dismissed out of hand with the words: 'Night fighting! It will never come to that!' This indifferent attitude did not change during the first months of the war, as is illustrated by the following anecdote. From 1 September 1939, Oblt Johannes 'Mäcki' Steinhoff served as commander of the still operational Versuchsnachtjagd Staffel 10./(N)JG26 flying Bf109s. At the end of the month, he was summoned to travel to Berlin, to attend a Luftwaffe meeting on the various problems faced by the experimental night fighting unit. Steinhoff was asked by Göring to explain why he had not succeeded in shooting down the few British night intruders. After Steinhoff had pleaded for better navigational equipment and interception procedures, the Generalfeldmarschall ordered him to sit down and then went on to belittle him with the words: 'You will have to gain much more experience before you will be able to join in this discussion'. Subsequently, nothing was done to solve the problems of experimental night fighting.

Due to the over-optimistic mood of the majority of the Luftwaffe leadership at the time, the possibility of an enemy air offensive by night was rejected as fantasy. Although, remarkably, the High Command did contemplate using Luftwaffe bombers by night. The night bomber featured prominently in Luftwaffe pre-war strategic planning, though this concept was not used operationally until the second half of the Battle of Britain, with the launch of the night *Blitz* on London and other cities in England.

After the successful campaign in Poland, Göring assumed that Germany would win the war within a year, and therefore did not see the need for spending large amounts of labour, resources and money on the development of new Luftwaffe equipment. Hence, on 9 February 1940, he announced a freeze on the development of any new aircraft and technical equipment that would not be ready for frontline duty within a year. This was accompanied by an order to the German aircraft industry to produce the maximum possible number of existing types, in an effort to force victory during 1940. As a result, almost all technological innovation in the German aircraft industry ground to a halt. The fatal consequences of this short term policy emerged after the summer of

Early Luftwaffe night-fighting experiments during 1939–1940 were carried out with the single-engined Bf109D-1 and Bf109E in 10./(N)JG26, 10./(N)JG53 and IV./(N)JG2, but to little avail. Depicted here is Bf109E 'Black 18' of 2./JG1, a similar machine to those used in the experiments. Underneath its fuselage the Peilgerät IV *is fitted, with which experiments were carried out during 1941. This was a radio transmitter and receiver to facilitate Identification Friend or Foe (IFF) and to guide these single-engined fighters from the ground. IFF remained a severe problem for Luftwaffe air defence, and especially for Nachtjagd, throughout the war.* Coll. Helmut Maul, via Rob de Visser.

1940 when the Luftwaffe was confronted with the beginning of the British strategic bombing offensive. The development of new aircraft, radars and other equipment for nocturnal interception had already been seriously delayed by the autumn of 1940 and the creation of a 'nightly roof' over Germany ran into serious difficulties.

Whilst attempting to attack German ports in daylight during the second half of 1939, Bomber Command suffered heavy losses at the hand of radar-directed Messerschmitt Bf109s and 110s. These painfully shattered the RAF pre-war strategic concept: apparently 'the bomber could not get through', or at least not by day. The RAF therefore decided that a future bomber offensive against targets in the Reich could only be conducted at night, as daytime losses simply were too heavy. At night, losses amongst the leaflet-dropping Whitleys had proved to be very light against the Luftwaffe flak and fighter defences. The devastating 1940 Luftwaffe raid on Rotterdam finally caused the British War Cabinet to exchange the leaflets for bombs. Thus, almost immediately after the German invasion of the Low Countries and France, Bomber Command commenced a series of night raids against military targets in

Germany. At last, the gloves were off. F/O. Bernard 'Max' Meyer joined 144 Squadron as a pilot at the beginning of 1939. He reflects on the first bombing attacks against targets in the Reich:

> On 11 May we were detailed to bomb the railway yards at München Gladbach in an attempt to slow up the German advance. These were really pioneering days for the RAF. Few people had much experience of flying long distances at night, sometimes in appalling weather conditions, let alone against highly efficient enemy defences. To find our way, we flew by dead-reckoning navigation and by map reading if we could see the ground. The sophisticated navigational aids did not become available until much later in the war. On the raid to München Gladbach we flew at about 3,000ft [900m] crossing the coast just to the north of Rotterdam. We were astonished and horrified to see so many places on the ground, on fire. I particularly remember seeing what appeared to be a large passenger ship lying beached in flames on the shore. The flight was in fact rather uneventful. We encountered searchlights and flak in the target area but no more than expected. In fact we received a much hotter reception from the British Navy when we flew over the top of one of our own convoys shortly before we crossed the English coast on our way back. Our next trip was to Dortmund in the Ruhr. The Ruhr was very strongly defended with numerous concentrations of searchlights and anti-aircraft guns of every description. Needless to say, it was not a popular target. However, perhaps the most frustrating thing about it was the thick industrial haze which, aggravated by the glare of searchlights, made it impossible to identify anything with any degree of accuracy.
>
> Nobody liked going to the Ruhr as you can imagine. With the retreat of the Allied armies the pace of our operations increased considerably with attacks on targets most likely to slow the enemy advance. By the end of June I had added a further ten sorties to my total. I believe it was about this time that we began to realize that this sort of tempo was likely to go on. We were suffering casualties of course, but morale in the squadron was good, and as far as I can remember there was little evidence of stress. It was always a shock of course, to lose a friend, but, we did not dwell on these things and were always 'optimists' as far as our own futures were concerned.
>
> With the fall of France and the looming threat of invasion our targets switched to the Channel ports and concentrations of invasion targets. Once that threat had passed, we began ranging much further afield to military and

144 Squadron aircrew posing with a Hampden I at Hemswell in July 1940. This unit kept flying the Hampden on operations until January 1943, by which time it had lost 109 aircraft. Coll. Max Meyer.

industrial targets in mainland Germany. I see on looking through my Flying Log Book that we 'visited' all the well known target areas like Hamburg, the Dortmund–Ems Canal, Cologne, Kiel, Hanover, Berlin, Leipzig etc. As the year went on the weather became progressively worse. Our meteorological forecasts were frequently completely wrong because no one could tell what was happening to the weather to the east of us and over Germany. Meteorological reconnaissance by Spitfires and Mosquitos was still a year or so away and so we really more often than not flew into the unknown – sometimes with quite frightening results.

I well remember such an occasion. Kiel was the target. The battlecruiser *Tirpitz* was reported as having moved into dock there. When we arrived over Kiel at about 11,000ft [3,300m] – we knew we were there because of the glare of searchlights and the amount of flak coming up – the whole area was covered by a thick layer of cloud. Having decided to go down to get below the cloud base to identify the target, I set the forecast barometric pressure for ground level on my altimeter, which had been given at the meteorological briefing, and set off down through the clouds flying by instruments. When we reached 2,000ft [600ft] according to the altimeter, and were still in thick cloud I eased the aircraft into a shallower descent as a precaution, which was just as well, because although we still had 1,000ft [300m] of height recorded on the altimeter, we shot out of the murk to find that we were no more than 200ft [60m] or less above the ground – the forecast barometric pressure was of course, way out. Looking back on those early days I would say that the appalling unforecasted weather we encountered at times was even more difficult to overcome than the highly efficient German defences, and probably accounted for a large percentage of our losses.

Max Meyer flew his final operation of his tour with 144 Squadron on 4 September 1940, a 'gardening' (minelaying) trip to Stettin in the Baltic. He concludes:

I was put down for another trip two nights later and was almost on my way out to my aircraft when my Squadron Commander came down to the Flights to say that my trip was cancelled. I was somewhat taken aback, thinking I had done something wrong, but he said I was not to go because I had done enough, and my tour of operations was ended. I was surprised because up till then there had been no such thing as a set number of operations for a 'tour' which was a word none of us had heard of before. We obviously talked about this amongst ourselves, and had assumed that we would just go on operating indefinitely. However, someone, somewhere, had decided that bomber crews would have to be limited to a certain number of 'trips' and from now on this would be thirty operations or 200 hours of operational flying.

One other crew was taken off that night, since we had both carried out thirty-seven operational sorties. So ended my first tour and after some very welcome leave, I was posted to the Hampden Operational Training Unit as an instructor engaged in training new crews.

To sum up, those of us who came through those early days of the war, flying obsolescent aircraft with poor equipment and few navigational aids, pioneering long distance night flying under war conditions and in often extremely bad weather, were generally surprised that we survived… I am sure I was.

Though the early raids were mere pinpricks compared to the devastating bombing offensive that came later, they soon laid bare the ineffectiveness of the German Flak arm. These Bomber Command attacks caused the Gauleiters of the German cities to complain to Adolf Hitler which in return politically embarrassed Göring. Hence, on 26 June 1940 during a meeting in The Hague, Generalfeldmarschall Göring ordered the establishment of a Nightfighter Arm or 'Nachtjagd'. The strategic task of the new arm was to shield German war industry and cities from night attack. Hermann Göring even stated on this occasion that air defence at night was 'the Achilles heel of the Luftwaffe'. Hauptmann

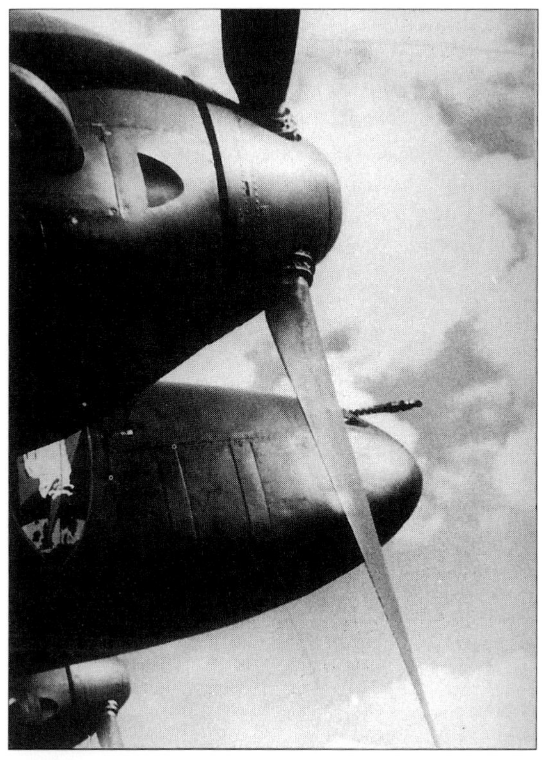

Bf110C of Hptm. Wolfgang Falck, St.Kpt. 2./ZG76, at Jever in early 1940. During this period, Falck and his unit experimented with night interceptions of British aircraft over Denmark, which in June 1940 led to his appointment as CO of the first nightfighter wing, NJG1. The family crest of Falck, seen here on the nose of his aircraft, later in 1940 formed the basis of the famous Nachtjagd crest. Coll. Wolfgang Falck.

Wolfgang Falck, who had gained experience with experimental interceptions of British bombers at dusk and at night earlier in the year, was appointed CO of the first Nachtjagdgeschwader (NJG1).

In order to improve the management of the rapidly expanding arm, the Erste Nachtjagd Division (First Night Fighting Division) had been established on 17 July 1940, with its HQ at Zeist in The Netherlands. Oberst Joseph Kammhuber was entrusted with the setting up of the division. Kammhuber was the right man in the right place. Although he had no previous experience with air warfare at night, he was given this command as he had won his spurs as an excellent organizer before the war. Moreover, he had personally gained some experience in blind flying when he served as CO of KG51 during the Battle of France. Kammhuber was now to further expand the new arm and create the conditions for technical and tactical development necessary to keep abreast of the RAF night bombing campaign.

At the outset Oberst Kammhuber was luckier than most senior commanders in the German armed forces. He was given ample powers, and with them, the opportunity to build up his night fighting organization without let or hindrance from any outside influence. He was in sole charge of all night fighting activity in the Luftwaffe. Additionally, when he was appointed General der Nachtjagd in April 1941 he also had a seat in the councils of the Higher Command, where he was able to push his own ideas through. This position carried two outstanding advantages in that demands for new equipment could be ratified and presented at once to industry and, secondly, operational experience gained by his Nachtjagd crews could be used immediately to bring about continuous improvements in tactics, equipment and organization.

Kammhuber envisaged a dual Nachtjagd concept as both a defensive and an offensive force. The offensive, long range, force (Fernnachtjagd) had a preferential status in his plans, as he stated in 1940: 'In the Fernnachtjagd, one looks up the enemy in his aerodromes and tries to destroy him there. A wasps' nest is best eliminated when one destroys it when the wasps are in it or by blocking the hole through which they fly in and out, so that the wasps cannot hive off at all. When one fails to do this, there is nothing else one can do but to chase after every individual wasp'. Yet, several circumstances prevented Kammhuber from forging Fernnachtjagd into an effective arm, as described in Chapter Two.

The second pillar of Nachtjagd was to be the defensive, short-range night fighting force or Nahe Nachtjagd. The Reich territory, and particularly the vital war industries in the Ruhr Valley, had to be provided with a nightly roof. For this purpose, the defensive Nachtjagd was being expanded rapidly by the end of 1940. Many units flying the twin-engined Messerschmitt Bf110C *Zerstörer* aircraft were converted to night fighting duties after the type's debacle during the Battle of Britain. The Bf110's heavy armament, speed, reliability and agility made it an ideal night fighting aircraft in 1940, although its effectiveness was reduced when Bomber Command was re-equipped with fast, four-engined heavy bombers, starting in 1941. However, in the absence of sufficient numbers of a better alternative, the 110 remained the backbone of Nachtjagd through most of the war. In addition to the Bf110C, the arm was equipped with modified bombers such as Dornier Do17Zs and Junkers Ju88Cs. A few Bf109Es also remained in service, as P/O. Churchill experienced on 2/3 September 1940, when he flew Hampden P4370 of 144 Squadron on a sortie to bomb Ludwigshaven:

> Flying in over Belgium, we were picked up by a large number of searchlights between Antwerp and Maastricht (on previous trips we had not

Oblt Werner Steib (on left) poses with two of his comrades of I./NJG1 at Gilze-Rijen airfield in the summer of 1940. Streib claimed the first official Nachtjagd victory in W.W.II. on 19/20 July 1940, when he shot down Whitley V P5007 of 51 Squadron west of Osnabrück. Streib went on to become Kommandeur of I./NJG1 on 7 October of that year and contributed decisively to the development of the infant arm during the pioneering years. He became Kommodore of NJG1 on 1 July 1943 and ended the war with sixty-eight confirmed victories. Coll. Gemeentearchief Arnhem via Wolfgang Falck.

seen many searchlights in this area). Evasive action was ineffective. No flak. After two minutes of aerobatics, we were attacked by an Me109 from astern. Three attacks were made, the first two without firing from the 109. My own rear gunner was firing continually. On the last attack a burst of cannon fire raked the aircraft. The gunners and W/Op. were killed, both engines and the fuselage were on fire, flames in the cockpit, and the tail was shot up. A shell through the artificial horizon took off the top of my navigator's head. The aircraft went into a vertical dive out of control, the hatch jammed half open and I was half-in, half-out of the aircraft but got stuck. I was finally pulled out by the parachute, minus boots, wrist watch, etc. My ankle hit on the tail plane.

P/O. Churchill ended up at Stalag Luft III Sagan, from where he escaped during the Great Escape. He was caught by the Germans again and was lucky not to be murdered.

On the German side, Ofw. Hans Rasper was one of Nachtjagd's pioneers. A pre-war professional

Due to the severe losses that the Bf110 Zerstörer *suffered in daylight operations during the Battle of Britain and in the first phases of the Russian campaign, many of these units were incorporated into Nachtjagd. 2. and 3./ZG1 formed I./NJG1 in the autumn of 1940; 1./ZG2 became 4./NJG2 in the same period, whilst parts of II./ZG2 were incorporated into II./NJG3 some time later. I./ZG76 became II./NJG1 at the end of August 1940, after having suffered severe losses in bomber-escort missions during the Battle of Britain. V./Lehrgeschwader 1 became I./NJG3 on 1 October 1940. II./ZG76 was incorporated into Nachtjagd as III./NJG3 at the end of 1941 and finally, I./ZG26 became I./NJG4 in April 1942. Depicted here is a formation of Bf110C-2s of 4./ZG76 during a daylight mission in 1941. This unit became 7./NJG3 in late 1941.* Coll. Rob de Visser.

Whitley T4134 GE–T of 58 Squadron took off from Linton-on-Ouse at 23.25 hours on 10 September 1940 for a raid on Bremen but no further message was received from it after take off. P/O. J.E. Thompson crash-landed the aircraft somewhere on the northern German coast and the crew were all taken prisoner. Coll. Peter Petrick.

pilot who joined the still 'under-cover' Luftwaffe at the end of 1933, Hans was trained as a fighter pilot during 1939–40. On completion of his final courses, he was posted to the 4th Staffel of the recently formed NJG1 at Gütersloh in the summer of 1940. Over the next year and a half, he flew on operations from Deelen, Schiphol, Bergen aan Zee, Leeuwarden and Wittmundhafen, amassing some 160 sorties. Rasper claimed a Wellington shot down into the North Sea off Egmond at 23.30 hours on 15 December 1940 as his first kill. This in fact was probably a Whitley, as Bomber Command lost two Whitleys, from 77 and 102 Squadrons, on this night. War reporter Klapproth wrote the following account of Rasper's first *Abschuss* (kill) for the German press:

> Now after he has gained a certain distance from the *Abschuss* of a Tommy, whose tail gunner put up a good but desperate fight and wrecked the right engine of his *Zerstörer*, Rasper speaks of the matter in such a calm way, as if it had been nothing to get excited about at all. With the same businesslike quiet Rasper has also told us about the time during his training days when he was forced to bail out of his training aircraft after a mid-air collision with the aircraft flown by one of his comrades.
>
> During the *Abschuss* of the Wellington it had almost come to another bailing out. The matter was as follows: Rasper and his aircraft had been directed to a British bomber, which Flight Control had detected. At medium altitude, he came across the adversary, heading in the same direction but a bit higher. The aircraft was recognized as a bomber of the Vickers-Wellington type by its rudder at the end of the fuselage that looked like a shark-fin. The British tail gunner did not seem to be very vigilant. In jest, his *Bordfunker* [radio

General Kammhuber (on left) hangs the much coveted Ritterkreuz around Major Walter Ehle's neck, who at that time served as Gruppen Kommandeur of II./NJG1 at St. Trond, 29 August 1943. During the pioneering days of 1940, Ehle had been one of the first Luftwaffe pilots to shoot down a British aircraft at night, a Wellington of either 37 or 75 Squadron on 20/21 July 1940. By late August 1943, he had accumulated thirty-four night and three daytime victories and was one of the leading lights of the Nachtjagd arm. Coll. Otto H. Fries.

operator], Uffz. Erich Schreiber, told Hans over the intercom: 'Now I want to see you make a sharp attack'. Rasper positions the aircraft almost underneath the Wellington, pulls up and hangs directly behind the Tommy. A burst of fire hits the Wellington in its body. Now the tail gunner definitely is wide awake, as from the tail turret, this dangerous hornets' nest, lines of tracer spray and bore into the fuselage and wings.

In a second attack Rasper aims for the left engine of the Briton. On no account should this big bird get home. Short flames flicker from the spots where the bullets have struck, the aircraft starts to burn. Once more the sprayer is opened, the salvoes lash into the fuselage and away over the right engine. The Tommy's slight evasive action has been of no use and the guns of the tail gunner now remain silent. 'It's on fire' has in the meantime been reported by the radio operator to the Ground Control Station, and now they watch how their adversary breaks up into three parts and like a giant torch crashes into the sea. On the surface of the sea the fire continues to burn. The mission has really cut in.

The flight back was a story in itself. The crew knows that their aircraft has been left with

Together with the Wellington, Blenheim and Hampden, the Whitley formed the backbone of Bomber Command during the pioneering years of 1940–41. Depicted here is a Whitley V, probably of 10 Squadron. Coll. Tom Thackray.

something from the return fire of the tail gunner, as the metallic 'click' of bullets smashing into their aircraft was only too audible. The number of revs of the right engine falls back all the time, finally Rasper has no choice left but to shut down the engine. Fortunately, the left engine performs normally. The hydraulics of the undercarriage are unserviceable. He can still pump it out, but to retract it is not possible any more. In the event of a possible touch-and-go, it would be curtains for the crew as this is hardly possible with the undercarriage folded out. The darkness makes landing even more hazardous. The crew considered whether or not to bail out, the *Funker* puts his radio documents and other navigational resources into the pockets of his flyer overalls and gets ready to bail out. Still, Hans is not ready yet to give it up. Over the radio the airfield has been informed of the impending emergency landing. Down on the ground, the fire-engine and the ambulance car stand in readiness. Hans is resolutely determined to save the valuable machine.

During the final approach he has to apply a bit of power to the damaged engine, and despite the fact that the number of revolutions is much too low, it works out for a while and this makes the landing easier. The aircraft has hardly touched down when the right engine cuts. It has only just held out long enough and it even is a smooth landing, the *Funker* congratulates his driver.

On a close inspection of the machine, twenty-two holes were counted, two fuel tanks had been shot through and near the right side-pedal a gaping hole was found in the fuselage

Fw. Hans Rasper of 4./NJG1, one of Nachtjagd's first aces with eight confirmed night victories from 1940 through to early 1942.
Coll. Hans Rasper.

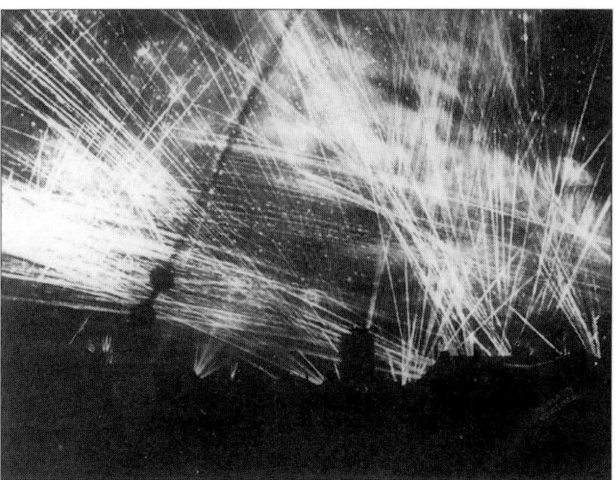

Until the end of 1941, Bomber Command's main foes over the Third Reich were searchlights and flak. A typical flak barrage is shown here during a night raid on Emden in 1941.
Coll. Emil Lechner.

> covering. Damn it, this could easily have been curtains for the crew. Next morning, both men were indemnified by the congratulations of the Geschwaderkommodore.

In the course of the next six months, Fw. Rasper went on to become one of Nachtjagd's first aces with four more Wellingtons, a Blenheim and a Whitley shot down. After his seventh *Abschuss*, Wellington T2996 of 103 Squadron (F/O. Chisholm and crew killed) on 12/13 June 1941, Göring (now Reichsmarschall) awarded him the 'Bowl of honour for exceptional achievements in the Air War'. His eighth victim, on 21 January 1942 was once more a Wellington. Aged thirty-one, Hans Rasper (now Oberfeldwebel) was then posted to a nightfighter training unit and served as an instructor for the next three years. He became operational once more in early 1945 in NJG101 and claimed a four-engined bomber as his ninth and final victim over Nuremberg on 30 March 1945. Later promoted to Leutnant, Rasper flew his last sortie, a ground-attack mission on 26 April 1945, when his aircraft was caught in radar-directed American flak at low level. He managed to bail out and was immediately taken POW, but his *Funker* was found dead near the wreckage of their aircraft.

The main problem the Nachtjagd pioneers Kammhuber and Falck faced was how to get their nightfighters to within firing range of the British bombers. The young arm had to overcome almost insurmountable barriers, as tracking down enemy bombers without the aid of specialized equipment was like looking for a needle in a haystack. Kammhuber realized that he needed a supporting organization to trace incoming British aircraft. For this purpose he set up the Flugmeldedienst. This organization consisted of listening posts equipped with acoustic aids to detect aircraft on the main routes of Bomber Command. In order to protect the industrial centres in the Ruhr, the Germans now turned to the most obvious instrument: the searchlights. During the summer of 1940, a belt of searchlights was constructed in this area, behind which nightfighters patrolled. Whenever a Flugwache (a listening post of the Flugmeldedienst) sounded the alarm, a nightfighter would be scrambled to patrol behind a battery of searchlights. Once a bomber was caught by a searchlight, the nightfighter had to shoot it down. This system was called Helle (illuminated) Nachtjagd, or *HeNaJa*. A second belt was constructed to the west of Berlin to protect the Reich capital.

After a few bombers were lost to the *HeNaJa* defences in the Ruhr, the British crews realized that they were ambushed in this area. To avoid this danger, the bomber crews began using more dispersed routes to the Ruhr Valley. Thus, Kammhuber had no alternative but to build a long chain of searchlights in north-west Germany, stretching from north to south. This defensive line, which was soon christened 'Kammhuber Line' by Bomber Command crews, was divided into separate boxes, or 'Nachtjagd Räume'. Each sector that was covered by a searchlight battery and one nightfighter aircraft constituted a Nachtjagd Raum. Kammhuber envisaged that the bulk of the incoming bombers would be shot down by nightfighters patrolling in the *HeNaJa* belt. Those enemy aircraft that succeeded in penetrating the defensive belt were to be destroyed by flak over the targets.

The most serious problem was, however, how to intercept Bomber Command aircraft in adverse weather conditions. *HeNaJa* had many disadvantages. Searchlights could only effectively illuminate their target aircraft on clear nights; the *Würzburg* radar that guided the searchlights only had a limited range, and only one nightfighter at a time could be deployed per Raum. Moreover, the Germans had not yet developed a reliable IFF (Identification Friend or Foe) system. Consequently, the fighter controllers in the Nachtjagd

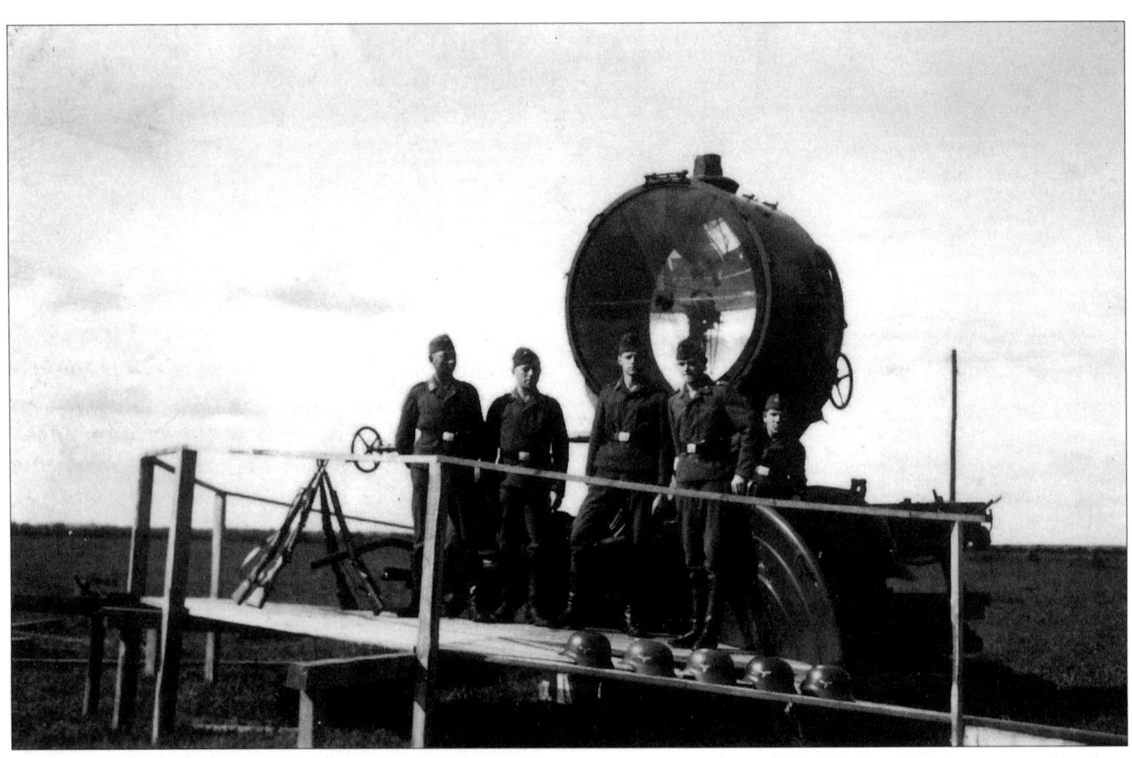

Searchlight with its five-man crew near Vechta airfield, 1941.
Coll. Engelbert Hasenkamp.

A few of the pioneers of the strategic bombing offensive. Aircrew from 51 Squadron pose in front of a Whitley V in early August 1941. Note the squadron badge, a wild goose. Sitting front row, fifth from left, is Sgt Brian Wildgoose (2nd pilot), who was shot down on his first operational sortie to Hanover, one day after his twentieth birthday, by Oblt Helmut Lent of 4./NJG1 on 14/15 August 1941. The whole crew of Whitley Z6819 perished in the North Sea off Schiermonnikoog Island. Coll. Geoffrey Kemp.

Räume often could not distinguish between friendly fighters and enemy bombers.

Kammhuber did not have any detailed technical knowledge of radar systems and the potential of radio detection, while the available *Würzburg A* ground radars were being claimed by the Flak arm for their fire control. Nevertheless, General Wolfgang Martini, who was in command of the Luftwaffe's Signals and Communications network, handed over six *Würzburgs* to the Nachtjagd for experiments in October 1940. During the same month, three experimental Nachtjagd Räume were created on the Bomber Command routes to the Ruhr. In these sectors, one *Würzburg* radar was used to get a fix on incoming bombers, while a second one would then direct the Raum's searchlights. The nightfighter patrolling in the Raum was the final link as it had to shoot the illuminated bomber down. The data coming in from the Flugmeldedienst were now being used to double-check the information from the *Würzburg* radars, and the Flugmeldedienst retained this position until the end of the summer of 1943.

This was how radar-directed Helle Nachtjagd was supposed to operate in theory. In reality, however, it usually turned out to be a different story altogether. The bombers used to pass the searchlight zone at full speed or they completely avoided the Kammhuber Line altogether. Thus, nightfighters laying in wait behind the sectors only rarely scored a kill. Don Bruce, Sgt Observer in 115 Squadron during 1942, wrote the following account on the shooting down of a Wellington of his squadron on the night of 10/11 May 1941 by a German nightfighter which clearly describes the Helle Nachtjagd interception method:

The weather in the British Isles on Saturday 10 May 1941 was fine with little or no cloud. Visibility was good and similar conditions obtained on the Continent with some high and medium cloud over north-west Germany. There would be a full moon that night. On the bomber squadrons the usual morning routine activities were taking place. Marham air base in Norfolk was reverberating with the noise of Wellington bombers bearing the code letters KO as 115 Squadron crews lifted off on short cross country flights to air test their machines, equipment and guns.

Twenty-six-year-old Sgt John Anderson touched down on the grass airfield around midday in Wellington R1379 KO–B having completed his air test. After taxying to his dispersal point he and his five-man crew clambered down the ladder to wait for transport back to the Flights. John Anderson, an experienced operational pilot, had recently taken command of this new, combat-inexperienced crew. He had flown three operational flights with them. The second pilot was a twenty-year-old Australian, Sgt Alex Kerr. Sgt David Fraser, also aged twenty, was the rear gunner. The observer, who carried out the dual role of navigator and bomb aimer, was Sgt Bill Legg. Sgts Geoff Hogg and Bernard Morgan as wireless operator and front gunner respectively completed the crew.

Back at the Flights John Anderson noted that instructions were chalked on the boards for the ground crew to fuel and bomb up his aircraft. It signified they would be on operations that night. In the late afternoon in the company of other participating aircrews he and his crew attended briefing and learned that orders had come through from Bomber Command HQ for an attack on Hamburg. 119 bombers were being dispatched to bomb the general city area, Altona power-station and the shipyards. Sixty of these aircraft would be Wellingtons. Hampdens and Whitleys, plus one Manchester, the forerunner of the Lancaster bomber, would make up the complement. The target for the crew of KO–B was the dock area at Hamburg.

Swinging round to line up with the take off strip at 22.17 hours the crew members of KO–B were very much preoccupied with thoughts of their immediate future. They could not know that the Luftwaffe had already begun a devastating fire-attack on the City of London. This attack, aided by good visibility from a full moon, and an abnormally low tide in the River Thames leaving firemen short of water, would create a 'second' Great Fire of London. They could not know that a lone German fighter was within six minutes' flying time of the British Isles. Bf110 coded VJ+OQ with Rudolf Hess the Deputy Führer of Germany at its controls was fast approaching its zero hour.

An uneventful outward flight punctuated only with a flak burst from an isolated battery along the route brought them to the port of Hamburg. Homing in on the target at a height of 11,000ft [3,300m] they began to make their bombing run, but fierce opposition from the defences in the form of close proximity flak threw them off course. Sgt Anderson turned to make another run across the target and this time Sgt Legg was able to release his bombs. Weaving out of the intense flak barrage they turned onto a predetermined course at full boost. Almost immediately they were picked up by three radar-controlled searchlights and coned in the beams of their attendant searchlight batteries.

The heavy flak now located and started hitting them. Hydraulic pipes in the aircraft were ruptured, releasing hydraulic fluid which caused the rear turret to jam at an awkward angle. David Fraser also reported over the intercom a fire in his turret. Further, his vision was obscured by hydraulic fluid and oil which had spread over the perspex windows of the turret. His electric gunsight had been put out of action. The observer, Bill Legg, made his way towards the rear turret with the cabin fire extinguisher. In the meantime David had stamped out the fire. As Bill made his way back to the cabin he could see Alex Kerr standing in the astrodome watching out for fighters. In the event of an attack Kerr would direct the pilot in his evasive action. Suddenly the flak batteries stopped firing. It signalled the immediate presence of a nightfighter.

Twenty-two-year-old Leutnant Eckart-Wilhelm von Bonin of 6./NJG1 piloting a Bf110 nightfighter had been vectored into the vicinity of the enemy aircraft. His task had been eased by the searchlights outlining the Wellington bomber. He was now manoeuvring into position for an attack from the rear starboard quarter. This was his first operational interception. He was keyed up and very apprehensive of the two guns in the bomber's rear turret. Von Bonin would eventually become a nightfighter ace with thirty-seven victories to his credit but he was now to be tested in battle for the very first time. Closing fast on the bomber he could not understand why the rear turret was not swinging in his direction. The enemy gunner must have seen him at this range. Tense, with the adrenalin pumping, he opened fire. As he did so he realized only his machine guns were firing. He had overlooked the firing button for the 20mm cannon. It was a blessing in disguise for the British crew.

Back in the bomber Alex Kerr heard David Fraser's terse voice over the intercom, 'Nightfighter on our tail'. He swung round in the astrodome and saw a dark shape moving rapidly into position on the starboard quarter. As he shouted instructions over the intercom to the pilot he felt Bill Legg brush against him as he returned from the rear turret. The fighter's nose danced with pinpoints of flame as the German pilot opened up. Kerr felt a heavy blow as though he had been punched simultaneously all over his body. He was knocked backwards on to the canvas bed in the aircraft. Before he lost consciousness he noticed a fire had started in the reconnaissance flares which were amidships on the starboard side. They were close to the oxygen bottles. The machine gun bullets had wounded him in ten places including a bullet in his liver. Bill Legg was standing next to Alex Kerr when the fighter attacked. He was off the intercom and didn't know what was happening. A hammer-like blow hit him in the lower part of the back. He twisted involuntarily and received several other hits. With blood oozing from his back and stomach he crumpled and fell unconscious to the floor.

John Anderson, aware of the bright yellow flame burning amidships, began to throw the Wellington about in an effort to blow out the fire. His efforts were unavailing. The bomber continued to burn fiercely. Fearing an explosion would blow the aircraft to pieces he gave the order to bail out.

Although David Fraser's turret was jammed at an angle he managed to squeeze through the narrow aperture left by the partly obscured door and gained access to the fuselage where his parachute was stored. As he made his way to the emergency escape hatch aft of the beam machine gun on the starboard side he saw Alex sitting in front of the hatch. He was obviously badly wounded and very dazed. A quick examination of Bill Legg who was lying further up the fuselage convinced David that he was dead. He returned to Alex, who in the meantime had managed to remove the cover from the escape hatch and was sitting with his legs dangling through the hatch. David placed Alex's hand on the ripcord and pushed him out. He was relieved to see his parachute open. David followed. By now Bernard Morgan and Geoff Hogg had both made good their escape. Having set the automatic pilot John Anderson scrambled down to the escape hatch and bailed out. Unfortunately he landed in the River Elbe and drowned. The aircraft continued on course burning brightly, carrying the badly wounded, unconscious figure of its observer.

The crumpled body of Bill Legg began to stir as he slowly regained his senses. He still wasn't sure what had happened and by an immense effort of will staggered to his feet and climbed over the main spar to get to the cockpit. He was amazed to find the pilot's seat empty. Slowly it dawned on him that he was alone in a burning aircraft some 9,000ft [2,700m] above Germany. He had to get out and get out quickly. His parachute was under his table. Having retrieved it he made his way forward to the main escape hatch. Carrying the parachute in his hand instead of immediately clipping it on his harness he stood over the escape hatch looking down into the night. At that moment his strength seemed to

Wellington R1379 KO–B of 115 Squadron near Tonning/Kiel, 11 May 1941. Sgt John Anderson and four of his crew bailed out but Anderson landed in the River Elbe and drowned. Sgt Bill Legg, the severely injured observer, landed the aircraft on its belly near Tonning. Coll. Thomas Hampel.

ebb. The chute slipped from his grasp. He watched with dismay as it fell through the escape hatch and into the darkness. His position was now desperate. He had never been officially trained as a pilot and had only taken over the controls of a Wellington briefly for a straight and level flight with one of his pilots.

Weakness brought on by his wounds dulled his senses. He didn't panic. With great difficulty he climbed into the pilot's seat and took over the controls. He released the automatic pilot and switched to manual control. As there was no possibility of surviving he decided to stick the nose down and crash, taking something or someone that was German with him. Losing height rapidly he found he could pick out rivers, fields and buildings in the bright moonlight. He pulled back on the stick and levelled out at about 600ft [180m]. One field appeared to be much larger than the rest. He decided to try to crash land in it. Easing back on the throttles, unable to employ flap because of the damaged hydraulics, he approached at a speed of 100 knots to avoid stalling. At a height of around 100ft [30m] he closed both throttles and braced himself for the crash. About three quarters of the way along the field the Wellington touched down, bumped along on its belly and stopped. Having released the pilot's escape hatch Bill found he was too weak to pull himself through it. Two German soldiers from a nearby flak battery climbed onto the burning plane and lifted him to safety.

In captivity Alex Kerr recovered from his wounds fairly rapidly and a year later on 11 May 1942 was recaptured after an attempted escape. With Bill Legg it was far more serious. Several operations were carried out on him by a fellow prisoner Dr Chatenay. Chatenay was a young French doctor who took a great interest in Bill's case. He carried out miraculous feats of surgery with limited medical supplies under primitive conditions. The open hole in Bill's back never healed, he has it to this day. Bill was repatriated in October 1943 under an exchange of POWs with the Germans. In August 1944 he recommenced flying duties as an instructor. The other crew survivors were repatriated at the end of the war.

Exactly fifty years after the original incident, on 10 May 1991, the three bomber crew members met Von Bonin at Hohn German Air Force base. It was a very emotional occasion. Von Bonin embraced them all. He said that in 1941 when he had attacked their bomber he had been very annoyed with himself because he had forgotten to arm his cannon. Meeting them now he was very pleased that he hadn't set the 20mm cannon button to 'Fire'.

Eckart-Wilhelm von Bonin eventually reached the rank of Major and was decorated with the Ritterkreuz (Knight's Cross) on 5 February 1944 when he had gained thirty-one victories. At that time he was Kommandeur of II./NJG1. He ended the war working for the Luftwaffe Inspector of Jet Aircraft. Although he had a splendid wartime career in the Luftwaffe, Von Bonin also personally experienced the dark side of war. Two of his brothers, also serving in the Luftwaffe, were killed on the Eastern Front. His father Bogislav von Bonin, an Oberst in the Luftwaffe, was captured by the Russians in March 1945 and since then remains missing. Eckhart-Wilhelm von Bonin died in January 1992.

Despite all the difficulties Nachtjagd faced during its first months of existence, the still infant arm could look back upon a hopeful start at the end of 1940. Up to 31 December, forty-two bombers had been destroyed, mainly in *HeNaJa*. Moreover, the Flak arm as its main rival

Twenty-two-year-old Lt Eckart-Wilhelm von Bonin of 6./NJG1 inspecting his first victim, Wellington Ic R1379 of 115 Squadron on 11 May 1941. Von Bonin ended the war as Major with thirty-seven kills to his credit. In February 1944, he was awarded the Ritterkreuz. Coll. Alfons Schmitt via Coll. Rob de Visser.

Burnt-out wreck of a Whitley which was shot down by a Marine Flak unit at Juist, probably during a Bomber Command raid on Emden in 1941–42. Coll. Emil Lechner.

could only claim thirty kills over that same period. These losses represented just under 2 per cent of all sorties dispatched, which was quite acceptable to Bomber Command. Still, these statistics did show that Nachtjagd had a future.

Behind the scenes, a lot of effort went into further perfecting the night fighting equipment. The *Würzburg* system, which had originally been designed as a fire control system for flak, was the only precision radar available. It had been rushed into service, but the data it supplied on the situation in the Nachtjagd Raum was quite inadequate. Kammhuber had to make do with this device, so to make the *Würzburg* data more useful to the fighter control officers in the Raum's HQ, the *Seeburg* table or screen was developed. On this table, nightfighters and bombers were depicted in different colours and their individual courses plotted on a translucent map. With the use of the information on the *Seeburg* table, fighter control officers directed their fighter by radio to the British intruder.

Despite the overall picture it created, it was a cumbersome system. The ironical thing was that during the autumn of 1940, German scientists had developed an excellent method for processing radar data. In this system, aircraft and their courses were immediately depicted on a map as they were registered by radar. This was a great step forward as it facilitated a quicker and clearer interpretation of the situation in the night sky. However, Hermann Göring himself held another view. When it was demonstrated to him in December 1940, he decided that such a technically complicated device need not be introduced into operational service as 'the war was nearly over anyway'.

Göring's statement illustrated the optimistic mood prevalent in the Luftwaffe High Command. The fact that Germany had lost the Battle of Britain did not shake Göring's, nor Generaloberst Hans Jeschonnek's (Luftwaffe Chief of Staff) belief that a victorious end of the war was still within reach. As a direct consequence of this euphoric mood, the technical branch of the Luftwaffe, led by 'General Luftzeugmeister' Ernst Udet, neglected the development of modern aircraft, radars and other equipment. Moreover, Göring considered the personal bravery of the individual pilots to be more important in the air war than the technical aids they were equipped with. This romantic notion was a remnant of his own experiences as a fighter pilot during World War I, yet, in the meantime, modern air warfare had rapidly evolved into a technically complicated subject. This development had passed almost unnoticed by the technological laymen Göring and Udet. Just over one year later, with the prospect of a lengthy war of attrition looming large upon them, the Germans would regret their neglect of the Luftwaffe's technological development.

In spite of these problems, Nachtjagd rapidly further developed into Germany's most important night defence system. *HeNaJa* was improved during 1941 by the introduction of improved radars (the *Würzburg Riese* with increased range) and a more sophisticated processing of radar information from the *Seeburg* tables. Also, the defensive line was broadened by the inclusion of the so-called Dunkle Nachtjagd or *DuNaJa* zones. In these zones, the same procedures for interception of enemy aircraft were being used as in the *HeNaJa*, albeit in complete darkness due to the absence of searchlights. In *DuNaJa*, the second *Würzburg* directed the nightfighter. As a final measure to improve *HeNaJa*, the belt in the oft-visited Ruhr Valley was extended in depth by

A number of successful Zerstörer *pilots went on to become laurelled night fighters. Lt Martin Drewes was one of these men. He is seen here with his* Bordfunker *Uffz. Fritz Hrachowina, preparing a mission in 4./ZG76 during 1941. He flew numerous missions with 4./ZG76 during 1940–41, gaining two victories. After becoming a night-fighter pilot in November 1941, he went on to claim forty-three night* Abschüsse, *plus four American* Viermots *in daylight. He ended the war as Gruppen Kommandeur of III./NJG1, decorated with the Ritterkreuz with Oak Leaves.*
Coll. Rob de Visser.

On 26 April 1941, a big celebration was held in the Amstelhotel in Amsterdam on the occasion of NJG1's 100th Abschuss. *The honour of this historic occasion fell to Oblt Egmont Prinz zur Lippe Weissenfeld of 4./NJG1, who destroyed Wellington W5375 of 12 Squadron over the Ijsselmeer on 9/10 April 1941. W/Cdr. Blackden and crew were all killed. Geschwaderkommodore Major Falck, seated in the middle, is obviously very pleased, as is Fw Hans Rasper to his right.* Coll. Hans Rasper.

some 12 miles (20km). This was a necessary improvement as Bomber Command's four-engined Stirlings and Halifaxes could cross the initial 6 mile (10km) zone in just two minutes and an interception had to be completed within this short stretch of time.

In an effort to combat the searchlight units in the *HeNaJa* belt, Bomber Command introduced so-called searchlight suppression sorties. On 28/29 August 1941, for example, six Hampdens of 49 and 106 Squadrons made searchlight suppression sorties in the target area of Duisburg, where sixty Wellingtons, thirty Hampdens and a handful of Stirlings, Halifaxes and Manchesters attacked railway targets. Sgt George Luke, WOp./AG. in Sgt Eric Lyon's crew in Hampden AE193 ZN–A of 106 Squadron, explains:

> We were to take off early and reach the target fifteen minutes ahead of the main force. These planes were called 'intruders', they would carry a small load of incendiary bombs but additional ammunition for the machine guns. Their purpose was to release the incendiaries on target at a height of 14,000ft [4,200m] then dive to low level and carry out machine gun attacks against the

Grieving Mr and Mrs Marsden of Blackburn visiting their only son's grave at Vredenhof cemetery on Schiermonnikoog Island for the first time in 1948, under the guidance of Mr Sake van der Werf, the founder of the cemetery. Sgt Edwin Marsden, a twenty-seven-year-old air gunner, served with 83 Squadron during 1941. On 25 July 1941, Sgt Draper had lifted Hampden I AD835 off Scampton's runway at 22.05 hours for a raid on Hanover. On the way back to base, Lt Lothar Linke of 4./NJG1 intercepted the bomber over Schiermonnikoog and shot it down at 03.57 hours. Sgt Draper, although injured, was the sole survivor.
Coll. Wyb-Jan Groendijk.

Portrait of Sgt Edwin Marsden, WOp./AG. with 83 Squadron, KIA 25/26 July 1941.
Coll. Wyb-Jan Groendijk.

searchlights on the target route, thus enabling the main bomber force to avoid the searchlight cones and the resulting attention of the German fighter and flak concentrations. The 'intruders' were to continue to harass the searchlights, hopefully keeping them out of action for one hour, allowing the main force to bomb, leave the target area and be well en route for home, then they would regain height and return to their bases.

Upon hearing that our crew had been selected as one of the three 'intruder' aircraft being dispatched from 106 Squadron the apprehension felt at the possible danger involved was counteracted to a degree by the feeling of pride, rather like being chosen for the first eleven at school.

We eventually took off at the designated time, made our way to the target and released the incendiary bombs, surprisingly meeting little opposition en route; we then dived to low altitude and commenced our attack on the searchlights. Personally I felt great exhilaration during the low level attacks, the sense of speed being so much greater, and in my position as under gunner in the Hampden I was kept extremely busy firing away left and right at searchlights as they were switched on. They were extinguished immediately, whether by our marksmanship or intentionally by the Germans, we were not sure.

We continued our attack, with the Wireless Operator also firing from the upper gun position, and felt that we were successfully achieving our purpose, although I do remember in the hectic activity taking place at that time catching sight of one of the main force bombers caught in a cone of searchlights and receiving a pasting from the flak batteries. We ourselves were meeting only light flak and machine gun fire from the searchlight defences; at low level and in the dark you are upon your target and gone almost before they can react.

The pace of events was so fast that the hour long attack seemed to last but a few minutes, then we regained height and set course for base. We had crossed the Dutch coast at about 10,000ft [3,000m] and were approximately 40 miles [64km] north west of Texel on our return to England, the time 3.15 a.m. on the morning of 29 August 1941, when as a result of a technical inability to switch fuel tanks we lost both engines and were forced to ditch.

Fortunately we all survived the ditching, the Skipper, in spite of awful conditions, having done a marvellous job in putting the old Hampden down. We took to the dinghy and started drifting. My Mae West [life jacket] was ripped in the ditching and was therefore useless, with the result that I swallowed gallons of sea water and was the last one to reach the safety of the dinghy. The sea water caused me to be terribly sick for the first few hours, I also suffered severe bruising and lost one of my flying boots. We fashioned paddles out of our parachute harnesses and endeavoured to paddle the dinghy in the direction of the Dutch coast.

Late on the second day and early on the third day, we sighted small cargo ships but visibility was poor on both occasions and they failed to see us. Had we had pyrotechnics of any kind we may have been rescued then. Late on the third day the Skipper was washed overboard and after a struggle we managed to haul him back in, but shortly after, the dinghy was capsized by choppy seas and we were all flung into the sea.

To our amazement, although unable to see land, we were in shallow water and actually walked on a series of sand banks towing the dinghy, until, as dusk was falling, we could just make out the coastline. That night I filled my remaining flying boot with sand, to act as an anchor, to prevent us drifting out to sea.

The following day, our fourth, we were all feeling near the end of our tether due to lack of water, not so much the lack of food, but the thirst was almost unbearable. However, we continued our walking when in the shallows, and paddling when out of our depth, towards the distant coastline, and finally spotted three small fishing boats.

We spent several hours waving and shouting, endeavouring to attract their attention and eventually, when we were on the point of collapse, one of them spotted us. It started heading in our direction and after what seemed an age, finally reached us and hauled us on board. The two Dutchmen aboard the boat were kind and concerned, giving us much needed water and what little food they had. I must admit that in spite of understanding that it was advisable to take only small sips of water after a long period without, I gulped and gulped it down until I had my fill, without suffering any ill effects.

As it was still broad daylight and we were well within sight of the coast and the other boats, plus our poor physical condition, the Dutchmen had no alternative but to hand us over to the German Naval Authorities in the small harbour of Zoutkamp where the Dutchmen hailed from; so late on 1 September 1941 we became *Kriegies* [POWs].

A second searchlight suppression Hampden which failed to return on 28/29 August was AD971 EA–O, a Mk I of 49 Squadron, which was shot down at 03.30 hours in the Waddenzee south of Nes (Ameland) by Oblt Helmut Lent of 4./NJG1. P/O. Bernard Fournier and his three crew were killed and were buried in Nes General Cemetery. The third intruder Hampden which failed to return was AE126, also of 49 Squadron, and piloted by P/O. Thomas Pratt, which was probably shot down by a nightfighter at 00.43 hours in the Waddenzee. Three of the crew were buried on Vlieland and Texel Islands, and Sgt Willis, under gunner, rests at Harlingen. In addition to the 50 per cent searchlight suppression losses, three Wellingtons, one Halifax, a Hampden and one Stirling of the Main Force on Duisburg were lost to flak and fighters.

Ameland Island received another unexpected arrival on the night of 7/8 September 1941 when L7380 EM–W, a Manchester of 207 Squadron based at Waddington, and flown by F/Lt Mike Lewis DFC, made a successful crash-landing on the North Sea beach in about five feet of water at 00.10 hours. En route to Berlin as part of a force of 197 bombers to attack the 'Big City', it had been attacked by a nightfighter at 23.55 hours and subsequently turned for home. L7380 was possibly hit by Uffz. Heinz Grimm of 4./NJG1, who claimed to have damaged a Whitley at 23.55 hours. At 00.09 hours a last message was sent by R/T (Radio Telephony) to

P/O. Jimmy Craig, 144 Squadron, running up the Bristol Pegasus XVII engines of his Hampden in October 1941. W/O.1 Frank Neale, his observer, is watching the proceedings. The aircraft is probably AD724, which served with 144 Squadron, CCDU, 1406 Flt, and 1404 Flt, and was finally written off on 11 September 1943 whilst serving with 517 Squadron when it swung on take-off for a Met. flight from St. Eval. Coll. Frank Neale.

base: 'Port engine smoking'. Sgt Charles Hall, the WOp./AG., recalls:

> On the night of my twenty-fifth birthday, September 7/8, we took off at 21.49 through the smoke and flames of the aircraft taking off immediately in front of us, which had crashed on take-off, and was clearly a blazing and exploding wreck. This was a very bad omen for our trip (my seventeenth), destination Berlin. In those early days, the captains took their own route to and from the target, and on this occasion had decided to track across the North Sea, avoiding the notoriously active German nightfighters, flak and searchlight belt over Holland on the outward leg, and only traversing it once on the return leg, when fuel conservation was a vital factor. I recall that we were always relieved to see the searchlights on Texel on our port side on the return journeys, for this meant that the traditional meal of bacon and eggs was not too far distant! We planned to cross the German coast west of Kiel and thence south west to Berlin avoiding the flak defences of Hamburg, Magdeburg and the Ruhr valley.
>
> The outward flight was uneventful until about midnight, when at about 13,000ft [4,000m], over the sea near Tonning in Schleswig-Holstein, Sgt Miller shouted 'Nightfighter astern', accompanied by the stutter of machine gun fire, and the sight of tracer and cannon fire which hit our aircraft in the area of the port engine. As Miller opened fire, the nightfighter (a Junkers 88 or Me110) continued over the top of the Manchester enabling me from my mid-upper gunners position, to fire into the belly of the enemy aircraft at very short range. F/Lt Lewis had immediately dived our aircraft and sought cover of thick cloud, and contact was lost with the enemy fighter.
>
> We took stock of the position – no crew casualties, and apart from bullet holes in the port wing, little signs of damage. However, soon, indications on the fuel gauges told us that we had a serious fuel leak. Thus we decided that the long flight to Berlin and back would not now be possible, so we decided to drop our 4,000lb [1,800kg] bomb and incendiaries on a searchlight concentration at Wilhelmshaven, which had given us much trouble on previous missions!
>
> We now set course for Waddington, having radioed them of the situation whilst keeping an anxious eye on the port engine. We were now travelling westward at about 9,000ft [2,700m] to conserve fuel, when we noticed that the port engine cowling was glowing red hot, then white hot, in turn. Lewis shut down the engine, feathered the airscrew, and activated the fire extinguisher within the engine cowling. This seemed to extinguish the fire, but thereafter twelve very anxious eyes were focussed on the port engine for signs of further trouble! Trouble, however came from another quarter...
>
> It soon became apparent that we were not capable of maintaining height on the one remaining 'Vulture' engine, so we gradually lost height. With the gunners keeping a sharp lookout, we descended to about 5,000ft [1,500m], but the descent continued through cloud, emerging at about 1,500ft [450m], with the inhospitable grey-black waters of the North Sea clearly visible. At this point Lewis decided that we were not going to make the English coast, and turned south aiming to reach the Frisian Islands.
>
> These islands eventually came into view, and turning westward again, Lewis kept the aircraft parallel to the shore. The inevitable loss of height continued, until we could see that we were almost in the water, and took up our 'crash' positions in the aircraft. The rear gunner, who was by now not connected up to the intercommunication system, was about to leap out of the escape hatch. I had to roughly pull him back to prevent him from taking a premature soaking. This was however not long delayed, for amidst noise, water and mayhem we hit the water, bouncing several times before settling in what turned out to be the surf of the north coast of an island, later verified as Ameland.
>
> After our unusual and unexpected introduction to Netherlands territory, our aircraft settled in about 6–10ft of water, temporarily rendering our captain unconscious, breaking the arm of our rear gunner, and generally rendering the remaining crew members in to an uncontrolled

Manchester L7380 EM–W of 207 Squadron on beach of Ameland in low tide, 8 September 1941. En route for Berlin, L7380 was damaged by a night fighter, possibly flown by Uffz. Heinz Grimm of 4./NJG1. F/Lt Mike Lewis DFC ditched the aircraft in some five feet of water. Coll. Frits Vos, via Hendrik Cazemier.

heap, washed by copious amounts of the North Sea, very wet and very cold.

Having climbed out on to the wings, and generally sorted ourselves out, we set about trying to set fire to the aircraft, and when that proved impossible, to destroy all items which may possibly be of interest to the enemy. The radio, gunsights, navigation equipment, instrument panel etc, came under the blows of the fire axes, whilst the wireless operators started to eat the codes printed on rice paper, until we realized that it would be just as effective to dissolve them in the sea, and less indigestible, too!

The dinghy, housed in the wing stub, had by this time automatically inflated, albeit upside down, so we waded ashore clinging on to its side, and pushing it before us. All the time we were conscious that the area may well have been mined. However, we arrived safely on the sandy beach, noting that our precipitate arrival had evidently not been noticed, or alerted anyone on the island. We attempted to dry out, shared out what few rations we had, and realizing that we were on an island, we set about looking for a suitable boat, with which to return to our shores.

A few kilometres from our embarkation point we came across a 25-feet solid-looking boat, set on a timber cradle, on half tracks, and wheels, suitable for launching by a team of horses. This boat contained a mast, engine, fuel, and a half bottle of rum. No doubt thanks to the latter item, we all set to with a will, to attempt to launch the boat, to continue our journey home. However, all prolonged attempts to move the boat proved fruitless, and by the time dawn was breaking on the horizon, we knew that we could do no more that night, and so settled in the boat, for the hours of daylight. We could just make out a village with a church and quay in the distance. We had previously agreed that we should not involve the local population on the island, for fear of repercussions on the local inhabitants by the Germans.

Before long however our look-out reported that an armed German soldier was approaching, who signalled to his patrol and soon had us surrounded. With rifles and revolvers at the ready they marched us to a small military outpost on the island. 'Dusty' Miller our rear gunner's broken arm was by now giving him some pain, so we asked, and received, medical attention. Mike Lewis was separated from the rest of the crew, and taken back to the site of the crash. There were by now only the tips of the fins of our aircraft visible, due to the incoming tide.

We were then all taken under heavy escort to a pier, to await a ferry to the mainland. To much shouting and pushing, the Germans evacuated the cabin of local inhabitants, and locked us therein, with two hungry looking Alsatian dogs on duty at the door.

On the mainland we were met by a Luftwaffe patrol again heavily armed and with dogs, and taken by truck to Leeuwarden airfield. We were taken to an office of a senior officer and provided with a cup of Ersatz coffee, and although communication was difficult, I sensed that there was a common acknowledgement that we were both airmen, doing their duty for their respective countries. Mike Lewis, our captain was taken to the Officers' Mess, and given a meal of sauerkraut.

At Leeuwarden airbase we were given a perfunctory interrogation and our valuables and flying clothing were removed. I still have a receipt for a watch and cigarette lighter but alas no sign of the articles, themselves never returned! I recall that we were treated in a relatively civilized manner, by the aircrew present, but we were warned by them that this would change appreciably when we were handed over to the Abwehr – a prophesy which proved to be too true.

We were then bundled into a truck and taken at high speed to, from what I remember, was another ferry journey and truck trip, to the centre of Amsterdam, to what I have since identified as the jail in Havenstraat. The jail was situated at the intersection of several busy streets and opposite a train station, a building of Napoleonic and sinister appearance, and where my three and a half years of captivity began.

137 crews claimed to have bombed their allotted targets in Berlin on the night of 7/8 September 1941. Fifteen aircraft went missing, and at least four are believed to have been brought down by nightfighters.

Apart from Helle Nachtjagd, Kammhuber developed a third nocturnal defensive system, the Kombinierte Nachtjagd (Combined Night Fighting) or *KoNaJa*. This system was dependent on the fact that the bombers had to fly straight and level for some two minutes on their bombing run to the target, during which time they were extremely vulnerable as they could not carry out any evasive action. *KoNaJa* was intended to take advantage of this situation. In combined night fighting, the bombers were to be destroyed over their target by a combination of flak, nightfighters and searchlights. To prevent the destruction of friendly aircraft, flak was ordered to fire below the nightfighter's operational altitude, which was usually at some 18,000ft (5,500m). The German fighters were directed to their adversaries by ground control with the use of

Prisoners: a British bomber crew at Vechta airfield, 1941–42. During W.W.II., Bomber Command lost 6,465 four-engined and 3,856 twin-engined aircraft. Of some 125,000 Commonwealth aircrew who served in the strategic night bombing offensive, 47,268 were killed in action, 8,195 died in accidents, 8,403 were wounded and 9,838 ended up in POW camps. Coll. Engelbert Hasenkamp.

radio and searchlights. The first *KoNaJa* belt was built up around Berlin in May 1941, followed by the cities of Kiel, Bremen, Hamburg and in the Ruhr Valley in the same year.

The co-operation between nightfighters, Flak batteries and searchlights was exemplary in theory and during exercises, but this was often not the case in the hectic turmoil of a raid. Many German nightfighters fell prey to flak, which often did not (or could not) distinguish between friend and foe. After a few surprising results during the summer of 1941, the number of kills in *KoNaJa* rapidly dropped towards the end of the year. In all, only a few dozens of British bombers were shot down by combined night fighting. From 1942 onwards, *KoNaJa* was only used around some industrial centres such as Frankfurt, Darmstadt, Cologne, Hamburg and Berlin. After the Battle of Hamburg in the summer of 1943, *KoNaJa* was abandoned altogether.

During the winter of 1941–42, the Kammhuber Line of *HeNaJa* and *KoNaJa* zones was completed. Sgt John Price flew his first operational tour as tail gunner in Wellingtons with 150 and 104 Squadron during 1941 and confirms the constant threat to the RAF night bomber crews of the combination of *HeNaJa* and flak:

> Often, the first thing you saw and heard was a very loud bang, a flash, a burst of smoke – this was usually the first 'marker' shell. If you were unfortunate enough, you would be 'coned' by about fifty searchlights – and a master searchlight. This one was a bright blue or purple colour on which all other searchlights converged – with you at the top of the cone. You felt like a fly impaled on a pin. Outlined by the searchlights, you were then a prime target for nightfighters and as the guns opened up, the bursting of the shells became closer and closer as the Germans put up what is known as 'box' barrage – hundreds of shells in a rectangle all around you, then all they had to do was to make the rectangle or box smaller and smaller. Eventually any shell that burst within 200ft [60m] or less would be enough to set you on fire, blow your aircraft up as fragments of red hot steel tore into the bomb casings or perhaps the engines and fuel tanks, and on the other hand kill the crew. Whenever this [coning] happened we would 'sideslip' down through the barrage and searchlights, by losing height rapidly – turning so that one wing always pointed to the ground, making us less of a target at the same time. I can tell you it was no way to spend a peaceful evening.
>
> I could actually smell the cordite from the bursting shells – that's when you start to pray. Of course we all pretended not to be afraid, in order to keep up the pretence we cracked jokes and sang dirty songs. Morale and discipline were everything.
>
> I never found a target in Germany that wasn't very heavily defended. On all our raids we tried every angle of attack we could think of, but the German defences were formidable. Lanes of hundreds of searchlights stretched all over Germany, with hundreds of guns in support – light and heavy flak, and apart from that every industrial centre [was] more heavily defended.
>
> Our driving force was fear of being thought a coward and pride in the thought that not even dread of death would prevent us from keeping our duty to our country and more importantly, keeping faith with our comrades.

When the complicated *HeNaJa* system finally started paying off in 1942, it was destroyed by Hitler himself. He ordered the searchlights to be concentrated around Germany's major cities after persistent pressure from Gauleiters of these cities suffering a number of heavy bombing raids. Thus, Kammhuber had to give up this essential link in his defence system, and *HeNaJa* was largely abandoned. The only remaining searchlight battery was deployed near Venlo and was used for continuing experiments with the *HeNaJa* interception method. Though Kammhuber protested strongly to Hitler against the retreat of the searchlights, he later realized that the step had actually been advantageous to the development of the completely radar-guided Himmelbett Nachtjagd system. After all, Helle and Kombinierte Nachtjagd suffered from too many disadvantages. After the first experiments with the fully radar-controlled Dunkle Nachtjagd, Kammhuber knew all

Sgt Ken Squire, WOp./AG. (Front Gunner) with 115 Squadron, was shot down in Wellington R1772 by a Bf110 over Kiel on 7/8 September 1941. Ken managed to bail out from the burning 'Wimpey' together with four other members of his crew, but the pilot, Sgt R.B.D. Hill, crashed to his death. He rests in Kiel War Cemetery. 115 Squadron lost another aircraft to a nightfighter on this night. R1798, on its way back from Berlin, fell victim to Oblt Helmut Lent of 4./NJG1 as his seventeenth Abschuss. *The 'Wimpey' exploded in mid-air at 04.58 hours near Drachtstercompagnie in Friesland province with the loss of Sgt Gordon and his crew.* Coll. Kathryn Squire.

too well that this was the only effective and lasting answer to the British night bombing offensive. So, although the number of nightfighter kills decreased immediately after the withdrawal of the searchlights from the Kammhuber Line, the arm recovered rapidly from this blow by the introduction of *Lichtenstein* AI (Airborne Interception) radar and the further extension of radar-controlled Dunkle Nachtjagd.

The year 1941 can be characterized as a transitional period in the air war over the Reich at night. Both Nachtjagd and its opponent Bomber Command grew rapidly during this year but with little progress in effectiveness on either side. The autumn and winter of 1941 were a critical period for Bomber Command as it became clear that its strategic bombing offensive had so far hardly produced any tangible results. On the other hand, the casualty rate had gone up. The primitive navigational equipment in the Bomber Command heavies was simply insufficient to find and hit small military targets, such as traffic junctions, factories and oil storage facilities, at night in blacked-out and unfamiliar territory.

Sgt Albert E. Robinson served as an Observer in 115 Squadron until his Wellington was shot down by a Bf110 nightfighter of 4./NJG1 piloted by ace Ofw. Paul Gildner on 31 October 1941. Albert further explains the difficulties experienced on the early night raids:

> Bombing by night presented a formidable barrier to the young crews of Bomber Command during the crisis years of 1940–41. So much so, that if groping blindly through the curtain of darkness which had descended over Europe was to be overcome, it became crystal clear that in these initial stages, an awful lot was going to depend on the crews themselves. Trial and error mostly, and such imposed vagary could only result in a situation which brought about a high casualty rate for the pioneer crews of the bomber.

Wellington BK307 KO-L of 115 Squadron in dispersal at RAF Marham, 1942. Coll. Ted Smith.

Unfortunately with little result for so great an effort. An effort which was a pot-pourri of calculated risk, personal skills, circumstances that favoured, and with the more successful crews an 'X' factor. A quality which lifted them high above average, a quality difficult to define, but one which enabled them to take advantage of more than a full share of luck.

But whatever the mixture, a common denominator united the crews almost without exception and that was a fierce determination to succeed in spite of the numerous setbacks. And with this resolution, the crews attempted to face up to their task. Not made easier by much talk by briefing officers about the necessity for precision bombing. Fanciful on many distanced targets set in the heart of Germany and it would not be too critical to suggest that some of these briefings were out of touch with reality. Certainly by truthful crews, to whom on many occasions in appalling weather, it was considered a reasonable effort if the city itself was found, let alone a positive sighting of a specific aiming point.

As a result of the disappointing Bomber Command raids on the Reich, strong voices were raised in the Royal Navy and Army calling for the Command to be dismantled. The bomber squadrons should now be employed in the Battle of the Atlantic, where German submarines threatened to cut off Britain's vital supply lines. The Army demanded bombers to support the campaigns in Northern Africa and the Far East. Bomber Command survived these critical months largely because of the unwavering strong support of the Prime Minister. Winston Churchill looked upon the strategic bombing offensive as the only way to keep pressure on Germany before any invasion could be successfully mounted on 'Fortress Europe'. Still, out of necessity, Bomber Command was directed, on 14 February 1942 by Chief of the Air Staff Sir Charles Portal, to virtually abandon the idea of precision bombing and devote most of its efforts to the general bombing of the most densely built-up areas of Germany's cities. Thus, the strategy of 'area bombing' was now officially adopted by Bomber Command.

1941 had been a troublesome year for Nachtjagd as well. Though rapidly expanding, it had been a period of laborious growth. Between January and December, its nominal strength had risen by some 90 per cent from four Gruppen (squadrons) and one Staffel, to seven Gruppen and one Staffel. Although this should have entailed a rise from 195 to 367 aircraft, the growth in frontline and combat-ready machines had only been from 106 to 159 nightfighters. This was largely caused by the failure of the Me210 as the intended successor to the ageing Bf110. In anticipation of this new twin-engined fighter aircraft, production of the Bf110 had already come to an almost complete standstill. The Me210 however proved to be a failure and no nightfighter units were equipped with the type.

As a consequence, Nachtjagd units received far fewer aircraft during the second half of 1941 than Kammhuber had originally intended, which in turn led to a serious decline in the frontline number of Bf110s. This grave situation was only remedied by the summer of 1942 when the Bf110 production lines turned out enough aircraft again to keep Nachtjagd at full strength.

Whilst awaiting the further build-up of Dunkle Nachtjagd, Helle Nachtjagd remained the most successful night fighting system during the transitional year of 1941, with fifty-nine *Abschüsse* during the summer months. *DuNaJa* was only slightly behind with fifty-three kills. By the end of autumn 1941, the roles had already been reversed, with *HeNaJa* destroying seventeen aircraft against twenty-seven by *DuNaJa*. By then, Kammhuber realized that the fully radar-controlled *DuNaJa* was the future.

Despite all the setbacks, Nachtjagd claimed 427 Bomber Command aircraft shot down during 1941. Even though the kill ratio declined sharply towards the end of the year, these statistics signified ever increasing losses for Bomber Command. Throughout the year, night bomber losses rose from 1.5 per cent to 3.5 per cent, typifying Nachtjagd's increasing efficiency. Under Kammhuber's inspiring leadership the infant arm had developed into a significant threat to Bomber Command.

CHAPTER 2

Fernnachtjagd: Night Intruders over Britain

Kammhuber was thinking along two lines when he founded Nachtjagd, intending to establish an offensive, long-range arm in parallel with a short-range Nachtjagd over the Reich territory. This long-range Fernnachtjagd would be employed to hunt Bomber Command over the British Isles, harassing the bombers on and over their airfields. Kammhuber preferred long-range intruders over the short range Nachtjagd as he felt they presented the most efficient way to combat the British.

On 17 July 1940, the day on which the First Nachtjagd Division was created, II./NJG1 was designated to fly intruder missions over the UK. Using modified Junkers Ju88 and Dornier Do17 bombers, this unit began flying offensive missions from Schiphol airfield. From early September 1940, the Gruppe operated from Gilze-Rijen airfield in the south of The Netherlands, being rechristened I./NJG2.

Kammhuber harboured ambitious plans for Fernnachtjagd. As a first step, Hauptmann Heyse, commander of II./NJG1, was ordered to expand his Gruppe to Geschwader strength. Kammhuber had obtained permission from Reichsmarschall

Ju88C 4R+CL of I./NJG2, the long-range night intruders, at Gilze-Rijen airfield, 1941. Coll. Kurt Frasch.

Göring to establish two complete Geschwader for Fernnachtjagd and a further third wing was authorized on 10 December 1940. This added up to a theoretical establishment of over 300 long-range nightfighter aircraft – but the reality was very different. Owing to shortages of suitable aircraft, the Fernnachtjagd force remained at Gruppen strength, with an average of only 20 machines available for intruder missions between August 1940 and October 1941.

During the late summer of 1940, the staff of I./NJG2 at Gilze-Rijen developed tactics for operations over the United Kingdom. The German Y-service (Signals Intelligence) was to monitor the radio frequencies used by Bomber Command and to warn I./NJG2 the moment they intercepted the test signals that indicated a Bomber Command raid that coming night. The Fernnachtjäger were then to operate in three waves. Firstly, British bombers were to be shot down whilst taking off from their bases. The second wave was to patrol over the North Sea to intercept the bombers on their way to and from the continent. Finally, a third wave of intruders would lie in wait for the returning bombers and shoot them down over their own airfields. The German aircraft were also armed with bombs to be dropped on RAF aerodromes. They soon discovered that they could harvest most profitably over the Bomber Command airfields. Flarepaths were often lit, and bombers circled their bases with navigation lights on, which made them very vulnerable to attack.

P/O. Ted Cox was one of the Bomber Command aircrew who received the unwelcome attention of a prowling Ju88 intruder. Ted manned the Vickers K-gun in the mid-upper turret of Blenheim IV R3905 with XV Squadron on the evening of 9 September 1940. P/O. Jimmy Kee piloted the aircraft on a bombing raid against shipping at Ostend, with Sgt Pickering as navigator. It was the crew's eleventh trip:

> We were over our home beacon in the circuit on returning to Wyton after a successful trip, with all nav lights on and the airfield all lit up, when I spotted an unlighted aircraft approaching from behind which appeared similar to a Blenheim. It came up from port quarter and gave us a good burst of tracer which hit the tail unit, damaging the rudder, ailerons, and trim tabs. I shouted evasive instructions to Jimmy Kee – turning in to the attack, and loaded up my K-gun with a pan of ammunition (it was a standing order, at that time, to unload guns when in the circuit). We got another burst from the Hun, which did little damage, and by that time we were down on the deck and evading madly. I got in two bursts at the intruder before we lost him. My pilot was having a job to fly the aircraft on an even keel. However, we managed to stagger back to Wyton and did an uneventful flapless landing at 23.15 hours.
>
> I remember getting out after landing and doing a war-dance round the tail-plane when I saw the damage! One splinter lodged in my W/T set and could have caused me serious damage if it had been a few inches higher! I always thought Jimmy Kee did wonderfully well to get us back without too much fuss.
>
> The enemy aircraft was a Ju88, I firmly believe, because of its similar profile, and single fin and rudder, but I was persuaded by others in the squadron to write it in my logbook as a Me110 as they, also, claimed to have seen it. Anyhow, I don't know how he failed to make a kill as he came so close. It was the nearest I came to 'buying it' whilst on XV Squadron. The intruder managed several other attacks the same night but I did not hear of any other damage.

In fact, Blenheim R3905 was claimed destroyed near Waddington at 23.15 hours by Fw. Hermann Sommer of I./NJG2. The German intruder pilot probably mistook the beacon at Wyton for that at Waddington which flashed a somewhat similar signal. It was Sommer's first claim in I./NJG2; he went on to claim seven more RAF bombers shot down over the UK during 1940–41. In all, he claimed nineteen *Abschüsse* in NJG2 and 102 from 1940 to early 1944, before he was killed in action on 11 February of that year.

The operational area of I./NJG2 in eastern England was divided into three sectors. Raum A

Tail unit of Blenheim IV R3905 N–Nuts of XV Squadron, extensively shot up by Ju88 intruder flown by Fw. Sommer of I./NJG2 in circuit of RAF Wyton on the night of 9 September 1940. Coll. Ted Cox.

comprised the whole of East Anglia, Raum B the Midlands and Raum C covered Yorkshire. Most of Bomber Command's operational airfields and also a number of training units were located in this area.

Despite these sound and promising tactical plans, the intruders did not make an auspicious start during the first five months of operations. For a mere eight aircraft claimed destroyed by the end of the year, the unit had lost twenty-one of its own, eleven of which were downed on operations. Thirty-two aircrew were killed or missing. As a direct result of I./NJG2's activities over the UK, Britain's air defences were reinforced during the winter of 1940–41. Radar equipped Bristol Beaufighters started exacting a heavy toll from the German intruders. This forced I./NJG2 to change its tactics; from June 1941 onwards, the German crews patrolled more and more over the North Sea and less over the increasingly dangerous British mainland. For example, eighteen out of a total of twenty interceptions in June 1941 took place over the North Sea.

Still, the successful formula of Fernnachtjagd was secured. Despite the heavy price I./NJG2 had to pay, it was able to inflict increasingly serious losses on the RAF, having a very successful spell during the summer of 1941. On the night of 26/27 June 1941, the intruders from Gilze-Rijen claimed their 100th *Abschuss.* This was a greater number of kills than claimed by all other German nightfighter units operating over the Reich territory combined. Moreover, the Gruppe now expanded its area of operations to mid-England where the majority of the RAF training airfields were located. Between January and October 1941, the crews of I./NJG2 claimed 125 enemy destroyed, for the loss of fifty-five aircraft and seventy-four aircrew. Dozens more RAF aircraft were damaged in intruder attacks, as F/O. David Penman experienced. David flew his final mission of his first tour in Hampdens with 44 Squadron on 15/16 February 1941. Seventy-three Wellingtons and twenty-seven Whitleys went to the Holten oil plant (with one Wellington and a Whitley lost), and thirty-seven Blenheims and thirty-three Hampdens to the oil plant at Homberg (without loss). David flew Hampden I P2917 as part of the Homberg force:

> We took four 500lb [900kg] and two 250lb [450kg] bombs to Düsseldorf where cloud and ground haze made aiming very difficult. Bombs were dropped and then we were held by searchlights and no results could be observed. On return to Waddington in the dark we were given permission to land and with all airfield and aircraft lights on we were flying up the grass landing area, marked with burning goose neck flares, at 1,000ft [300m] prior to making our left hand circuit for landing.

General Kammhuber (on left) chats with Ofw. Wilhelm Beier (middle) and Major Wolfgang Falck on the occasion of the award of the Ritterkreuz to Beier on 10 October 1941 at Gilze-Rijen airfield. Beier received the coveted decoration after his twelfth to fourteenth long-range night fighting victories with 3./NJG2 on the night of 8 August 1941. Coll. Gemeentearchief Arnhem via Wolfgang Falck.

There was a very sudden rattle of cannon fire as tracer bullets streamed into our starboard wing and engine. As I swung the aircraft violently in a diving turn to the left the faint shape of a Me110 went past us. I switched off all lights and broadcast a warning of intruder in the circuit. All lights on the airfield went out.

My considerable knowledge of Waddington enabled me to continue the circuit, land the aircraft, swing off the landing area and shut off the engines. We got out of the aircraft; no one had been hit, but petrol was pouring out of the starboard side. Looking up we saw another Hampden with lights on joining the circuit with the Me110 following him and opening fire. The Hampden was hit and the pilot S/Ldr Smalies was lucky that a bullet which came his way hit the large metal box holding his parachute straps together and did not damage him. Fortunately his aircraft was not badly damaged and, the Me110 having left, he landed safely.

It was an exciting end to my Hampden flying and I was honoured to go to Buckingham Palace and receive the Distinguished Flying Cross from King George VI, with my mother watching.

The 44 Squadron Hampden flown by S/Ldr Smalies was claimed destroyed near Waddington by Oblt Bönsch at 01.25. The German intruder pilot, who flew a Ju88 and not a Bf110 as David Penman states, misidentified Hampden I X3025 as a Blenheim. Two Oxfords of No. 2 FIS were also damaged at Fulbeck by intruders of I./NJG2, but both were able to land in one piece. The RAF was furthermore harassed by bombing and strafing attacks on the airfields of Bircham Newton, Feltwell and Sutton Bridge.

As a direct result of the Fernnachtjäger operations, the RAF was forced to end night flying training in East Anglia, Yorkshire and Lincolnshire. Moreover, I./NJG2's continuous presence over England had a huge psychological impact on RAF aircrews. Many aircraft were lost in crashes due to rushed landings on their bases for fear of being shot down. This clearly proved the point that the General der Nachtjagd was trying to make: Bomber Command could be challenged most effectively by venturing into the lion's den. Kammhuber next planned in mid-1941 to use the Dornier Do217J over Great Britain as this type had greater endurance than the Ju88. Also, these long range heavy fighters were to be equipped with their own AI (Airborne Interception) radar to reap even more havoc in the night skies over Great Britain.

It therefore came as a great shock to General Kammhuber and his intruder crews when on 12 October 1941, Hitler himself ordered Kammhuber to halt all Nachtjagd operations over the UK and the North Sea. The Führer reasoned: 'One

Hampden AD837 'E' of 83 Squadron preparing to take off on a sortie from RAF Scampton, July 1941. Note the two 250lb (113kg) bombs on each wing. This aircraft was lost on 17/18 August 1941 when it ran out of fuel and ditched off Holy Island, Northumberland on return from a raid on Bremen. Coll. Len Wood.

cannot expect any results by the Fernnachtjagd. If the Fernnachtjagd really would have been successful, the British would have copied it a long time ago, as they imitate anything that works well'. Hitler also stated on this occasion: 'The German citizen, whose house was destroyed by a British bomber pilot, would rather see the British flyer shot down by a German nightfighter in such a way that he can see this British machine lying next to his burning house'. A final consideration was that Hitler did not believe in the effectiveness of I./NJG2 because there had been no noticeable decline in the Bomber Command raids on targets in the Reich.

Ju88C-5 in Zerstörer *configuration, developed from the C-4* Zerstörer*/nightfighter series in early 1941. Clearly visible is the nose armament of one MG151 20mm cannon and three MG17 machine guns. Just ten of these machines, fitted with 1,560hp (1,164kw) BMW801 engines were built, as these engines were almost exclusively intended for the Fw190 fighter. Its successor, the Ju88C-6 series (developed from the Ju88A-4) was fitted with the 1,410hp (1,052kw) Jumo 211J engines and reached a top speed of between 310–340mph (500–550kph). Equipped with the* Lichtenstein SN-2 *AI radar, this series saw extensive service in the night fighting arm from autumn 1942. Total Ju88* Zerstörer *and nightfighter production amounted to 3,964 aircraft by the end of the war, 2,518 having been built during 1944.*
Coll. Theo Boiten.

After having gained permission in late 1940 to expand the long range nightfighter force to a more formidable opponent for Bomber Command, Kammhuber had been denied all practical support to realize his ambitious plans. His efforts to build up a truly effective force constantly met with opposition from the Luftwaffe High Command, which already was plagued by too many requests for reinforcements at this stage of the war. Another reason for the opposition was that the Luftwaffe High Command still did not take the looming threat of a large-scale British night bombing offensive seriously. Why bolster the Reich's air defence at a time when the Luftwaffe desperately needed all its resources at the Eastern Front and in North Africa?

Expansion of the Fernnachtjagd force was further hampered by the low production rate of Junkers Ju88 airframes. Kammhuber had envisaged this type as the standard aircraft for the intruder force, but production of the Ju88 nightfighter during 1940 amounted to a mere sixty airframes. This barely even sufficed to compensate for the losses of I./NJG2. This serious situation improved somewhat after the winter of 1940–41, though hardly enough to make a

Hptm. Karl Hülshoff (in middle), his crew, and the two groundcrew responsible for maintaining the aircraft, pose in front of their Ju88C-4 at Gilze-Rijen in early 1941. Hptm. Hülshoff was CO of the night intruders of I./NJG2 between 24 November 1940 and 31 October 1941, leading his men from the front. He scored four confirmed kills over the UK in I./NJG2 during 1940–41, adding another seven in NJG2 before the end of the war. Coll. Werner Kock.

significant change for the better. Due to these circumstances, the operational strength of the Gruppe at Gilze-Rijen always remained below thirty serviceable aircraft.

Adolf Hitler and others in the High Command were not the only critics of Kammhuber's Fernnachtjagd. Sperrle, the man responsible for all Luftwaffe attacks on the UK disapproved of it because he did not want any Luftwaffe units operating in 'his' territory that were not under his direct command. After the war, Kammhuber gave a more rational reason for the end of long-range night intruding. By the autumn of 1941, the Luftwaffe was already stretched to the limit as it operated on many fronts simultaneously. Of necessity, choices now had to be made where best to deploy its assets. Hence, it was decided that I./NJG2 would be of more use to the war effort in the Mediterranean than in the air defence of the Reich, as Bomber Command did not yet represent an immediate threat to the German cities and war industry.

Lt Völker, pilot of 3./NJG2, congratulates Ogefr. Groschwitz, groundrew, on his good maintenance work. Völker and his crew of Fw. Gärtner (FE.) and Fw. Brehne (WOp.) claimed three Blenheims destroyed near RAF Lindholme on 25 April 1941. In background, hangar and tail unit of Ju88C with seven Abschuss*-markings. Gilze-Rijen, 1941.* Coll. Kurt Frasch.

An immediate result of Hitler's orders in regard to Fernnachtjagd was that Bomber Command could now expand without interference over the UK. Moreover, the RAF aircrew training centres and OTUs (Operational Training Units) could get about their business of training thousands of young men that would serve in Bomber Command, without the threat of lurking German night intruders. The fact that the RAF was allowed to operate with its bases undisturbed from late 1941 until early in 1945 (when intruder operations were again undertaken for a brief period of two nights) must be considered as an important factor which contributed to the final crippling of Germany. Kammhuber supported this view in 1945. He expressed the opinion that this omission was a substantial factor in the destruction of Germany's homeland, and thus its ultimate defeat. Luftwaffe General Major Walter Grabmann, commander of the 3rd Jagddivision in the air defence of the Reich expands on Kammhuber's observations:

> Considering the highly complicated and weather-sensitive landing and taking off procedures used by the RAF in its ever increasing nightly bomber activities, a well developed system of German long distance night fighting would have had an excellent chance of success. The fact that Germany refused to produce such an arm while it still had the chance must be held against the Nachtjagd as one of its most serious omissions.

Kammhuber next intended to employ the experienced Fernnachtjagd Gruppe in the radar-controlled GCI (Ground Controlled Interception) system that he was busy building up in the Reich territories. But he could not convince his superiors of the soundness of this idea. At the end of October 1941, I./NJG2 was transferred to the Mediterranean theatre for night fighting operations from Sicily and North Africa. In September 1942, it looked as if Fernnachtjagd was going to be reinstated when the Gruppe was transferred back to The Netherlands. With the aim of thwarting the build-up of the American 8th Army Air Force in the UK, I./NJG2 was to carry

Ju88C of 3./NJG2 at Gilze-Rijen in early 1941, with groundcrews, (l–r): Ogefr. König; unknown; unknown; Ogefr. Groschwitz. Coll. Kurt Frasch.

out night intruder missions over Britain again. However, these plans were also brushed off the table and in November of the same year I./NJG2 was once more transferred to Sicily.

The 'Angriffsführer England' ('Attack Leader England'), Oberst Peltz, was now assigned the task of long range night intruding. Still, as Peltz only had (fighter) bombers at his disposal and no nightfighter aircraft, this came to nothing in reality. The only long range night fighting sorties that were flown in this period were the so-called 'Lange Kerle' sorties. These consisted of an occasional pursuit by nightfighters based in the Low Countries over and even across the North Sea. An organized Fernnachtjagd however no longer existed, all that remained were sporadic individual sorties. Kammhuber was forced to fight his nocturnal air war over the mainland of western Europe.

Bomber Command's strategic bombing offensive reached its first climax in the spring of 1943 during the Battle of the Ruhr. Between March and July, the Command conducted a series of devastating raids against the industrial heart of Germany. The area was soon dubbed the 'Valley of Death' by the bomber crews due to the severe RAF losses. As a direct result of these heavy raids, early in July, Air Marshall Erhard Milch urged Hitler to renew the Fernnachtjagd over Great Britain. The Führer, however, would have nothing of it as 'the nightfighters would not be able to find the enemy bombers anyhow'. Heinz Rökker, who served in I./NJG2 from May 1942, ending the war as Hauptmann with sixty-four confirmed victories and holder of the Ritterkreuz with Oak Leaves comments:

Left to right: Hptm. Paul Semran; Lt Heinz Strüning; Ofw. Alfons Köster; Lt Wilhelm Beier. This photo was taken on 9 November 1942, on the occasion of the award of the Ritterkreng to Strüning and Köster. These four men amassed between them 168 Abschüsse, *all but one at night against Bomber Command. They had all been blooded on operations over England during 1940–41 in the long-range nightfighter role. Semran shot down nine aircraft as Fernnachtjäger; Beier had been awarded the Ritterkreug in October 1941 for his fourteen kills over England with 3./NJG2. Eleven of Köster's kills were gained as Fernnachtjäger; Strüning gained nine victories over England in 1940–41. Beier was destined to be the only one in this group of nightfighter* Experten *to survive the war. Semran was killed on 8 February 1945; Strüning on 24/25 December 1944; Köster died in a landing accident on 6/7 January 1945.* Coll. Hans-Jakob Schmitz.

> At the latest by early 1943, the German long-range intruding over Great Britain should have been built up again, because it was a well-known fact that the British operational aerodromes were fully lit-up during the take off and landing procedures. Furthermore, during the assembling process of the bomber stream, the bomber crews, against regulations, often switched on their navigation lights for fear of collision. To hunt them under these conditions would have been the ultimate dream of the German long-range intruders.

On 15 September, 1943, Joseph Kammhuber was relieved from command of the Nachtjagd. He was removed from his post having been unable to prevent the destructive raids launched during the Battle of the Ruhr and the Battle of Hamburg. By this time, the inefficiency of the Reich's air defence had caused considerable concern within Germany's war leadership. Generalmajor Joseph 'Beppo' Schmid was now put in command of Nachtjagd after Kammhuber's dismissal, and Schmid made almost daily attempts to rehabilitate Fernnachtjagd. In this effort, he was supported by Milch, who, during September and October 1943, again dedicated himself to promoting long range night intruder operations over the UK. On the night of 2/3 October, for example, some twenty-two Fernnachtjäger of V./KG2 were active over England. Nevertheless, Hitler again prohibited the continuation of these operations when he heard of the matter. On this occasion he stated: 'These actions may cause some confusion among the British bombers, but they keep coming all the same'.

A renewed Fernnachtjagd appealed to Schmid as he was now provided with an excellent tool for these operations. During the winter of 1942–43, Bomber Command aircraft had been fitted with the *H2S* navigation radar. *H2S* helped the navigators in Bomber Command as it provided them with a picture of the terrain the aircraft flew over, albeit an incomplete and often inaccurate impression. Within a matter of only weeks, during February 1943, the Luftwaffe had recovered one of these sets intact and German scientists immediately developed a device that homed onto *H2S* emissions, the Funkgerät 350 *Naxos Z.* With the aid of *Naxos,* the Germans could determine the grouping pattern and courses of the British bombers. Even though *H2S* was soon outdated by the introduction of more precise route and target marking techniques, the device remained in service on a large scale. Bomber crews were unaware that the German air defences could accurately trace their aircraft by the *H2S* emissions from the moment they took off. With the aid of *Naxos,* the Germans could even track individual 'heavies'.

Schmid now intended to surprise the bombers over their fully illuminated bases on a few carefully chosen nights with a strong force of between 600 and 700 Fernnachtjäger. Using *Naxos* to determine the course of the bomber stream, the bombers were to be attacked on their return flight, right up to their bases in East Anglia. Just like in the days of the long range night intruders of I./NJG2, the nightfighters were to operate over England in successive waves. Bomber Command airfields were to be attacked with bombs, gunfire and caltrops, and in the ensuing chaos and confusion as many bombers as possible should be destroyed. Schmid assumed that he should be able to inflict at least one devastating blow on Bomber Command. After all, the bombers were by this time used to returning to their fully lit bases without any interference. The night fighting General expected to destroy a minimum of some 100 bomber aircraft in one blow. As a beneficial side-effect, the operation would undoubtedly force the RAF to reinforce its night air defence over the UK at the expense of a further development of the strategic night bombing offensive. This renewed Fernnachtjagd was not intended to become a routine effort as in 1940–41, as German intelligence assessed British air defences to be too strong in the long run. The plan was to deliver one or two devastating blows by surprise.

In December 1943, Schmid went to see Hermann Göring to present his plans for a renewed Fernnachtjagd. Göring refused to give the go-ahead. He told Schmid that long-range intruder operations over the United Kingdom were not his business but this was for Generalmajor Dietrich Peltz to decide upon. Undaunted, Schmid turned to Generalmajor Hans Stumpff on several occasions during January and February 1944. (Stumpff at that time was responsible for the Reich's Air Defence). However, he was not interested in Schmid's plans either. Firstly, he insisted that the recently introduced AI radar *SN-2* was on no account to fall into enemy hands; it was the only German radar that the RAF was not yet able to jam. Stumpff's second reason for his refusal was simple: Hitler himself was fundamentally opposed to Fernnachtjagd. Schmid was left with no choice but to shelve his plans.

Despite Hitler's orders, II./KG51 under the command of Major Dietrich Puttfarken (who was killed in action near Cambridge on 22/23 April 1944) was granted permission in March 1944 to commence Fernnachtjagd missions from Soesterberg airfield in the Netherlands. In the few short months between March and July 1944, the crews demonstrated the potential of long-range intruding over East Anglia. They destroyed forty Allied aircraft for the loss of twelve crews, and on many a night created chaos and confusion in the skies over England.

After the might of the Allied forces had been unleashed in the long-expected invasion in June 1944, Major Heinz-Wolfgang Schnaufer (Kommodore of NJG4) urged Schmid once more to try and get a sympathetic ear in the Luftwaffe High Command in regard to a renewed Fernnachtjagd. This time, he was successful. In view of the by now overwhelming Allied bombing offensive and the decreasing effectiveness of the Nachtjagd over the Reich, Hitler was at long last convinced of the need for a last desperate effort to stop the crushing bombing raids. The scheme of the operation was identical to the one proposed six months earlier. Under the code-name 'Gisela' the greater part of the Luftwaffe nightfighter force was to inflict at least one crushing blow to Bomber Command in a surprise intruder attack. With the full support of the inspector of Nachtjagd, Oberstleutnant Werner Streib, hundreds of crews were trained for the mission.

Ju88G-1 of 2./NJG2 fitted with SN-2 *radar and experimental* Schräge Musik *heavy calibre cannon in the nose of the aircraft, Holland, Summer of 1944.* Coll. Heinz Rökker.

By the end of November 1944 their training was completed, but the execution of the plans was postponed time and again by the Supreme Command. Luftwaffe intelligence had discovered that their adversaries were expecting a Fernnachtjagd operation. And more seriously, the Reich's fuel reserves were all but exhausted by this time. When on 21 February, 1945, the green light was finally given for 'Unternehmen Gisela', the operation was bungled by Peltz. On 3/4 March, he only committed some 142 Ju88Gs of NJG2, 3, 4 and 5 to the intruder operation; far too small a force to inflict a serious blow on Bomber Command. Some seventy to eighty crews actually operated over Britain in several waves. They intercepted a force of 234 bombers returning from a raid on the synthetic oil plant at Kamen and 222 aircraft returning from an attack on the Ladbergen aqueduct.

Twenty-seven-year-old Leutnant Arnold Döring at this time served as a pilot in 10./NJG3 at Jever in north-west Germany. Before he joined the nightfighter arm in the summer of 1943, he already had an incredible career behind him. Döring had completed 348 operational sorties as a bomber pilot in KG53 and KG55. He had seen action during the Battles of France and Britain and in the Russian campaign. Amongst his feats of arms were ten Russian fighters and bombers destroyed in air combat whilst flying a He111 bomber aircraft. As a *Wild Boar* pilot in JG300 *(see later)* he claimed a further eight aircraft shot down during 1943/44, and Döring went on to claim three more night victories in NJG2 and NJG3. He flew one of the Ju88Gs on Operation Gisela:

In January 1945, 'Operation Gisela' was planned. It was to be a long-range night fighting and bombing effort over England. With a British night bombing raid in progress, our nightfighters and bombers should cross the North Sea at very low level and intrude on the British over their aerodromes whilst they were landing. The whole thing had been planned to render the south of England unsafe first, then central England and finally the north. Thus, our comrades who operate over south and central England would drive the diverting Tommies into our arms.

Our reconnaissance aircraft had discovered that the Tommy flew around his 'dromes in almost peacetime fashion and with all lights on, both in the air and on the ground. Moreover, from the statements of prisoners of war, one had an exact picture of the take off and landing procedures. We received a thorough instruction on the airfield lighting systems, the Drem airfield circuiting and the T-system, as well as information on dummy airfields, the routes that the bombers used over England, flak and balloon-defended areas, and our own routes to fly in and out. Our Geschwader Kommodore, Oberst Radusch, went into the operation in depth, and after some time the Division Commander, General Major Ibel tested our knowledge. This all proceeded under the strictest secrecy. In spite of all this, something must have leaked out, as a little later a married couple of agents were taken into custody due to the vigilance of one of our pilots. Their aim was to spy on Operation Gisela.

Gisela was continuously shoved forward, the Englishman had got wind of the affair and tricked us by transmitting the popular song 'Tonight, I only dance with Gisela' on the soldiers' radio station Calais.

Then, finally, on the night of 3/4 March 1945 Operation Gisela is finally mounted. Some 150–200 British bombers have flown into the Reich, released their loads on Münster and we join the returning stream over the North Sea, whilst flying at a height of less than 50m [160ft], which should fool the enemy radar defences. We are heading for the peninsula of Flamborough Head, our sector to penetrate the British mainland. This is the same route that the returning bombers belonging to the British 100 Bomber Group are taking, in the area NW of Hull. We are ordered to keep absolute radio silence, the Tommy should not notice anything. Neither are we allowed to engage any *Viermots* [four-engined bombers] in combat over the North Sea, as we must succeed in totally surprising them.

Shortly before we arrive over the coast, we climb to a height of some 1,800m [5,800ft] and throw out bundles of *Düppel* [aluminium foil, known to the British as *Window*] to counter the AI of the Mosquitos. I cross the coast a little to the north of Flamborough head, over the small harbour town of Scarborough and watch how in this penetration zone an aircraft is hit by the flak hosing up and crashing in flames. I also observe a lot of fires from aircraft crash-landing on the enormous emergency landing ground, which is used by damaged *Viermots* that are not allowed to touch down on their regular 'dromes to avoid the danger of these aircraft blocking the runways. This once more proves that the true losses of the Tommies are bigger than one can assess in Germany from the wreckage of shot down machines on the continent.

Walter Hoyer, my *Funker*, makes notes of a series of *Abschüsse*, so that we can confirm the times of claims on our return. We identify a row of airfields on which bombs are dropped and see a lot of aircraft being shot out of the sky. Lines of tracer hiss down into targets on the ground, as we are ordered not to bring back home a single bullet from our frontal guns.

I descend steeply to some 600m [1,900ft] and as I approach two illuminated airfields, they both switch off. Three others are still in operation, on the ground red lamps flash the night intruder warning signal .-. .-. .-. = R for Raider. Yet many *Viermots* are still flying around with all navigation lights on.

This 'drome flashes its identification DH in white capital letters, the landing system is a Drem-system, and over the airfield it is a frantic affair. I position myself beneath a *Viermot* with all his navigation lights on, it is a B-17 as I can see from its wide tailplane. I aim a burst from my oblique cannons into the fuel tanks, the fuselage and wings. The bomber starts to burn, the fires in its fuselage flicker up and then become fainter. The crew probably switches on the fire-extinguishers. On the edge of the Drem system, the *Viermot* crashes hard in a pile of dust and smoke, but without a fire. We clearly see it in the bright moonlight, as we fly low and away over the wreckage.

Despite the fact that we fly very low, the navigation lights of a bomber even flash past beneath me. As I am not familiar with the surroundings and the moon disappears behind a bank of clouds, I let this *Viermot* escape and attack another one on its final approach. I destroy this Lancaster with my oblique cannons; it immediately bursts into a bright fire and crashes in an enormous sheet of flames.

The other Tommies now finally take notice and switch off their navigation lights. I engage a Lancaster from head-on and can only just climb over it before I could open fire. Despite the fact that my fuel is getting low, I circle the airfield that is the only one with its flare path still in operation, a couple of times, but can see no more adversaries. Neither can I discern anything on the ground, as the moon disappears completely.

Since we are allowed to attack anything on the ground, I eliminate a double morse identification beacon, attack some trucks on a mountainous road, shoot a train on fire and get rid of my remaining ammunition in storage sheds at Scarborough. A convoy is assembling on the sea just off the town, I can only just clear the masts of the anchored vessels and then set off for home, flying as low as possible. We still have a sea-crossing of some 600km [370 miles] ahead of us.

The Tommy takes revenge in another way, as he jams our radio beacons and switches on other beacons with the same identification as ours, but situated on British territory. Still, as I can recall this trick from my bombing missions back in 1940, they don't fool me, and I keep on course, heading east. After one and three-quarter hours we enter a zone of bad weather, with low cloud, which our 'weather frog' had not predicted. Soon, we overfly the Dutch coast. On dead reckoning, we reckon to be in the area of Jever, but my *Funker* can't get through to the homing station, as twenty-five machines are still waiting before us and some of them are in an emergency. There must be a desperate muddle over and on all aerodromes in the area of the German Bight due to the increasingly worsening weather conditions. As I only have fuel left for some fifteen more minutes, I send out an emergency call, I get a bearing which however is very weak, and moreover is far behind me, so I decide to touch down on an airfield I can see in front of me. It turns out to be Nordholz. We have an operational sortie of over five hours behind us.

I get a phone connection with Jever and report our successes. Olt Förster has also bagged two, Fw. Misch has one *Abschuss* and the other crews have either seen nothing, didn't get in a shooting position or haven't returned yet. Division wants to know everything, I have to give them an exact picture of my sortie, on the weather on both the way in and out, on my crossing of the coast, times, enemy defences, *Abschüsse*, etc. etc. etc. I finally drop down on a bed, I am exhausted but due to the too strong strain of the nerves I can't fall asleep. And the telephone kept ringing, first my Gruppe, then the Geschwader, again the Division, and even the Jagdkorps, they all want to know details of the operation. These inquisitive chairborne Staff stallions should have flown on the mission themselves, then they would know how things looked over there.

Probably the weather frogs had a lot to explain, as they had completely mispredicted the weather, and we had encountered the opposite of what they had told us, as sad to say so often had happened before. Our own losses among the returning crews must be enormous, as can be deducted from the many emergency calls over the radio and as later phone calls confirmed.

Next day, I receive a whole 500 litres of juice, fly back to Jever and on landing we have to shake lots of hands. Everybody is of the opinion that I now should get the Ritterkreuz.

The Gruppe had suffered severe losses: the Kommandeur, Major Ney was forced to bale out on the way back as he couldn't find an airfield to land on in the atrocious weather and he was badly injured in the process. The result was a paraplegia from the waist. His crew was safe. The Staffelkapitän of the 12th is missing. Uffz Lohse and his crew are missing. Uffz Kowalski and crew crashed shortly after taking off for Operation Gisela from Marx airfield due to an engine fire. The pilot and his *Funker* Wiebranitz are dead, his FE could bale out and thus saved his skin. Furthermore, many other aircraft are damaged in emergency landings, as these machines were landed in desperation with their last drops of fuel.

Hauptmann Heinz Rökker, Staffelkapitän of 2./NJG2 experienced a frustrating night during Operation Gisela. By this time, twenty-four-year-old Rökker had scored sixty-one kills, mainly *Viermots* in the *Tame Boar* (*see later*) night fighting over the Reich during 1944 and early 1945. He was decorated with the Ritterkreuz in July 1944:

Six crews of our Gruppe I./NJG2, led by Gruppenkommandeur Hptm. Raht, took off at 23.00 hours from Twente in Holland. We flew the Ju88G-6 with a four-man crew. Our aircraft were loaded with two AB 50/10 cluster bombs. In order to avoid being detected by British radar, we were briefed to cross the North Sea at a height of less than 100m [320ft] whilst heading for our allotted area of Grimsby-Lincoln. Only when in sight of the enemy coast, we were to climb to our operational height of between 500 and 1,000m [1,600 and 3,200ft].

Flying at low level over the North Sea at night was a nerve-racking business, as we had the impression that we might crash at any time into the white-crested waves which were well visible. I had to concentrate fully on the compass course and on the altimeter. I dared not switch on the more accurate electrical altimeter for fear of being located by the British. Luckily, the weather did not pose us any difficulties at this time. The sky was partly overcast, partly clear.

Hptm. Heinz Rökker, St.Kpt. of 2./NJG2 from 1 April 1944. Rökker's first Abschuss *was a Beaufort over the Mediterranean in June 1942 in daytime, followed by sixty-three kills at night. Among these were fifty-five Bomber Command* Viermots, *all shot down in the Reichsverteidigung between August 1943 and 15 March 1945. His sixty-fifth and final victim was a Mosquito which he shot down at 21.34 hours on 15 March 1945 over St. Trond. He was awarded the Knight's Cross on 27 July 1944 and the Oak Leaves on 12 March 1945. Here he is depicted whilst concentrating before taking off on a mission in early 1945 at Twente airfield.* Coll. Heinz Rökker.

After being airborne for some one and a half hours, we reached the British coast, which revealed itself from afar with several light beacons, both at sea and on land. I now climbed to operational height, and keyed up, we awaited what would happen to us. It was quite a ghastly feeling to fly over enemy territory, where at any time something unexpected might occur. After all, up to now we had almost exclusively flown on operations over friendly territory. Still, nothing happened. We encountered no visible defences like searchlights or flak. Of course we had to be prepared to be attacked at any time by British nightfighters, as we knew that the Mosquito fighter aircraft had been equipped with a very sophisticated AI radar. We did not switch on our *SN-2* radar, as we expected to encounter British aircraft with their navigation lights on. Besides, the emissions of the *SN-2* could be picked up by the British nightfighters.

Still, the skies remained dark, with only occasionally lights flickering on the ground. After groping around the skies for around half an hour without any success, we suddenly spotted the navigation lights of a single aircraft underneath us, and at a considerable distance. For us this was quite an unusual sight, as it bordered on suicide to fly with one's navigation lights switched on over the Heimat [home] territories. If one did, it was only a matter of time before one was finished off by a British intruder. For me, therefore, it was only a matter of time before this frivolous bird would plunge out of the sky in flames. I gave full throttle and soon, I was within range of the target. It was a four-engined aircraft, either a Lancaster or a Halifax, flying imperturbably on a straight and level course from north to south at a height of some 800m [2,600ft]. After having adapted my speed to the target, I positioned myself underneath the aircraft, in order to shoot it down with the oblique cannons, as I had done so many times before. Everything went according to plan. When I had it firmly in the reflector sight over my head, I pushed the button of my *Schräge Musik*. However, I noticed from the trajectory of the glim-ammunition that the whole burst flew past the aircraft. We could not observe any hits. In the same instant, our adversary had noticed our attack and switched off its navigation lights. The bomber pilot immediately turned the crate upside down, but against the clear starlit sky, I could still discern it clearly. Stupidly, I tried to stay beneath the machine and get in another burst. But of course, whilst diving down steeply at an angle of some forty degrees, it was quite impossible to get it into my sights again. When I finally conceived the bright idea to shoot my adversary down with my frontal guns, I naturally forgot to switch on the reflector sight in front of me. When at last I had done this, the Tommy had in the meantime disappeared under the horizon.

This whole action had brought me down to a height of only some 300m [970ft], and I could clearly distinguish houses and trees, so it was about time that I should regain some height. Undoubtedly, the British bomber crew must have thrown quite a party to celebrate their lucky escape. It was the only time in my nightfighting career that I did not hit my target with the oblique cannons. Later on, it became clear to me that I had wrongly estimated the distance to the target because of its navigation lights. As I could clearly see the aircraft through its lights, I had positioned myself too far below it, which had caused the burst to sweep past my adversary.

We flew on for around another hour in our allotted area, without detecting any further aircraft. In the end however, we spotted a lit up airfield, on which we dropped our bombs. We could not observe any results as after all we did not have a bomb sight and had to aim at our target visually. The airfield lighting was switched off briefly, but soon they came on again. I assume that one or several machines wanted to land there, but to my disappointment none of them had their navigation lights on.

By now, we had to start thinking of our return flight. Whilst flying eastwards again, we overflew a town in which the street lighting had been turned on. Since we had not encountered any defences so far, I blew out the lighting of a row of streets with my frontal guns for want of other targets and then set out to fly back to base. At low level we sped home over the North Sea. With this tactic we intended to shake off any nightfighters that might have been directed onto us. When we arrived back at Twente, the weather conditions had worsened considerably.

Rain was pouring down from a solid layer of clouds, with a ceiling at only 300m [970ft]. This front of bad weather was fatal for many inexperienced crews. They could not find their bases, crashed whilst attempting to land at other airfields, or were forced to bail out because they had got completely lost. It was rumoured that the British had jammed our radio beacons and also the R/T traffic. Nevertheless, my *Funker* Carlos Nugent had no difficulty in obtaining a bearing from our 'drome at Twente.

After having touched down at 03.10 hours, I wrote my combat report of the mission and told of my failed attempt to shoot a bomber down. It turned out that Ofw. Winn's crew had spotted the same British aircraft and had pursued it. When they had come into firing range, Winn witnessed my futile attack and how the machine had switched off its position lights. Of course, he was very annoyed that I had spoiled an almost certain kill for him. Hptm. Raht was more successful, as he reported two *Abschüsse*. He was the only successful pilot of our Gruppe on this night.

In all, thirty-three Ju88G night intruders were lost during the execution of Unternehmen Gisela. Five German aircraft crashed on British soil and eight other crews were posted missing. Three further crews perished in crashes on German territory, six crews baled out due to lack of fuel and eleven crashed on landing. Most of the losses on the return flight to Germany were due to adverse weather conditions, lack of fuel and faulty navigation at low level. These heavy losses were hardly compensated by a meagre twenty-four *Abschüsse*; thirteen Halifaxes, nine Lancasters, a Flying Fortress and a Mosquito had all fallen victim to the Fernnachtjäger. The intended knock-out blow had failed to materialize. Operation Gisela had turned out to be Nachtjagd's swan song.

Although Bomber Command mounted no major raid on the next night, a handful of experienced German crews again were briefed for an intruder operation over the United Kingdom, as Heinz Rökker recounts:

Of our Gruppe only Hptm. Raht and I took off for a Fernnachtjagd operation. We started at 18.30 hours at dusk on 4 March. One hoped that we could slip in and mingle with the bombers whilst they were in the process of taking off. When we crossed the Dutch coast on the way out, we were shot at by our own light flak, fortunately we were not hit. Certainly, the report of our flight taking place had not filtered through to the last flak position.

Our allotted night fighting area lay between Grimsby and Norwich. We headed for our target

Major Bertold 'Petz' Ney, Gruppenkommandeur of IV./NJG3 with nineteen victories broke his back on bailing out when he returned from Operation Gisela. The result was paralysis from the waist down. Ney remained bed-bound for the next fifty-one years, finally passing away in February 1996. Coll. Werner Kock.

area in good weather conditions. When we had arrived there, we hung around the area for over one and a half hours, without coming upon any defences. Despite our searching diligently and flying around we neither discovered any aircraft with navigation lights on, nor any illuminated airfields. In the far distance however, we saw how a German nightfighter shot an aircraft on fire with its oblique guns.

When the time had arrived for us to start on our return journey, there was a brightly illuminated city beneath us, in which we could even distinguish a number of streetcars. For want of better targets, and keeping in mind the German cities that by now had been turned into heaps of rubble and ashes, I dropped my bombs on this city. As quickly as possible we then dashed for it and sped back home. This time, we did not fly so low any more, as our presence must have surely been determined a long time ago. When we arrived over the sea again, our Observer, Fritz Wefelmeier, thought he had spotted an aircraft behind us. As we had to bear in mind the British nightfighters, to be on the safe side I turned in a full circle and changed over to the unpleasant low level flight for some time.

At 23.05 hours we landed safely at Twente, after a sortie of some four and a half hours duration. Hauptmann Raht had already landed before us, also without any success.

As a tactical concept, the deployment of Fernnachtjäger came much too late to bring the hoped-for success. It was, like so many other missions near the end of the war, a desperate attempt to contain the superiority of the enemy air force. However, by this time the defeat of Germany was already clearly recognizable.

Major Schnaufer, Germany's most successful nightfighter ace, had planned another operation similar to Gisela. He intended to commit his entire NJG4, some sixty aircraft in all, to a mass interception of a bomber stream over the Channel whilst the heavies were on their way back from a night raid. He fully realized that he might only pull it off once, but he expected to be able to destroy at least some 100 bombers. He had the detailed plans for this 'Unternehmen Feuersee' (Operation Sea of Fire) all worked out by January 1945, but, as he declared after the capitulation a few months later: 'The war was already over by the time I got the go ahead through the official channels'.

Due to Adolf Hitler's short-sighted point of view, the full potential of Fernnachtjagd never got a real chance to reach maturity. As Kammhuber had predicted as early as the autumn of 1940, the RAF bomber offensive could have been nipped in the bud by exploiting all the possibilities of long-range intruding over the United Kingdom. The Führer's negligence in this matter may well be regarded as his most serious strategic blunder with regard to Nachtjagd in World War II.

CHAPTER 3

Himmelbett, *Lichtenstein* and Bomber Streams: GCI Nachtjagd

From the start of the strategic night bombing offensive in the late spring of 1940, individual Bomber Command crews were briefed to find their own way to and from their assigned targets. Consequently, the bombers groped their way over the Third Reich in a widely dispersed front. When Nachtjagd was created, the planners of the new German arm devised their defensive measures to counter these British tactics. The German plan was to create a chain of adjacent nightfighter 'boxes' along the main routes of Bomber Command, and deal with enemy aircraft one by one as they crossed these zones. After some initial experiments with GCI (Ground Controlled Interception) radar, Kammhuber was quickly convinced that Nachtjagd could only achieve a maximum number of kills if it were completely guided by both ground and airborne radar. There was no other option, as Helle and Kombinierte Nachtjagd were proving to be too much effort for little result, especially on cloudy nights or in smog conditions (e.g. in the Ruhr Valley).

In co-operation with General Martini, head of Luftwaffe Signals and Communications, Kammhuber issued an order to German industry in the autumn of 1940 to develop an improved *Würzburg* radar with increased detection range and enhanced bearing accuracy. He also urged the development of an airborne radar and an

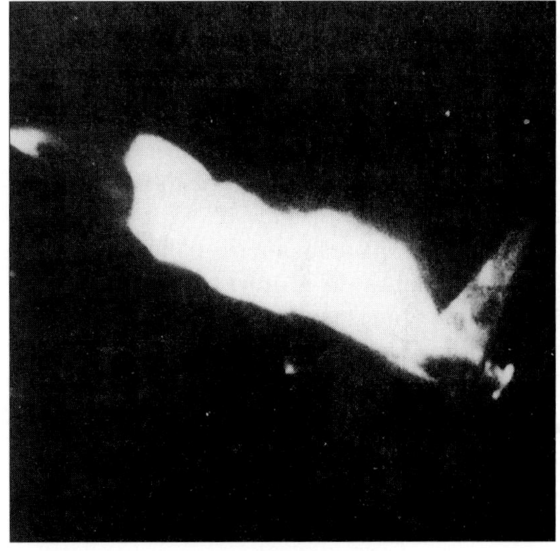

The first radar-controlled DuNaJa *kill. Wellington L7844 KX–T of 311 Squadron, bound for Kiel, fell victim to a Dornier Do17Z-10, flown by Lt Ludwig Becker and his* Funker *Uffz. Josef Staub of 4./NJG1 on 16 October 1940. The Wellington crashed in flames at 21.45 hours near Oosterwolde (Gld./The Netherlands), killing P/O. Bohumil Landa and three of his Czech crew. It was Becker's first* Abschuss, *the first of forty-four confirmed kills before he went missing in action on 26 February 1943.*
Coll. Douwe Drijver.

improved plotting table for processing data in the battle control centres of the night fighting zones. The modernized ground radars (*Würzburg Riesen* or *Giant Würzburg*) and *Seeburg* plotting tables were initially employed in the *HeNaJa*.

Kammhuber's ambitious plans met with some resistance among the Luftwaffe leadership. On the one hand, Luftwaffe Chief of Staff Generaloberst Hans Jeschonnek was aware of the need to develop a large-scale Nachtjagd to halt the Bomber Command offensive. On the other hand, he realized that a fully expanded offensive and defensive air force was beyond Germany's grasp. During this phase of the war, the emphasis of Germany's war machine was still on attack rather than defence, and since Bomber Command did not yet pose a significant threat, little attention was paid to countermeasures. Hans Jeschonnek had a blind faith in his Führer, and in his assumption that the war would be brief and victorious. Hitler demanded an offensive air force for the duration of the war, and for Jeschonnek this meant that the demands of the front lines where the German armies were advancing always prevailed over those of the air defence of the Reich. He even went so far as to neglect an adequate long-term training organization for the Luftwaffe in order to satisfy the immediate needs of the front.

This attitude was evident in continued opposition to the expansion of Nachtjagd into the truly effective force Kammhuber and his staff envisaged. Under these circumstances, the far-reaching plans for Fernnachtjagd over the United Kingdom could not be realized, while the expansion of a defensive Nachtjagd over the Reich met with the same continuous resistance. After the Battle of Britain, all attention was devoted to Russia, so the Luftwaffe's deployment in the east was given priority. As long as Bomber Command constituted no real and present danger, Göring and Jeschonnek did not see the need to meet Kammhuber's wishes for strengthening Nachtjagd. Two incidents during 1941 and 1942 demonstrate this opposition and lack of interest. In May 1941, Kammhuber was summoned to meet Göring at his Karinhall estate, where he was told that the invasion of Russia was imminent and that he had to redirect half of his nightfighter force to the Eastern Front. Kammhuber's protests were of no use, although eventually, due to other circumstances, the order was not carried out and the disastrous consequences the transfer would have had on the development of Nachtjagd did not materialize. Six months after this first incident, Kammhuber unfolded his plans to Hermann Göring and Hans Jeschonnek to expand his force to eight Nachtjagdgeschwader and a radically enlarged ground control organization. His two superiors still would have nothing of it and rejected his plans as utterly Utopian.

Kammhuber was convinced that a nightfighter force of this size was sorely needed to repel the

Hampden Is of 61 Squadron being serviced and bombed up at RAF Hemswell prior to an operation. This squadron lost fifty-six Hampdens during some two years of operations from September 1939 till July 1941, when the unit started conversion onto the ill-fated Manchester. Coll. Alex H. Gould.

increasing Bomber Command offensive. He based his conclusions on estimates of aircraft production figures in Great Britain and on the recent growth of Bomber Command. Nevertheless, his realistic plans stood no chance with his superiors. After the launch of Operation Barbarossa in June 1941, the Eastern Front took priority over the needs of the air defence of the Reich and seriously curtailed the implementation of Kammhuber's plans for the build-up of Nachtjagd.

In spite of all the opposition from Hitler, Göring and Jeschonnek, Kammhuber worked as hard as he could, with the limited means at his disposal, to provide the Reich with a roof that would be as 'waterproof' as possible. During 1941, the *HeNaJa* belt was expanded in depth with *DuNaJa* zones. Most nightfighter crews actually preferred to intercept bomber aircraft with the aid of searchlights in the *HeNaJa* belt, where they still had some limited freedom of manoeuvre and could see what was going on. By incorporating *DuNaJa* zones in front of the *HeNaJa* belt, Kammhuber encouraged his crews to start their interception patrols under guidance of radar directed ground control. Should this method fail, then the individual crews could always have a final attempt at the illuminated bombers in the searchlight belt. Under this scheme, Luftwaffe nightfighter crews got their first valuable experience of GCI operations.

The partially overlapping *DuNaJa* boxes gradually increased in number during 1941. By the end of the year, these boxes covered almost the whole of the Netherlands and the coastal areas of north-west Germany, which were the most frequented routes of Bomber Command during raids on the Ruhr Valley and German ports. The effectiveness of the radar-controlled *DuNaJa* was rapidly demonstrated. Every ninth nightfighter sortie in a *DuNaJa* box led to a kill, whereas in *HeNaJa* this ratio was forty-one to one. The fully radar guided interception technique in the *DuNaJa* boxes was code-named Himmelbett ('four-poster bed'), and during the spring of 1942 the technique had become so sophisticated and successful that Hitler's decision to remove the searchlight batteries from Nachtjagd's defence system did not have any serious consequences. One result was that Kammhuber was forced to expand the existing chain of Himmelbette, both in width and in depth. As a first measure, the Himmelbett belt along the north-west European coastlines was further expanded, followed by the areas around Bomber Command's major targets and along the bombers' main routes over the Reich territory. It was Kammhuber's intention not to leave any gaps in the night roof over the Reich that could be used by an aircraft to sneak in undetected. Moreover, this concept enabled his nightfighters to intercept and destroy both incoming and returning bomber aircraft.

Himmelbett station 'Hering' (Herring) near Medemblik on the western coast of Holland. The Freya *radar is flanked by two* Würzburgs, *one of which is visible on the right. 'Hering' was one of the first Himmelbett stations to become operational, in late 1941.* Coll. Günther Heise, via Johan Schuurman.

Kammhuber was soon forced to enlarge his Himmelbett zones further, after the British bomber crews learned to respect the danger zone over the Netherlands and switched to penetration routes to the north and to the south of the main air defence line. As early as March 1941, the Himmelbett-zone stretched to the Danish border; just over a year later it had expanded from northern Denmark down to Paris. By the end of 1942, the major industrial centres in Germany's hinterland were also protected by GCI boxes. Himmelbett Nachtjagd stood at its peak in the summer of 1943, when the major part of the Third Reich in the west was covered by Himmelbette.

Each individual Himmelbett site had a *Freya* early warning radar with an effective range of between 75 to 95 miles (120 to 150km), and which provided early detection of a target. Two precision radars, the *Würzburg Riesen,* were used for the actual interception. One tracked the bomber as it overflew the box, and the second directed the box's allocated nightfighter to the enemy aircraft. The heart of the central operations room of a Himmelbett box was formed by a *Seeburg* table which displayed the air situation over the box. The operational procedures for a Himmelbett interception were as follows: the moment an enemy aircraft was detected with the *Freya* long-range radar, one nightfighter was scrambled from a nearby airfield. The nightfighter was then ordered by ground control to proceed to a radio beacon in the Himmelbett box and await further orders whilst circling the beacon. As soon as the *Würzburg* plotted the incoming British aircraft, the nightfighter was directed to the bomber with the aid of the second *Würzburg.* The ground controller had a direct radio connection to the fighter pilot, and would guide him to the bomber by skilfully interpreting the radar data depicted on the *Seeburg* table. An experienced pilot co-operating with a familiar and equally experienced ground controller, could be brought to within visual range of a bomber and shoot it down in only a few short minutes.

During 1941 and the first months of 1942, this procedure was executed almost completely without the aid of airborne radar in the nightfighter aircraft themselves. Although Kammhuber was convinced

The two cornerstones of the Himmelbett GCI system:
(A) A rotating Freya-Köthen *early warning radar was used for long range detection of bomber aircraft.* Freya *was named after the warrior wife of the Nordic war-god Wotan. Aircraft flying at a height of 6,500ft (2,000m) could be tracked at a distance of some 40 miles (65km); when flying at a height of 32,500ft (10,000m) this was increased to some 140 miles (230km). The set shown here was in use in the Himmelbett station 'Schlei' at Schiermonnikoog Island, a box which became operational in early 1942.*

(B) In the Himmelbett boxes, the Freya *radar was flanked by two* Würzburg Riese (Giant Würzburg) *GCI radars. This precision radar had an effective range of some 37 miles (60km), with an accuracy of some 100yd (m). It measured 26ft (7.9m) high and 24ft (7.5m) wide. One* Würzburg *was used for tracking an enemy aircraft and the second one for guiding a nightfighter to the bomber.* Coll. Wyb Jan Groendijk.

that Himmelbett Nachtjagd could only come to full fruition by a combined use of both ground and airborne radar, this idea did not meet with much enthusiasm from his crews. Aircrew would rather rely on the 'Eyeball Mk I' than on unfamiliar radar gadgets, while the weight of the equipment and the drag from the aerials mounted on the aircraft's nose severely limited a nightfighter's performance.

Kammhuber's specifications had led to Telefunken developing an AI radar device with a forward scanning range of between 200 and 3,300yd (200 and 3,000m). The radar was called *Lichtenstein BC* and was to be operated by the navigator/air gunner, or *Bordfunker* in the nightfighter crew. A first *Lichtenstein* set was installed into the Dornier Do215 coded G9+OM of Oblt Ludwig Becker of 4./NJG1. Whilst operating from Leeuwarden airfield, Becker and his *Bordfunker*, Uffz. Staub, scored six kills between 8/9 August and 29/30 September 1941. These were Becker's second to seventh victories. This success convinced many sceptical crews of AI's huge potential. It took quite some time to introduce *Lichtenstein* on a large scale, and was not until the spring of 1943 that some 95 per cent of nightfighter aircraft were so equipped. Consequently, Nachtjagd was deprived of an excellent opportunity to exact an even heavier toll from Bomber Command during 1942 than the arm already did. At this time the British bombers still flew their sorties in a widely dispersed formation and thus represented ideal targets for a combined use of both ground and airborne radar.

Uffz. Heinz Huhn served as *Bordfunker* in Lt Karl-Heinz Völlkopf's crew in the Leeuwarden Gruppe, the Nachtjagd unit that was the first to be fully equipped with *Lichtenstein BC* in the spring of 1942. Heinz noted in his diary on his crew's first Himmelbett AI kill:

> Mission on 1.6.42. Take off at 23.30 hours. Get course to steer from ground control. Clouds beneath us. Moon very big, very clear sky. *Kurier* [bomber] still far away to the west. We approach him, on incoming heading. Pick it up in *Li*-set at distance of 4.5km [2.8 miles]. We turn round and chase him. Marie 2 [Luftwaffe code for distance

Before the Lichtenstein *AI radar was introduced into operational service during 1942, Nachtjagd had to make do with various less successful devices to trace the RAF bombers. Depicted here is a belly-landed Bf110 of II./NJG1 near Paderborn, equipped with an infra-red detection device known as* Spanner *mounted forward of the cockpit.* Coll. Alfred F. Weinke.

to target], slow down, slow down, can't see anything. We've overtaken the *Kurier*. Start the whole procedure again. Marie 4, Marie 3. Pick him up in Li-set at 2.6km [1.6 miles]. Height 3,000m [9,700ft]. I lead my pilot towards him. Marie 300m [970ft]. Karlheinz: 'I have him!'. We lose height. Underneath *Kurier*. It's a Hampden. Dangerous, can see and fire downwards. We climb ever more. Distance some 100 to 150m [110 to 160yd]. Attack. Keep firing. Burst of fire aimed very well. *Kurier* is burning. Sieg Heil! Karlheinz congratulates me: a *Lichtenstein* victory! I am feeling very pleased.

Receive new course to steer from ground control. Marie 3. Change pans of ammunition for cannons. Marie 2. Turn round. Marie 5.4 and picked him up. Lead pilot towards him. Marie 500m [550yd]. I roar: 'Slow down!' Völlkopf throttles back. Radar echo disappeared. *Kurier* not visible. 'You are leaving sector' from ground control. Flown too far. Nothing to do any more. I announce returning to base a little later. No reply from ground station. Steer for radio beacon. On 2.6.42 Hptm. Lent presents me with the EKI [Iron Cross First Class].

The victim of the Völlkopf/Huhn crew was Hampden AT191 'A' of 408 Squadron. P/O. Charlton and crew had taken off from Balderton at 22.58 hours as part of the 1,000 bomber force bound for Essen, and after the nightfighter attack the Hampden crashed in flames into the Ijsselmeer, with

Wreckage of Wellington Mk II Z8370 of 12 Squadron on the North Sea beach of Terschelling island. Oblt Ludwig Becker shot down this aircraft as his ninth victory on 20/21 January 1942 during a raid on Emden. F/Lt W.H. Thallon, captain of Z8370, and three of his crew survived the crash-landing at 21.00 hours to be taken prisoner, but Sgts Edmund Fowler, 2nd pilot, and William Rutherford, the tail gunner, were killed and buried on Terschelling. Whilst operating in the Himmelbett sector 'Tiger' on Terschelling, Becker went on to shoot down, within forty minutes, two more Wellingtons of 142 and 101 Squadrons into the North Sea. There were no survivors. Coll. Douwe Drijver.

Uffz. Heinz Huhn, Bordfunker *to Oblt Völlkopf, in his Bf110 of II./NJG2, Leeuwarden airfield, 1942.* Coll. Heinz Huhn, via Rob de Visser.

Himmelbett night fighting aces of 6./NJG2 (Leeuwarden), summer 1942. (l–r): Lt Robert Denzel (nine victories, shot down and killed by a Beaufighter intruder on 25/26 July 1943); Lt Eberhard Gardiewski (five victories, POW 25 July 1943); Oblt Ludwig Becker, Ritterkreuz, (St.Kpt. with forty-four night Abschüsse, *missing on 26 February 1943); Lt Josef Schauberger; Lt Wolfgang Kuthe (eight victories, killed in flying accident on 14 April 1943).* Coll. Heinz Huhn, via Rob de Visser.

Uffz. Fritz Abromeit, Lt Gardiewski's Bordfunker *in 6./NJG2 and 12./NJG1.* Coll. Rob de Visser.

the loss of the whole crew. F/Sgt Womar DFM, one of the crew's gunners, was flying his fifty-sixth sortie on this night. Of the thirty-seven RAF aircraft lost on the second 1,000 bomber raid on Essen, at least five were claimed by nightfighters.

Another *Bordfunker* in IV./NJG1 at this time was Uffz. Fritz Abromeit, who joined the 12th Staffel with his pilot Lt Eberhard Gardiewski in the summer of 1942. He recalls his first contact with the enemy in the Himmelbett:

> On the night of 4/5 September 1942 we took off from Leeuwarden for the Xth time for a patrol in the night fighting box Tiger [Tiger was the codename for the area around Terschelling Island]. We already had a few missions under our belt, but had never had a brush with the enemy, no success. It was no small feat to find an enemy aircraft on a dark night. Our machine was not equipped with a *Lichtenstein* radar set yet.
>
> It was in the second half of the night when we took off in our Bf110. Dawn was not far off any more, as the sky in the east was already becoming slightly lighter. The night fighting controller of Tiger sent us on a north-easterly heading, as a straggler was expected to be heading in our direction, coming back from Germany. After a few corrections of our course, we started peering towards

the horizon for the enemy aircraft. Only a short while later we spotted the bomber, and moments later we flew some 100–150m [110–160yd] underneath it. We identified it as a Halifax. My heart was missing a beat, and I expected my pilot felt the same. At long last, the anxiously awaited moment had come for us to make an *Abschuss*! We lowered our voices over the intercom – the enemy might hear us! The bomber droned on a steady course in the direction of England, which was a good sign, its crew had not noticed us.

'I am going in to attack', my pilot said and slowly pulled up the machine. I barely had time to announce 'Pauke, Pauke' over the R/T. I heard from the front of the aircraft 'Shut up Fritz' and already our two cannons and four machine guns were bellowing. Two or three seconds later, it rumbled and flashed frighteningly in our machine. Splinters of glass, mixed with dust flew through the cockpit. We obviously had not hit the enemy well, perhaps through inexperience, and possibly also by our excitement. Now our adversary had successfully hit back!

Leutnant Gardiewski pulled our machine away in a steep curve to the left. We then noticed black smoke belching from both our engines. Still, the propellers were turning. We assumed that the coolers had taken hits. Due to the excitement and having to pay attention to what happened to our own aircraft I didn't keep an eye on the Halifax. It probably flew back home with a few hits – or perhaps not! We never found out what happened to this aircraft.

I proceeded to get in touch with the ground station to report the bad shape we were in, but unfortunately, the radio transmitter was u/s. Thank God the intercom was not damaged. We were well aware of the fact that the engines would only work properly for a short time yet before they would pack up. So, we had two options: bail out, or try and glide towards the coast. We decided to go for the latter; with engines throttled back we glided in a southerly direction. These were tense minutes. Would we have enough height to reach the coast?

It was now almost daybreak and on the horizon we spotted land. We had some height left – the air combat had taken place at some 3,000m [9,700ft] – so nothing much could go wrong any more. With a final effort of the engines, or rather of one engine, we reached the island of Terschelling. Skilfully, my pilot belly-landed the Bf110 on the soft sand of the dunes. We were down on terra firma again!

Bf110 nightfighter of 6./NJG2 belly-landed by the Gardiewski/Abromeit crew on Terschelling's North Sea beach, 5 September 1942. Coll. 't Behouden Huys.

Pilots and their pet dogs, Leeuwarden airfield, spring 1943. Left: twenty-two-year-old Lt Karl-Heinz Völlkopf, who was killed in a low-flying accident on 21/22 June 1943. Between April 1942 and May 1943, Völlkopf scored six Himmelbett Abschüsse *in II./NJG2 and III./NJG1. Right: Lt Eberhard Gardiewski, pilot with 6./NJG2 and 12./NJG1. Gardiewski had five confirmed victories to his credit as a nightfighter pilot, before he and his* Funker *Fritz Abromeit were shot down by B-17s on 25 July 1943, on their very first daylight sortie. After a successful ditching off the Frisians, they were picked up by Royal Navy MTB621 and taken prisoner.* Coll. Heinz Huhn, via Rob de Visser.

> Happily, we both jumped out of the crate. From underneath both the engines smoke was ascending and we heard hissing sounds. The driving gears had done their duty till the last moment!
>
> The fighter control officer, I think it was Leutnant Schulz, had followed us on his radar sets from the moment we had engaged the enemy till we had come down.

On the night when Lt Gardiewski and Uffz. Abromeit were shot down, their unit, IV./NJG1 claimed three Halifaxes and five Wellingtons from a force of 251 bombers bound for Bremen. Among their victims were Lancaster R5682 of 61 Squadron (crashed near Wartena), and Halifax W1220 of 103 Squadron, which crashed just North of Leeuwarden. In all, Bomber Command lost twelve aircraft, 4.8 per cent of the force. The increasing efficiency of the nightfighter force during this period is clearly illustrated by the fact that the majority of the Bomber Command losses in this night fell to fighters.

After their inauspicious debut, Gardiewski and Abromeit further perfected their trade and over the next few months accumulated five night kills. The end of this crew's night fighting career came on 25 July 1943, when they were sent off in a force of some sixteen Bf110 nightfighters to engage American day bombers returning from Hamburg. Whilst attacking a B-17 flown by Lt Baker in the high squadron of the 303rd Bomb Group, they were hit in both engines by return fire and soon after ditched in the North Sea off Texel. They survived the rough landing at nearly 120mph (200kph), and spent the next four hours in their dinghy. During the following night, they attracted the attention of a gaggle of ships, but these turned out to be British MTBs prowling off the Dutch coast. The German crew were picked up by MTB621, were well treated and survived a gun battle with a German convoy some six hours later. They were landed next day at Great Yarmouth and spent the next two years in a POW camp in Canada.

Nachtjagd had matured into a mighty force during 1942, and wherever Bomber Command aircraft penetrated, they ran a great risk of being intercepted in the Himmelbett boxes or in the *KoNaJa* over Germany's major cities and industrial areas. On 10 August 1941, the strapping Nachtjagd Division and its battle control organizations were grouped to form a Fliegerkorps of their own, the XIIth. Some nine months later, on 1 May 1942, Kammhuber was forced to split up his bulging Nachtjagd Division into three separate units; the First, Second and Third Jagd Divisions. This splitting up did not entail a decentralization of control, as the entire arm remained centrally led from Kammhuber's HQ at Zeist in The Netherlands.

Despite the ever mounting number of losses that his crews managed to inflict on Bomber Command during 1941 and early 1942, Kammhuber was not a satisfied man. After all, there was no apparent decline in the number of bombing raids on the Reich. Moreover, losses inflicted on the bombers represented an average of a mere 4 per cent of the night sorties dispatched by the RAF, with an occasional peak of 5 per cent or more during deep penetration raids. Kammhuber knew that an average casualty rate of five per cent or more would put a stop to the numerical growth of Bomber Command. And if he could inflict a sustained loss rate of 10 per cent, the British strategic bombing offensive would grind to a halt. The General der Nachtjagd was also well aware of the fact that Bomber Command was busy converting from light and medium twin-engined aircraft to a new generation of four-engined heavy bombers. Great Britain's offensive potential would be greatly enlarged with the Stirling, Halifax and the Lancaster. But although he was supported in his ideas by Milch, Kammhuber was quite unable to convince anyone in the Oberkommando der Luftwaffe (OKL) of this looming threat. Neither Reichsmarschall Göring, nor Generaloberst Jeschonnek expressed any desire to shift the main Luftwaffe effort from attack to defence. In the autumn of 1941, Göring strikingly explained his views on Kammhuber's continuing requests for an expansion of Nachtjagd: 'This nonsense will no longer be necessary the moment I have returned my fighter units to the West' (after the defeat of Russia).

On 22 February 1942, Air Marshal Arthur Harris was appointed C-in-C Bomber Command, taking over from Air Vice Marshal Baldwin. 'Bomber' or 'Butch' Harris enthusiastically prosecuted the newly adopted area bombing policy. He was to lead Bomber Command for the rest of the war, vigorously bringing the war to the German economy, its leaders and people by massive area bombing raids. During the early months of 1942, British intelligence had sorted out how the Himmelbett system worked. As a result, Harris had come to realize that by sending his aircraft to penetrate German air space in a compact 'Bomber Stream', he could exploit Himmelbett's one weak spot – only one or two nightfighters could be directed onto bomber targets in any one GCI box. And with the aid of improved navigation methods, like the *Gee* system, by May 1942 his men had the capability to use the new tactic. A further advantage of the bomber stream was that Harris expected to inflict much more damage on his

The geodetic construction is clearly visible in this burnt-out Wellington. The aircraft is possibly Z1290 of 460 Squadron which crashed at Tondern, Germany on 28/29 April 1942 with the loss of F/Sgt L.M. Shephard RAAF and his Australian crew. Coll. Peter Petrick.

targets by concentrating each raid into a short period of time.

During the first three 1,000 bomber raids on Cologne, Essen and Bremen in May and June 1942, the weakness of the Himmelbett system became painfully apparent to Nachtjagd's leadership. The huge forces employed on these raids flew in a compact stream and carried out concentrated attacks on these major cities. Apart from the Bremen raid when nightfighters interfered in force due to the stream spreading out, only small losses were incurred by the Main Force. Individual Himmelbett boxes were completely swamped, and, consequently, Nachtjagd was unable to put up a good fight. The bomber stream tactic had clearly borne fruit. S/Ldr John Russell DFC flew Whitley V Z9307 of 1502 Flt from Driffield, one of only nine aircraft falling victim to nightfighters on the successful Cologne raid of 30/31 May 1942:

> Two attacks from below by NF. Nothing heard from Tail Gunner. Port nacelle and inner wing burning – fires beyond control so gave the word to jump at 1,100ft [330m]. 2nd Pilot handed me my parachute and immediately port wing disappeared with loud explosion. A/c turned onto her back and started to spin. Flames now everywhere, cockpit full of smoke and tangled up crew. Feeling very dazed and stupid and still pulling at controls to try and correct spin. Another explosion and I am alone in space, with moon, fields, canals etc. chasing one another round and round. Now very wide-awake and cool as I am airborne and have my parachute firmly gripped in my right hand.

Debriefing in 'Ops' Room of II./NJG2 at Leeuwarden airfield. Oblt Ludwig Becker, St.Kpt. of 6./NJG2 has just returned from a mission, probably on 17/18 August, 1942. On this night, he claimed Stirling BF330 of 214 Squadron at 01.46 hours, some 19 miles (30km) north of Terschelling Island (Sgt A. Fleming RCAF and crew all killed), and Wellington X3654 of 101 Squadron at 02.02 hours near Harlingen (P/O. E.H. Brown RCAF and crew all killed). Coll. Horst Diener, via Ab Jansen.

> Clip it on very gingerly and pull rip-cord. Two swings and I hit heavily breaking my right leg. A/c hit a few seconds later (most of it) about 200yd [m] away. WOp. arrived later, being the only one to get his parachute on before being blown out of the A/c. 2nd Pilot undoubtedly saved my life and lost his own through fetching my pack before trying to put on his. He and Navigator fell some distance away. Tail gunner was either killed or incapacitated by gunfire. His body was still in the turret with cannon shells through the thorax.

The unfortunate Whitley crashed near Hoboken in the south-west suburbs of Antwerp. P/O. Box RNZAF, 2nd pilot, F/Sgt Godbehere RCAF, navigator and Sgt Orman, tail gunner were killed and buried at Schoonselhof. S/Ldr Russell DFC and his WOp. F/O. Foster DFM were taken prisoner, ending up at Sagan POW camp.

Apart from the safety in numbers offered by the concentrated bomber stream, the British bomber crews had another tactic at their disposal to evade a nightfighter attack: the corkscrew manoeuvre. F/Lt Stanley Freestone served as a pilot with 142 Squadron flying Wellingtons in 1942, and with 199 Squadron in Stirlings in 1943. He experienced no encounters with fighters whilst on Wellingtons, but this changed when

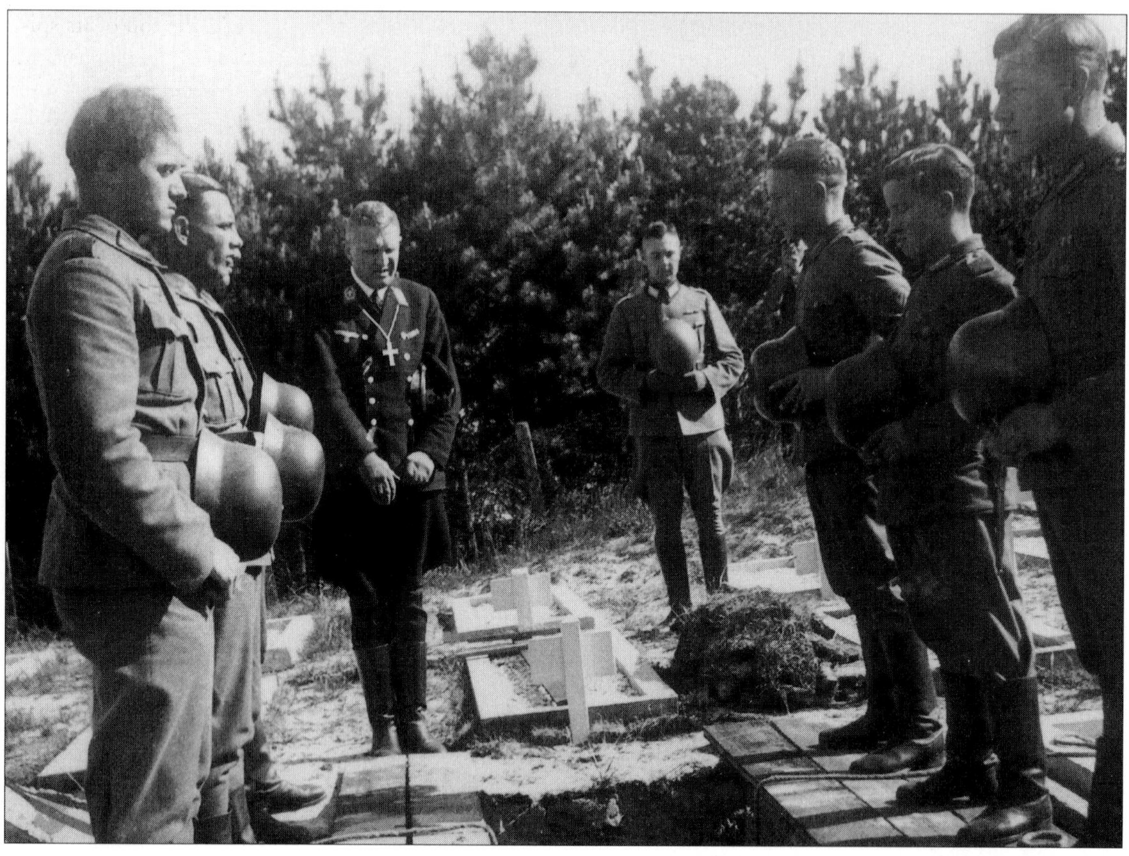

Kriegsmarine vicar saying a prayer at the grave of F/Lt Reginald Turtle at Vredenhof cemetery on Schiermonnikoog Island, during funeral ceremonies with full military honours. Twenty-six-year-old F/Lt Turtle, a veteran with forty-six 'ops' under his belt, flew Stirling N3761 of 214 Squadron to Emden on 6/7 June 1942. His aircraft was intercepted by a Bf110 night fighter of II./NJG2 and shot down into the North Sea off Terschelling at 01.47 hours. The whole crew was killed, with five men washing ashore on Schiermonnikoog, Vlieland and Terschelling islands. F/Lt Turtle was posthumously awarded a DFC. Coll. Wyb Jan Groendijk.

he came to fly Stirlings. During August 1943 he experienced no less than four nightfighter attacks. Twice, on 10 and 12 August, his crew claimed a fighter damaged. Stanley comments:

> To obtain a fighter downed confirmation was very difficult since it required some confirming observation from another crew. That is an observed aircraft going down or on fire. Time and position would have to be logged to clear all doubt.
>
> The prime purpose was to save your bomber aircraft – not engage a highly manoeuvrable aircraft which could always outgun you anyway. Many German nightfighters were armed with 20mm cannon.
>
> We were taught and used a basic defensive manoeuvre once attacked by a fighter. It was called a corkscrew and so named since one flew a pattern in the sky akin to flying the line of a corkscrew. It was actioned by the pilot as soon as he was given

the requisite command by his observing air gunners. As soon as the attacker was spotted the gunner noted the direction from which the intended attack was coming and the turn was actioned in that direction. The whole purpose of this was to increase the angle of deflection (aiming off) and decrease the time that the attacking fighter could bring his guns to bear on the bomber.

The pilot of the bomber thus had to roll the aircraft steeply and rapidly in that direction and at the same time increase engine power and push the aircraft nose down to further increase rapid acceleration. After a heading change of some fifty degrees the aircraft was rolled to the opposite bank and initiate some climb, thus making a twisting/corkscrew flight path. Then the whole procedure was reversed again as the aircraft reached the top of its spiral, and down one went again. It was seldom necessary to execute more than one complete spiral. Usually by this time the fighter had overshot his target and would be concerned about presenting a target to the bomber's guns and would break away.

Sgt Stanley Freestone (right) and his crew on completion of Wellington training at RAF Lossiemouth, posing in front of their Nissen hut. Coll. Stanley Freestone.

As a personal addition to this manoeuvre I used excessive rudder control in the turns to exaggerate the apparent turning movement. This caused the bomber to slip into the turn and hopefully give the attacking fighter a false sense of the true direction. This tactic seemed to work because on more than one occasion I observed fighter bullets going over the top of my cockpit canopy, in other words the fighter pilot was not aiming with enough deflection. Further proof it cannot be luck, in four attacks I never sustained any real damage as a result of these fighter encounters.

In corkscrewing a heavily laden bomber, at night and flying on instruments, it was very easy to overstress the airframe and/or lose control. Through overbanking in the corkscrew the pilot could take the wings past the vertical and stall the aircraft in an inverted position. This could result in an almost unrecoverable spin or a dive during which one could exceed the safe maximum speed of the airframe. This could lead to complete loss of control and structural damage. Bear in mind these pilots in the main had well under 300 hours total flying experience.

However all the foregoing is the experience of a crew that survived an attack. Many never knew what hit them as a short burst of cannon fire took away a complete wing. I personally have seen an aircraft explode completely at cruising height, possibly having received a direct hit from anti-aircraft or perhaps suddenly 'jumped' by a fighter. It was a terrible sight. A huge ball of fire and as the flaming debris plunged earthwards a huge waterfall of fire and explosions reaches down thousands of feet. It is not dramatizing the event but one would hear a comment from your own crew of something like 'Poor bastards'. A most derogatory remark upon the immediate death of some of your colleagues or more correctly comrades in arms.

Australian W/O. Bill Pearce served as WOp./AG. in F/Lt Andy Pelly's crew flying in Lancasters with 100 and 156 Squadrons during 1944–45. He further comments on corkscrewing:

> On my 12th op with No.100 Squadron in September, 1944, to bomb the railway marshalling yards at Frankfurt we survived four separate fighter attacks. The fact that we survived these four attacks was due, I feel sure, to the vigilance of my two gunners and the skill of my pilot.
>
> The corkscrew manoeuvre was a very violent one. I sat with my knees jammed under my small desk. At the bottom of the dive my stomach was forced down, as was my body; at the top of the climb I tended to float, but my knees under the desk prevented this. My parachute pack, lying on the floor beside me floated up in the air, and as we commenced to dive again, it dropped slowly down, to settle again on the floor.
>
> And all the time I was listening to the sound of our guns; this came through the intercom as a 'tick-tick-ticking' sort of sound. I smelled the burning cordite as it drifted through the fuselage. And I felt the fear. Sitting in the cabin, virtually hanging on grimly, waiting for the worst to happen, and hoping like mad that it wouldn't. All else was obliterated from my mind; I was taking no part in the action, merely waiting, more than anxiously, for whatever might happen.
>
> And then a gunner called that the fighter had broken off the attack, and it was OK to level out. I breathed again!

Bill Pearce now comments on another danger that threatened the bomber crews: being hit by bombs from 'friendly' aircraft in the bomber stream over the target:

> I witnessed one very frightening incident on a daylight raid to Walcheren Island on 29 October 1944. We had dropped our bombs and were circling in the target area in support of the Master Bomber. I was standing in the astrodome, which was above my position in the Lancaster's cabin, watching, somewhat in awe, sticks of bombs falling from other aircraft above us. Luckily, for us, none of these bombs were falling close enough to threaten my aircraft. However, as I watched, I saw a 'cookie' (the 4,000lb/1,800kg 'blockbuster'), I saw it fall down and hit one of the lower aircraft. There was a huge explosion: the aircraft virtually disappeared into a cloud of black smoke. I looked at it, fascinated, with an awful sickly feeling in my stomach and kept an intense and anxious watch in the sky above us. That black pall of smoke hung there in the sky throughout the duration of the attack.
>
> We left this target area and I returned to my duties at the wireless desk. I could not get the sight of this explosion out of my mind's eye: I thought 'How often does this happen on our night time ops, when no-one can see it happening; no-one can record or report it. How many bombers which were reported as "Missing" were destroyed in this way?' With hundreds of bombers, at, usually, three different levels, put on a target in virtually a matter of minutes, this sort of thing must have happened far too often. There have been aircraft which have survived being hit by a bomb from above, and which have managed to get back to base with a gaping hole in a wing, or the fuselage, or with an incendiary sticking out of a wing, which, luckily, had not ignited. So, there were other hazards, apart from enemy action, and the weather!

The initial large area bombing raids during the spring of 1942 had clearly pointed out to the German war leaders the painful consequences of their neglect of the Reich's air defence. Yet, little was done to remedy this situation. Milch's and Kammhuber's repeated requests for strengthening Nachtjagd only met with opposition from their superiors. Göring simply refused to believe the statistics on British production of four-engined bombers, which were presented to him by Milch. Hitler just observed that Kammhuber's Nachtjagd had obviously failed in warding off the *Terrorflieger* area raids. After having hauled Jeschonnek over the coals for failing to prevent the 1,000 bomber raid on Cologne, Hitler ordered him to launch a series of retaliatory raids against cities in Britain. This course of action was typical of Hitler's views:

During the pioneering years, many Nachtjagd aircraft were lost in accidents. Here Bf110C D5+HN of 5./NJG3, flown by Ofw. Dingeldeih and his Funker *Gebhardt has come to grief at Grove airfield in 1942. No* Lichtenstein *AI radar has been fitted to this aircraft yet.* Coll. Peter Petrick.

the best way to deal with a terror bombing attack was to respond in kind. The air defence of the Reich was hardly strengthened and the Luftwaffe remained primarily engaged in the campaigns in Russia and the Mediterranean.

That the German war leaders refused to shift the emphasis to defence was mainly due to the fact that the RAF bombing offensive had only caused minor damage to Germany's war industry and cities until the spring of 1942. In retrospect, Hitler, Göring, and Jeschonnek can be blamed for refusing to recognize the threat of the ever mounting British, and later American, bombing offensive, despite the clear indications that Kammhuber and Milch supplied them with. Moreover, even if these three war leaders had been inclined to shift the Luftwaffe emphasis to the defence of the Reich, by now they would have hardly been able to do this in practice. At the end of 1942, the fourth year of war, the Luftwaffe was heavily engaged on three different fronts: Russia, Northern Africa and in Germany itself. The Luftwaffe could not possibly meet the demands of all three sufficiently; its reserves had been stretched so far that it could not even achieve air superiority over one front. An adequate strengthening of the air defence of the Third Reich was almost completely out of reach already, unless a completely new defensive overall strategy was adopted by the German armed forces. The serious strategic defeats at Stalingrad and El Alamein had signalled the end of Germany's offensive power. Following these, the German war machine found itself at a crossroads: its reserves

Two photos of the wreckage of Halifax Mk II W7884 of 102 Squadron, shot down at Laumersheim near Worms during a raid on Frankfurt am Main on 2/3 December 1942. The victor was twenty-one-year-old Lt Heinz Hadeball of 8./NJG4, who noted in his log book on his eighth kill 'Abschuss of a Halifax on 03.12.1942 near Laumersheim from a height of 4,400m [13,000ft]'. 'Hannibal' Hadeball went on to become an ace with thirty-three night kills with NJG1, 4, 6 and 10 and was awarded the Ritterkeuz in July 1944. '"It is heading straight at us…" a frightened citizen of Laumersheim shouted, as a burning four-engined bomber thundered over the old Laumersheimer mill at very low level. The inhabitants feared a catastrophe if the bomber crashed into their village. At the break of day, a horrifying scene was revealed to the inquisitive. The machine had crashed on the slope of a vineyard, 300m [970ft] to the right of the municipal cemetery of Laumersheim. The aircraft was almost completely burnt out and two of the crew were dead.' (Eye-witness Peter Menges, then a fourteen-year-old boy living at Laumersheim).
Coll. Peter Menges.

F/Sgt Cyril John Pope, mid-upper gunner in F/Sgt Chapman's crew of Halifax W7884 was killed on 3 December 1942 and buried at Laumersheim. After the war, he was re-buried at the British Military War Cemetery at Rheinberg, Germany. Coll. Peter Menges.

in manpower and material had been seriously eroded, and, after more than three years of prolonged war, its offensive strategy had not brought about a victorious outcome. The prospect for the German people was now one of a lengthy war of attrition, and a reversal in strategy, from offensive to defensive, had become a pressing necessity. A defensive strategy was the only way to be able to retain the territory they had already conquered, and, in the long run, the only possibility for the survival of the Reich.

Germany's only chance to prevent a second front in western Europe was to bring the Allied air offensive to a halt, but neither Hitler, nor Göring or Jeschonnek made a determined effort in this direction. Hans Jeschonnek became increasingly aware of the need to strengthen air defences, but he did not want to be disloyal to his Führer by arguing for a shift in strategy. Göring's main concern was to hold his position now that his Luftwaffe was exposed to ever increasing criticism from Hitler. The end result was that after the debacles at Stalingrad and in North Africa no radical changes occurred in Germany's war strategy. All that happened was a series of indecisive measures that could neither solve the problems of the hour, nor safeguard the future of the Third Reich.

Despite the weaknesses in the rigid Himmelbett GCI system, the German nightfighters exacted an increasing toll of RAF bombers

A matt black Bf110C of II./NJG3 starting up its engines at Grove airfield, 1942. The night fighting crest is clearly visible on the nose. Coll. Peter Petrick.

Tail gunner's view of the sleek hunter. BF110C of II./NJG3 flying above cloud in 1942. Coll. Peter Petrick.

during 1942 and in early 1943. This was mainly due to two major developments: a growing number of nightfighter aircraft had been fitted with the *Lichtenstein BC* radar sets, while the co-operation between the nightfighter crews and the ground controllers in the Himmelbett sites was improving daily. Moreover, Kammhuber had strengthened his defences in depth by providing the Reich with still more Himmelbett GCI stations. Thus, on 10 September 1942, Kammhuber's XII Fliegerkorps proudly reported its 1,000th *Abschuss. DuNaJa* claimed the majority of these victories with 648 aircraft destroyed, *HeNaJa* claimed 200 bombers shot down and the Fernnachtjagd another 141 victories. Eleven other aircraft had been brought down by searchlights through blinding the pilots. Only nine months later, the 1,700 mark was reached. These tremendous successes pulled the wool over the Luftwaffe leaders' eyes in the spring of 1943: why increase the Reich's air defence when the existing Nachtjagd was able to achieve such good results?

With hindsight, this view is belied by the facts: the increasing RAF losses during 1942 and in early 1943 'only' indicated a rise of the average loss rate from 3.7 to 4.3 per cent. Only if the average losses rose to a figure of more than 5 per cent, with an occasional loss of more than 10 per cent, would Bomber Command be confronted with serious problems in maintaining a strong force. A steady loss rate of some 4 per cent would mean that Bomber Command would be entangled in a prolonged war of attrition with Nachtjagd, able to continue its strategic offensive while growing in size and striking power. After all, the reserves, both in manpower and material, of Britain and its Commonwealth, combined with those of the United States, were many times larger than those of Germany. Once more, Hitler's decision to halt the Fernnachtjagd in October 1941 was paid back with interest. As a direct consequence, Bomber Command was able to expand virtually undisturbed into a formidable force of four-engined heavy bombers. RAF training centres churned out thousands of aircrew who would serve in Bomber Command during 1943–45 without any intruders disrupting the training process.

By early 1943 the rigid Himmelbett GCI system had reached its peak of efficiency with a maximum of some six *Abschüsse* for every hundred RAF bombers penetrating the Reich's airspace. Under the most favourable circumstances, only six nightfighter crews could be guided in any one Himmelbett box per hour. Although Nachtjagd gradually increased in size over this period, only a relatively small part of the force could be

Some of the cream of Nachtjagd at Leeuwarden, probably in early 1943. Sitting, (l–r): Oblt Greiner; Oblt Drewes; Hptm. Ruppel (OC Eisbär Himmelbett GCI station); Hptm. Jabs; Major Sutor; Oblt Schnaufer. Standing, (l–r): Lt Grimm; Lt Rühle; unk Hptm. Oblt Weissflog; Hptm. Sips; Lt Potthast; Oblt Bredereck; Lt Rolland; unk Hptm.; unk Lt. The seven identified pilots in this photo amassed 324 victories, mainly at night. Grimm, Pottharst and Rolland were killed in action whereas Greiner, Drewes, Jabs and Schnauf er survived the war highly decorated. Coll. Hans-Joachim Jabs, via Rob de Visser.

employed in the Himmelbette through which the bomber streams passed. For example, during the first 1,000 bomber raid on Cologne o n the night of 30/31 May 1942, a mere twenty-five night-fighter crews out of the available force of 230 could be guided onto the giant bomber stream: eight in every nine crews had to remain inactive!

A relatively small number of very experienced crews were almost always given a preferential treatment in the Himmelbett Nachtjagd. These *Experten* were employed in the most profitable boxes and accumulated many kills against Bomber Command. One of these aces was Oblt Paul Gildner, one of the founding members of Nachtjagd. Together with Hptm. Ludwig Becker (forty-four GCI kills), Major Werner Streib (some forty-five Himmelbett Abschüsse), Hptm. Reinhold Knacke (forty-four kills) and Major Helmut Lent (some sixty Himmelbett victories), Gildner was the most successful exponent of Himmelbett GCI night fighting. Of these aces, only Werner Streib was destined to survive the war. Uffz. Heinz Huhn, an experienced radar operator crewed up with Ritterkreuzträger Gildner in early 1943. Gildner assumed command of 1./NJG1 at Gilze-Rijen airfield after Hptm.

Oblt Helmut Lent, at twenty-three years of age Gruppen Kommandeur of II./NJG2, briefing his crews in the Operations Room at Leeuwarden airfield in early 1942. By June 1942, when Lent received the Oak Leaves to the Ritterkreuz from the hands of Adolf Hitler, he was Nachtjagd's top-scoring pilot with forty-two kills, of which thirty-four were by night. Helmut Lent went on to become Kommodore of NJG3 and destroyed 113 aircraft in air combat (105 by night), before he was mortally injured in a crash due to engine failure on final approach to Paderborn airfield on 5 October 1944. Coll. Heinz Huhn via Rob de Visser.

Reinhold Knacke had been killed in action on 3/4 February 1943. By this time, Gildner had thirty-eight confirmed victories to his credit. Heinz recorded in his diary:

> Gildner and I are posted to Gilze. In Gilze-Rijen we are at readiness on every night, and we also have successes. On 14/2 we destroy a Wellington and a Boeing in sector Hamster [Domburg/Holland]. There is no radio beacon in operation and we fly without being able to orientate ourselves. Our bearing set is unserviceable. Thank God we can still communicate over R/T with the ground station. Finally, a thought crosses my mind: could it be the *Lichtenstein* that jams our bearing set? I switch off the *Li*-set. Sure enough, I can now obtain a bearing. We proceed towards the box flying at a height of 3,000m [9,700ft]. We receive a course to steer straight away but the *Lichtenstein* is not in operation. We fly between two layers of cloud, above us the clouds are very thin. We therefore climb above these clouds and get a visual on a Wellington. 'I engage', Gildner announces and attacks directly from behind. The enemy is on fire in its left engine and wing, pulls up steeply and plunges down. We observe it crashing into the water: 'Sieg Heil'.
>
> Immediately, we receive a new course to steer from the ground station. The moon brightly illuminates the sky, it is as if it were daylight. I experience interference in the R/T communications with ground control. At last, we obtain visual contact. 'I engage'. Gildner gets into attacking position and opens fire. The *Kurier* is identified as a Boeing. It is burning in the left engines and dives down out of control. It crashes into the sea. 'Sieg Heil!' We are vectored onto another aircraft. We get a visual but we're too fast. We turn around to get into a good attacking position but contact is lost with the *Kurier* in the process. We're low on fuel, so we set course for home right away. A smooth landing. Oblt Gildner's thirty-ninth and fortieth night victories.

Gildner's thirty-ninth victim was probably Wellington HE169 of 196 Squadron, which crashed into the North Sea at 21.48 hours some 12 miles

(20km) west of Schouwen. F/Lt Milne and his crew remain missing. The 'Boeing' was probably in fact Stirling BF438 WP–D of 90 Squadron which also found a watery grave 30 miles (45km) west of Flushing at 22.07 hours, with the loss of the whole crew.

Uffz. Huhn continues:

On 18/2 we are ordered to take off and head for box Gorilla. When the order comes through, I am busy drawing maps. I quickly put on my flying clothing and gear and get into the aircraft. Gildner has already been ready and waiting for me for some time. He applies full power and off we go. Mist and bad visibility. Where are my radio orders for the day? How terrible, I've forgotten the radio orders! I tell Gildner that we must return to base immediately. I fire off the colours of the day and also a red flare to let them switch on the flare path of Gilze-Rijen. Thank god I can remember the notes I made on the bearings and frequency. I get a connection on R/T. We execute a touch-and-go manoeuvre six times, the duty officer fires off flares which dazzle us. Oblt Gildner tells me we'll proceed to Leeuwarden. I don't know the radio frequency for Leeuwarden but we get there all right. I fire off the colours of the day once, a smooth landing follows. But what a terrible disgrace for me.

Next day we can't get away, as the weather at Gilze is too bad. We're in the Operations Room that night. A thick layer of mist and bad ground visibility prevail. Enemy bombers are reported approaching Wilhelmshaven. We can't take off. Still, Gildner wants to get after the bombers, if necessary he will fly the Dornier. The bombers fly back through the boxes in our area. We decide to take off all the same. There's a full moon. The Dornier is not fitted with flame dampers, so from the engine exhausts long flames trail back. The radio and radar equipment of the aircraft is completely worn out. I switch off the *Lichtenstein* and we have to search without it. We immediately get a course to steer for a mission in box Tiger. The first *Kurier* is a Halifax. Suspecting no attack, it's crew must feel

Uffz. Heinz Huhn in full flying gear, including 'Mae West'. Huhn survived his three pilots (Oblt Völlkopf, Oblt Gildner and Lt Köstler) but after his third pilot was killed when Lancaster ED618 of 101 Squadron exploded in the crew's face on 9/10 April 1943, Heinz decided he had had enough and never flew again. For the remaining years of the war, he served as Operations Officer at Bergen/Alkmaar and St. Trond airfields. Coll. Heinz Huhn, via Rob de Visser.

quite safe. Gildner attacks, the *Kurier* starts to burn and at 21.05 hours it crashes into the North Sea, 'Sieg Heil'.

The reflector sight has broken down and only one cannon still fires. We are guided onto another aircraft. At 21.10 hours we obtain visual contact. A Halifax. A giant pillar of smoke from our first kill rises from the water. An attack, the

Kurier trails a long banner of smoke, it explodes and crashes into the sea. Time is 21.16 hours.

We are vectored onto another aircraft, this time we engage a Boeing. R/T connection is very bad, as a transmitter on the ground has broken down. I am dripping with sweat, have to switch all the time and tune the radio set. And my helmet fits miserably. Nevertheless, we're still in business and remain in visual contact with the enemy bomber. We get into attacking position. Gildner opens fire, only three machine guns are still working. The aircraft is not burning yet. We charge in again and fire another burst, then have to turn away as a second *Kurier* is flying only 200m [yd] away from us. So, this one is getting away. We can only claim a damaged. Our own aircraft has been hit by return fire in the propellers.

We immediately turn back for home and safely touch down. In the Operations Room we have a big party that same night with champagne and red wine. Jabs has shot down three bombers, all Short Stirlings. Our third probably didn't make it back home either as it sent off an SOS. In the afternoon of the 20th our lightning visit to Leeuwarden comes to an end and we fly back to Gilze.

Despite the dreadful weather conditions on 19/20 February 1943, three experienced crews had been given permission to take off from Leeuwarden to try and intercept the returning Wilhelmshaven force in the Himmelbett boxes Schlei (on Schiermonnikoog island) and Tiger (on Terschelling). Lt Wolfgang Kuthe managed to destroy a Stirling at 22.25 hours, probably R9276 WP–G of 90 Squadron over the North Sea. Jabs' three victims were all Stirlings of 15

Lancaster W4308 'C–Charlie' of 460 (RAAF) Squadron was shot down on 23/24 January 1943 by the Bf110F night fighter of Oblt Kuthe and Uffz. Helmut Bonk of IV./NJG1 at Warns village in Friesland. Bordfunker *Helmut Bonk poses in front of the burnt-out remains.* Coll. Luit van Kampen.

Squadron: BF457 (at 21.00 hours), BF378 (at 21.14), and BF411 (destroyed at 21.45 hours). There were no survivors among these four Stirling crews. Both 'Halifaxes' which Gildner claimed were in fact Lancasters, of 83, 156 or 467 Squadrons. The 'Boeing' in Huhn's story was a Stirling, probably BK627 of 90 Squadron. Little could Oblt Paul Gildner suspect that he only had four more days to live. On 24/25 February, his Bf110G-4 crashed on final approach to Gilze-Rijen due to engine failure. Uffz. Heinz Huhn managed to bale out at low level, but for Gildner it was too late. For Kuthe the end came on 14 April 1943, when he was killed in a flying accident.

Stragglers were very vulnerable to the Himmelbett defences. They could easily be picked up by GCI radar and then intercepted and destroyed by a *Lichtenstein*-equipped nightfighter. At 18.45 hours on the evening of 14 February 1943, F/Sgt John Gow RNZAF lifted Stirling W7638 OJ–R of 149 Squadron off from Lakenheath for his crew's fifth operation. Loaded with eight 1,000lb (450kg) bombs and 2,000lb (900kg) of incendiaries, they were part of a 243 strong force sent to bomb Cologne. There was a problem with one of the engines on the way over which slowed the Stirling down, and John Gow couldn't get the aircraft any higher than 16,000ft (4,900m) due to icing. Needless to say this made the crew late over the target. Canadian F/Sgt Cecil Loughlin was the Nav./BA. in John Gow's crew:

> Two planes had been hit and were on fire a few miles ahead of us. It looked like nightfighters as there was no ack-ack [anti-aircraft fire]. As we made our run in on the target the plane was shaking from the ack-ack explosions all around us. Two planes exploded to our right. We had to keep the plane straight and level as we made our run in to bomb on the green marker flare, Bombs Gone and we made a left turn for home when we were boxed by ack-ack and searchlights. John threw the plane into a corkscrew dive at 300mph [480kph] diving and climbing all the time, turning for seventeen minutes. We

Paul Gildner as a twenty-eight-year-old Oberleutnant in early 1943. As the third Nachtjagd pilot, he had been awarded the Ritterkreuz on 9 July 1941 after his fourteenth Abschuss. *By 20 February 1943, Gildner had risen to Staffelkapitän of 1./NJG1 with some forty-four victories, two during the day in the Battle of France, and forty-two at night, all in some 160 sorties. Whilst on a GCI sortie on 24/25 February 1943, the port engine of his Bf110G-4 suddenly caught fire. Gildner broke off the sortie and tried to make an emergency landing at Gilze-Rijen airfield. It didn't work out and Gildner ordered his* Funker *Uffz. Heinz Huhn to bail out on final approach from some 800ft (240m). Huhn observed the Bf110 slideslipping over its port wing, and Gildner crashed to his death. He was awarded the Oak Leaves two days after his death.* Coll. Horst Diener.

could get out of the searchlights but the ack-ack was exploding all around us. We could feel the shrapnel hitting us and smell the explosive all through the plane. John was really breathing heavy as it was hard work weaving and diving for such a long time.

All of a sudden it became quiet except for the roar of our engines, so we set course for home all the time taking evasive action. We started to check out the condition of the crew. The plane was operating beautifully so we had not been seriously hit.

All of a sudden Jim Brigden, mid-upper yelled 'You bastard'. We felt the cannon shells hit our plane. The fighter had come up beneath and Jim didn't get a crack at him until he was breaking off and it was too late. All this time we had not heard from the rear gunner Bill Summerson and I believe he must have been a casualty of the ack-ack. We were on fire and the Skipper gave the order to bail out about 22:00. I got my chute and went down to open the escape hatch which was in the front of the plane behind the front turret. I was just going to open the hatch when Val Tully, who had been sitting beside the pilot, hollered at me to wait until he got his chute out of the front turret.

Then I opened the hatch and bailed out. Val was beside me and was ready to jump next. I tumbled out and pulled the rip chord and the chute opened OK. and I started to float down. Our plane flew on straight and steady for three to four minutes, still burning, and then went into a long curving dive and into the lower clouds. I came through the cloud and saw a fire burning a few miles away which I took to be our plane. I landed in a field, buried my chute and Mae West and started walking west. It was the loneliest time of my life; in enemy territory, in the dark all alone and hearing the other planes above returning to England.

F/Sgt John Gow RNZAF (left) at the controls of a Stirling of 149 Squadron, early 1943. On the the right, in second pilot's seat, Sgt John Brigden, mid-upper gunner, with two groundcrew in foreground. At age twenty-seven, John Gow was killed when his Stirling W7638 OJ–R was shot down by a Bf110 of I./NJG1, probably flown by Oblt Martin Bauer, near Boxmeer/Holland on return from Cologne on 14/15 February 1943. John Brigden escaped to become POW.
Coll. John Brigden.

Stirling W7638 OJ–R of 149 Squadron was shot down at 21.30 hours by a Bf110 of I./NJG1, probably flown by Oblt Martin Bauer, and crashed near Boxmeer, as one of the nine aircraft lost from the Cologne force. At least six of these heavies fell victim to nightfighters of I. and II./NJG1 manning Himmelbett boxes in the southern Netherlands and Belgium. Three crew members of W7638 were found dead at the crash site next day; Skipper John Gow, Sgt Paul Oldham, engineer, and Sgt William Summerson, rear gunner. The four survivors were all rounded up, taken to the interrogation centre at Frankfurt then sent to Stalag Luft VIIIB at Lamsdorf, where they stayed until 1945.

CHAPTER 4

American Combat Boxes and the Ruhr

While Kammhuber and his Himmelbett Nachtjagd tried to ward off the Bomber Command night offensive, a new threat to Germany emerged in early 1943. On 27 January, fifty-five B-17 Flying Fortresses of the American 8th Army Air Force carried out their first raid on Germany, with a daylight attack on Wilhelmshaven. It now became clear that not enough day fighters were available in the west to successfully combat the growing strength of the England-based American bombers. As a result, Oberkommando der Luftwaffe decided to use their nightfighter force against these daylight raids. They reasoned that these heavily armed twin-engined aircraft with a much longer range than the Bf109 and Fw190 single-engined dayfighter aircraft could undoubtedly deal effectively with the unescorted American 'combat boxes' (close formations of bombers).

Yet, during the 8th AAF raids in February 1943, the opposite proved to be true. The large and cumbersome nightfighters, with their crews who were scarcely trained in daylight interception tactics, suffered heavy losses. Large numbers of valuable radar-equipped aircraft were shot down, along with their crews. Some of the most experienced and indispensable *Experten* fell victim to the massive defensive fire of the American combat boxes, including Hptm. Ludwig Becker, at the time of his death the Luftwaffe's top-scoring nightfighter ace with forty-four kills. Crews who had been in action in daylight were often ordered to be on duty the next night as well, and were burning themselves out rapidly. Despite the serious consequences for the combat readiness of the nightfighter arm, OKL did not countermand its decision, although some slight changes were made. The new policy from April 1943 onwards was that the *Spitzenbesatzungen* (crews with more than twenty night kills to their credit) were grounded for the risky daylight missions. This measure was intended to preserve the experienced backbone of Nachtjagd for the night battles with Bomber Command.

Lt Peter Spoden, a twenty-two-year-old pilot with 5./NJG5, and who started his night fighting career with four RAF heavies shot down in August and November 1943, comments on the daylight missions:

> I flew several missions in daylight during the first months of 1944. Only crews with few night victories were selected for these sorties, as the aces were too valuable for the powers that be. We youngsters usually just came into readiness at night, as in the Himmelbett night fighting system, the most successful crews were scrambled in the first waves. Nevertheless, those daylight missions were quite exhausting, as we were also

Bf110Gs of 5./NJG5 formatting during a daylight mission against the US 8th AAF in January 1944. Coll. Peter Spoden.

at readiness at night. What's more, we were too slow in daylight with our 110 equipped with *Lichtenstein* and flame-dampers, and tactically we were at a disadvantage due to our approach from behind. When we came into firing range of the heavy defensive fire of the American bombers, it was like flying into a shower! The 109 and 190 on the other hand attacked the *Pulks* [bomber formations] from head-on and out of the sun. Consequently, the losses among our nightfighters were horrendous.

Lt Martin Drewes, a former *Zerstörer* pilot who was transferred to Nachtjagd at the end of 1941, served in 7./NJG3. By early 1943, his tally stood at three victories, and he was one of those young nightfighter pilots who were ordered to fly against the American bombers. He recounts a particularly dicey daylight sortie on 19 May 1943:

Late in the morning I had flown from my operational airfield Kopenhagen-Kastrup (7./NJG3) to Stade, to settle various things for the Gruppe. My radar operator had immediately gone to the big hangar to take a shower. Then all of a sudden – Alarm! – a strong formation of *Viermots* was reported flying in the direction of Kiel. A Hauptmann told me that the order for take off was only for a specific number of aircraft of the unit that was based at the 'drome. Still, I felt that I had to scramble and walked towards my Me110. An officer mechanic asked me if he could fly with me and confirmed that he knew all about how to operate the R/T and the weapons systems. So we took off at 13.13 hours.

The last machine to take off before me was flown by the excellent Oberfeldwebel Leschnik. I tried to catch up with him, but he was climbing with full power and the distance between us

Peter Spoden, shown here in 1942 as a newly-commissioned Leutnant. Spoden became one of the leading Tame Boar *pilots, claiming twenty-four RAF bombers from August 1943 to March 1945, plus a probable B-17 in daylight on 6 March 1944. He finished the war as Gruppenkommandeur of I./NJG6.* Coll. Peter Spoden.

wasn't reduced. Weather: bright sunshine, good visibility and at a height of some 1,000m [3,200ft] an 9/10th veil of cloud. We climbed to a height of 7,000m [22,700ft]. Leschnik, who flew some 500m [1,600ft] in front of me, had come into shooting distance of the last *Pulk* of Boeing B-17s. I watched the exchange of fire, then Leschnik's machine plunged down steeply – no parachutes.

Without any doubt, a number of 'Gun Ships' flew along in the *Pulk.* I was now alone with the thirteen B-17s in the last box and fired off a burst at the bomber that flew in the middle and in the back and registered some good hits. Suddenly I received strong return fire and heard bullets smashing into my machine, from the frame of my canopy creeping back to the tail unit. I glanced into the mirror but couldn't see my companion any more, and the intercom remained silent. He must have bought it... My Messerschmitt was responding to the controls, so I went into the attack again. The Boeing that I fired upon was sheering out of the formation, jettisoned it's bombs... suddenly it turned onto its back and dived down steeply in order to reach the safety of the layer of cloud. I went after it, and despite strong return fire I shot it on fire with a couple of bursts. It then plunged down. The clouds prevented me from observing it crash into the sea.

I flew back to Stade. While I overflew the base, someone signalled to me from the ground that my tyres were in one piece. A quick touch-down, and I taxied towards the hangar. Then I suddenly saw the pale face of my companion appearing in the mirror. Thank God, he was still alive. I switched off the engines, and already he jumped out onto the wing. He exclaimed: 'I will never fly with you again!' and off he was. What had happened? After he saw the aircraft in front of us going down, he had laid himself flat on the floor of his cockpit. The burst of gun fire that next hit my Me110, had flown over him with only inches to spare. The intercom was shot to pieces.

I drew up my combat report, *Abschuss* of a B-17 at 14.12 hours some 80km [50miles] NW of Heligoland. I explained to the officer in the Operations Room that the aircraft had gone down and thus never would drag any more bombs to Germany. As far as I was concerned, that was the main point. I requested that he took care of the further formalities, as I really had to leave.

Although I had a companion on board, who was not injured, he had observed nothing! A flak ship had heard the air combat raging overhead at the same time I claimed the *Abschuss,* and further confirmed that the bombers were not on their way back yet. One had fished some smashed pieces of aircraft out of the water. Still, no firm claim could be submitted due to the layer of clouds.

From a superficial inspection of my machine it appeared that although it had been hit numerous times, no vital parts seemed to have been damaged. The route back to Copenhagen was monotonous, as shortly before I had been in combat, even though I was told not to. Really pleased with myself, I travelled along on a straight course, at a height of some 300m [1,000ft]. A wide turn before reaching Malmoe, approach, touch down, the machine bounced ...bounced...bounced. At the dispersals, the NCO in charge of the groundcrews was of the opinion that anyone could perform a bad landing from time to time. I told him to climb onto the wing and to get hold of the control column. During touch down and the pulling back of the column, the elevator control cable had completely snapped; it had obviously been severely damaged during the air combat. Only the slightest sudden manoeuvre during the flight back to Copenhagen would have caused my machine to have immediately crashed into the ground. For a long moment I kept sitting quietly in my aircraft and did not take off on a mission that night!

Reichsmarschall Hermann Göring talking to three ace pilots of the crack nightfighter unit IV./NJG1 during a visit to Leeuwarden airfield in October 1943. The three pilots are from left to right: Hptm. Jabs, Oblt Schnaufer and Oblt Drewes. Both Jabs and Drewes regularly flew on daylight missions against the US 8th AAF during 1943.
Coll. Ab Jansen.

Martin Drewes was posted to 11./NJG1 a few days after this episode, a unit he led as Staffelkapitän from August 1943. By the end of the year, he had shot down six British night bombers, a B-17 in daylight, and shared in the kills of three more B-17s. In early 1944, a B-24 claim followed and two more B-17s on 11 January. On 1 March, he was appointed Kommandeur of III./NJG1, and his score mounted fast during *Tame Boar* night fighting missions. After his forty-eighth kill, he was awarded the Ritterkreuz on 27 July 1944. A few days before, he had been shot down and wounded himself over the Dutch border after claiming two Lancasters. He ended the war as Major, with forty-nine confirmed *Abschüsse*, including six daytime victories, and decorated with the Ritterkreuz with Oak Leaves.

Losses among the less experienced nightfighter crews still ordered to fly against the Americans after April 1943 remained serious. For example, on the famous raids against Schweinfurt and Regensburg on 17 August 1943, and on 18 August, when the fighter airfields at Ypres and Woensdrecht were raided, twenty-one nightfighter aircraft and crews were lost. A further twenty-one aircraft landed with serious battle damage and with dead and wounded crew members on board. Still, the daylight sorties against the American combat boxes by Nachtjagd crews continued, although German losses rose to an even more alarming level once the first Allied fighter escorts appeared on the scene. Lt Norbert Pietrek, a pilot in 2./NJG4, flying Bf110s from Florennes airfield in southern Belgium, recalls the introduction of Allied fighter escorts during the summer of 1943:

> These were very tough weeks for us. During daytime we couldn't leave the Operations Room, as we were practically on readiness twenty-four hours a day. I recall one day, when I was scrambled three times during the night and again twice on the following day, without getting into combat with the enemy as they flew in and out again a considerable distance away from Florennes. We hardly saw the inside of our quarters during these weeks, we slept in full flying gear folded up in the arm chairs in the Operations Room and also took our meals there.
>
> During one daylight sortie I did in fact get into combat with the enemy. It was 25 August 1943. During the previous night I had been ordered to take off for a patrol in box 7B, but no Tommies showed up and thus the Fighter Control Officer kept me busy in the box for over an hour with a practice target interception flight. On landing from this sortie, we were not allowed to retire to our quarters as our names were on the battle order for daylight readiness the following morning.
>
> The names of six crews had appeared on the battle order: those of my Staffelkapitän Rudi Altendorf, Hptm. Erwin Kowalzik, Oblt Heinrich Schulenburg, another comrade whose

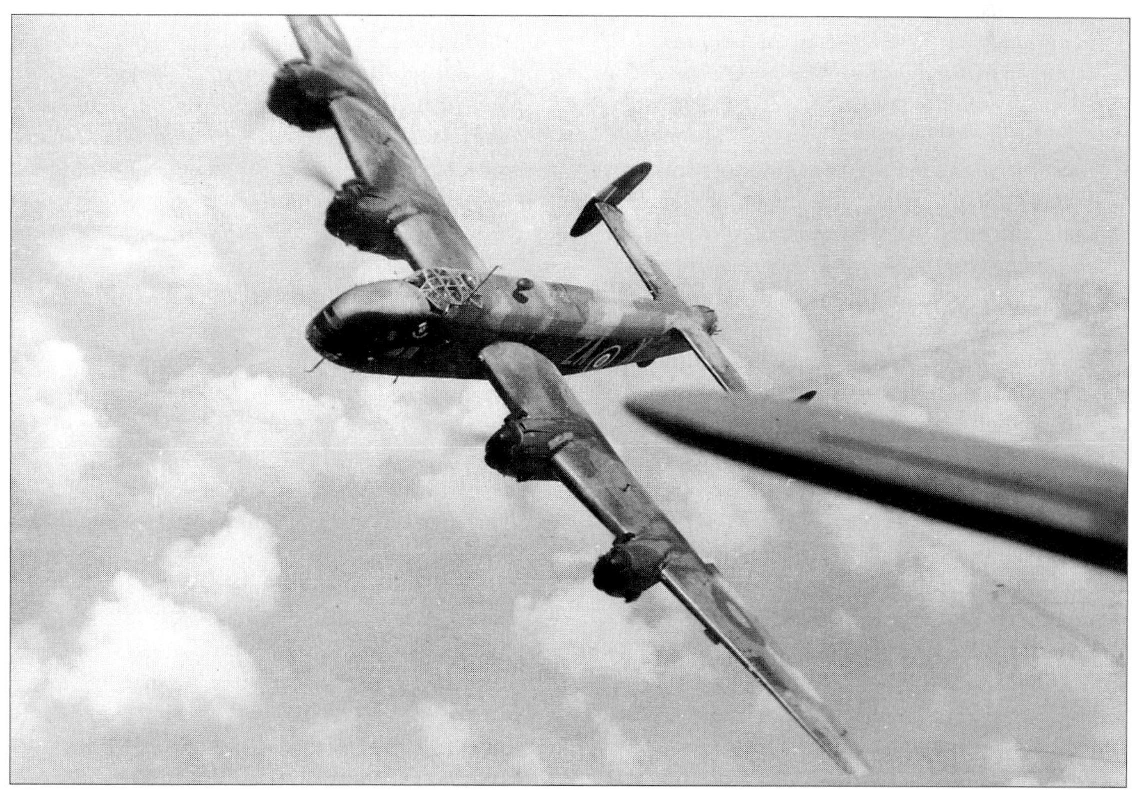

Halifax II 1A BB324 ZA–X of 10 Squadron. This aircraft was shot down by a nightfighter into the North Sea some 15 miles (25km) west of The Hague on 22/23 June 1943 during a raid on Mülheim in the Ruhr Valley, with the loss of Sgt Pinkerton and crew. Thirty-seven aircraft, or 6.6 per cent of the attacking force, were lost on this raid. At least fifteen of these bombers fell victim to nightfighters. Coll. Tom Thackray.

name I have forgotten, Fw. Paul Gralmann, and finally me. It had been determined that Altendorf and three other crews would form a flight to attack the bombers, and I would form a fighter cover flight together with Paul Gralmann as my wing man.

Shortly before supper time, we were ordered to take off. We had been briefed to attack two American bomber formations which were on their way back from a raid. So, we ran outside towards our machines and strapped ourselves in. Gralmann experienced starting up problems, which took too long to Altendorf's liking and he ordered us to take off as soon as possible and catch up with the rest whilst his flight in the meantime scrambled. However, almost half an hour passed before Gralmann finally came taxying into my sight and we could proceed to take off. Altendorf and his flight meanwhile had disappeared out of sight for a long time. Therefore I headed in the direction which ground control had ordered me to fly and soon I spotted both bomber formations, with a distance of some 20km [12 miles] between them, and with the rear box some 100m [yd] higher than the first one. I was scanning the sky for Altendorf's flight, which should be engaged in air combat somewhere in front of me by now. Meanwhile I neared the first box ever more. We were somewhere over the border of Germany near Belgium, a bit to the south of Aachen.

Then, out of the blue, we were suddenly attacked by a gaggle of Spitfires. It was quite clear that we did not stand a chance in our cumbersome Me110 against four Spitfires, and therefore Paul Gralmann and I tried to form a defensive circle. Yet, there were only the two of us, at least two too few. Over the R/T, I ordered Paul to try and climb into the vapour trails, which the first bomber formation that had just passed over us had left in the sky. We almost made it, but I watched, powerless to help, how Gralmann was squarely hit by a Spitfire and plunged down with both engines on fire. I had no option but to climb as fast and steeply as possible into the vapour trails, where I would become invisible to the enemy. Good old Paul, my *Funker*, fired off long bursts like mad with his backwards firing machine gun, but still, I could see over my left shoulder how one Tommy got into firing position. I caught a glimpse of its underbelly and then all of a sudden it exploded! One or two seconds later I vanished into the vapour trails, but still I was able to see how Gralmann, despite the fact that both his engines were on fire, had performed an Immelmann loop and actually had managed to shoot the Spitfire off my tail. I thanked him over the R/T, bade him a safe landing and now conferred excitedly with good old Paul on what to do next.

We were still over the Continent and flying on a westerly course when we stuck our nose out of the upper ceiling of the layer of vapour trails and we saw the second American combat box about one kilometre behind and below to the right of us. As we had to return to our home base at Florennes on an easterly heading, I considered making one head-on attack straight through the second formation and then to return to base if the defensive fire of the combat box had not upset my calculations.

So, I increased my speed and flew on ahead, until I believed to be in a position some two kilometres in front of the box. I then made a 180 degrees right-hand turn and sped towards the formation with around 250kph [150mph] on the clock, took aim at the leading bomber and fired off a short burst with all my six frontal guns, then fired at a machine in the middle of the combat box. Miraculously, we received no return fire at all! Then, with a right-hand turn I swiftly returned to the safety of the vapour trails from the first box. 'Well, Paul,' I exclaimed, 'that went off smoothly! Let's do it one more time, but this time we'll undoubtedly get a warm reception'. He just replied: 'I don't give a shit, Herr Leutnant!', but I knew quite well that he was just as excited and scared as I was. Again I headed on a westerly course for some time, whilst from time to time I peeped out of the upper ceiling of the vapours and already I caught a hazy glimpse of the British coastline dead ahead. Underneath us, there was nothing but water. I didn't consider for

Oblt Norbert Pietrek, whilst serving with IV./NJG5 during the summer of 1944. Coll. Norbert Pietrek.

one moment the fact that for some obscure reason we had forgotten to bring our Mae Wests and dinghy with us!

Once I had overtaken the formation far enough, I once again headed for the box in a steep right-hand curve. This time however, I throttled back and reduced speed until my aircraft almost stalled, in order to have more time to fire a long and well-aimed burst from all my guns. I took aim at just one bomber in the middle of the formation. At a distance of some 500m [550yd], I had its cockpit area squarely in my reflector gun sight, and I fired a long burst into it. I saw how the shells struck home and how the cockpit was smashed to pieces. Out of control, the bomber lurched upwards and to the left. To avoid ramming it, I was forced to pull up steeply like in an Immelmann turn. I slid over the stricken bomber with a margin of perhaps 5m, and could clearly see how the cockpit area had been smashed up completely, and both pilots torn up by my cannon shells hanging in their seats. That was a close escape!

Through steeply pulling up and by the recoil of my six frontal guns I had lost so much speed that I hung in the air suspended with my nose pointing upwards 'like a ripe plum', just as in the highest point of the Immelmann turn. This was my good luck, as in this instant I saw an apex of red tracers from the gunners in the combat box some 20 to 30m in front of me. If my forward speed would have been only 10kph [6mph], we would have been riddled. In a reflex, I put my aircraft into a left-hand spin and observed how the gunners' firing ceased immediately. Obviously, our adversaries believed that they had hit me. After three full spinning turns, I regained control over my machine and put its nose down in a powered dive, I waggled my wings and soon reached a speed of some 750kph [470mph]. The *Amis* now noticed that their defensive fire had been off the mark, and once more opened fire. I watched how their lines of tracer very slowly overtook me; I could have grabbed them.

After this final encounter, I flew back to base and over the telephone proudly reported on my successful mission to the 'Small Kadi', the affectionate nickname for our Kommandeur Hptm. Wilhelm Herget. Instead of commending me on my success, as I had expected, he chewed me out. What had got into me, to fly out over the middle of the Channel without Mae Wests and without a dinghy, to engage single-handedly a great big combat box of heavily armed Flying Fortresses? I was very disappointed with his reaction at first, but soon it dawned on me what risks I had taken without consulting anyone, and I had to agree with him. After all, I had not just endangered my own life, but also the life of good old Paul and my aircraft, for which as the captain of the crew I was responsible.

We had not been able to watch our American bomber crash, since we had to take to our heels so fast, and we had no witness in the air as not a single German fighter was to be seen anywhere in the area. Moreover, the combat had taken place at such a long distance from the Belgian coast that no-one else could have observed it. Therefore, much to my regret, I did not submit a combat report this time, which was a shame as it would have been my fourth confirmed victory, and which would have earned me the EKI [Iron Cross First Class].

Nevertheless, we received a warm welcome from everyone still present in the Operations Room, first of all because of our successful mission, and secondly because we were the only crew out of the six to have taken off on this mission who had reached base again safely, as we were now told. What had happened to Altendorf and his flight? Just like us, when they had approached the enemy combat boxes, they had been intercepted by a superior number of escorting fighter aircraft. They had immediately formed a defensive circle, a well-tried *Zerstörer* tactic, which did not permit the adversary to get onto the tail of any of the machines in the circle without being popped off by another 'destroyer'. The one thing not to do in this tactic was to break out of the circle in an effort to try and shoot down an adversary who acted as a decoy. In that case one enemy fighter filled this gap in the circle and could snip away the remaining fighter aircraft in the circle one by one. Therefore, in the defensive circle, a strict discipline was required.

This tactic worked well for quite a while, until finally Hptm. Kowalzik could not resist the temptation and broke away from the circle to try and shoot down an enemy fighter. That did the rest of them in, and all four were shot down. Unfortunately, Hptm. Kowalzik paid with his life for his lack of discipline, whereas all the others managed to save their necks by bailing out.

Uffz. Paul Gärtig, Lt Norbert Pietrek's Bordfunker *in 2./NJG4 during August 1943.* Coll. Norbert Pietrek.

The two American combat boxes which Norbert Pietrek and his comrades had encountered were twenty-one B-26 Marauders of the 387th Bomb Group (9th AAF) returning from a raid on the Rouen power station, plus thirty-one more from the 322nd BG that had attacked the Luftwaffe fighter airfield at Triqueville. The Marauders of the latter formation bore the brunt of the Luftwaffe fighter attacks on this day. For two damaged aircraft, the gunners of the 322nd claimed one Luftwaffe fighter destroyed, plus eight probables and one more damaged. Bf110 4762 coded 3C+KB, flown by Hptm. Erwin Kowalzik and his *Bordfunker* Uffz. Bernard Budke of I./NJG4 was completely destroyed when the aircraft crashed at Rescheid, killing the pilot. Uffz. Budke was wounded but escaped to fight another day.

The drain on Nachtjagd continued in daylight through the second half of 1943 and into 1944, as Lt Peter Spoden recalls. On 7 January 1944, his Gruppe was scrambled to intercept a force of 502 B-17s and B-24s bound for Ludwigshaven:

This time, we nightfighters arrived on the

scene too late, and all I could see were pieces of wreckage and between seven and ten American airmen in life jackets floating in the sea. They signalled towards us. They were in the sea between Bremen and Heligoland: we immediately alerted the German coast guard and stayed with the Americans, who kept waving towards us. And now the terrible thing happened; by the minute the movements of the men in the water became slower and in the end they didn't move any more at all. We could already see the German marine craft approaching and flew as low as we dared in an effort to keep the men awake. We were later told that no-one survived and that all had died of hypothermia. From that day on, I always flew with a one-man dinghy, which was firmly attached to my body, even on bailing out.

On the 6 March 1944 the US 8th AAF attacked Berlin in force, and Spoden's Gruppe was ordered once again to intercept the home-bound bombers over the North Sea. Lt Spoden by this time had become an ace with nine confirmed night victories:

I was the leader of a formation of four Me110 nightfighters of II./NJG5 detailed to attack from behind with four aircraft in line abreast. We had discussed this tactic beforehand, because we had been equipped with new rockets which were fixed under our wings. We called these devices *Dödels*. Whilst measuring the distance to target with our *Lichtenstein* we should approach to a distance of 2km [1.2 miles] and then aim for the centre of the combat box. With a successful rocket launch this should lead to the loss of several B-17s.

At a distance of approximately 3km [1.9 miles] from a combat box of twenty or more B-17s, I already saw the first lines of tracer curling towards us, and only moments later I received the first hits in the wings of my aircraft. I was not used to this, as at night one doesn't see the hits in one's own aeroplane, these are only reported to the pilot after the sortie by the groundcrew mechanic.

I gave the order to fire when we were still 2.5km [1.5 miles] distant from the bombers. I pressed the firing button but nothing happened. The rockets had been wrongly loaded, or the electrical system leading to the rockets had been hit. I now fired with all my frontal guns, however I did not observe any hits. Over the R/T I heard my comrades shouting for help, but could not come to their aid as my left engine packed up after being hit. Two of our four nightfighter aircraft plunged down into the water. With a lot of difficulty I made it back to base at Parchim in Mecklenburg. This action took place between Rügen and the Danish coast, in broad daylight.

Oblt Viktor Sorko and Ofw. Walter Kammerer and their radar operators of II./NJG5 were killed when their Bf110G-4s crashed into the North Sea. Of a force of 730 B-17s and B-24s that bombed targets in Berlin on 6 March 1944, no less than sixty-nine fell victim to the flak and fighter defences. This represented a loss of 686 fully trained aircrew dead, missing or in captivity. Although II./NJG5 was hit hard, the Luftwaffe as a whole paid a relatively light price with only eighteen aircraft shot down on this day.

Despite the ever mounting losses, Nachtjagd units continued to be employed in daylight during the first few months of 1944. By this time however, P-38 Lightnings, P-47 Thunderbolts, and P-51 Mustangs had appeared in numbers as escorts for the combat boxes. These American fighter aircraft took such a high toll that the Luftwaffe leaders were finally forced to withdraw the Nachtjagd crews from the daylight battles. Lt Spoden concludes:

Another factor that contributed to our losses were the long-range Mustang and Thunderbolt fighters that escorted the bombers in ever increasing numbers during early 1944. The 110 was no match for these aircraft, just as had happened with the Spitfire in combat with the 110 during the Battle of Britain in 1940. Due to the heavy losses the daylight missions of the nightfighter units were prohibited in April 1944.

Bf110F-4s of 5./NJG1 on a ferry flight to Berlin, 1943. On G9+HN, the FuG 202 Lichtenstein BC *radar aerials are clearly visible.* Coll. Otto H. Fries.

At the end of 1942, Nachtjagd consisted of five Geschwader with fifteen Gruppen. By June 1943, the arm had been expanded into six Geschwader, plus one training Geschwader (NJG101), with a total of twenty-two Gruppen. Despite all the opposition from his superiors, General Kammhuber had created a formidable force of some 350 aircraft and crews ready for action on the eve of the Battle of Hamburg, plus some 200 reserve aircraft – a twofold increase compared to the situation of early 1942. The striking power of these aircraft had also been significantly increased over this period, as some 95 per cent of the nightfighter force had been fitted with the *Lichtenstein BC* AI radar.

Uffz. 'Schorsch' Kraft and his radar operator Uffz. Erich Handke of IV./NJG1 operated in the Himmelbett Box Eisbär (Polar Bear) in Friesland province on the night of 3/4 April 1943 when Bomber Command attacked Essen. The crew's Bf110F had been fitted with a *Lichtenstein* AI radar set in March, but this did not guarantee success, as Handke recalls:

> In the night of 3 April 1943 we patrolled in Box Eisbär. After we had switched over to another radio beacon and changed to another frequency (because of jamming), ground control homed us onto a target flying in at a height of 5,000m [16,200ft], which I picked up in my *Lichtenstein* set at a distance of 3.8km [2.4 miles]. It was weaving a little, but I led Schorsch to the target well, until he spotted it, flying some 300m [330yd] to the right and over us (it was a bright night, with a clear starry sky and no moon). We identified it as a Halifax.
>
> I had messed up only shortly before, as I had pushed in the converter button five minutes

'While we manoeuvred under it, I identified it as a Halifax. We adapted to the weaving pattern of the bomber and travelled along with it until it had steadied its course a bit. Schorsch then pulled the aircraft up and pressed the gun tit'. Coll. Tom Thackray.

before the tubular heating, as the inscription had moved. Fortunately, this time the set had not been damaged. When I had switched it on correctly, I immediately had the echoes of the target on the screen at a distance of some 4km [2.5 miles].

Schorsch blasted away from below and behind from a distance of 50m [yd]. The Halifax immediately peeled away in a steep dive, but Schorsch kept shooting, until a fire was started in the bomber's fuselage. We pulled our aircraft out of the dive and watched the Halifax still plunging down, until we hardly could see it any more. By the time we thought that it must have reached the ground, we saw a huge explosion. This was in the south-easterly corner of the Zuiderzee.

On the edge of the coast, a large bomb-crater was found, nothing else. We had no witnesses on the ground. Moreover, the exact crash location could not be ascertained by Eisbär. In this area, four other Halifaxes had crashed, but these were all claimed by crews from another Gruppe. Because it was very hazy, we could not ascertain whether we had land or sea beneath us. The outcome was that we didn't get this one as a confirmed kill. Hauptmann Ruppel (OC Eisbär) asserted that the Halifax must have jettisoned its bombs and had continued its flight.

We were then homed onto a second target which I got into my set but at a distance of 800m [870yd] I suddenly lost it. A third target was found for us, which I picked up at 3km [1.9 miles] and in spite of it weaving strongly I managed to lead my pilot to the bomber to a distance of 250m [270yd]. Yet Schorsch couldn't see it.

Lent took off in this box after us and managed to shoot one down. Once more, we had not been able to get a kill, which was a pity as it would have been our first with AI.

Uffzs Kraft and Handke received a new Bf110G in late April 1943, which was a much more deadly night fighting machine, as Handke explains:

The G-series had more powerful engines (Daimler-Benz DB605s), and therefore was a

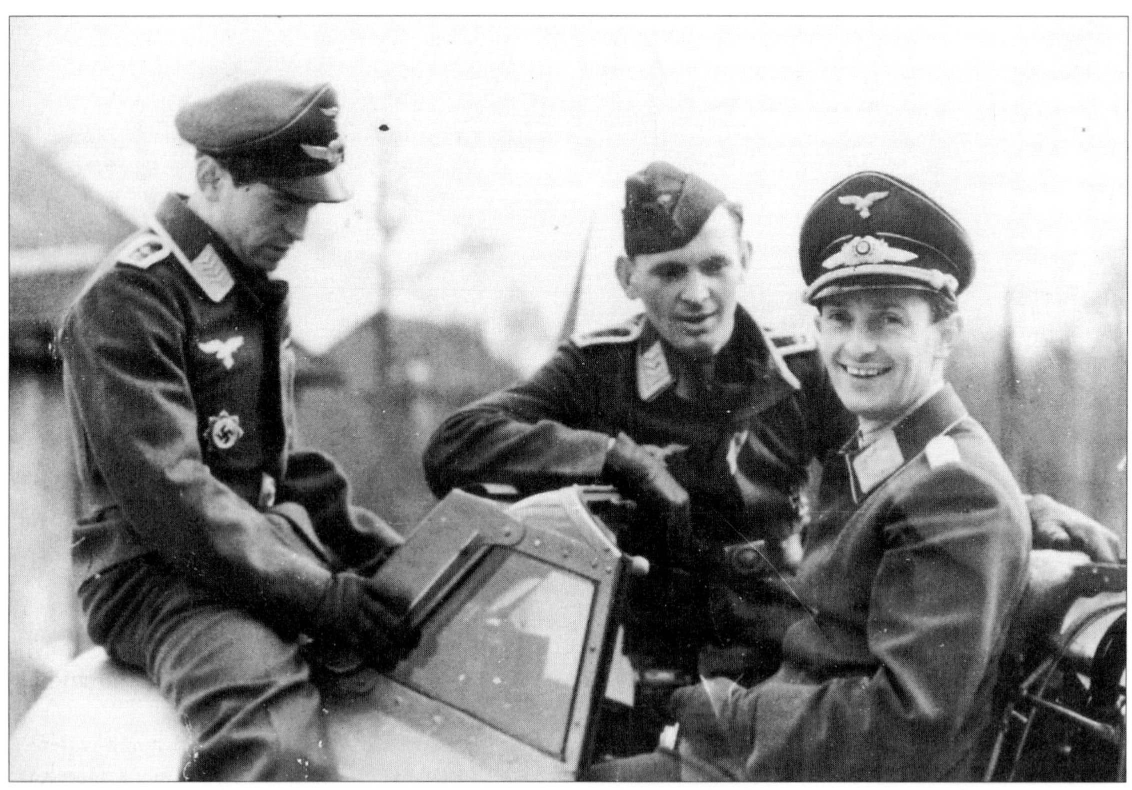

*Left to right: Uffz. Hans Liebherr (*Bordfunker*); unk gunner; and Major Wilhelm Herget (Kommandeur I./NJG4) sitting on their Bf110G in 1943. Starting his Luftwaffe career as a* Zerstörer *pilot in ZG76 with twelve victories during May–September 1940 (including nine Hurricanes and Spitfires during the Battle of Britain), Herget became a nightfighter pilot in mid-1941. Affectionately nicknamed 'Der Kleine', or 'The small one' because of his stature, he went on to become one of the leading men in Nachtjagd, gaining a further fifty-eight night victories, and three more day* Abschüsse. *His final night victory was a Mosquito on 14/15 June 1944. Wilhelm Herget scored most heavily against Bomber Command during 1943 with thirty-three* Abschüsse, *reaching the peak in his night fighting career on 20/21 December 1943, when he destroyed eight four-engined bombers within forty-five minutes during a British raid on Frankfurt. Herget didn't get away unscathed however: he was shot down three times and survived another four crash-landings. He ended the war flying in Galland's elite Me262 jet unit JV44, claiming a P-47 Thunderbolt as his seventy-third and final kill of the war on 27 April 1945.* Coll. Frau Erna Liebherr via Rob de Visser.

bit faster than the Bf110F with a cruising speed of 380 against 360 kph [236 against 224mph] and with better climbing performance. Our new machine was equipped with an improved AI (*Lichtenstein G6*) and above all with more powerful armament: the four MG17s of the F-series, with four additional belt-fed 20mm cannons and a higher rate of fire (600–800 shells per minute). The painstaking task of drum-feeding the guns was now something of the past, and the radar operator had more space. Each gun had 300 shells. The *Funker* had a twin MG81, also belt-fed and firing at a rate of 1,500 bullets/min. Yet the third and fourth cannons were not yet installed in a gun pack under the fuselage; Lent and Vinke always flew without them as the machine was faster without the added gun pack.

In this new machine we took off from Leeuwarden on the night of 26 April and headed towards box Salzhering [Salted Herring, at Den Helder]. When I had finally managed, after twenty minutes, to get radio contact with ground control, they sent us on to box Tiger (on Terschelling island). After we had arrived there, the situation worsened, as it took me half an hour to establish contact with the ground. We had already decided to call it a day when at last I got R/T contact with the box and they homed us onto the very last one to fly back, which was coming back from the Ruhr. Hptm. Jabs had already been sent after this machine but had not succeeded to get a visual on it and it had got away. At a height of 3,900m [12,600ft] we got a course to steer to the southwest towards this target.

Already flying past it, I got a fleeting blip of it at a distance of 3,200m [3,500yd], but soon after I lost it. We curved after it and after a short search I found it back at a distance of 2,000m [2,200yd]; it waved quite violently, but I managed to steer my pilot towards it well. We flew over the clouds which were dimly lit up by a weak moonlight and this enabled me to spot it already some 500m [550yd] away, in front and over us. While we manoeuvred under it, I identified it as a Halifax. We adapted to the weaving pattern of the bomber and travelled along with it until it had steadied its course a bit. Schorsch then pulled the aircraft up and pressed the gun tit. However, the first shells all went past the bomber, some 5m under it, due to a faulty calibration of the Revi [reflector gunsight]. Schorsch quickly pulled up even more and kept firing with glow-ammunition (incendiary bullets are blinding at night), until its right wing burst into flames. We intended to fly with it for a while and see what happened, but had to break off and head for home immediately as the red warning lights were already showing that we only had fifteen minutes juice left (as the DB605 engines burned more fuel, our range had been reduced to only two instead of three hours). On turning away I saw how the burning Halifax went down into the clouds. It was seen to crash into the sea from Texel Island, as our seventh *Abschuss*. When we got back to Leeuwarden, we found that our right undercarriage had hung half out of its gondola during the whole of the sortie.

Kraft and Handke's victim was Halifax JB918 DY–T of 102 Squadron which had taken off from Pocklington at 00.41 hours for Dortmund. Sgt James George Grainger RCAF and his crew were all killed when their aircraft crashed into the North Sea off Texel at 04.29 hours. The pilot washed ashore on Vlieland Island and rests there, four others were interred at Texel Island and at Esbjerg in Denmark.

The Nachtjagd crews still mainly flew improved marks of the Bf110 and Ju88 types that had been converted into nightfighter aircraft as a temporary solution in the autumn of 1940. Joseph Kammhuber realized that these by now rather obsolescent aircraft could not be kept in front-line service for much longer. Their overall performance was too poor to successfully combat the new generation of British four-engined bombers, especially the Halifax and the Lancaster. Furthermore, the Bf110 and Ju88 were absolutely inadequate to successfully deal with the British 'wooden wonder', the de Havilland Mosquito. Introduced in 1942, the small, fast and versatile Mosquitos were almost immune from interception, and quickly became one of Nachtjagd's worst nightmares.

F/O. Norman Black RNZAF and crew of 76 Squadron, shot down by Lt Denzel of II./NJG1 some 25 miles (40km) west of Texel on 1/2 March 1943 whilst on a mission to Berlin. A fading signal was received from Halifax DT556 'MP–V' saying Jack Ryder, tail gunner, was badly shot up. Despite a search by other 76 Squadron Halifaxes next day, nothing was found. Hundreds of Bomber Command aircraft were shot down by nightfighters into the North Sea during the war, with most crew members remaining missing. Coll. Ted Strange.

As early as the late summer of 1940, Kammhuber had requested German industry to develop an aircraft specifically designed to meet Nachtjagd's demands. In 1941, the Heinkel company had developed a formidable nightfighter aircraft, the He219 Uhu (Owl). Kammhuber was impressed with the aircraft's potential and planned for the type to become Nachtjagd's standard nightfighter. Fast and heavily armed, this machine would provide the arm with an excellent tool to deal with Bomber Command's four-engined bombers. It was to be fitted with improved radar, and was to be the first combat aircraft in the world equipped with ejection seats for the crew. Kammhuber planned to have his Bf110 and Ju88 units completely converted to the He219 by the spring of 1944 – but it was not to be.

In September 1941, Hitler and the Reich's Air Ministry had taken the far-reaching decision to bring the war to a successful end with the types of aircraft currently in front-line service. Existing types could easily be mass-produced, while a new generation of machines could only be manufactured in numbers after a prolonged period of development and testing. With the wisdom of hindsight, this decision can be heavily criticized, as the war did not end quickly, as expected by the Nazi leadership. However, it is more understandable when one considers the contemporary circumstances. Germany was faced with an acute shortage of resources and vital raw materials, so needed to concentrate on making the best use of these in the production of as many aircraft as possible to meet the Luftwaffe's ever rising demands. The Air Force had actually been thrown into a major conflict too soon, some three years before it would be properly equipped.

Consequently, Milch, who was now the man responsible for Luftwaffe equipment, decided that updated versions of the Bf110 and Ju88 would remain in service as Nachtjagd's standard fighters. The He219 project was postponed indefinitely, despite Kammhuber's strong protests. As a result, from the end of 1943 onwards, Nachtjagd was confronted with an adversary superior both in quality and in quantity.

The Heinkel He219 Uhu was never to become Germany's standard nightfighter. While it did eventually enter limited manufacture, production totalled no more than 268 of these state-of-the-art aircraft, which mainly equipped I./NJG1. Further production was delayed as an insufficient number of DB603 engines were available. Another blow was the bombing of the factory in Vienna during

Rescued. A dinghy with three undoubtedly very relieved Bomber Command aircrew is spotted by a German flak ship of the 13th Vorpostenboot Flotilla off the Dutch Frisian Islands during a rain storm, 1942–43. Coll. Helmut Persch.

Evidence of an Abschuss. *The main wheel of a British bomber is recovered from the North Sea by the crew of a flak ship of the 13th Vorpostenboot Flottilla, 1942–43.* Coll. Gerhard Schubert.

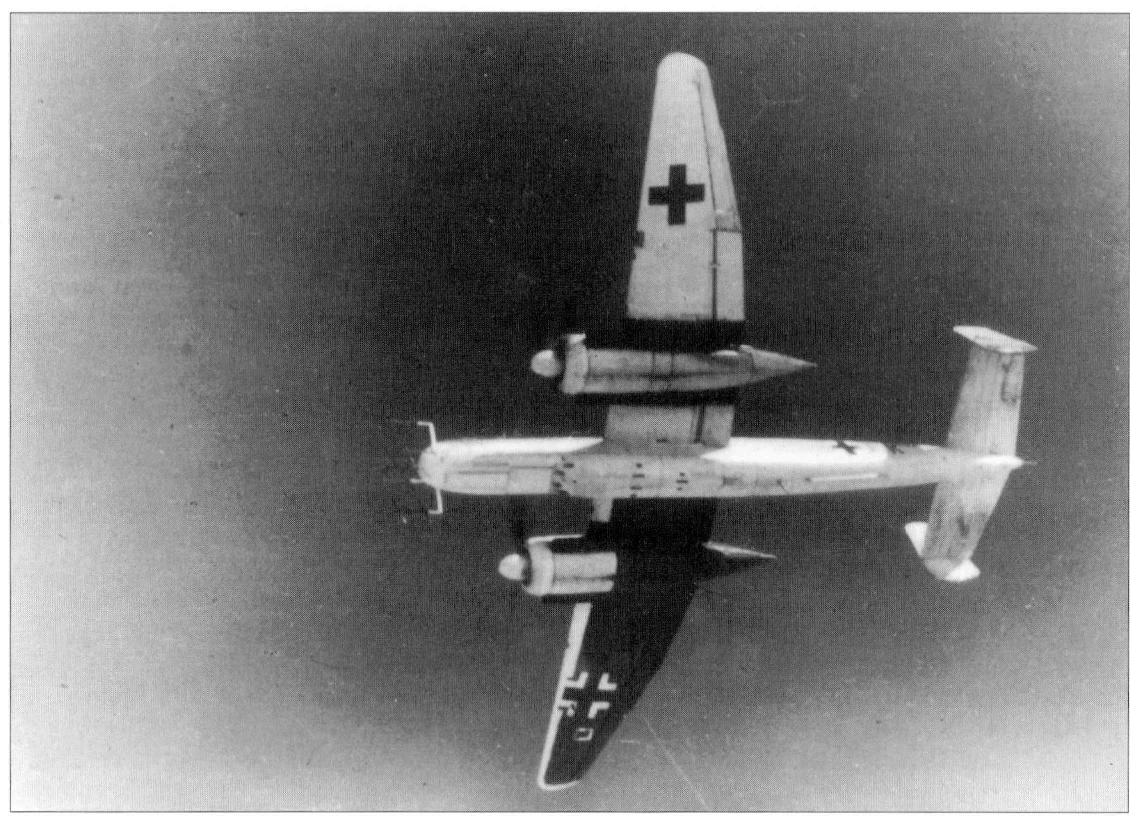

He219A-0 flown by Oblt Ernst-Wilhelm Modrow, St.Kpt. of 1./NJG1 between 1 April 1944 and May 1945. Modrow, an experienced pre-war Lufthansa pilot, joined the nightfighter arm in October 1943. He claimed thirty-four night kills in 109 sorties between March 1944 and January 1945 and was awarded the Ritterkreuz. The single black wing underside scheme depicted on this Uhu was adopted to identify German night fighters to Flak defences. Note the heavy 20mm MG151 cannon armament in the belly of the aircraft and the SN-2 *radar aerials.* Coll. Otto H. Fries.

April and June 1944, from which the He219 programme never recovered. And in the desperate circumstances of January 1945, He219 production was stopped in favour of the older Ju88G.

Bordfunker Fw. Fritz Habicht first flew in the Bf110 when he joined 3./NJG1 at Venlo airfield in the summer of 1943. He converted onto the He219 in March 1944:

> The Me110, the former daytime *Zerstörer* aircraft, had proved its value during the short range GCI night fighting. In the long range freelance Nachtjagd, which had to be carried out in often adverse weather conditions and with our old *Lichtenstein BC* heavily jammed, successes were very hard to gain in the 110. In March 1944, we converted onto the He219, a specially designed night fighting machine with a long range and fitted with the jam-proof *SN-2* AI radar. The mounting number of kills with this aircraft lifted our spirit considerably.

Within Nachtjagd itself, much thought was given to how to improve the striking power of the arm.

The shortcomings of the Himmelbett system were apparent now that Bomber Command had successfully introduced the bomber stream tactic, carrying out a series of concentrated and devastating raids during the first half of 1942. General Wolfgang Martini, Head of Luftwaffe Signals and Communications, proposed in May 1942 to use the Y-navigation system to facilitate the guidance of two or more nightfighter aircraft simultaneously in one Himmelbett GCI box. This concept, it was hoped, would result in at least a 50 per cent rise in successful interceptions. When it was tested operationally however, the outcome was disappointing, with the Y-system proving to be too inaccurate and too vulnerable to jamming. Still, there was to be a future for the Y-system in Nachtjagd as it would be successfully employed in the *Tame Boar* night fighting after the Battle of Hamburg.

A second solution to the problems Nachtjagd was facing in this period, was offered by Major Hajo Herrmann. A brilliant and very experienced bomber pilot, Ritterkreuzträger since October 1940 and a real 'Draufgänger' (daredevil), twenty-nine-year-old Herrmann was the spokesman for a group of bomber pilots who, just like himself, were looking for a new challenge now that they had been posted to desk or instructing jobs. Among several ideas, Herrmann had set his eyes on night fighting. In February 1943, he suggested to Kammhuber that he could use large numbers of single-engined day fighters over the target cities themselves. Aided by searchlights and the burning infernos in the cities, the fighter pilots would be able to find and attack the illuminated bombers. Herrmann was convinced that with this tactic, at least some 5 per cent of the attacking force could be destroyed over their targets. Combined with the existing Himmelbett Nachtjagd, Kammhuber could expect to shoot down some 10 per cent of the RAF bombers on any one raid. Kammhuber did not agree, and refused Herrmann permission to experiment with this idea. In his view, all night fighting should be strictly controlled, as he feared chaos would reign over the Reich with extensive uncontrolled freelance operations. Kammhuber also objected on 'ethical' grounds to the basic principles of Herrmann's tactics, as his system would only work if German cities were already on fire. Herrmann and a couple of other pilots only received grudging permission to practice night flying in the Berlin area during their spare time throughout May and June.

But in June 1943, with the Battle of the Ruhr reaching a climax, Milch recommended to Göring that Herrmann should be given permission to test his concept with an experimental *commando*. The Reichsmarschall favoured the idea of the *Wild Boar* irregulars (as they were soon dubbed), so Herrmann rapidly got together a group of experienced volunteer pilots and Bf109 and Fw190 aircraft. In the night of 3/4 July 1943, this group claimed twelve RAF heavies shot down over the blazing city of Cologne. The next morning, Göring ordered Hajo Herrmann to establish a complete Geschwader, JG300, of these *Wild Boar* nightfighters.

Kammhuber still remained strongly opposed to this new tactic: *Wild Boars* did not fit in with his neatly organized and closely radar-controlled Himmelbett Nachtjagd. He was convinced that these tactics would not bring success in the long run and that they offered no permanent solution to the problems he was facing. Though he was eventually to be proven right in his contemplations on *Wild Boar*, he was not able to check the expansion of the freelance night fighting arm. And when the go-ahead for *Wild Boar* was given, Kammhuber was not even consulted by his superiors, a sure sign that his own star was on the wane.

A third solution put was forward in order to improve Nachtjagd's efficiency, one which resembled Herrmann's ideas. Obstlt Viktor von Lossberg, Milch's adviser on Nachtjagd matters, suggested that Kammhuber should try and infiltrate a number of fast nightfighters, like the He219, into the incoming bomber stream. With skilful use of their AI radar, these aircraft could then 'swim' with the bombers for as long as they could, and chase and destroy as many aircraft as possible along the way. A running commentary, broadcast by radio stations throughout Germany would keep the nightfighter crews informed of the development of the air situation. Oberst

51 Squadron Halifax Mk II, ready for take-off at dusk. Coll. Robert Ramshaw.

Falck, who by that time was serving in the staff of Luftflotte Reich as Kammhuber's right-hand man, supported these ideas. He advised Kammhuber to employ the available nightfighter force more concentratedly than just in the widely dispersed and rigid Himmelbett system.

However, Kammhuber would have nothing to do with these sound proposals. He argued that without the Himmelbett ground control system, the individual nightfighters would not be able to find the bombers, and would also run the risk of being shot down by the German flak defences. He uncompromisingly held on to his radar-controlled and static Himmelbett system and rejected any plans for loose forms of Nachtjagd.

In early 1943, while these arguments were going on, Bomber Command carried out its first concentrated battle, which has gone down in history as the Battle of the Ruhr. Destruction of the industrial centres in the Ruhr valley had been given first priority from the start of the night bombing offensive in 1940, but it was not until two and a half years later that Bomber Command finally had the tools to effect this. Arthur Harris was convinced that his command had now grown sufficiently, both in size and in hitting power, to destroy the Reich's industrial heart. Equipped with the new and accurate navigation and bombing system *Oboe*, and led by the new Pathfinder Force, his Main Force carried out a series of devastating raids on targets in the Ruhr area between March and July 1943. Damage to cities as a result of these raids was enormous, causing considerable anxiety among Germany's war leaders. But even now, when both Milch and Kammhuber urged Hitler to reinforce the air defence of the Reich, it was to no avail. The Führer flatly refused to believe the Anglo-American aircraft production figures which Kammhuber presented him with. He exclaimed:

> If the figures of 5,000 a month were right, you would be right too. In that case I would have to withdraw from the Eastern Front forthwith, and apply all resources to air defence. But they are not right! I will not stand for such nonsense!

By this time, Hermann Göring shared Kammhuber's and Milch's worries, but he dared not argue with Hitler for fear of further forfeiting his fading goodwill with him. After the Luftwaffe's defeats in the Battle of Britain, at Stalingrad and now in the Battle of the Ruhr, Göring's prestige with his Führer had been eroded considerably. From the summer of 1943 onwards, the influence of the Reichsmarschall on Germany's conduct of the war had become marginal. As a result Hitler himself increasingly interfered in matters concerning Luftwaffe strategy and tactics.

Although the Battle of the Ruhr was a slap in the face for the Reich's war leaders, Bomber Command suffered heavy casualties during this series of raids. From 23,401 night sorties despatched, exactly 1,000 failed to return in the period from 5 March to 24 July 1943. This represented an average loss of 4.3 per cent per raid. The majority of these losses were inflicted by Nachtjagd, which reached a peak of efficiency in the Himmelbett over this period.

On completion of his nightfighter pilot training, Lt Norbert Pietrek joined 2./NJG4 on 1 January 1943. Being stationed at Florennes airfield in southern Belgium, on one of Bomber Command's main routes to and from the Ruhr Valley, his unit was amongst those scoring heavily against the RAF heavies during the Battle of the Ruhr. On the evening of 16 April, for example, 271 Wellingtons, Stirlings and Halifaxes went to Mannheim, with another mixed force of 327 Halifaxes and Lancasters dispatched to bomb the Skoda armaments factory at Pilsen. When the Luftwaffe Flugmeldedienst (Air Traffic Reporting Service) reported two main forces approaching over the Channel at around 22.00 hours, dozens of nightfighters were scrambled from their bases in Belgium and northern France to take up waiting positions in their allocated Himmelbett boxes. Pietrek was scrambled for a patrol in Himmelbett box 'Kater' or 'Tomcat', near Florennes airfield. At first the crew experienced difficulties getting a clear connection over the R/T

Luftwaffe personnel inspecting a crash-landed Stirling. Coll. Peter Petrick.

with Oblt Brockmüller, the Fighter Control Officer in the box, due to strong British jamming. After a few anxious minutes, Pietrek's *Funker*, Uffz. Otto Bauchens, finally found a clear wavelength and the crew could commence their GCI patrol:

> The weather is fine, no clouds, a star-spangled sky and the moon in its last quarter, so visibility is almost unlimited. Shortly before arriving over the radio beacon in box 'Tomcat', I receive orders to stand by: 'I have a *Kurier* for you, turn starboard 105!' Behind me, Otto rejoices: 'Man, hopefully it will work out right this time!' Brockmüller's instructions are excellent, as on completing the right-hand turn, I see a *Viermot*, a Lancaster, some 200m [yd] to my right and somewhat higher. We assume it must be a Pathfinder, because the Lancaster has only recently entered operational service in small numbers and is a pretty fast aircraft. I therefore push the throttles through the gate to catch up with him and then, as I have learned during training, to position myself exactly underneath it, adjust my speed to that of the bomber, pull up and then fire a long burst through a wing between the engines into its fuel tanks.
>
> This chap however must have spotted us in the clear visibility and in a powered dive he speeds downwards steeply. He dives under my horizon and I lose sight of him for a few seconds, but luckily I find him again soon by his exhaust flames. We are both travelling at the same speed, which simply prevents me from getting underneath him. When Otto reads me our altitude from the altimeter: 300...250...200...150m, the matter gets a bit too risky for my liking, since the hills surrounding the River Meuse can't be far away any more! I therefore decide to turn away to the left and keep a distance of some 250m [270yd] between us, in the hope that my adversary assumes that I have given up the chase and he will climb back to his operational height and thus will lose some speed.
>
> This goes on for a while, we are speeding eastward at low level in darkness, the Lancaster in front of me whilst I keep an eye on the four red dots of its exhaust flames. When the Tommy shows no intention of pulling up after a couple of minutes, I decide to give in. After all, this Pathfinder carries no bombs, and those bombers following this one through 'Tomcat' do. Since my box is *de facto* unoccupied, because I have travelled eastward and out of its range, I break off the chase and pull up steeply.
>
> At this instant, my machine 'H' receives such a hard punch in its belly that we are all pushed hard into our seats. I am completely blinded for a number of seconds and have great difficulty in controlling my aircraft. The Tommy must have flown into a hill on the banks of the River Meuse, and I was so closely behind him that surely I would not have been able to pull up in time if I had not decided only seconds previously to turn back. So, this is my first kill. It certainly saved me ammunition. Really, it is quite a splendid matter to chase one big *Viermot* into the ground without firing a single bullet. However, there is no time for such reflections, I must get back to 'Tomcat', since masses of Kuriers will still pass through my box, and surely, all these want to get shot down.
>
> 'Hurry up, Otto, get me a connection with "Tomcat", we must push on!' 'Roger, roger, head for the radio beacon by the visual set.' Whilst I am steering for the beacon, Otto endeavours to re-establish contact with Brockmüller. Damn this jamming, to hell with it! My 'H' is strenuously climbing, since I must regain altitude as soon as possible. Well, my comrades obviously have a field day again tonight. Everywhere around me, I see exchanges of fire, burning torches falling earthwards and sheets of flame where aircraft have just crashed. 'Come on, Otto, when is my connection with "Tomcat", coming along, soon the trade will all be gone!' 'I can't get in contact with him, he can't hear us.' I try and call him a number of times myself, I even hear his distorted voice calling out for us, but obviously he cannot receive our reply. I have now completed my first orbit around the radio beacon.
>
> And then – well, well, what is that? I am so astonished that I stare at it open-mouthed. 'Eh,

Otto, look over there, what an enormous barn-door!' 'My God what a giant, it's a Short Stirling!' From my left to the right, a Short Stirling skims over me with only metres to spare, as if it indicates to play, but this game is deadly serious.

Since this barn-door appeared into my field of vision completely unexpected, I pull on my control column too hastily and I loose off a few 20mm cannon rounds which explode in front of the Tommy. Its crew has obviously spotted me now, and a wild twisting and turning begins. Much too close for comfort, green lines of tracer from the Tommy's tail turret swish past me. We climb and turn, a steep spiral to the left, pull up, the same manoeuvre to the right, up again, and so it goes on and on. Never could I have imagined that one could carry out such wild manoeuvres with a giant kite like this. Its two pilots must be slaving away as never before! The gunners of the Stirling crew put up a spirited defence, they blaze away from the tail turret, from the turret on top of the fuselage, I even get the impression that it is equipped with waist guns. Still, in such a wild combat, it is hard for both parties to register any hits, the more for me since I am still a green pilot! A lot of bursts flash past without doing any harm, but I manage to score one or two hits. Look, a cannon shell explodes in its right outer engine. 'Hurrah, it's on fire!' However, the next moment the flames are gone, has the fire been extinguished? The tail gunner gives me lots of trouble, well, take this! Ratatata… I only pull away at point blank range and my tracers disappear into the belly of the aircraft. I get no return fire from him. He's probably had it. 'It's on fire all right!' Otto exclaims, but the next moment the fire in its right wing is gone.

This goes on for quite some time, every now and then the flames flicker up and then die down again. That pilot must be a madman! He still flies eastward despite one dead engine and a fire in his wing, and is obviously determined to press on and discard his load of bombs on a German city. Well, my dear boy, there is no way that you will pull that off! And the twisting and turning continues, we have been combating each other for at least fifteen minutes now. We started out at a height of 4,500m [14,600ft], went down to 500m [1,600ft] and are now at 2,500m [8,000ft]. Up and down, full throttle, I throttle back, lower my flaps and even my undercarriage, raise it again, raise the flaps halfway, push the throttle through the gate again, raise flaps, on and on it goes, it never ends. In my back, Otto is slaving away with the heavy pans of cannon ammunition and manages to get one cannon ready for action every time I go in. What it is like to change these pans of ammo can only be assessed by the *Funker* of the Me110. One moment he lies on the floor of the cockpit with an empty pan, the next instant he is glued to the cabin roof. I have seen your hands afterwards, Otto, they were full of bloody cuts!

Suddenly, I burst into loud laughter. I visualise how the two men in the front of the Stirling are hauling on their control column and are stamping on their pedals like mad, just as I am doing in my own aircraft, it must look like two puppets hanging and dancing from a wire.

Damn it, that was close! I can only just dive underneath the lines of tracer from the mid upper turret. Wait a minute, young man! I creep up on him from beneath, pull up and level out swiftly and I fire a burst exactly over the top of the fuselage, a ball of fire, and the turret has disappeared. That's what you get when you cause me so much trouble! My next volley squarely hits the left outer engine, then the Tommy has no other choice than to jettison its bombs and turn back for home. Only its two inner engines are still in operation, and he now makes a last desperate attempt to escape destruction. The twisting and turning has finally stopped, the tub is now on a steady westerly course.

Well, my little brother, the game is up! Just like in training, I dive underneath it to assume an ideal attacking position, pull up, aim at the left inner engine… Taktaktak… Shit, I have run out of ammunition, apart from one machine gun, and I empty my last ammo in the Stirling's engine. But who knows where the bullets hit; the 1,000 rounds are too much for my machine gun barrels; after the prolonged bursts of fire, they look more like rubber hoses. As I found out later, after having landed back at base, all four machine gun barrels had been so severely bent that every one of them had to be replaced. One red-hot barrel had been bent back at an angle of ninety degrees, and one bullet had gone straight through the side of it.

Both Otto and I are completely exhausted. All I can do now is take up a position to the Tommy's right and carefully look it over. It is quite clear that this Tommy will not make it back home. It is struggling at only 220kph [140mph] at a height of 1,500m [4,800ft], and loses 3–5m of height per second. It is a strangely beautiful sight, the wounded big black bird, in which right wing flames are still flaring up from time to time. I see how burning parts are regularly falling away. Well comrade, your fate is sealed, that will be clear to you chaps inside that wounded bird too.

'Otto, give me a course to steer!' I can peacefully let the Tommy fly, as I am quite certain that it will crash-land on the Continent, or that its crew will bail out. There is no need to accompany it until it comes down, because if I fly back home fast, I can have another go at the returning bombers. In the meantime, Otto has got in touch with the bearing station, and, after three changes of course, I arrive over the airfield and come in to land.

Unfortunately, I did not get confirmation of the Lancaster that had crashed into a hill as my first victory at night. The Lancaster had come down in the area of a neighbouring Himmelbett box, and was assigned to a comrade who claimed a Lancaster destroyed in that area around the same time. It was his third claim for the night. However, I did get confirmation of my Stirling *Abschuss* as my first kill at night, and was awarded the EKII [Iron Cross Second Class]. It was later reported that the Stirling had crashed soon after I had left it to its own. Three crew members had bailed out safely and were taken prisoner. Before they were transported to the Luftwaffe interrogation centre at Oberursel, the captured crew members were brought to Florennes, where Hptm. Wilhelm Herget, my Gruppen Kommandeur, had a drink with them to get over the initial shock.

From the Mannheim force, eighteen aircraft failed to return, and the Pilsen force lost thirty-six aircraft. These were the highest losses for Bomber Command so far in the war, even exceeding the losses on the third 1,000 bomber raid on Bremen of 25/26 June 1942, when fifty aircraft failed to return. There was slight comfort for Arthur Harris that the Mannheim force had carried out a concentrated and effective attack, but the Pilsen raid was a failure.

German nightfighters accounted for at least fifteen bombers destroyed on 16/17 April 1943. As for Lt Pietrek's Gruppe I./NJG4: this unit claimed six bombers shot down. Pietrek's Stirling victim in fact was BK653 BU–A of 214 Squadron, which F/O. D.E. James had lifted off from Chedburg at 21.50 hours. Sgt E.M. Lee, the tail gunner was killed in the prolonged battle with Pietrek's Bf110. The seven survivors of the Stirling crew finally abandoned their aircraft, which crashed at 23.45 hours at Bonneuil-les-Eaux in the Oise district. F/O. James and three of his crew evaded capture, but F/Sgt J.A. Smith and Sgts C.G. Walton and G.B. Gallagher were taken prisoner. Lt Pietrek went on to claim Lancaster W4236 of 61 Squadron (Sgt J.C. Whitley and crew) and Halifax HR872 of 405 Squadron (F/Lt K. MacG Gray RCAF and crew all killed), both destroyed on the night of 9/10 August 1943 during another raid on Mannheim. Just over two weeks later, Pietrek came back from a night sortie on one engine. When he tried to belly-land his Bf110 4762 coded 3C+BK at Kitzingen, he crashed and received severe head injuries. Barely recovered, he was again involved in a crash-landing in October the same year, and once more suffered head injuries. Although he returned to his unit in March 1944, he would never fly on operations again. In October 1945, Norbert Pietrek was arrested by the Russians in Erfurt and spent the next ten years in captivity. His war was only over in 1955.

Sgt Ken Goodchild's experiences are perhaps typical of the thousands of young Bomber Command aircrew who failed to return from a raid in the 'Valley of Death' between March and July 1943. Ken was the WOp. in Sgt B. Brown's crew, who in late April 1943 had joined 51 Squadron

Funeral of Oblt Wolfgang Kuthe, an ace with eight victories in 11./NJG1 at Leeuwarden. Kuthe was killed in a flying accident on 14 April 1943 at Leeuwarden airfield. Hptm. Lent, Gruppenkommandeur of IV./NJG1, is adressing the aircrew gathered at the grave. Coll. Manfred Eidner.

at Snaith in Yorkshire. In the afternoon of 12 May 1943 they were briefed for their first trip, a raid on Duisburg in the Ruhr Valley. Typical bomb load consisted of two 1,000lb [450kg] GP HE, forty-eight 30lb [14kg] incendiaries and 630 41lb [19kg] incendiaries. Fuel load was 1,636 Imp gallons [7,436l]:

> We took off from Snaith at 22.54 hrs in Halifax Mk II JB806 and headed to Scotland. This was to enable us to gain enough height before crossing the North Sea as not enough distance was available to allow us to reach our operational height of 20,000ft [6,100m]. All went according to plan and in due course we reached the Dutch coast at Egmond.
>
> We headed for our pinpoint position but on the way we started to experience heavy flak and during this period I was in the cockpit keeping a watch to assist the skipper in case enemy aircraft were about. To our starboard was a Lanc which had been coned by searchlights and was taking a beating from the flak and eventually he must have taken a direct hit in the bomb bay because he suddenly blew up in a cloud of flame. The crew did not stand a chance.
>
> In order to understand the next sequence of events an explanation of the layout of the Halifax would help. The pilot, Sgt B. Brown flew the aircraft from the left hand seat with the wireless operator (me) directly beneath him, and the upper and lower flight decks were connected by a three-step staircase. The navigator, Sgt W.B. Henderson RAF sat sideways on in front of the wireless operator and finally the bomb aimer Sgt Rae RAF was forward of the navigator and in front of him was the front turret. The flight engineer, Sgt A.L.G. Knight RAF was located behind the pilot.
>
> A short while after the Lanc incident, I was back in the wireless position taking a routine group broadcast when I felt a blast of air close to my right elbow, and upon investigation found a large hole in the staircase and reported the matter to the skipper who replied that he also had a large hole in the cockpit roof. A shell had passed right through the aircraft missing me and the pilot by about a foot, and what is more amazing it had not exploded. Next, we were approaching our Dutch pinpoint when a shell exploded in front of us and all but wrecked the front turret creating an enormous gust of wind throughout the aircraft. We managed to close the front bulkhead door and carried on. By now we were losing fuel from the port wing tanks but as the leak did not seem too bad we pressed on. A few minutes later I noticed

the navigator slump forward, he had been hit by shrapnel coming through the outer wall of the airframe to which his seat was attached. I called for assistance and the flight engineer came forward and we took him aft to the rest position and gave him a shot of morphine. We thought he had a punctured lung as he was spewing out a sticky fluid from his mouth. When I got back to my seat I wiped my hands of the sticky substance only to discover it was chocolate. In the green lighting of the aircraft it had not been possible to identify the substance. He had been eating chocolate when he was hit and it had dribbled out. Fortunately his wound was less serious than we had thought and he eventually recovered.

We now flew on to the target and bombed the docks and oil refinery without any more excitement. We turned away from the target and headed home. Flying along the Belgian–Dutch border we were starting to worry about our fuel losses and were now facing a barrage of searchlights ahead. I went into the cockpit to keep an eye out for nightfighters when the rear gunner, Sgt De Bourbon RCAF called the pilot to weave as we were being attacked from two quarters by fighters and I went into the astrodome to direct the gunners. A converging attack developed by a Fw190 and a Ju88 and I was amazed to see how seemingly slowly the incendiary bullets seemed to approach us. I could see flames coming from the port wing in the shape of falling balls of fuel and the rear gunner shouted he could see the wing was on fire. The skipper called for assistance as the control column had jammed. The flight engineer and I tried to help the skipper by all pulling on the control column together but it was no use, and when the port outer engine decided to detach itself and go it alone the skipper told us to bail out.

We got the navigator to the escape hatch and attached his ripcord to a static line and threw him out, followed by the bomb aimer. Next to go was the flight engineer who sat on the edge of the hatch fiddling with something and as I was waiting to jump, gave him a push. Out I went, pulled the ripcord and what seemed a long time found myself upside down and wondering if the chute was ever going to open, which it did eventually and I found myself being circled by a fighter. I was so furious I reached for my revolver which luckily I had lost, for if I had fired at him he may have replied with his machine guns.

Sgt Ken Goodchild, Wireless Operator in 51 Squadron, who was shot down and taken prisoner on 12/13 May 1943. Coll. Ken Goodchild.

I landed in a hay stack, a softer landing could not have been chosen. Shortly I met up with my flight engineer and the reason he had been delayed in jumping was because his helmet was tangled in the aircraft structure and when I pushed him I nearly strangled him. The whole crew survived the war as POWs.

The aircraft crashed on a bakery in Weelde, Belgium, killing the baker's wife and one of his young daughters. The baker survived but his niece was badly burned and was in hospital for two years. After the war the baker remarried and had a son by his second wife who now runs the business. I visited the bakery in May 1992 and was given a royal welcome. Also I met the niece, now a mother herself, and saw some of the dreadful scars she has which I helped to create. I also met an eighty-nine-year-old gentleman who had rescued the little girl from the inferno. Another memorable call I made was to the prison in Turnhout where I was held pending interrogation and sat in the actual cell I had occupied forty-nine years earlier.

Ken Goodchild's Halifax may very well have been one of the victims of I./NJG1. Lt Beier, Lt Schön, Hptm. Liedke and Ofw. Eikmeier each claimed a Halifax shot down from the Duisburg force. In all, this Nachtjagd unit, operating from Venlo, claimed twelve bombers shot down on 12/13 May 1943. 51 Squadron was especially hit hard on this raid, with four Halifaxes failing to return and a fifth crashing whilst coming in to land at base. In all, Bomber Command lost thirty-four aircraft, 5.9 per cent of the force, during this raid. Despite these heavy losses, the fourth raid on Duisburg during the Battle of the Ruhr was deemed a great success. Pathfinder marking was near perfect and the Main Force bombing was well concentrated, causing widespread damage to the centre of the city and to the port area just off the River Rhine. 1,596 buildings were completely destroyed and 273 people killed. After carefully studying the damage assessment reports, 'Bomber' Harris decided that it was not necessary to attack Duisburg again during the Battle of the Ruhr.

As a result of the Battle of the Ruhr, Milch became firmly convinced of the pressing need to deploy the Luftwaffe primarily in the Reich's defence. Should this fail to materialize, he felt that the German war industry and cities were doomed. Milch therefore repeatedly advocated the necessity of this fundamental change in Luftwaffe strategy with Hitler, but the Führer still did not want to see the point. In addition, Milch also argued for an extensive reorganization of the uneconomical Himmelbett system. The available nightfighter force should be employed *en masse* against Bomber Command in an effort to inflict more serious losses on the night bombers. The crux was that too many nightfighter crews remained idle on the ground as only a small number could be directed at one time in the Himmelbett boxes: this situation had to change.

Only weeks after the successful conclusion of Bomber Command's first major 'battle', Nachtjagd suffered a devastating and far-reaching blow. During the night of 24/25 July 1943, 728 Bomber Command aircraft attacked the ancient port of Hamburg, dropping 2,284 tons of bombs in just fifty minutes. For the first time, during the course of this raid the bombers threw out mil-

Oblt Rudolf Szardenings (in middle) with his WOp. and Flight Engineer/Gunner posing in front of their Ju88C.

The airmen in the previous picture climbing on board their aircraft. Szardenings rose to Staffelkapitän of 6./NJG3, scoring twelve confirmed kills during 1943–44 and survived the war, gaining the rank of Hauptmann. Coll. Peter Petrick.

lions of strips of aluminium foil, each 11in by 1in (27cm by 2cm). A cloud of thousands of these strips (codenamed *Window*) would create the image of dozens of aircraft on German radar screens, and Nachtjagd's *Würzburgs* and *Lichtensteins* were quickly swamped with echoes. The principles behind *Window* (called *Düppel* by the Germans) had been known by both sides for some time, but each was reluctant to use it as they feared its subsequent use against themselves. But the losses suffered by the RAF during the Battle of the Ruhr were so high that the arguments against its use were overruled, and clouds of aluminium rained down over north Germany. The results were disastrous for Germany's air defence system. The Himmelbett radars could not pick out the real targets from the thousands of false echoes, and a clear impression of the RAF bomber routes could no longer be obtained. Moreover, ground control of the nightfighters became impossible and the *Lichtenstein* AI radars had been rendered all but useless. Chaos and confusion reigned – Nachtjagd had been thrown back into the 'dark ages'. The Kammhuber Line, on which unprecedented amounts of manpower, energy and funds had been spent over the preceding three years, had been rendered obsolete in the course of just one night.

CHAPTER 5

Hamburg and the *Wild Boars*: Nachtjagd Reorganized

Under the appropriate code-name 'Operation Gomorrah', huge parts of Hamburg were destroyed in four devastating raids between 24/25 July and 2/3 August 1943. Apart from large-scale destruction in residential areas, almost half of the industrial facilities in the largest port of Europe and Germany's second-largest city were wiped out in the course of just over one week. During the night of 27/28 July 1943, 729 heavies dropped 2,326 tons [2363 tonne] of HE bombs and incendiaries on the heaviest raid of the war to date. The concentrated bombing, combined with the extremely dry and warm weather conditions, created a firestorm in the eastern residential districts of the city. Some 40,000 Hamburgers died, and after the fourth consecutive raid, on 2/3 August, over a million inhabitants fled their doomed city. Albert Speer, the Minister of War Production, warned Hitler that the Third Reich would have to surrender if Bomber Command could carry out another six such heavy raids on major German cities. Nachtjagd and the Flak arm had been rendered almost completely impotent by *Window*: only 2.8 per cent of the attacking force being lost during these four raids.

Several months before the Battle of Hamburg, the possibility of *Würzburg* radars being jammed by *Düppel* (the German counterpart of *Window*) had been brought up at a conference of Nachtjagd ground-control officers. German scientists had independently developed this simple countermeasure in early 1943. During testing against *Würzburg* precision radars, it was found that *Düppel* rendered these vital cornerstones of the Himmelbett GCI system almost completely useless. When Göring and Martini were informed of these test results, both were so shocked that they prohibited any further research into the possibilities of *Düppel*. They decided on this course of action, as only the tightest security could prevent the Allies learning of this effective countermeasure to German air defences. However, as a result of the ban on testing, German engineers had no chance to work out a response to this deadly tactic until Bomber Command began using it in late July 1943. Ironically, the British had already known all about the principles of the new countermeasure for some time, but until now had themselves refrained from using it for similar reasons to the Germans.

But *Window* was not the only electronic countermeasure used by the RAF. German Air Force leaders had been given warning of the impending large-scale jamming of their radar equipment, from as early as December 1942. This was when Bomber Command had started experiments with the *Mandrel* active jamming system which was intended to blind the German *Freya* early-warning radar.

The British wanted to capitalize on the paralyzing effects of *Window*, so apart from the four raids on Hamburg, two other German cities were also attacked at the same time. Essen was bombed on 25/26 July, and Remscheid followed five nights later. Sgt Ron James flew as mid-upper gunner in Canadian F/O. Bill Day's crew with 90 Squadron. Ron vividly recalls his crew's first trip to Essen on 25/26 July 1943, and gives a graphic description of what it was like to fly on night bombing operations in this period of the war:

> There it was on the Battle Order – F/O. Day in Stirling 'R–Roger' EH908. It was to be a 'maximum effort' that is to say that every available aircraft was to take part. Someone once said 'That you always remember the first time', and this was our initiation. Of course the person who made that remark had a different circumstance in mind, one with a sexual connotation – a loss of virginity! But in a way it aptly applied to our own situation, for the events of that night robbed us of our innocence and preconceived ideas of what war was like, and mentally we reached maturity in a few action packed hours – this experience was still to come!
>
> We hurried out to our aircraft to carry out the daily inspection and ensure all equipment was in working order; soon to be joined by Bill and Mitch. With the crew all available, we took up 'Roger' for an air test, and to our satisfaction found no snags or problems. Everything was now set for the evening's raid.
>
> Over lunch we asked Mitch for details of the previous night's operation (he went to Hamburg as rear gunner in another crew), but he was rather noncommittal. 'It's like something you have never experienced before, but tonight you will find out for yourselves.' This reticence on Mitch's part was so unlike him that we asked no other questions; just put it down to tiredness and fatigue. The thought did occur to me however that he may have been holding something back, and the forthcoming operation would have a few surprises awaiting us.
>
> The afternoon should have been one of rest and repose, but we had too much on our minds just to sit around and take it easy. Time dragged, and it seemed that we checked our watches every few minutes. You could have likened us to five greyhounds fidgeting in the traps, anxiously waiting for the hare to appear, and ready for the off.
>
> Later that afternoon we made our way over to the Sergeants' Mess and had our pre-flight meal, and when finished, walked over to the Briefing Room. This room was a large Nissen hut not unlike the one we were housed in. It held I should say about 160 to 200 people, and on this occasion it was quite full. Most of the space was filled with seating for the aircrews, but at one end there was a stage, and beyond on the wall itself, a curtained area. A buzz of conversation filled the air: some men were joking, some serious, others unconcerned, and the sound of forced laughter was strident and nerve jangling. It was an amalgam of noise and sound, but the underlying theme was one of expectancy and anxiety.
>
> Wing Commander Giles our CO now entered followed by his section heads. He walked onto the stage and pulled back the curtains to reveal a large map of Europe. 'Gentlemen your target for tonight is Essen.' A gasp went up from the aircrew, they knew this would be no pushover for Essen was one of the most heavily defended cities in Germany, right in the heartland of the Ruhr. A place where you could expect losses! The wall map was a revelation: it had all the defended areas marked in red; pins were stuck in to show fighter beacons and gun concentrations, and a ribbon of red tape stretched from our aerodrome, right across to the target and out again, returning by a different route. It did not need an expert to tell you that there was no easy way in; whichever route was taken, at some point the defences would have to be breached. The CO and his section leaders all had their say on different aspects of the raid and at last it was over, now it was up to us to go and get on with the job. From the easy and nonchalant manner that the briefing had been conducted this should pose no problems. On reflection how could it have been handled otherwise? It was better to set out in hope and

good spirits, than to languish in despair – morale was the governing factor.

We next went to the locker-rooms to leave our personal belongings; put on flying clothing, and collect various other items: parachute, escape kit, flask of coffee and sandwiches etc., before trooping out to the waiting crew bus.

At 'Roger's' dispersal the ground crew were there to greet us, and we sat on the grass with them having a talk and smoke whilst waiting for the allotted hour. Once the Station Commander came out in his car. He had probably heard that this was our first trip and had come out to 'wish us all the best'. 'Hello lads, I believe that you are the new crew aren't you? And you must be flying officer Day' to Bill. 'Very pleased to meet you all. I hope that you have a good trip. I will see you back at de-briefing – the best of luck' and he was off to another aircraft.

It was almost the time of our departure, so we carried out the usual routine of urinating on the tail wheel. 'Just for Luck' we said, but this was our last chance for several hours. There was an Elsan aboard, but to use it at night, especially on Ops was difficult if not downright dangerous.

Entering the aircraft, we took up our crew positions, whilst Bill and Jock started up on their cockpit procedure. Bill leaned out of the side window and gave the 'thumbs up' to the ground crew standing by the battery cart. 'Port outer: Contact.' He lifted the cover from the starting button and pressed it down, waiting for the puff of grey smoke shot with flame, the cough and roar as it fired. At last, with all four engines running, he checked the oil pressure and tested the throttles, checked revolutions and magneto drop. 'All OK Chief' Bill said to the flight sergeant fitter standing just behind him. 'Let me have the form 700 then we will be on our way.' Bill signed the form which stated that he had received 'R-Roger' in good order, and the NCO departed with his clipboard to join the rest of his crew on the dispersal. After checking that all hatches were closed, Bill signalled the ground staff to remove the chocks, and we were moving. The air was filled with the roar of engines as the Stirlings made their ungainly way along the perimeter track, to marshal in line astern at the end of the take-off runway.

Soon came the signal that we were waiting for: a green Very light shot high in the air, above the control tower – radio silence was necessary, as transmissions between controllers and aircraft could be monitored by the enemy – and the first Stirling in the line turned onto the runway for take-off.

Soon it was our turn, and as we rumbled along the tarmac I had both fingers crossed, hoping that 'Roger' with its extra weight of bombs and petrol would 'unstick' in time before we reached the end of the runway. The ground flashed by, and looking out from the turret I could see the rapidly diminishing figures of our compatriots waving us goodbye.

Once airborne we climbed for height; levelled out at about 4,000ft [1,200m], and after a couple of circuits set course for Cromer. Around us in one long stream were fellow travellers all heading for the same destination – Essen. In total 700 aircraft were taking part in this operation. The plan: to attack in three waves, and timed to be completed in less than twenty minutes; by doing so swamping the German defences. No. 3 Group, the Stirling squadrons, would lead the attack, not because they were better than any other Group, but because of their antiquated aircraft. By sending in the Stirlings first they would not be bombed by the Lancs and Halis above, or so it should have worked in theory, and a head start on the others on the way back would offer some protection and chance of survival.

It was a beautiful summer evening: light clouds in a blue sky, and below, the Suffolk countryside bathed in the sun's dying rays, slipped peacefully by. Looking at the churches, villages, and fields with cattle grazing, it was hard to imagine that we were flying out on a mission of destruction, and only the nearness of other aircraft reminded us of the task ahead.

'Coast coming up skipper' from Don in the nose. 'We have Cromer about three miles on the port bow.' John the navigator gives us a new course setting. We are heading out to sea now and the light has started to fail. 'Pilot to gunners, you can test your guns now.' We point the guns downwards and fire off two short bursts. 'All OK skip,' from both of us. We settle down to maintain intercom silence. My thoughts are on the firing that we have just carried out. Surely it is a dangerous procedure to fire off guns in darkness with hundreds of other aircraft in close proximity? Some poor bugger was bound to cop it sometime? But I expect that our leaders have taken account of this hazard like they have of mid-air collisions. A risk worth taking, only a small percentage loss, and after all we are expendable! You cannot make an omelette without breaking eggs!

We are nearing the Dutch coast and it seems we are completely alone, only the buffeting as we hit someone's slipstream tells us that we are in the 'stream' and to be ever vigilant. It is now time to reach operational height; up to now we have kept low to avoid detection by radar, but as we climb several searchlights pierce the night sky in front of us. The Pathfinders have alerted the defences, and now the AA guns come into play, their bursting shells punctuating the darkness in balls of fire. 'Enemy coast ahead skipper' I report in the time honoured ritual, and just to let Bill know that I am not asleep. As it was he would have been blind anyway to have missed knowing our location. 'Thank you mid-upper – hold tight lads here we go.' He put the nose down and we were in among the flak. It was heavier than we had expected but we came safely through unscathed. 'Navigator,' from Don, 'I have a pinpoint – we have just passed over Den Helder and the Ijsselmeer is coming up'. 'Thanks Don, we are on course and all right for the next turning point.'

As we neared Germany more and more searchlights lightened the sky, until at last we were confronted by a zone many miles long and several miles deep. This was the famed Kammhuber Line. It stretched from Denmark right down to Paris and protected the Ruhr on all sides. It was an area of concentrated light: bristling with hundreds of guns, and patrolled by waiting nightfighters. It was an awesome sight, and a barrier that had to be crossed. In my wildest dreams I had never envisaged anything of this magnitude. Even as I looked I saw three bombers 'coned', and no matter how they twisted and turned the tentacles stayed with them, until at last fire from the massed guns below brought about their demise, and they fell in flaming wreckage to the ground.

To say that I was apprehensive would be an understatement – I was shit scared! The flak was now bursting all around us, and at times we heard a noise like stones rattling off a tin roof – that was pieces of shrapnel hitting the sides of the plane – but no serious damage was done, and no one was hurt. The most surprising thing was, we were wearing masks and breathing in oxygen, yet we could still smell the cordite from the bursting shells. We were now nearing the target, and as I was rotating the turret I spotted a nightfighter coming straight at us on a reciprocal course. It was too sudden to bring the guns to bear, and I am sure the German pilot did not see us until the last moment. In that split second as he passed by, it was like a moment frozen in time. A Messerschmitt 109, dappled grey in colour, and the pilot looking across at me. We must have been close to colliding for I saw his face quite distinctly. That was the last we saw of him thank heavens!

Before we had fully recovered from the near miss, our attention was directed to the panorama in front of us: it was one of foreboding, danger, and unbelievable destruction. The PFF [Pathfinder Force] had dropped their large green and red markers and bombing was already underway. Most of the early arrivals like ourselves, carried mainly incendiaries, and these had set whole districts ablaze. With the combined light of these fires, fighter flares, and searchlights, it is no exaggeration to say that we could have easily read a newspaper in our aircraft.

Even though Essen was being heavily bombed it did not stop the AA from sending up a large and lethal amount of hardware. It formed a box barrage right through the bombing run. 'Surely,' I said to myself, 'There is no way we can survive this. Now I know how the gallant six hundred must have felt when they started their charge'.

'Pilot to bomb aimer! TIs [Target Indicators] coming up, are you ready to take over?' 'OK turn to starboard – hold it – more to starboard – hold it – now straight and level.' 'What the hell was that?' from Bill, as 'Roger' was hit as from a blow, and he fought to regain control. He brought the aircraft back on course, and we were back on the run-in. It was only then I became aware of the bombs cascading around us: not only were we under fire from the enemy, but our own side was giving them a helpful hand. What, of course, had happened was that the other Groups had arrived early and had no intention of hanging around, so had come in to get rid of their loads, and we poor souls could only hope and pray that none would hit us. At last 'Keep her steady, bombs gone!' 'Roger' lurched upwards on release of its bombs, and we were through another hurdle.

Once we headed for home a fresh peril confronted us – they had plotted and marked our return route with flares – now the nightfighters lurked in the shadows awaiting their pickings. They infiltrated the 'stream' and soon combats started around us: first a string of tracer would snake through the night sky, followed by a dull red glow when someone was hit; this glow would intensify, until at last an explosion took place, and flaming debris announced yet another casualty. This was our lucky night as we did not have one encounter.

With all the action that had been taking place, it was not until we had left Essen far behind that we could check to see if all was well with aircraft and crew. I could not see any structural damage from my position, and all the rest of the crew confirmed that they were OK, that is all except Mitch in the rear turret, he had been silent for some time. Bill called him up on the intercom but received no reply. The wireless operator went back to check, and reported damage and oil spill at the rear end. He had tried to get through into the turret but the doors were jammed. It was now my turn to get through to Mitch; Jimmy meanwhile took over my position. Frankly, we all thought that Mitch was dead or badly injured, and I did bang on the turret but got no answering knock so expected the worst. In the end I did manage to prize open the doors with an axe, and found Mitch no worse for wear. His intercom had gone u/s, and damage to the doors had jammed him in so that he was unable to turn around – he was glad to see me!

Even as we crossed the Dutch coast we could still see Essen burning, and knew that this raid was something out of the ordinary. We could now relax or so we thought, and got out the flasks and sandwiches. But fate had still one final card to play: for as we were approaching the English coast near Cromer, a gigantic explosion occurred in front of us; two bombers had collided in mid-air. Later we were to learn that in one of these was our Flight Commander, Squadron Leader Dugdale – he had arrived on the squadron only a few days before ourselves, and was just starting out on his second tour.

What a relief to finally land at Wratting Common, all our fears now behind us, and replaced with one of euphoria. We gathered on the tarmac, and made a cursory inspection of 'Roger' before the crew bus arrived: there were plenty of holes in the fuselage, but part of the tailplane had gone near the rear turret; severing the hydraulics and intercom. It was obvious that a bomb had hit us, and for Mitch it had been a very close thing indeed.

On that night's raid Bomber Command only lost twenty-six aircraft, and this was put down to *Window* which had recently been introduced. It certainly was a good counter to the enemy's radar, and did pose a problem to them throughout the rest of the war.

Although the night's raid had proved traumatic it had in no way affected our spirit. Even the near thing of being almost downed by one of our bombers was soon forgotten. We had performed well as a crew on our first major assignment, and considered that apart from a stroke of ill luck as befell our Flight Commander, nothing the enemy could do would stop us from completing the tour. I suppose 'it was fools rush in where angels fear to tread' in our case: we were so inexperienced, so confident and full of resolve. Only future events would prove that our trust was misplaced, and survival was subject to the vagaries of fate.

The 25/26 July 1943 raid on Essen indeed caused severe damage to the industrial areas in the eastern parts of the city. The Krupps works suffered its most damaging raid of the war, and fifty-one other industrial buildings were destroyed, with another eighty-three heavily damaged. The price was twenty-six bombers, or 3.7 per cent of the force, of which at least twelve were destroyed by nightfighters.

The Luftwaffe High Command now searched feverishly for ways to prevent any further catastrophes like Hamburg, and to get Nachtjagd back on its feet again. Kammhuber still firmly held on to his orderly Himmelbett system as the standard method of combating Bomber Command. He therefore ordered German industry to look for a solution to the jamming of his *Würzburg* and *Freya* GCI radars. Additionally, Milch ordered new ground- and AI radars that operated on jam-proof wavelengths to be developed forthwith. These new AI radars should also equip Herrmann's single-engined *Wild Boar* nightfighter aircraft. As a final measure to overcome the crisis, expansion of the existing network of the Y-system was also taken in hand to ease the infiltration by *Tame Boar* nightfighter aircraft into the bomber stream.

Reichsmarschall Göring was very distressed by the Hamburg catastrophe. On 1 August 1943, he declared that strengthening the Reich air defence was to take priority over all other Luftwaffe commitments. His resolve was confirmed during a Luftwaffe conference held in late August. A unanimous decision was taken to devote all Luftwaffe resources to stem the Anglo-American bombing offensive. Once this goal was realized, the Luftwaffe was to be employed again in Russia and on the southern front. Everyone at the conference was fully convinced that, as Milch put it, 'it was five minutes to twelve for the Third Reich'. If no fundamental change in Luftwaffe strategy was adopted forthwith, Germany was doomed. After the conference, Göring went to see Hitler to get the Führer's permission to adopt this new defensive Luftwaffe strategy. Hitler flatly rejected this proposal and told his Reichsmarschall that attack was still the best defence: 'Terror can only be smashed with terror'. He then gave Göring and his Luftwaffe one final opportunity to vindicate themselves with a renewed bombing offensive against Great Britain. This campaign should be launched immediately. In the end, Göring did not possess the stamina to resist Hitler's ill-fated wishes. The 'Führerbefehl' still ruled, and the helm was not radically altered in favour of the air defence of the Reich. Thus, the last and only remaining chance to save Germany's cities and war industry from near-total destruction was missed.

The development of new radars and the implementation of the other long-term plans would take weeks, if not months. Kammhuber therefore had to resort to temporary measures to counter Bomber Command raids, now that his Himmelbett Nachtjagd had been rendered virtually useless. Oberst von Lossberg, supported by Göring, finally convinced Kammhuber of the validity of *Tame Boar* tactics and from 1 August 1943, this system was employed operationally. The approximate course of the RAF bombers could still be tracked by ground radar, and with the use of this general information, nightfighters were to be directed to radio beacons and then infiltrated into the bomber stream. The nightfighter crews would get up-to-date information on the situation through a running radio commentary, which was broadcast by ground stations throughout Germany. It was then up to the skill of the individual crews to hunt and destroy their RAF adversaries.

The second interim tactic came from Major Hajo Herrmann, who was also ordered on 1 August to throw his *Wild Boar* single-engined day fighters into the battle and practice his target area night fighting. Kammhuber still expressed strong objections to Herrmann's ideas, but he was overruled by Göring and his immediate superior, Generaloberst Weise. These men were very enthusiastic about Herrmann's *Wild Boars*. Bearing in mind the Hamburg catastrophe, they welcomed any practical form of night fighting that could be implemented without the aid of radar. Kammhuber was left with no choice but to give Herrmann the go-ahead. After all, for as long as Nachtjagd's radars were still jammed, the only effective night fighting tactic seemed to be to intercept and destroy the RAF bombers over Germany's burning cities.

These *Wild* and *Tame Boar* tactics had been proposed before the Battle of Hamburg took place, although Kammhuber had prevented their adoption into Nachtjagd. He still felt strongly that only a tightly organized and fully radar-controlled system could yield lasting results, and he regarded these new tactics as merely temporary solutions. However, during the month of August 1943, immediately following the Battle of Hamburg, both the *Wild* and *Tame Boars* claimed a record number of 200 kills. Freelance night fighting clearly paid off rapidly! Over the same period, in the traditional Himmelbett Nachtjagd only forty-eight bombers were shot down.

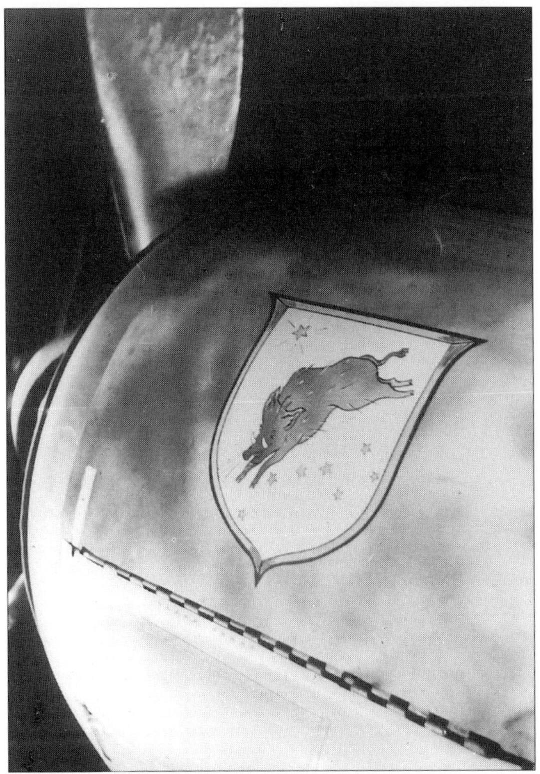

The pilot of this Fw190 nightfighter had his personal Wild Boar *emblem painted on the nose of his aircraft, 1943–44.* Coll. Hans Bredewold, via Ab Jansen.

With this record number of *Abschüsse* during August, the Luftwaffe leaders were slightly optimistic again. It appeared that the catastrophic tide had been turned to some degree. Still, during September 1943, the first inklings of optimism soon turned into pessimism again. Alarmed by the mounting losses in August, Bomber Command introduced three new tactical measures. First of all, 'spoof' raids were introduced to disguise the main target of attack, often using fast, light Mosquitos. This made life very difficult for the German fighter controllers, who had to decide in the early stages of a raid where to send the bulk of the nightfighters in order to counter the British Main Force. Secondly, new electronic countermeasures were introduced. Finally, raids were carried out in poor weather whenever possible, as the *H2S* navigation radar had made it possible for the bombers to find their targets in virtually all conditions. The result was a drop in Bomber Command losses at the same time as German nightfighter losses mounted. The number of *Wild Boar* pilots killed in action rose dramatically from September 1943, mainly because they had to operate in the adverse autumn weather conditions.

The outcome was a crisis in the Nachtjagd leadership. Göring had completely lost his confidence in Kammhuber's ability to ward off the Bomber Command offensive, and strongly felt that the General of Nachtjagd had backed the wrong horse, the Himmelbett Nachtjagd, for too long. Kammhuber had obviously failed in shielding the German cities and war industry against the devastating Bomber Command raids of the past months, and had proved himself unable to adapt quickly enough to the difficulties arising after the Battle of Hamburg. Consequently, he was removed from his post as C-in-C of XII Fliegerkorps on 15 September 1943.

Kammhuber's relations with both Hitler and Göring had been strained for quite some time: his persistent requests for full-scale reinforcements

On the left, General Joseph 'Beppo' Schmid, who replaced General Kammhuber as AOC of XII Fliegerkorps on 15 September 1943. Fw. Heinz Vinke, one of Nachtjagd's leading aces with fifty-four night kills in 5./NJG2 and 11./NJG1, is sitting to his left during an official dinner in Amsterdam. Twenty-three-year-old Heinz Vinke fell victim to roaming Spitfires whilst on a daylight sortie to the northwest of Dunkirk on 26 February 1944, and remains missing. Coll. Rob de Visser.

of his arm had regularly led to clashes with his superiors. At the height of the Battle of the Ruhr in May 1943, Kammhuber had finally pleaded with Göring for a quadrupling of his existing force. The Reichsmarschall's reply was clear: 'You must be a megalomaniac. You clearly want to have the whole Luftwaffe, so why don't you sit right down in my chair?!' Kammhuber's days as General of Nachtjagd had been numbered from then on..

Göring appointed General Joseph 'Beppo' Schmid as Kammhuber's successor. Schmid had been head of the Luftwaffe Intelligence between 1939 and 1942 and had become a personal friend of Göring. At the latter's request, Schmid had written a report in August 1943 on the inefficiency of the Reich's air defences. He had concluded that one of the main causes of Nachtjagd's shortcomings was the peculiar organization of the arm. Until that time, night air defence had been conducted by 'two separate worlds': Hugo Sperrle in Luftflotte 3 was responsible for the defence of France, and Kammhuber's XII Fliegerkorps controlled the defences in the Low Countries and Germany. This splitting up of the Nachtjagd command had led to an inefficient co-ordination of resources. Schmid further concluded that the Himmelbett Nachtjagd was over-organized and inefficient and needed a thorough reorganization. He advised Göring to place the air defence of the

Third Reich in the hands of one body, and to incorporate Luftflotte 3 into this centralized organization. Schmid, a self-assured and persuasive man who possessed a sharp tongue, convinced Göring that he was the right man to command this new body. Göring wasted no time and ordered Schmid to take over command of XII Fliegerkorps on 15 September 1943.

Joseph Kammhuber was allowed to retain his title and responsibilities of General der Nachtjagd for two more months before he was completely shunted off in November 1943 to take command of Luftflotte 5 in Norway. The German war leaders did not make use of his wide experience in night fighting matters for the remainder of the war. According to Major Ruppel, one of Nachtjagd's most skilful fighter controllers, Kammhuber was the finest night fighting strategist there was. But the reign of the founding father of Nachtjagd was definitely over.

Under the aegis of Kammhuber, the arm had been systematically and steadily developed along predetermined lines. It had been a period of continually mounting successes against a still limited British night bombing offensive employing unimaginative tactics. But the future, in which Schmid would hold the reins, would be characterized by continuous hasty improvizations in an often desperate effort to overcome the deficiencies of a machine which had been thrown out of gear by British countermeasures. Both countries would put their highest scientific ingenuity and tactical skills to use in the titanic struggle for supremacy in the night skies over the Third Reich.

In mid-October 1943, one month after Schmid had been appointed commander of XII Fliegerkorps, a reorganization of Nachtjagd was finally implemented. However, the result was quite the opposite to what Schmid had in mind when he wrote his report in August. XII Fliegerkorps, which until then had been centrally controlled from Zeist in the Netherlands, was split up into three separate commands: I and II Jagdkorps, and 7th Jagddivision. Hajo Herrmann's *Wild Boar* units were incorporated into a fourth independent command, the 30th Jagddivision. This restructuring heralded the end of a centrally controlled Nachtjagd. From then on, four separate command centres operated in the nocturnal air defence of the Third Reich, each one independently executing its own defence of a part of Germany and the Occupied Territories. Schmid

Ofw. Willi Bleier, Heinz Strüning's Bordfunker *in NJG1 & 2 during 1940–43. On the night of 6 September 1943, St.Kpt. Oblt Strüning's He219 G9+FB of 3./NJG1 was damaged in both engines by return fire, whilst on a sortie in the Ludwigshafen–Mannheim area. Both Strüning and his* Bordfunker *and friend bailed out; Heinz Strüning hit the tail unit of his 'Uhu' and broke several ribs. Willi Bleier was less fortunate; he probably also hit the machine and was found dead the next day with unopened parachute. By the time of his death, Bleier had participated in the destruction of some forty RAF bombers.*
Coll. Hans-Jakob Schmitz.

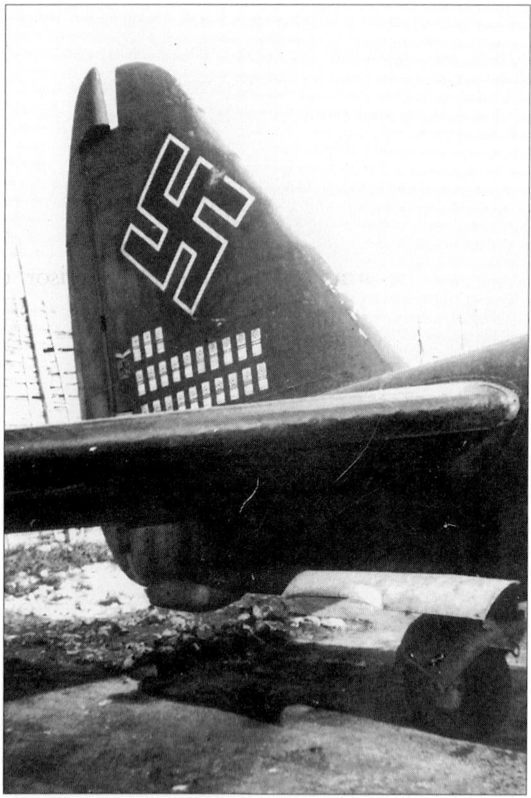

Tail unit of the Ju88 flown by Lt Heinz Strüning of 4./NJG2, showing twenty-three victory symbols and Ritterkreuz, awarded to Strüning on 29 October 1942. Coll. Hans-Jakob Schmitz.

was put in charge of only part of the Nachtjagd; he was appointed commander of I Jagdkorps, covering roughly the Low Countries, Germany and Denmark. Although this was the main air defence command, Schmid had no control whatsoever over II Jagdkorps in France, which firmly remained under Hugo Sperrle's control. The splitting of responsibility often made a co-ordinated night fighting operation impossible, and the reorganization was a disaster for the Reich's air defence. The adverse effect on efficiency was so great that Schmid had no difficulty in obtaining the resubordination to himself of 7th Jagddivision on 1 February 1944. Much of his remaining time in office was spent in an only partly successful effort to reclaim the full and effective command of the nightfighting force enjoyed from the onset by his predecessor.

In an effort to create a reasonably reliable impression of the build up of RAF raids in the chaos immediately following the Hamburg battles, Kammhuber had fallen back on the primitive system of listening posts, or the Flugmeldedienst. These posts, equipped with acoustic aids which had been introduced during the first year of the war, registered the engine noise of RAF aircraft. In order to reduce response time and thus create a more efficient Nachtjagd, Schmid wanted direct access to the Flugmeldedienst. He requested full control over the Flugmeldedienst, intending to incorporate this service into his I Jagdkorps. However, until now the Flugmeldedienst had formed part of General Wolfgang Martini's Luftwaffe Signals and Communications Organization. The procedure was that Schmid had to request *Fluko* (Flugmeldedienst) data from Martini's HQ, during which valuable time was wasted. Martini refused to countenance any change to this system: *Fluko* was his, and he intended to keep it so.

Martini also hindered Schmid's use of another form of early warning information. A few months before the Battle of Hamburg, the Germans had captured intact a British *H2S* navigation radar set. The Luftwaffe 'boffins' soon found that using the existing Luftwaffe Y-system, they could home in on *H2S* transmissions, enabling them to accurately track the flight patterns of the bomber streams, from the moment the bombers took off until they landed again. The crisis caused by *Window* could thus be solved at a stroke. However, the Y-system was a cornerstone of Martini's organization. Schmid received permission to use the vital tactical information supplied by the Y-system only on the day following a raid! Thus, the tactical importance of this information was for the greater part lost to Nachtjagd. Schmid made it perfectly clear to Martini that he needed the *H2S* reports from the Y-service for the co-ordination of his nightfighter defence, but Martini kept refusing this. He even went so far as to forbid the officers in his Y-system to have any direct contact with Schmid and his subordinates. This stalemate now led to a grotesque situation. Schmid secretly contacted a high-ranking Y-officer who was stationed at a Y-site near I Fliegerkorps HQ at Zeist and persuaded him to covertly supply him direct with the much-needed *H2S* reports. It did not take Martini long to find out about this secret liaison, but instead of letting Schmid have the information he so badly needed, Martini transferred the whole Y-site from Zeist to Paris! And as even Göring did not feel like intervening in this matter, Schmid had no option but to build up his own Y-organization! After an intense period of training, two Y-sites were established near Zeist and Berlin, and Schmid finally had the vitally important *H2S* reports directly at his disposal. It is pertinent to note that this bizarre struggle for power between the Generals Martini and Schmid, which the latter after the war labelled as 'tragicomic', took place at the time when Nazi Germany was being pounded by a series of heavy raids during the Battle of Berlin.

With the jammed *Freya* and *Würzburg* radars largely neutralized after July 1943, the Y-system had become vitally important for Nachtjagd. But the struggle between Schmid and Martini prevented a sensible pooling of resources, and provides yet another example of that striving by individuals to retain or gain empires which had so adverse an effect on German policy-making during the war. It was not until Göring himself finally intervened to change this pathetic and disruptive situation that Schmid had his way. On 28 February 1944 Göring incorporated part of Martini's Y-system, and the whole Flugmeldedienst, into I Jagdkorps. At last, Schmid was able to coordinate the night air defence of the Reich as well as he could – but four valuable months had been lost in the process.

Nachtjagd had lost its independent position during the reorganization of October 1943 because Göring had lost faith in it. This meant a severe dent in the prestige of the proud night fighting arm and Schmid consequently experienced a serious neglect of Nachtjagd's interests. It was quite clear to him that Göring no longer believed that the arm could play an effective role in warding off the Bomber Command offensive: the Reichsmarschall even went so far in the chaotic situation after the Battle of Hamburg to consider abolishing Nachtjagd altogether. As a clear indication of Göring's negative attitude, the function of General der Nachtjagd became defunct, and Adolf Galland, the General of the day fighter arm was appointed supervisor of Nachtjagd. Thus, Nachtjagd was placed under the supervision of a day fighting specialist who knew next to nothing about night fighting. It did not take Galland long to realize that these two widely diverging responsibilities could not be reconciled by one man, and he therefore requested that Göring separate them. However, he need not have bothered; this impractical construction was maintained until Galland himself fell out with Göring and was dismissed from high command in February 1945. In an effort to fill his two-fold job satisfactorily, Galland appointed Hajo Herrmann, the Father of the *Wild Boars*, to the post of Inspector of Nachtjagd. Herrmann held this position until March 1944, when Werner Streib took over.

A reorganization of the air defence of the Reich could have been effective if Nachtjagd had been drastically reinforced at the same time. What was needed were more modern nightfighter aircraft; trained crews; unjammable ground and AI radars and radio beacons; Y-sites to take care of the running commentaries and also of the infiltration of the German aircraft into the bomber streams. These were not supplied, which in effect made the reorganization a half-hearted attempt. The direct consequence of the 'Führerbefehl' of August 1943 was that Luftwaffe priority remained with its offensive tasks, at the expense of the Reichsverteidigung (Reich defence). The results of this omission, as we shall see, painfully emerged a few months later during the Battle of Berlin.

In the late autumn of 1943, General Schmid had introduced *Wild* and *Tame Boar* night fighting as the standard Nachtjagd tactics for the coming winter period. Despite all the protests from Kammhuber, the *Wilde Sau* (*Wild Boar*)

'Geschwader Herrmann' or JG300 had been established in July 1943. The *Wild Boars* soon were so successful that Major Hajo Herrmann was ordered in September 1943 to establish two further complete Geschwader: JG301 and JG302. These three Geschwader, each comprising some eighty aircraft and pilots, were respectively stationed near Berlin, Frankfurt and Munich to protect these areas with target area night fighting. The 30th Jagddivision was set up to co-ordinate the independent *Wild Boar* operations under Herrmann's command.

Each *Wild Boar* Geschwader comprised three Gruppen. One Gruppe was equipped with standard Fw190 and Bf109 day fighter aircraft. The other two Gruppen were so-called 'Aufsitzer-

Ofw. Reinhard Kollak (pilot, 8./NJG4, on left) and Major Walter Ehle (Gr.Kdr. II./NJG1, on right) receive the Ritterkreuz at St. Trond on 29 August 1943. General Kammhuber, the Commanding General of Nachtjagd, who was under a lot of pressure at this time due to the recent Hamburg catastrophe, salutes in the middle. Thirty-year-old Major Ehle and his crew were destined to be killed on 17/18 November 1943, when, on finals to St Trond, the flarepath was suddenly extinguished. Ehle's Bf110G-4 G9+AC crashed near Horpmoel in Belgium. At the time of his death, Major Ehle had accumulated thirty-nine victories. Ofw. Reinhard Kollak, on the other hand, survived the war with forty-nine night Abschüsse *in NJG1 and NJG4, all but ten of them* Viermots. Coll. Otto H. Fries.

*Funeral ceremonies on 17/18 November 1943 of Major Ehle and his crew of Ofw. Leidenbach (*Bordfunker*) and Uffz. Derlitzky (gunner).* Coll. Otto H. Fries.

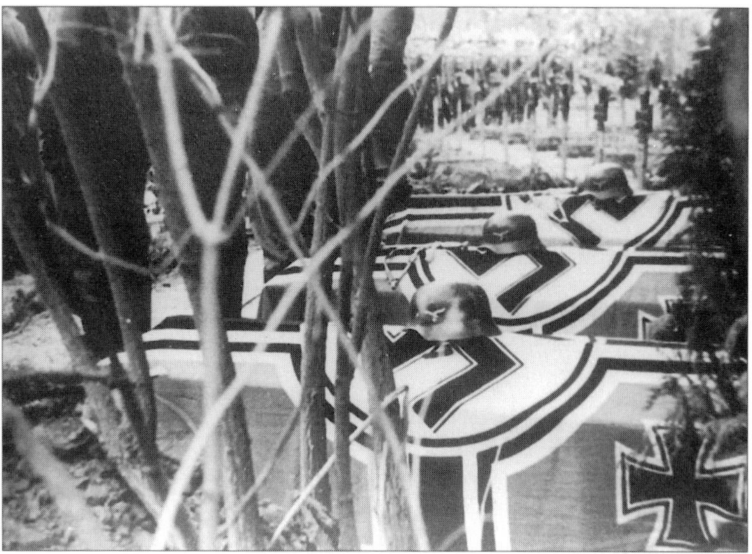

gruppen' or 'lodger units', which had to share their Fw190 and Bf109 aircraft with other day fighter units. For example II. and III./JG300 shared the Fw190 and Bf109s of II. and III./JG1. The Aufsitzergruppen wore out these shared aircraft at a rapid rate; Major Herrmann deployed his *Wilde Saue* relentlessly, insisting that his aircraft should take off even in conditions that grounded the better-equipped twin-engined nightfighter aircraft. Own losses did not matter, only results did. This regularly led to friction with the day-fighter units.

The spectacular results of JG300 in September 1943 made Herrmann and his pilots national heroes, and the German propaganda machine went out of its way to elaborate on their achievements. It seemed that *Wild Boar* night fighting was the solution to the severe problems of the arm. What was forgotten in the euphoria of the moment however, was that the large majority of *Wild Boar* kills were scored by a small nucleus of very experienced pilots. Pilots with less experience in night flying achieved precious little. Experts who kept accumulating *Wild Boar* kills were men like Oblt Friedrich Karl 'Felix' or 'Nose' Müller, a former pre-war captain in Lufthansa and now Operations Officer in JG300, and who scored twenty-nine *Viermots*

Lt Otto Fries, pilot of Stab II./NJG1 carrying the decorations of Major Walter Ehle during the funeral ceremonies in late November 1943. Coll. Otto H. Fries.

and a Mosquito in just fifty-two sorties. Müller received the Ritterkreuz for these feats of arms in July 1944. Major Herrmann himself shot down nine *Viermots* in some fifty sorties. Another *Wilde Sau* legend was Oblt Kurt Welter of 5./JG301, who claimed seventeen *Viermots* shot down in only fifteen sorties between September 1943 and early April 1944.

Lt Kurt Lamm, an experienced fighter pilot instructor, volunteered for *Wild Boar* duty in August 1943:

> I knew Oblt Kurt Welter from our instructing days at the Pilot Training School at Quedlinburg. We were both very experienced in flying on instruments. During August 1943 we were trained in the *Wild Boar* illuminated night fighting on the Me109 and Fw190. Kurt Welter was a brilliant pilot, and soon after our posting to 5./JG301 he scored his first kills in the Schleswig–Hamburg area. Only experienced pilots were able to achieve successes in the single-engined Nachtjagd, as became clear over the following months. They had to do the flying, navigating, calculating, reading the phosphorescent dials and digital clocks and interpreting the often strongly distorted and jammed information which came in over the R/T single-handedly. Moreover, they had to interpret the flares and waving searchlights correctly, combat the bombers, avoid being deluded by the glaring searchlights and finally, find an illuminated airfield and land with the last remaining drops of fuel. This all bordered on the limits of what our brain and body were able to cope with.

After the initial wave of euphoria had blown over in October, the casualty rate amongst the Wild Boars rose quickly. After all, their aircraft were not equipped with any blind-flying aids, which proved fatal to many pilots when the bad autumn and winter weather set in. Losses of 50 per cent were not uncommon on a night of *Wild Boar* operations. Besides, as a countermeasure to *Wild Boar*, Bomber Command radically concentrated attacks in space and time over target. A bombing raid by between 400 and 900 heavy bombers now only took less than half an hour to be executed. This measure effectively curtailed any successful target area night fighting.

In all, JG300 pilots scored some 173 *Wild Boar* kills between July 1943 and March 1944. JG301 flew *Wild Boar* missions on twenty-one nights from September 1943. For eighty-seven *Abschüsse*, this Geschwader lost fifty-eight pilots killed or severely injured. From November 1943, Fw190s and Bf109s of JG302 were dispatched on twenty-two nights, and for forty-three pilots lost the unit claimed seventy bombers shot down. In 1945, General Schmid estimated *Wild Boar* losses at some 45 per cent between 1 August 1943 and 1 February 1944. Such heavy losses, at a time when every fighter pilot and aircraft

Ofw. Günther Migge with his Fw190A-5 'White 9' of 1./NJGr10 at Werneuchen airfield. Ofw. Migge shot down eight British bombers whilst serving with the Wild Boar *JG300 and NJG10 & 11.* Coll. Fritz Krause.

counted in the Reich's air defence, could not be justified any more. Consequently, Herrmann's 30th Jagddivision was dissolved on 16 March 1944. JG300, 301 and 302 and the surviving pilots were transferred to the day fighter arm. Small scale employment of the single-engined Fw190 and Bf109 at night continued throughout the last year of the war, especially in an attempt to engage the elusive RAF Mosquitos. But due to their obvious limitations, they achieved precious little. Kammhuber had been proven right when he commented in July 1943: '*Wild Boar* night fighting may be cheap, but it costs a lot of blood'. The relative significance of *Wild Boar* Nachtjagd is shown by the fact that it could only claim 3 per cent of all Nachtjagd kills during the war. Therefore, the employment of single-engined day fighter aircraft in Nachtjagd must in the long run be considered a tactical failure. On the other hand Herrmann's brainchild must also be considered as a catalyst in the revitalization of Nachtjagd after the Hamburg catastrophe. Partly due to Major Herrmann's efforts, the rigid Himmelbett Nachtjagd was largely given up during the autumn of 1943 in favour of the freelance Nachtjagd, or '*Bewegungskrieg*' (war of movement) as Herrmann termed it.

Twenty-two-year-old Willi Reschke entered the Luftwaffe in February 1944, and on completion of his fighter pilot's training in June, he was posted to 1./JG301. By the time Willi joined the Reichsverteidigung, JG301 had given up night

Oblt Fritz Krause of 1./NJGr10 and his Wild Boar *Fw190 A-5 'White 11' at Werneuchen airfield, early 1944. Note the FuG 217-J2* Neptun *radar array.* Coll. Fritz Krause.

fighting completely. Ofw. Reschke rapidly proved himself to be an outstanding day fighter pilot, accumulating twenty-eight kills (including eighteen *Viermots*) in seventy sorties which earned him the award of the Ritterkreuz on 20 April 1945. Willi further comments on *Wild Boar* night fighting:

> As the fighter pilots who had been instructed in normal day-fighting did not have the required blind-flying training for these night fighting missions, one fell back on airmen who had served as bomber pilots and in that capacity had the required experience in blind-flying. Additionally, on the Night Fighting School 110 at Altenburg, pilots who had already been trained as day-fighter pilots were instructed in night flying.
>
> Since the three *Wild Boar* Jagdgeschwader were equipped with the Bf109G-6 and the Fw190A-8, the bomber pilots now began converting onto these fighter aircraft, to which they were not accustomed. This often was a very problematical process. A number of pilots were killed during the conversion phase, as mastering the fast fighter aircraft proved to be more difficult than the powers that be had assumed beforehand.
>
> In contrast to the traditional nightfighter wings which were radar-directed to the enemy by Himmelbett ground stations, the *Wild Boar* units were not guided by any radar from the ground. The machines were equipped with the FuG 16Z and FuG 25 to keep contact with the central radio station, and to enable them to land on a radio beam on specially equipped 'dromes.
>
> Attacks on the enemy bombers were executed by visual contact, aided either by searchlights in the target area, or by making use of good visibility during clear moonlit nights. As by the nature of these tactics success or failure depended largely on chance, many a pilot never got into contact with the enemy.
>
> JG301 was formed at Neubiberg near München in September 1943, and JG302 followed in November 1943 in the Hamburg area. During the first few months both Wings were solely employed in nightfighter defence. From March/April 1944 the first day-fighting missions were flown and from May 1944 only daylight operations were carried out. The Luftwaffe leadership had increasingly realized that the initial successes of the *Wild Boar* Geschwader could not be maintained. On the contrary: the kill versus loss ratio had become so negative that this forced a decision to be made. Of course, this negative spiral had been largely caused by the bad weather conditions in the autumn and winter. Despite a thorough blind-flying course the pilots in their fast fighter aircraft often found themselves incapable of successfully dealing with these extreme weather conditions. Moreover, the small endurance of the aircraft often forced them to give up a good attacking position and due to lack of fuel had to make for the nearest available airfield. During this phase at times serious losses were incurred among the pilots and aircraft and the initial enthusiasm ever more made way for resignation. Only a handful of very experienced experts were able to deal with the circumstances and remained successful, but their number also diminished from day to day.

The second Nachtjagd tactic with which the Germans hoped to overcome the setbacks after the Battle of Hamburg was *Zahme Sau*, or *Tame Boar* night fighting. In early 1943, Oberst von Lossberg had already tried unsuccessfully to win Kammhuber over to his *Tame Boar* ideas, but now he obtained permission to test the concept operationally. Von Lossberg intended to infiltrate small groups of fast twin-engined nightfighter aircraft into the bomber stream at the earliest possible moment, if possible over the North Sea before the stream even penetrated German airspace. The leading and experienced nightfighter crew in each group would be led into the stream by the Y-navigation system, and some four or five other crews had to keep in visual contact with the leader until the bomber stream had been found. Thus, from the early stages of a British raid, complete formations of Luftwaffe nightfighter aircraft could swim with the bomber stream, and fly along in the stream during the inward flight, over the target area and on their flight back to the United Kingdom. Equipped with the *Lichtenstein SN-2*

AI radar, the German crews could fight the bombers in a running battle and exact a heavy toll from the raiders. The *SN-2* radar, which had recently been developed by Telefunken, was resistant to jamming by *Window* and was to prove of vital importance to the *Tame Boar* Nachtjagd. The whole operation would be directed and supported by a running commentary on the situation during a raid and which was broadcast by radio stations throughout the Reich. Using this procedure, the Nachtjagd leaders hoped to direct some forty to fifty He219, Ju88R and Ju188 aircraft into combat and to engage and destroy between eighty and 100 heavy bombers from each deep penetration raid. Such numbers would represent bomber losses of between 20 and 25 per cent on each raid, and if Nachtjagd could inflict such casualties on a number of consecutive raids, Bomber Command would cease to exist as an offensive force.

However ambitious and optimistic, 'Verfolgungs-Nachtjagd' (Pursuit Night fighting) could hardly be realized before the winter of 1943, as mass-production of the *SN-2* was severely behind schedule. Furthermore, the nightfighter crews needed a few months to convert effectively from the short-range and fully radar-controlled Himmelbett Nachtjagd to the long-range and freelance *Wild* and *Tame Boar*. Crews who had almost always operated in favourable weather conditions and hardly ever at distances of more than fifty miles from their home base now had to learn how to operate over long distances, in bad weather, without strict ground control and land at various strange airfields far away from home. This fundamental changeover demanded extensive training time, and the training alone caused casualties among the nightfighter crews.

Oblt Hermann Greiner (left) and his Bordfunker *Uffz. Kissing in* 'Abschuss*-pose' in front of their Bf110G of IV./NJG1, 1943. Note the flame-dampers on the 1,475hp (1,100kw) Daimler Benz DB 605 engines. Greiner joined Nachtjagd in October 1941 and although he only claimed two bombers shot down in the Himmelbett Nachtjagd during 1942, he was one of the nightfighter pilots who came to full maturity in the* Tame Boar *fighting from mid-1943. By the end of the war, he had risen to Kommandeur of IV./NJG1 with fifty-one victories (forty-seven at night). He was awarded the Ritterkreuz after thirty-six* Abschüsse *in May 1944.* Coll. Ab Jansen via Hermann Greiner.

Consequently, the Germans had to resort to target area night fighting for the time being. Single- and twin-engined nightfighter aircraft tried to intercept and destroy the bombers over the blazing infernos of the target cities in true Hajo Herrmann fashion. The first real success of *Wild Boar* target area night fighting occurred on the night of 17/18 August 1943 when 596 heavies of Bomber Command set out to destroy Hitler's rocket development complex at Peenemünde. Although the V-2 rocket development and production programme was delayed by at least two, and possibly even six months, by a successful low level precision bombing attack, some thirty nightfighters arrived over the target during the raid's final phase. Aided by bright moonlight conditions they claimed twenty-four bombers destroyed in the immediate vicinity of the target. A further eighteen were shot down from the returning force.

Sgt Ron James, mid-upper gunner in F/O. Bill Day's crew with 90 Squadron had just been to the Fiat Works on the 16/17 August 1943, and was ready for a few days rest, but this was not to be, as they were told by their Flight Commander, S/Ldr Freeman:

> 'Sorry to tell you lads but you are ON tonight, it's another maximum effort. Grab a bite to eat, and report for briefing in just over an hour's time – you will see all the details on the notice board'. From all the activity that was going on around us we knew that this was something out of the ordinary: an Air Commodore from Group HQ, SPs guarding the approaches to the Briefing Room, and the Erks [ground crew] scurrying around like blue-arsed flies – what had they cooked up for us this time?
>
> As the wall map was exposed a gasp went up – Berlin? no, someplace on the Baltic – but there is no town there! The Group Captain got to his feet and began. 'I realize after yesterday how tired you must be, but tonight's target must be totally destroyed. The Germans have a factory here,' pointing to the map, 'that is producing nightfighter equipment which is so sophisticated that if it is put into general use we could lose the air war. It is so important that not only we are going to bomb it to extinction, but we are going to get the scientists too. And that will be your job. Our Group will go in first, flying much lower than usual and carrying armour piercing bombs. You bomb aimers will be given detailed maps of the living quarters that have to be attacked. PFF will mark the target as normal, but in this case a master bomber is to be used for the first time. He will talk you through the raid on an open frequency so there should be no slip ups. If any crew does not feel up to the task after a sleepless night I quite understand and they can see me after briefing, but I have to warn you that if this target is not obliterated tonight, you will have to go again tomorrow and every succeeding night until the job is done – I know that I can rely on you and that you will not let me down. Good luck to you all!'
>
> Of course no crew bothered to see the Groupie afterwards. The briefing continued, with the Intelligence Officer telling us that only twelve light calibre AA guns protected the site, and, as we would be operating in full moonlight, the target would be easily discernible. Someone asked 'What is the name of this place we are going to?' He replied – 'Peenemunde'.
>
> It was water nearly all the way: across the North Sea, then south of Esbjerg in Denmark, and along the shores of the Baltic. Surprisingly even flying in perfect conditions some of our crews managed to stray over the defended areas of Lubeck and Rostock, and were given a hot reception at both places.
>
> We arrived early at Rugen Island, a designated turning point for the run-in to the target, and, although PFF had not yet put down their markers, it was rapidly approaching H-Hour. Bill decided to press on, expecting the markers to be released before we came into bombing range. What happened was that we overshot Peenemunde, and the TIs went down behind us. Apart from circling to get back into the 'stream', a dangerous manoeuvre in this situation, it also meant that we would be late in arriving. Bill informed us that he was going back on a reciprocal course and would fly below the incoming bombers to avoid a head on collision. Down we went to about 2,500ft [760m] and back into the fray. That run-in was perilous in the extreme. There was a mass of machines concentrated above over a very small target, and despite the bombs whistling down – a situation which we were quickly coming to terms with – the explosions from the ground tossed us around like a cork. Meanwhile, the Germans had found a few score guns to supplement those twelve we had been led to expect. They didn't have to aim; just hosepipe straight up.
>
> One Halifax, which must have overshot too, was keeping us company barely thirty yards

away. He received a direct hit and dived into the ground; but our luck held, and we came through without a scratch. The Mosquitos over Berlin did a grand job, by drawing off the enemy fighters. We in the first wave made good our escape, but, once they [the nightfighters] realized that Peenemunde was the target, they arrived in time to intercept the following groups. They pursued us along the Baltic and combats occurred right up to the North Sea. Due to the moonlight conditions they had a field day and forty-four bombers were lost, twelve of which I saw shot down.

It had been a costly day for the Allied air forces: the Americans losing sixty bombers on the Schweinfurt raid, and the RAF's total bringing it over the one hundred mark. The Americans were taught a valuable lesson that day: that long range penetration over Germany without fighter cover all the way, was not a viable proposition. Unfortunately, it took the British longer to realize that by sending out a large bomber force during a full moon period, was a recipe for disaster. Later raids on Berlin and Nuremberg would hammer home this point. Only the spoof raid on Berlin, which drew off the enemy fighters whilst we bombed Peenemunde, saved us from being massacred.

Not until much later did we learn that the pre-emptive strike on Peenemunde was to destroy Hitler's V-weapons, the V-1 and V-2. At the time all we lads could think of was, 'Thank God it's over, now maybe we can get some sleep'. Forty-eight hours without shut-eye is a long time, and when we eventually did get our heads down we slept through until evening.

Despite this success for the *Wild Boars* over Peenemünde, aided by the good weather and fine visibility; in the deteriorating autumn and winter weather conditions, the single-engined Fw190 and Bf109 aircraft could hardly be employed successfully in Nachtjagd any more. And as the Flak defences did not distinguish between friend and foe, scores of German nightfighters were falling victim to the flak over the bombers' targets. In an effort to minimize losses, the ceiling of fire for the Flak batteries over the German cities was reduced to 14,600ft (4,500m), just like in the old days of *KoNaJa* (Combined Night Fighting). However, this scheme did not work in practice as the Flak arm was not placed under a unified battle control as had been done in the KoNaJa of 1941–42. During night raids, Flak units tended to ignore the agreement with Nachtjagd, and fired as high, as much and as long as the local Flak commanders considered necessary. As a result, between 15 September 1943 and 20 April 1944, at least fifteen German nightfighter aircraft were destroyed by friendly fire and many more limped back to base badly damaged with dead and wounded crew members on board. In December 1943, General Schmid made another determined effort to ensure close co-operation with the Flak arm and reduce the losses among his crews in the target area. But he overplayed his hand by demanding direct control over the local Flak units during a British raid on any given city. This of course was quite unacceptable to the Flak commanders, and co-operation between the two arms became virtually non-existent.

Sgt Ron James describes a very narrow escape from *Wild Boars* over the 'Big City', during the Berlin raid of 23/24 August 1943. Although he had seen the MO about a rash that had appeared on his body, and which was diagnosed as shingles, Ron decided to join his crew for an operation – their 13th! – that night:

I decided I was going with them. It was not an entirely brave decision, for I realized, that if at the end of our tour I still had Ops to make up, it would mean I would have to fly with another crew to finish my quota – rather a daunting prospect if that crew was fresh out of Conversion Unit.

Berlin, or the 'Big City' as we used to describe it, was never easy, in fact it was bloody hard; and here I was a willing volunteer! 'At least,' I thought to myself, 'here we are flying through 7/10th cloud cover; only sixty miles from the target, and no sign of trouble'. Then it happened! We hit a real bad storm, and started to ice up. The only way through was under it, so down we went, and, by the time we had fought a way out, there was Berlin stretched out before us.

Hundreds of searchlights were sweeping the sky, a sky now completely clear of cloud. It is perhaps perverse to say that there was no sign of flak, but this could only mean that nightfighters were up in force.

By the time we had dropped our bombs we had barely reached our normal ceiling, and thus far we had been lucky, but now that luck changed. A Master Searchlight caught us spot on, and within seconds we were held by at least thirty others, and were well and truly 'coned'. If AA guns had been used I think our chances of survival would have been minimal, but on this particular night it was the turn of their fighters. 'Gunners watch out – a *Boozer* warning' [*Boozer* was a device which detected nightfighter radar signals. A red signal lamp in the cockpit would be activated when a fighter was on your tail]. Even as Bill was throwing 'Roger' into a series of turns and dives, he still managed to keep us informed – not that we needed it.

'Fighter astern and below – corkscrew – Go!' from Mitch as a Fw190 came into attack. The fighter closed, and raked our aircraft with his cannons, but Mitch caught it with a well aimed burst from his Brownings, and we saw him break-up and fall away. All this action was happening within seconds, and even whilst the combat was taking place, I reported two other 190s coming in to attack: one on the port side, the other on the starboard. It was unfortunate that our port inner engine, the one which powered my turret, was knocked out by the first burst of cannon fire – so, apart from giving evasive action commands, I was unable to help Mitch in any way.

Once again we were hit; and now in a vertical dive. Someone screamed: there was a smell of burning, and petrol fumes. This, I thought, was the time to get out; convinced that the aircraft was out of control. Even as I struggled from my seat, it was obvious from the G-force that no way I was going to make it. I relaxed, and a great calm came over me as I sat waiting for the inevitable. What happened next I can only describe as miraculous – my mind floated clear of my body, and I could see myself sitting in the turret. 'If this is death,' I thought 'what is there to be afraid of? It is wonderful; but what will the folks think back home – I am too young to die'. (In later years I often relived this moment, and can only put it down to a severe traumatic shock.)

Suddenly, I became aware that the aircraft was levelling out. How we survived that dive I shall never know, the wings would have dropped off on a less sturdy plane. Our attackers had disappeared, and now flying low over Berlin's suburbs we could see houses and gardens quite clearly. It was time for taking stock of the damage, and our chances of returning home. Jimmy Fenn the W/Op. had 20mm shell fragments in his legs, but nothing serious: the port inner engine was out of action, and a fuel pipe cut; the pilot's control panel damaged, and many instruments u/s, with general damage in the fuselage and bomb aimer's compartment. Our worst fear was that the escaping high octane fuel was awash right down the length of the fuselage, and one spark would have finished us off.

The homeward course took us once more over the Baltic Sea, and on our starboard side we could see the Swedish coast. 'This is the pilot to crew – we have a problem' (an understatement if ever there was one). 'There is no way we can tell how much fuel we have left, and it seems unlikely that we are going to make it all the way home. We have two alternatives: bail out over Sweden, or go as far as we can; send out a "Mayday" and take to the dinghy'. Bill asked us for our opinion on which course to take; and I said, 'With all the damage to the wings, I think that it is probable that the dinghy will be u/s. Frankly, I'm for Sweden, it's a neutral country, and as we know, it is easy to get back to the UK from there'.

Two other members agreed with me, but three others were willing to take a chance. Then Bill with the casting vote said 'Let's press on'. Mark you, I do not think we had any choice, I am sure Bill had already decided his course of action; he was just sounding us out.

Somehow we limped – I think that would be the right word – across the North Sea; very lucky indeed not to have received the attentions of the enemy. By waiting until the engines cut, then quickly switching from one wing tank to another, we had almost made it! A 'Mayday' call was sent out, and an answering message told us to return to base. We replied that our fuel was almost exhausted and we would not make it. We tried again but still the same answer. It was now up to us. Why we had not been given another 'drome near the coast to make a diversion was a mystery to us.

Bill was now convinced that at any moment we would drop out of the sky. All fuel tanks had been drained dry and there was no telling of how much was left in the last tank. 'Crew, stand-by! We have just crossed the coast, and in a few minutes I am going to head "Roger" back out to sea, but I will give you time to make your jump.'

As if on cue a row of lights appeared below us illuminating a runway. 'Hold tight lads – take crash positions, I'm going in.' Almost before we had time to reach our stations we were landing. We touched a small hill on the way in and slithered to a stop at the end of the airfield. A second miracle happened that night; despite all the fuel loose inside the aircraft we did not blow up. Our Guardian Angel must have been looking after us, for even one spark in the right place would have seen our early demise.

The next thing we knew was, that many helping hands were assisting us to vacate the aircraft. Mitch was unconscious, and I was very dazed and in no position to help him or myself for that matter. We had landed at Bodney, Norfolk; only taken over that day by a Thunderbolt squadron of the 352nd Fighter Group USAAF. It was only through the initiative of a private first-class that we had been able to put down at all. At the time he had been in the control tower looking around when he had heard our distress call. Not knowing the lighting system, he had started throwing switches, and succeeded in illuminating the runway with one line of lights. For our skipper Bill there was another surprise in store, for the first man he saw, was one of his best friends from back home in Canada. This friend was now a fighter pilot serving with the American forces.

The crew told us later that they had been entertained like Royalty by the Americans, but Jimmy and I were soon away to hospital; Jimmy to Ely and myself to Stradishall. Apart from suffering from severe concussion, the Shingles were now a mass of blisters encircling my body (It took years for the scars to disappear).

Skipper F/Lt Bill Day received an immediate DFC, the Australian rear gunner Sgt Colin Mitchinson the DFM. Stirling EH908 'R–Roger' was repaired and finally written off on 12 November 1943, when the control column jammed and it crashed at Hundon near Stradishall.

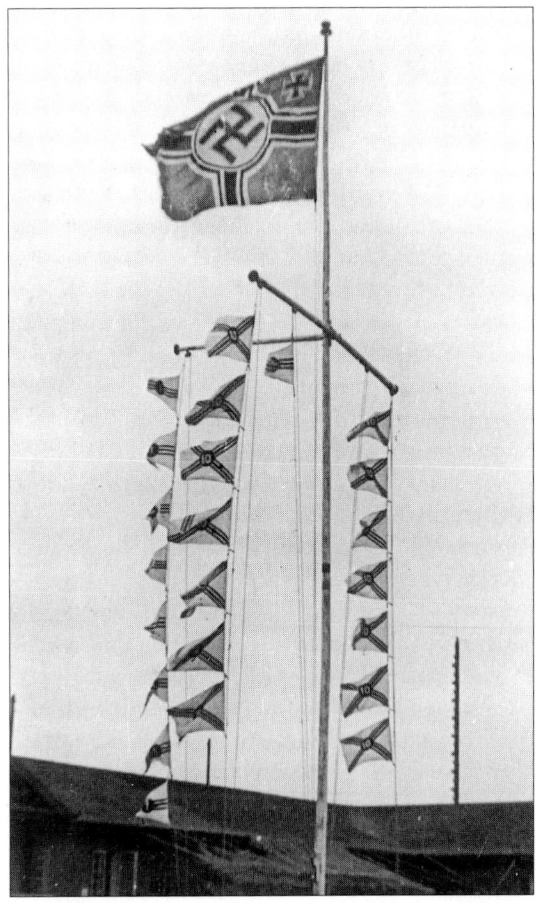

Victory banners of II./NJG3, 1943. Each banner stands for a British bomber shot down. Coll. Peter Petrick.

The 23/24 August 1943 Berlin Raid cost Bomber Command twenty-five Halifaxes, twenty Lancasters and seventeen Stirlings shot down, or 8.7 per cent of the force dispatched. Thirty-one bombers fell to fighters in the target area with another seven crashing on the way back as a result of fighter attacks over Berlin. It was Bomber Command's biggest loss of aircraft and crews in one night so far in the war. These losses clearly illustrated that the German night defences had not been rendered impotent by the effects of *Window*: on the contrary, freelance night fighting clearly had the future.

Nachtjagd however, did not escape unscathed on the same night, although the arm's losses were comparatively very small. In the whirling chaos of dozens of bombers and fighters, illuminated at any one time over the target by hundreds of searchlights and by the blazing inferno below, and with lines of tracer going in every direction, five Luftwaffe fighters were lost to return fire and to Flak. A sixth force-landed at Hanover after a combat with a bomber on the inward flight, and a seventh, a *Naxos*-fitted Bf109 of II./JG300, crashed in Sweden. Another six Bf110s of NJGs 1, 2 and 3 carried out emergency landings at Berlin-Werneuchen airfield with flak damage.

Twenty-two-year-old Lt Peter Spoden served as a pilot with 5./NJG5 from Parchim airfield. He had gained his first confirmed kill, a Lancaster on the Peenemünde raid of 17/18 August 1943 and was now to experience his first *Wild Boar* mission over Berlin. Next day, he drafted the following combat report:

> On 23.8.43 I was ordered to take off on a mission over Berlin in Bf110 CA+KP. After being in the air for around one hour I saw a four-engined enemy aircraft with two tail fins which was illuminated by searchlights. I fired several bursts from a distance of some 200m [yd], and as a result the aircraft plunged down in flames. I next engaged an enemy aircraft over the city at a height of 4,000m [13,000ft]. The results of my bursts of fire however could not be observed. The last enemy aircraft I could determine was a Short Stirling, which turned into me and so I was forced to attack it from head-on. My bursts of fire were aimed so well that the aircraft dived down steeply and approached the ground fast. In the meantime, the enemy rear gunner fired at my own aircraft and inflicted a number of clearly audible hits in the fuselage, so that it started to burn. I myself was hit by a bullet in the upper part of my left thigh which caused the shattering of the bone. I immediately checked if my crew was all right, but received no reply any more. When the heat from underneath me became unbearable, I loudly and clearly ordered them to bail out four or five times. After some more time had expired, I jettisoned the cockpit canopy and got out. I got stuck to the tail plane and whilst exerting all my strength, being hampered by my injured upper thigh I only came loose at a height of 1,000m [3,250ft]. After pulling the rip cord of my parachute I lost consciousness and only some time later I found myself in an air-raid shelter at Grunewalddamm 69.

Peter Spoden adds fifty-three years later:

> My combat report was written in a very businesslike manner. In actuality I was terribly frightened whilst I was held pinned against the tail unit and cried for my mother, as many young soldiers, injured and in mortal fear, do.

Lt Spoden's gunner Uffz. Franz Ballweg was found dead in the remains of the Bf110 but his *Funker* had bailed out safely. Spoden recovered, and with one leg shorter than the other he rejoined his unit in late November to claim his fourth victim, a Lancaster, on 23 November during another raid on Berlin. He went on to become Gruppenkommandeur of I./NJG6 and ended the war with twenty-four confirmed victories.

As soon as Sgt Ron James had recovered, he was on operations again. But as the crew lost their Skipper Bill in September for a while through a motorbike accident, they were 'spare bods', and were for the time being crewed up with Flight Commander S/Ldr Freeman. They did a 'ropey op' to Hanover on 22/23 September, and the next night, their names appeared on the Battle Order again:

> It was really hard luck for us next morning, to find we were on Ops again, we had hoped for a stand-down after the last night's effort. The good news was we were with our own crew once more. Mannheim was the target; always a difficult one, and on this night I wondered whether the Germans had prior knowledge of the route we were to take.
>
> From the enemy's coast, right through to the target, a line of flares marked our passage, on both sides of the bomber stream, and the fighters scored heavily. We lost thirty-two bombers that night – six less than the previous raid.
>
> Our hut-mates, Sandy Lowe and crew, were shot-up on this particular raid, and it was only a few nights after, that we were to witness some of the stress and tension they were living under. On this night we were in bed when our neighbours returned from an operation. Their arrival woke us up, and we found it difficult to get back to sleep, but they, being very tired, soon dropped off.
>
> To our amazement, what happened next was hard to believe. Sandy, in his sleep, started to do a pre-take off check. As if on cue the flight engineer responded, followed by the rest of the crew when their turn arose.
>
> It did illustrate to us the effect that the mental strain of operational flying could have on one.

Maj. Friedrich-Karl Müller, here depicted with his son in late 1944 when he served as Kdr. of I./NJG11. 'Felix' or 'Nose' Müller was the most successful Wild Boar *pilot with thirty kills in just fifty-two sorties.* Coll. Fritz Krause.

Bill Day and his crew were lucky, for in late November 1943 all finished their tour with 90 Squadron. Five went on to do a second tour; Ron James in B-17s in 214 (Bomber Support) Squadron (100 Group). Ron reflects on his first tour:

> We were loath to leave. After losing a total of forty-three aircraft in six months, or to put it another way, two complete squadrons, to say that we enjoyed our stay seems rather paradoxical; but it was the truth.

Himmelbett night fighting remained in operation after July 1943, but at a much smaller scale than before the Battle of Hamburg. On the Berlin raid of 23/24 August 1943, for example, six RAF heavies were destroyed in coastal Himmelbett boxes whilst returning from this raid in a widely spread out front. As soon as General Schmid assumed command of XII Fliegerkorps in September 1943, he drastically reorganized the Himmelbett Nachtjagd. He significantly reduced the number of staff personnel in the Divisional HQs and disbanded most of the Himmelbett sites. The *Giant Würzburg* radars from the disbanded stations were distributed over Germany and the occupied territories. Only the sites in the Netherlands and north-west Germany remained intact as here the hunting conditions were still favourable for the Himmelbett GCI type of night fighting. Over these coastal areas, RAF bombers

Uffz. Walter Schneider, Bordfunker *from 6./NJG1 1944–45. As* SN-2 *radar operator in Hptm. Hager's crew, he contributed towards the destruction of thirteen Lancasters and Halifaxes. Johannes Hager was St.Kpt. of 6./NJG1 during 1944–45 and claimed a total of forty-eight night bombers between February 1943 and March 1945. He was awarded the Ritterkreuz.* Coll. Walter Schneider.

often returned from raids in Germany in a scattered stream, and individual aircraft could thus be picked off relatively easily and destroyed by prowling Himmelbett nightfighter crews.

For *Wild Boar* night fighting to be effective, the Nachtjagd leaders had to identify the main target of the incoming bomber streams as early as possible; only then could sufficient fighters be directed to intercept the main bomber force in time. This often didn't happen during the autumn of 1943: as a direct result of the reorganization of Nachtjagd in October 1943, unified co-ordination of the air defences was impossible. The various Jagdkorps and Divisions operated without any real contact, which had far-reaching and detrimental consequences for the Reich's air defence. Bomber Command made life even harder for its adversary by jamming the R/T communications and radars of the Nachtjagd divisions and of the Flugmeldedienst. Moreover, almost every major raid was accompanied by diversionary 'spoof' raids on other less important targets. These were mainly carried out by the elusive de Havilland Mosquito.

One of the electronic countermeasures the RAF brought into action in October 1943 was 'Operation Corona'. In the RAF monitoring station at Kingsdown, Kent, a duplicate of the Nachtjagd battle control centre at Stade had been built. The idea was to give the RAF bombers penetrating deep into the Reich support by transmitting false instructions for the German nightfighter crews. On the night of 22/23 October, Corona made its operational debut with German-speaking Czechs and Poles broadcasting false instructions. Although experienced Nachtjagd crews recognized the orders issued by Corona as false because of their faulty pronunciation, they still created considerable confusion at Stade and amongst other, less experienced crews, and disrupted the defence against a devastating raid on Kassel. Still, Bomber Command lost forty-three aircraft or 7.6 per cent this night, thirty-nine of them shot down by *Tame Boar* nightfighters. When interrogated on the efficiency of Corona immediately after the war, Major Schnaufer declared: 'Corona never fooled us. We recognized the voices as unfamiliar. We also thought it was most unimaginatively done by the RAF'. One must bear in mind that these are the words of the most successful nightfighter pilot ever, and there is no doubt that Corona caused an additional headache for many a Nachtjagd crew and controller during the ensuing months.

Arthur Harris fully realized that electronic warfare would be a decisive factor in the giant night air battles against the Third Reich, so one month later, all Bomber Command electronic counter-

The Mighty 'M' Stirling EF122 GI–M of 622 Squadron, second half 1943. EF122 flew eight operations with 622 Squadron before being transferred to 1661 CU. It was written off in a crash at Carnaby on 10 November 1944. Coll. Gene Thomason.

measure efforts were concentrated in the newly formed 100 (Special Duties, later Bomber Support) Group. 100 Group was tasked with making a concerted electronic countermeasures effort to disrupt the German night fighting organizations. Spoofing also became a major task, and the Group came to control radar-equipped Mosquito intruder squadrons which were sent to hunt down nightfighters over the Reich. The importance Harris attached to the activities of 100 Group was underlined in December 1943, when the Group was given priority in formation and equipment over all other Groups in Bomber Command.

From early 1944, 100 Group combated Nachtjagd with a wide range of ELINT (Electronic Intelligence) and RCM (Radio Countermeasures) activities, both from British soil and from jamming aircraft in the night sky over the Reich. German radar and radio communications, like the running commentaries for the *Wild* and *Tame Boars*, were jammed with ever increasing effectiveness. What made matters even worse for Nachtjagd was the rising toll that the omnipotent Mosquitos exacted from the Luftwaffe nightfighters and crews.

At first sight, the balance of the second half of 1943 appeared to be very unfavourable for Nachtjagd. Five factors contribute towards this impression. First of all, the operational strength of the arm rapidly declined during the autumn and winter. This decline had set in immediately after the Battle of Hamburg, as the increasing pressure resulted in rapidly mounting losses amongst the Nachtjagd crews. Whereas losses had amounted to only twelve crews in June 1943, during the next month, losses rose to thirty-eight crews (6.8 per cent of strength). In August, fifty-seven crews were killed, missing or severely injured (9.8 per cent) and losses remained at this level in September with fifty-three crews (7.7 per cent) permanently out of action. Kammhuber therefore strongly urged Göring in October 1943 to strengthen the existing training facilities of the arm, as he feared Nachtjagd would gravely lose battle strength. The Reichsmarschall however brushed aside this serious situation with the words: 'Today, there is a war going on, and losses are inevitable'. Training a fully operational Nachtjagd crew was a time-consuming business, as Walter Schneider recalls:

> Aged 18, in October 1941, I was posted to the Air Signals Group at Augsburg. For my *Bordfunker* training I stayed at Signals School 3 at Pocking from the autumn of 1942 until spring 1943 and subsequently till June 1943 at Blind Flying School 3 at Prag–Rusin.
>
> For my night fighting training I came to NJG101 at Kitzingen in the summer of 1943. As this aerodrome was under reconstruction we were diverted to Unterschlauersbach in the vicinity of Nuremberg. I flew on all the practice flights with a Leutnant who was about the same age as myself and we stayed together as a night fighting crew. During our training days here, one third of all the crews under training were killed in Bf110 crashes, all due to accidents. This was a rather sobering fact that made us reflect on the causes. Apart from a lot of luck one needed an excellent pilot to survive the training course. On looking back at our night-fighter *Bordfunker* training, I now even consider it to be more backward, as I experienced it in 1943. No high demands were made on the *Bordfunker*, we just did the most simple triangular flights on a pre-determined course. Moreover, we were precisely guided on these flights by the *Würzburg* radars. The large-scale bombing raids with 1,000 *Viermots*, like the raid on Cologne in May 1942, had by mid-1943 not brought about a change in this useless practice. Besides, a preparation on the navigational procedures in the *Wild Boar* type of night fighting had been long overdue. Small wonder that even experienced *Bordfunkers* who had gained operational experience in GCI night fighting were often unable to gain further successes in freelance night fighting.
>
> On completion of the final phases in our training at Manching and Schleissheim, we were

Due to the lack of training facilities for Nachtjagd, the number of new crews fell sharply during the first half of the Battle of Berlin. Here Göring is seen inspecting instructors of training wing NJG101 at Ingolstadt in 1944. To Göring's right is Ofw. Hans Rasper, who ended the war with nine confirmed night victories. Coll. Hans Rasper.

posted to II/NJG1 at St. Trond in early 1944. Even at our very first visit to the aerodrome on 25 February 1944, I was very unpleasantly surprised by a Marauder raid.

Due to the deficiency in training facilities for the nightfighter arm, the number of combat crews in Schmid's I Jagdkorps, the main Nachtjagd command in the Reichsverteidigung, declined steadily. Between 15 September 1943 and 31 January 1944, it fell from 339 to a mere 179 aircraft and crews, a reduction in strength of almost 50 per cent! The changeover from Himmelbett to freelance night fighting took its toll, as did the continuing daylight missions against the American combat boxes.

Additional losses were caused by Mosquito night intruders that shielded the bomber streams from prowling Luftwaffe fighter aircraft. From July 1943, the British intruders, under the codename of 'Operation Flower', patrolled the German nightfighter bases whilst a heavy raid was developing. Thus the German crews always ran the risk of being shot down during take off and landing. In the same period the 'Bomber Support' operations were initiated. Equipped with AI radar and *Serrate*, a device that homed onto the emissions of the German *Lichtenstein BC* AI radar, the fast and heavily-armed Mosquitos roamed the night skies over the Third Reich and posed an increasingly deadly threat to the nightfighters. A countermeasure to the British intruder offensive was to add a gunner to the Nachtjagd crews. Although this added a welcome third pair of eyes, the additional load posed a problem especially to the performance of the already overloaded and ageing Bf110, which still formed the backbone of the German nightfighter force. Nevertheless, the

Bf109G-6/R3 of I./JG300 being serviced, summer 1944. By this time, JG300 had completely abandoned Wild Boar *night fighting, and flew solely against the Americans in daylight.* Coll. Gerhard Stamp, via Gebhard Aders.

Mosquitos operated in only small numbers for the time being, and would only pose a major threat to Nachtjagd after the Battle of Berlin.

A second cause of the decline in hitting power of Nachtjagd was the disappointing performance of Major Hajo Herrmann's *Wild Boar* pilots once the bad autumn and winter weather had set in.

Thirdly, the increasing British electronic countermeasures campaign seriously curtailed Nachtjagd's performance from the autumn of 1943.

And fourthly, Bomber Command raids could have been dealt with much more efficiently in this period if the power struggle between Schmid and Martini had been resolved, and Schmid given full control over the *Fluko* and Y-services.

And last but not least, the effects of the splitting up of I Jagdkorps into three separate and largely autonomous commands often rendered a successful co-ordination of the defence against Bomber Command raids impossible. And as if this division of control did not cause enough chaos and confusion already, Sperrle stubbornly held onto the independent status of 'his' Luftflotte 3 in France.

All these factors contributed towards a decline in average Bomber Command losses to a level of 'only' 2 per cent, whereas the Nachtjagd losses rose to an average of 3 per cent. The situation looked grim for the Luftwaffe nightfighter force by late 1943.

CHAPTER 6

From Berlin to Nuremberg: The *Tame Boars*

Against British expectations, Bomber Command losses rose considerably during December 1943. The Command had, by introducing *Window*, actually forced the Luftwaffe arm to operate more efficiently. Nachtjagd leaders had out of necessity largely abandoned the inflexible Himmelbett system and now concentrated on the *Wild* and *Tame Boar* Nachtjagd. These flexible tactics enabled the Germans to bring their available nightfighters into action in quantity at any chosen spot over the Reich. Thus, the available force could be deployed much more efficiently than had been done in the Himmelbett Nachtjagd. Moreover, in the Himmelbett night fighting, most of the time only the most successful *Experten* had been guided onto the RAF bombers, whereas in the freelance night fighting, the young and eager crews at last got every opportunity to score against Bomber Command. After the war, many Nachtjagd crews even went as far as to state that *Window* was the best thing that had ever happened to Nachtjagd!

By the end of the year some one third of the force had been fully trained in the freelance *Tame Boar* tactics. Not only did they now have more opportunities to combat the British bombers, but their aircraft were also better equipped than before. The 'unjammable' *SN-2* AI radar and the *Naxos* and *Flensburg* devices had become widely available. The latter two enabled Nachtjagd crews to home onto the emissions of the British *H2S* navigation radar and *Monica* tail-warning device respectively, systems which were fitted to the majority of the British bombers. German crews could thus track down individual bombers with deadly precision. These technical aids clearly illustrate the growing complexity of night combat which had developed in only a few years.

In the autumn of 1943 the majority of Nachtjagd aircraft were fitted with '*Schräge Musik*'; cannons mounted in the fuselage behind the cockpit, and firing upwards at an oblique angle. Until now Luftwaffe nightfighter pilots usually attacked their British opponents from below and behind, a method of attack which made them vulnerable to return fire from a vigilant tail gunner. The problem was solved by mounting *Schräge Musik* within the nightfighter fuselage, and giving the pilot a special sight above his head. Once a bomber had been spotted, the German crew could now take up a position directly underneath the bomber, aim for its fuel tanks, and fire without running the risk of being hit by return fire or debris from his victim.

With the extra burden of *SN-2*, *Naxos*, *Flensburg*, R/T equipment, *Schräge Musik* and auxiliary fuel tanks fitted under the wings for the long-distance freelance sorties, plus the extra weight of a

Bf110G in full night fighting trim for Tame Boar *operations, probably at Leeuwarden airfield in late 1943. Note the* SN-2 *radar aerials, nose armament, long-range auxiliary tanks, flame-dampers, armoured glass windscreen, and the absence of camouflage.* Coll. Luit van Kampen.

gunner, the Bf110 and Ju88 nightfighter aircraft suffered from a drop in performance. However, this was more than compensated by the increase in hitting power.

By the turn of the year, General Schmid ordered the incorporation of 'Fühlungshalter' or (contact-keeper) aircraft into Nachtjagd. As their name implies, these Ju88 and Do217 aircraft were tasked with monitoring the bomber streams. Once infiltrated into the stream by the Y-system, their crews had to keep in contact with the bomber stream with the use of their *SN-2* and *Naxos* sets. The vital information they gathered on the movements of the stream and indications of the possible target of the bombers was passed on to their Jagddivision HQs. This information was then broadcast in the running commentary to the nightfighter crews, who were directed to the best area for engaging the main bomber force.

As a final innovation, Nachtjagd's battle control organization was improved by the end of 1943, both in quality and in quantity. The 'unjammable' *Wassermann* and *Mammuth* early warning radars had entered service in numbers and the Y-service gathered all possible information on the development of each raid. This in turn was used for processing into the running commentaries for the benefit of the *Wild* and *Tame Boar* crews. This then was the reorganized and re-equipped Nachtjagd that was to combat

Ju88G-6 of 7./NJG3, early 1945, with the single 20mm MG151 Schräge Musik *cannon clearly visible on top of the fuselage. Also note the second MG151 cannon in the cupola manned by the rear gunner.* Coll. Peter Petrick.

the British night bombing offensive during the winter of 1943/44.

By November 1943, Arthur Harris considered his Bomber Command to have grown strong enough to achieve his ultimate goal: the destruction of Berlin. The recent successes in the Battles of the Ruhr and Hamburg had confirmed his views that the time was ripe now for the 'Final Battle', the destruction of the capital of the Third Reich. With the aid of *H2S* Berlin was easily identifiable from the air at night and the long winter nights made the deep penetration flights to the 'Big City' possible. Harris had calculated that the Battle of Berlin would cost his Command between 400 and 500 heavy bombers and crews, but he believed that the destruction of Berlin would force Hitler to capitulate by April 1944.

The battle officially began on 18/19 November 1943, when Bomber Command despatched 440 Lancasters and four Mosquitos (to drop dummy fighter flares) to Berlin. Both marking and bombing were carried out blindly as Berlin was completely cloud covered, and as a result the bombing was scattered. No serious damage was inflicted to major industrial premises in the city, although considerable damage was caused by fire in residential suburbs. German fighter controllers on the other hand were unable to bring any significant number of *Wild* and *Tame Boar* nightfighters into action against the bomber

Taking aim. Lt Kettner, Technical Officer of 9./NJG4 peering through the reflector sight of his Bf110. Coll. Werner Kock.

stream bound for Berlin, and only nine Lancasters were lost from the Berlin force, all to flak – a mere 2 per cent. The German *Wild Boar* force lost the Geschwader Kommodore of JG301, Major Helmut Weinreich on this night. His Fw190 had been badly damaged in combat with a British bomber and when Weinreich attempted to force-land his crippled machine at Rhein-Main airfield, the Fw190 struck the ground short of the runway, killing the pilot. While the Lancaster raid on Berlin took place, 395 bombers, mostly Stirlings and Halifaxes from 3, 4, 6 and 8 Groups were attacking Ludwigshafen am Rhein. This city however was also covered by cloud and their results were similar to the Berlin raiders – a scattered attack which caused some damage. Twenty-three aircraft, or 5.8 per cent of the Ludwigshafen force were lost, thirteen to flak and ten to nightfighters.

P/O. John C. Adams, an Australian pilot serving with 50 Squadron since August 1943, flew brand new Lancaster DV368 'S–Sugar' as one of twenty-one aircraft his squadron contributed on the opening Berlin raid:

> Our Lancasters had been loaded to an all up weight of 65,000lb [29,500kg]. This consisted of enough fuel for us to stay airborne for nearly nine hours and our bombload was the usual 4,000lb [1,800kg] 'cookie' surrounded by nearly 6,000lb [2,700kg] of incendiaries.
>
> We had been briefed to take the most direct route to the target – 'straight in' – which took us over Holland and north of most of the defended areas such as the Ruhr and the cities east of it. Our return track was to take us north after leaving the target. When we reached the Baltic we were to fly due west over Denmark.
>
> We left the English coast near Mablethorpe and headed across the North Sea until we came to the coast of Holland. By this time we had climbed to 18,000ft [5,500m]. After a short time over land we were again over water, the Zuider Zee. It was a very dark night and we were only just able to make out shorelines. There were no features on the ground which we could distinguish. By this time we had left the effective area of our *Gee* navigation system so that the coast of the Zuider Zee was the last chance we had of fixing our position. From there to the target it would be a matter of flying by dead reckoning using the wind strength and direction obtained from the last position fix.
>
> The weather had been fairly clear over England

but as the flight progressed we found patches of cloud at around the height we were flying. I was flying the Lancaster for most of the time on instruments. There was very little to be seen by looking out. On clear nights I looked on the Pole Star as a good friend. It was very often nicely positioned just over my left wing tip on our way to the target. However on this occasion there was too much cloud around for it to be visible.

We were well into Germany, somewhere to the north-west of Hanover, when I was startled by another aircraft which flashed in front of my windscreen. It was close enough for me to see that it was twin-engined and it seemed to be travelling very fast, about a hundred miles an hour faster than we were. It came into my field of vision from our left and disappeared off to the right a few metres in front of my right wing tip. I think that its course would have been at an angle of about sixty degrees to our own. It was close enough for me to see the flames from its engines and, whether I imagined it or not, I believed that I heard their roar as it was crossing in front of us.

This close encounter happened so fast that Tom Midgely, our Flight Engineer was the only other member of the crew who saw it. When the other members of the crew heard what had very nearly happened, there was some excited chatter over the intercom but it soon died down. I told the boys to forget about it. That one had missed us!

I wondered if the enemy pilot had another Lancaster on his radar and was hurrying to catch up with him or whether he had just been vectored into the bomber stream. To this day I wonder if that enemy pilot was aware that he had come within of a split second of being part of a fireball in the sky.

When we arrived we found the city covered in cloud and because of the difficulty of accurately identifying the target area, the markers were quite scattered. We bombed on what appeared to be the main concentration of reds and greens. With the cloud cover, searchlights were not a problem but the defences put up a very heavy barrage of predicted flak. We had no chance of obtaining a picture of the aiming point, we just came back with a nice picture of cloud which was lit up by the fires under it and some lines of light which represented the target indicator flares. We saw no fighters and we managed to come through the flak barrage without damage although some bursts were fairly close.

We left the target area and the trip home from then on was without incident. We felt the usual relief at leaving the enemy occupied Danish coast behind. Then began our slow let-down over the North Sea. When we passed through 10,000ft [3,000m] it was time to break out the

P/O. John C. Adams RAAF. John served with 50 Squadron in Lancasters between August and 26 November 1943, when he was forced to ditch his Lancaster off Wilhelmshaven after a collision with another aircraft. P/O. Adams and four of his crew were taken prisoner. Coll. John C. Adams.

coffee – we no longer needed to be on oxygen and we could take off our masks to drink it. This was a time of relaxation. I had 'George' the automatic pilot engaged and all I had to do was correct it when it wandered off course. There was plenty of chatter over the intercom – very little of it about the raid on Berlin. I reminded Bill, George and Cyril to keep a good lookout for other aircraft – I was always nervous about a collision. At about this time we were within range of *Gee* and this enabled Jimmy to get a fix. We were fairly close to track and he gave me a small alteration to course to bring us in over the coast between Mablethorpe and Skegness. A few minutes later we were letting down to join the circuit around Skellingthorpe. I called up 'Black Swan' and Blackie answered and gave me landing instructions. I found our place in the landing system and we were on the ground at 01.31 – just three minutes short of eight hours from take-off. When we reached our dispersal we were greeted by the groundstaff who anxiously asked if all was well with their lovely new 'S–Sugar'. We told them that she had performed perfectly except that *Monica* was u/s. They said that it was not their worry – the radar people would have to fix that. We were discussing this when the crew bus arrived to pick us up. As we piled in, the groundcrew were already starting to work on servicing 'S'.

The episode of the near miss made me even more nervous about the possibility of colliding in the dark with another aircraft. These fears were realized eight days later, on the night of the 26th, while on our sixteenth operation in Lancaster DV178. Another Lancaster came down on us. Its tail section took out the windscreen and wrecked the two port motors. This occurred about twenty minutes after we had dropped our bombs on Berlin. About two hours later, the damage we sustained led to us crashing in Wilhelmshaven Bay. We were lucky that we only suffered the loss of two members of the crew. The bomb aimer, Bill Ward, was killed on impact and Cyril Billett the rear gunner, was drowned. We survivors spent the remainder of the war as prisoners.

Oblt Fritz Engau, St.Kpt. 5./NJG1 in 'Sitzbereitschaft' (cockpit readiness) in the cabin of his Bf110G-4 at St Trond, autumn 1943. Coll. Fritz Engau.

The 18/19 November raid was followed by another fifteen heavy raids on the German capital and sixteen more on other German cities over the next four-and-a-half months. Just a week after the opening raid, Harris was forced to withdraw his Short Stirling squadrons from the battle, as losses amongst the eldest of the four-engined RAF heavies had become too high. The units equipped with the early type Halifaxes met the same fate during February 1944 – decisions that caused a 20 per cent loss in Bomber Command's hitting power. Despite this severe setback for Harris, the Battle of Berlin had got off to a promising start. The majority of the first raids in November caused severe damage to the Reichshauptstadt against only small losses amongst the RAF heavies. But this situation was soon to change: equipped with *SN-2*, *Naxos* and *Flensburg*, the *Tame Boar* nightfighters started exacting a rising toll from the British raiders during December and January. Additionally, weather permitting, large-scale *Wild Boar* operations were also carried out over the cities under attack. Even though losses to the Luftwaffe nightfighters remained high, this was (partly) compensated by their growing hitting power.

On completion of their nightfighter training, Lt Otto Fries with his *Bordfunker* Uffz. Fred Staffa was posted to II./NJG1 at St Trond in January 1942. Under the prevailing conditions of the Himmelbett GCI system, the green crew had hardly been given a chance to prove their ability in combat, as only the most experienced crews patrolled in the most 'profitable' boxes. Therefore, by August 1943, Fries and Staffa had only had fleeting encounters with a British bomber on two occasions, without being able to score a confirmed kill. The luck was finally changed on 10/11 August 1943 when the crew shot down Halifax JA716 of 97 Squadron at Hanzinelle/Belgium in a traditional Himmelbett interception. F/Lt Covington DFC and crew all bailed out safely. A second victim followed on 22/23 October 1943, when Fries destroyed Lancaster III EE175 EM–R of 207 Squadron which was bound for Kassel. S/Ldr McDowell, a Canadian from Vancouver, and his crew were killed when Lancaster EE175 crashed at Nettersheim at 20.30 hours. All are buried in Rheinberg War Cemetery. Halifax LK932 of 76 Squadron followed on 3/4 November, with F/Lt Hornsey and crew escaping alive. Stirling LJ442 JN–F of 75 Squadron fell victim to Fries on 19/20 November at Horrues/Belgium. Four of the crew were killed. Lt Otto Fries, Uffz. Fred Staffa and their gunner Uffz. Konrad Deubzer were again on readiness at St Trond on 29 December 1943, when Bomber Command attacked Berlin with 709 heavies and three Mosquitos:

Lt Otto H. Fries, pilot with I. and II./NJG1 during 1942–44. Over this period, he claimed eighteen Abschüsse *whilst flying the Bf110 and He219.* Coll. Otto H. Fries.

> During briefing for the mission, the codeword 'Temporary Crow' was given. This meant that due to adverse weather conditions we should not expect an order to take off for the time being. In case of an expected improvement of the weather at a later stage the codeword 'Pheasant' might be given to order us to take off on the mission. On the other hand, in the case of lasting bad weather over the 'drome or even further deteriorating weather conditions, the codeword 'Definitive Crow' might be issued to announce the end of our state of immediate readiness.
>
> By 17.00 hours the first enemy aircraft were reported flying in. This was far off to the north in the operational area of the Fourth Gruppe, but these comrades were not able to take off either due to the bad weather. Thus, the whole Geschwader had to sit and wait at their bases for the bombers coming back in some three or four hours, silently hoping that by that time the

weather conditions would have improved so much that they would be able to start.

The Operations Room regularly announced the position of the front of the bomber stream – they assumed that Berlin must be the target for the night. The weather intelligence people affirmed that the weather was gradually improving from north-west to south-east. Nevertheless, this didn't show at the 'drome yet. From the Jagddivision HQ they learnt that the units in northern Holland would be able to take off and land shortly.

Shortly after 20.00 hours the crews who were on the battle order to patrol in both the northern night fighting boxes were taken by surprise by the order for cockpit readiness, even though the codeword 'Temporary Crow' was not yet cancelled. On this night, [Fries and] his crew were allocated to the wave to patrol in box 'Chamois'.

The crew bus drove six of them over to the dispersal area, where they immediately boarded their aircraft. All the checks before take off, already carried out hundreds of times before, were performed with the confidence of a sleepwalker. Having completed the check list and having been strapped in, they sat and waited in their machines. The NCO groundcrew sat and waited with them on the edge of the narrow cockpit rim. In the end, he got a sore behind and he slid down onto the wing.

Cockpit readiness is a nerve-racking business. The more unfavourable the weather conditions on take off and landing are, the stronger is the tension and the greater the pressure on the nerves. Still, once the machine is in the air and the props are turning quietly and smoothly, the pressure is gone and left behind on the ground. The fascination of night flying is always a new and wonderful experience!

Then, all of a sudden, the green lamp on the front edge of the hangar is blinking: the order to take off!

The NCO groundcrew jumps up and shuts the cockpit roof, he [Fries] locks it from the inside. On the seat of his pants, the groundcrew slides down from the wing and runs towards the battery trolley, which he plugs in. One after the other, the engines burst snorting into life. Cable removed – battery trolley rolled aside – chocks away – aircraft free! He [Fries] cautiously taxies out of the camouflaged hangar and turns off towards the taxi track whilst applying a bit of extra power.

'Eagle 98 taxies to starting point – switch on flare path!'

'Roger-Roger – you may proceed!'

The moment he arrived at the take off point he turned sharply to the left and paused for a few seconds to check the time of take off on the clock in the instrument panel. It indicated 20.42 hours.

'Eagle 98 taking off – will go on small lantern right away!'

'Roger-Roger – Horrido and good hunting!'

'Horrido – thanks!'

Taking off was done in the same way as on that afternoon when they had tested the aircraft, with the difference that now complete darkness prevailed. This meant that after lifting off, he had to change over to flying on instruments immediately and complete the take off procedure quickly, in order to have his eyes and brains free for blind flying.

Changing over from flying on sight to flying on instruments is always a battle between feeling and reason. The feeling points out that the aircraft is listing to the left, so push the stick to the right to restore level flight again! The reason responds: no way, the instruments indicate that the machine is flying in a completely normal fashion! Many a young and less experienced pilot has met his fate as a result of this internal conflict, by reacting instinctively and causing the aircraft to slip down over one wing and smash to pieces on the ground.

Even before the lamps of the second artificial horizon (which were positioned 5km [3 miles] beyond the end of the runway to ease the switching over from visual flight to instrument flying) had disappeared below his wings, he went into a flat curve and set course for the radio beacon in box Chamois. When he had reached a height of 80m [260ft], the machine was swallowed up by the clouds. The *Funker* pulled in the transmitter and aligned the bearing loop aerial diagonally – this was the simplest method finding the shortest route to the waiting position in the box.

The needle of the altimeter had almost reached the 2,000m [6,500ft] mark when they surfaced from the clouds and had a brilliantly clear starry sky over them. They concluded that the upper limit of the cloud layer had sunk considerably since that afternoon, a clear sign of the forecast improvement in the weather. Only the lower limit of the clouds had not lifted yet. He had not noticed any icing up.

'Eagle 98 to Barrabas – we're approaching, please come in!'

In answer he only heard a mutilated rasping.

'Eagle 98 to Barrabas – I cannot understand you – please come in – please come in!'

There was a murmuring and hissing in their headphones and then, still a bit faint, box Chamois responded: 'Barrabas to Eagle 98 – please come in!'

'Eagle 98 is approaching.'

'Roger – ask heading – ask altitude.'

'Head eight-five – height three-two.'

'After a short break, Chamois came in again:

'Turn ten degrees starboard, ten degrees port!'

'Roger.' He alternately banked to the left and right several times.

'Barrabas to Eagle 98 – I have established contact – head nine-zero and climb to height four-five.'

'Roger-Roger!' He turned onto a course of ninety degrees. When the needle on the altimeter indicated 4,000m [13,000ft], he clipped on his oxygen mask and ordered both his crew members to do the same. A few minutes later, he had reached the demanded height. He stopped climbing, changed over to level flight and throttled back to economic cruising speed. He then trimmed the aircraft and synchronized the engines.

He was well aware of the fact that they had only been scrambled as a precautionary measure, and that the British aircraft coming back took a much more northerly route. Still, possibly one bomber or another might stray towards his area, as perhaps its compass had been damaged by shrapnel – this did happen once in every while.

They received instructions to orbit the beacon and change course every eight to ten minutes by 90 degrees. He didn't feel very well physically. For lunch he had enjoyed a nourishing pea soup with bacon; and for supper a farmer's meal, richly laced with onions had been dished up. Now the peas battled with the onions for the available space in his intestines, but he was firmly strapped into his confined cockpit and was suffering. It felt as if it would tear him apart. He tried everything to distract him from the pain, but just didn't succeed: the piercing pain in his bowels became more unbearable every minute. When he indicated to his crew that he might have to break off the mission and also told them why, he received some sniggering remarks. He had no

Lt Otto H. Fries (left) posing with his Funker *Uffz. Alfred Staffa in front of their Bf110G of 5./NJG1 at St Trond, September 1943.* Coll. Otto H. Fries.

choice but to suffer in silence.

In the course of the next half-hour, he talked with the ground station several times on the whereabouts of the *Kuriers.* And always, he got the same stock answer: 'Please wait – *Kuriers* are still on their way'. Thus, he felt ever more and more that no enemy aircraft would stray into their hunting grounds this time – by now, they had been airborne for more than an hour. He took the decision to break off the mission, since the revolt in his bowels had become unbearable.

Just when he intended to press the microphone to announce his decision and ask for a course home, the excited voice of the fighter control officer came in: 'Barrabas to Eagle 98 – I have a *Kurier* for you – steer eight-zero – target at height six-three – increase speed – increase speed.'

He glanced at his clock: it was exactly 22.00 hours.

The pain had instantly disappeared – at last, he could get into action again; what a stroke of luck! He pushed the throttle forward and adjusted the propellers to fine pitch. He steered onto the indicated course in a steep curve. From the variometer he read off a climbing speed of between seven and nine metres per second. When he had reached the operational height, he throttled back a little.

'Barrabas to Eagle 98 – turn 360 degrees port at two-eight-zero – increase speed – increase speed!'

He went to a reciprocal course in a steep left-hand turn. During the turn he switched on his weapons systems. As soon as the machine was heading on the new course, he raised his seat and switched on the lighting in the reflector sight.

'Target height six-three – ten degrees starboard – target range three-five-zero – increase speed – increase speed!'

'What does your *SN-2* indicate? Don't you have an echo yet?', he asked his *Funker.*

'One moment, there's a lot of jamming, the tubes are flickering considerably!'

'Barrabas to Eagle 98, twenty degrees port – target height six-three unaltered – target range three-zero-zero.'

'Yes, I have him in my set – the large echo there, must be it, range three Ka-Em.'

'Eagle 98 to Barrabas – I have contact on Emil-Emil – over and out!'

'Roger-Roger – good hunting!'

The bomber was flying 3km [1.9 miles] in front of him. It was amazing that it was flying at such great height, normally they cruised at between 4,000 and 5,000m [13,000 and 16,200ft] high, at times even at 5,500m [18,000ft], but over 6,000m [19,500ft], he had never experienced this before.

'A bit to the right – a little higher – distance nineteen hundred.'

He steered ten degrees to the right and pulled the machine up a bit.

'Target dead ahead – almost same height – distance twelve hundred.'

They approached rapidly, so he throttled the engines back a little.

'Left a bit – little higher – distance seven hundred.'

The expanse of the star-spangled sky hung brilliantly clear over them, only the horizon was a bit indefinite through a thin bank of haze, which defined the clear sky from the darker depth.

'Slightly left – a bit higher – distance four hundred – we're approaching rather fast!'

He throttled back even a bit more.

'Tell me his exact position!'

'He is now immediately ahead – just a little over us – drifting a bit to the left – distance three hundred.'

He screwed up his eyes and peered intensely forward. He scanned the horizon from right to left. There he is! Just a shadow, thin like the back of a knife, just above the layer of mist which outlines the horizon. He distinguished the four engines, the relatively slender fuselage and the double tail unit – Lancaster or Halifax? Probably Lancaster – the Halifax was more cumbersome. He came in a bit closer and clearly saw the engines protruding from the front of the wings and their weakly glowing exhausts. It definitely was a Lancaster!

'I can see it – you can switch off your set! A Lancaster – make a note of the time, it's 22.05 hours.'

'Eagle 98 to Barrabas – I engage!'

'Roger-Roger – Horrido!'

The bomber flew some 150m [yd] in front of him and slightly to the left. He removed the safety lid from the control column and moved in a bit closer. Just when he wanted to launch his attack, the Lancaster turned sharply to the right and flew exactly through his sights – its crew must have spotted him. Almost automatically his right forefinger bent and all the machine guns and cannons blazed away. He didn't register any hits – it had all gone much too quickly. 'Write down the time! It's 22.07 hours.'

'Eagle 98 to Barrabas – have made Pauke-Pauke – will keep in visual contact!'

'Roger-Roger!'

The tail gunner had simultaneously opened fire, he saw the muzzle fire flashing up in the turret and how the lines of tracer of the four machine guns fanned out against the night sky through the wild manoeuvres of the bomber. The tail gunner hardly had a chance to score any hits on his machine during such extreme manoeuvres.

He swiftly pulled the throttle back and plunged down to the right and after the bomber, always endeavouring to stay below the aircraft so as to be able to keep an eye on it against the clearer sky.

All of a sudden, the Lancaster pulled up to the right, and just as unexpectedly slid down again to the left, followed by sharply pulling up to the left and plunging down to the right again. Both the bomber and fighter aircraft rapidly lost height and accelerated very fast.

Riddled with bullets from a nightfighter, Lancaster ED438 EA–R of 49 Squadron has come to grief on 3/4 November 1943, probably near the target of Düsseldorf. This aircraft had come to 49 Squadron on 28 December 1942 and was shot down on its fifty-seventh 'op'. Five of the crew, including the pilot, F/Lt Cecil G. Thomas, were killed and eventually buried in Rheinberg cemetery. Coll. Peter Petrick.

'Keep your eyes on the needle of the speedometer Fred and tell me when it approaches the red mark! I have to keep my eyes glued to this lad up front, otherwise he's gone!'

The Lancaster danced the corkscrew and he danced with it – it was a foolish game, which not only took a lot of nerves but also sheer strength. He felt sweat pouring from his temples and he started to steam all over his body. Behind him, the two men were roaring, but he could not understand them as they both shouted at the same time. The gunner's makeshift light folding chair had collapsed. Depending on the manoeuvres of the machine, he was glued to the cockpit roof or the next moment he was pressed to the floor through the centrifugal forces. Fred's *Bordfunker* case had unlocked and its contents were flying through the cabin. The ammunition belts of Konrad's twin-MGs had crept out of their boxes and hissed through the cabin like crazy snakes. The chaos was complete!

'Let him go and take the next one – you're not going to get this one, the way he's turning – everything is in a mess here with us in the back!'

'Not now!' he muttered.

All of a sudden the Lancaster slid down over its left wing – this had nothing to do with a corkscrew! He dived down after it, they raced down steeply, he had almost lost the bomber in the darkness.

'Are you crazy! We almost have 700 on the clock!' his *Funker* yelled! He glanced at the speedometer, and indeed, they travelled far beyond the 600 mark! Almost as suddenly as the bomber had plunged down, it pulled up again, it zoomed up all but vertically. Taken by surprise by this manoeuvre, he pulled the stick against his breast and stalled his machine so badly that it sheered off to the side. The Lancaster had already disappeared from his view, when he saw it sliding past, only a few metres over his machine. The bomber pilot had stalled his machine as well. He immediately went after it and wondered how one could cut such capers in a heavy kite like the Lancaster.

'What bloody game are you playing!' the *Funker* exclaimed, 'cut this damned dog fighting now, you can't win!'

He was right, it was an idiotic game, in which the bomber undoubtedly held the best cards. Its pilot laid down the rules of play, he knew what he intended to do the next second, which flying manoeuvres he wanted to perform. The chasing hunter always hobbled split seconds, if not whole seconds, after it, as the pilot had to adapt to the next manoeuvre of the bomber and react accordingly. Whilst he was twisting and turning, he pondered on how to get into a firing position. He only saw one possibility: when the bomber had reached the highest point in the corkscrew and prepared to roll to the other side, it hung still into the air for one short instant – he had to seize this opportunity. It would undoubtedly be hard and the chance to hit the bomber squarely at this moment surely was not big, but he had to try! The game could not go on for much longer as they steadily lost height, and if the Lancaster succeeded in reaching the safety of the clouds, it would escape for certain!

He concentrated fully on the movements of the bomber and at the next moment when it hung as if suspended, he fired a burst into its left wing. He believed he saw a hit, but no fire erupted. The tail gunner replied with a volley but the tracer flew past their machine. Aiming accurately was hardly possible for the British gunner in the wild manoeuvring of the bomber.

'22.12 hours – height 4,200', reported the *Funker*.

The corkscrewing of the Lancaster became even more feverish. It also lost height rapidly, and he had the impression that it wanted to reach the layer of clouds at all cost – he would have done the same in their position.

With his third burst of fire, he got it in its right wing – the right inner engine was on fire, it trailed a banner of smoke like a ribbon.

'22.14 hours – height three-three – you had better watch your speed!'

The bomber's corkscrew flattened out; it was quite clear that the 'comrades from the other side' desperately wanted to reach the safety of the cloud layer. They were certainly travelling much faster than was permitted in the type's manuals.

Nachtjagd aces at St Trond, Belgium in the early spring of 1944. From left to right: Major Helmut Lent (Kommodore of NJG3; by this tme his tally stood at some eighty-five confirmed victories); bandmaster; Oblt Heinz-Wolfgang Schnaufer (Kommandeur of IV./NJG1) and Hptm. Hans-Joachim Jabs (Kommodore NJG1 with some forty-five kills). By this time, Schnaufer was earning himself the nickname 'Night Ghost of St Trond'. After receiving the Knight's Cross on 31 December 1943 for forty-two night victories, he was awarded the Oak Leaves on 24 June 1944 for amassing eighty-four night Abschüsse. Coll. Martin Drewes, via Rob de Visser.

Now that the Lancaster was hardly curving any more, he could quietly aim. Very slowly he approached the aircraft – the bomber's pilot must have pushed the throttles through the gate, he noticed the vibration of his wings – and he let the crossing lines of the reflector sight wander between the engines in the right wing. A short burst set the wing on fire – it was like an explosion, he must have hit the fuel tanks squarely.

He rolled away to the right and then went over into a sharp left hand turn. He saw how the Lancaster plunged down over its right wing. The fire reflected in the clouds and disappeared. Moments later the layer of clouds lit up as if illuminated by a flashlight. All that remained was the typical dull red burning spot.

'Height 2,800 – time 22.16 hours – I have made full notes for the combat report. Congratulations! That really was a tough cookie!'

'Ugh! Indeed it was!'

'Eagle 98 to Barrabas – have Sieg-Heil! – do you have position?'

'Barrabas to Eagle 98 – congratulations – Roger-Roger – position is noted.'

Fred got a little overconfident: 'Eagle 98 to Barrabas – next one please!'

'Roger-Roger – we do our best – proceed to height five-five – head nine-zero.'

He increased the manifold pressure, steered a course of 90 degrees and with eight metres per second he started climbing. He was exhausted! His arms and legs trembled from the strains of the combat. Never would he have suspected that a bomber could twist and turn like that – perhaps its pilot had been the aerobatics champion of England! He was bathing in his own sweat, really, he had had enough for one day! Yet, perhaps another one would stray into their box, who knows?

When they had reached a height of 5,000m [16,200ft] he attained level flight again and throttled back to economic cruising speed. They had used up a lot of fuel in the combat, but there was still enough left for another one and a half hours. They flew squares again over box Chamois.

'Barrabas to Eagle 98– Kuriers have gone to bed – return to base – head two-five-zero – good night – over and out.'

'Roger-Roger – good night – over and out.'

He steered the indicated course, throttled back a bit and trimmed the elevator so that they headed for base whilst descending some three to five metres per second. The *Funker* picked up the radio beacon of the home base in the bearing receiver. After having been on their way for some ten minutes, the *Funker* called the Operations Room of their Gruppe.

'Eagle 98 to Tango – come in please – come in please!'

'Tango to Eagle 98 – Roger-Roger – come in!'

'Eagle 98 returning to base – switch on flarepath in ten minutes.'

'Tango to Eagle 98 – you cannot come to garden fence – head for Home 46 – garden fence has thick soup!'

'Oh damn it! That's what we need! Where is Home 46 – surely somewhere in Holland?'

'One moment – Konrad, hold the lamp please!'

The *Funker* thumbed through his documents. With his finger, he run through a table.

'It's Leeuwarden!'

'On no, that's the other end of the world! Well, let's see.' He checked the remaining fuel. 'We won't make it, in the combat we've used rather too much juice. As a last resort I would perhaps risk it, but what the heck, the weather can't be that bad! If it's the same as on take off, we'll make it! So, let's go home!' He pressed the microphone on his stick: 'Eagle 98 – are very thirsty – cannot go to Home four-six – must come to garden fence – switch on flarepath in five minutes!'

'Roger-Roger – curtain at zero-seven – nothing else changed!'

'Well, the lower limit of the clouds at 70m [230ft], weather otherwise unaltered, hardly a problem!' He had always found that landing in bad weather at night was less complicated than at daytime, as the lamps were more visible - and after all, flying on instruments was their nightly bread!

On approach to the base radio beacon, their machine dived into clouds at some 1,000m [3200ft]. He concentrated completely on his instruments. With the aid of the radio altimeter he felt his way toward the ground using the Roland system. The needle of his altimeter was between the seventy and eighty mark when he finally saw the flickering of the lamp on top of the radio beacon. Whilst holding his altitude, he carefully curved until he was on course of 270 degrees, then he levelled the machine and throttled back a little. When the first lamp of the flare path turned up, he pulled back the throttle, and lowered the undercarriage and the flaps. With a speed of some 300kph [186mph] he headed towards the 'drome along the path of lights whilst taking great care to hold his altitude. The first and outer artificial horizon turned up – another five kilometres, then the arrow to indicate the right direction came into view. When the inner artificial horizon disappeared beneath his wings, he fully throttled back and lowered full flaps. Just like in training, he put down the machine on the concrete runway with a three-point landing. The clock indicated 22.55 hours.

'Tango from Eagle 98 – Luzie-Anton completed!'

'Roger-Roger' – congratulations!'

'Thanks!'

'My congratulations too!' said the *Funker*,

'This time on a perfect landing!'

'Thank you too – practice makes perfect!'

He rolled his aircraft on to the end of the runway and then turned off to the right onto the taxi tracks leading to the dispersal area of his Staffel. In front of his hangar he switched off the engines.

The ground crews of the Staffel who were on night duty came walking towards them and climbed onto the wings. With a hearty 'Hallo' they congratulated the crew on their victory. He was barely able to get out of his machine, his knees were very shaky from the strain of the mission and from the nervous tension of the landing.

They just set off to walk over to the operations room of the Staffel to report their return and give a first account of their mission, when they heard the noise of engines over the 'drome, which seemed to come from the direction of the approach route. There, from the haze an Me110 turned up with its landing light blazing and navigation lights switched on. It glided in much too high and touched down far too late, almost in the middle of the runway, its speed much too high. 'This is definitely going wrong!' The wheels only just touched the concrete and the machine bounced high into the air again. Brakes were squeaking, the aircraft raced towards the fence. They instinctively ducked – presently there would be an excruciating cracking and tearing! Still, only a muffled sound was heard, a grinding and rasping – then it became deathly quiet. Seconds later, one heard a canopy roof slammed open. Loud and clear, it resounded in the quiet: 'Shit, damn it!'

His friend Willi had also landed!

The wreck of the Lancaster was found near the Dutch village of Tungelroy some 18km (11 miles) west of Roermond. The HQ at Venlo airfield laconically reported on the fate of the bomber crew: four men dead, one man prisoner, rest probably on the run.

Lt Fries' fifth victim was Lancaster II DS834 KO–F of 115 Squadron, which had departed from Witchford at 17.28 hours. F/Sgt J.Y. Lee and his crew were on the way back from Berlin when they were intercepted by Fries. Lee and Sgt Pike, his navigator were taken prisoner whilst Sgt A.F. Gunnell evaded capture. The four other members of the crew who had put up such a brave fight were less fortunate and were killed. F/Sgt Keith S. Bell RAAF (bomb aimer) and Sgts Laurens H. Jones (WOp.), Arthur M. Wilkinson RCAF (mid-upper gunner) and Graham Johnson (rear gunner) were killed and buried in Weert Roman Catholic Churchyard. Bomber Command lost twenty-one Lancasters and Halifaxes on that raid, of which at least six were destroyed by nightfighters. Among the forty-three Bomber Support sorties despatched there were no losses. The adverse weather had prevented more nightfighters from taking off and intercepting the Berlin force. Nachtjagd lost three aircraft shot down or crashed in bad weather. Otto Fries and Fred Staffa would add another thirteen victories to their tally before the end of the war.

Over this period, the paradoxical situation arose where Nachtjagd, despite its diminishing numbers, was able to inflict ever increasing losses on Bomber Command. With hindsight, one must conclude that if Nachtjagd had been able to grow numerically during the winter of 1943/44, it would have inflicted such heavy losses on Bomber Command that Harris might have been forced to break off his strategic offensive. But the neglect of the Nachtjagd leaders, brought about by the 'Führerbefehl' of August 1943, and combined with the loss of centralized control, was coming home to roost. As a result of the general neglect of nightfighter pilot and *Bordfunker* training, the arm suffered a chronic shortage of fully trained operational crews throughout the Battle of Berlin. During this winter period there weren't even enough replacement crews and nightfighter aircraft becoming available to compensate for operational losses, which in turn increased the severe decline in Nachtjagd's numbers.

But even with reduced numbers, Nachtjagd could still hit hard. After the first few successful raids on Berlin, Bomber Command inflicted less and less damage, whereas its losses mounted to some 10 per cent during deep penetration raids. On those nights when the German ground

Stirling Mk III EF411 of 149 Squadron, a veteran of seventy-three missions with 15 and 149 Squadrons during 1943–44. After a spell with 1653 CU, this aircraft was finally 'struck off' on 24 April 1945. After they sustained an average of 6.4 per cent losses during the initial stages of the Battle of Berlin, Harris was forced to withdraw the Stirling squadrons of 3 Group from the Battle. Coll. Roy Abbott.

controllers managed to identify the main RAF target at an early stage of the raid, they often succeeded in infiltrating the nightfighters in force into the bomber stream. Experienced nightfighter crews could wreak havoc amongst the RAF heavies under these conditions. It was not uncommon for an expert crew to shoot down six, seven or even eight Halifaxes and Lancasters in the course of one sortie whilst swimming along with the bomber stream.

Twenty-year-old Werner 'Red' Hoffmann started his career as a fighter pilot in ZG52 (later ZG2) in August 1938, claiming his first victim, a Spitfire of 54, 74 or 92 Squadron over Dunkirk on 24 May 1940. After a spell of instructing, he joined Nachtjagd in early 1942 as Staffelkapitän of 5./NJG3, and flew with *Bordfunker* Ofw. Rudi Köhler. Their tally mounted steadily, with eight night bomber kills in the illuminated and Himmelbett night fighting between June 1942 and the eve of the Battle of Hamburg. Hoffmann was appointed Gruppenkommandeur of I./NJG5 on 5 July 1943, one of the Gruppen of NJG5 stationed in the vicinity of Berlin. He and Köhler claimed a Lancaster to the north of Berlin as their ninth *Abschuss* at 00.32 hours on 4 September 1943 (Lancasters of eight different squadrons crashed in this area during the raid). Their first *Tame Boar* kill was followed by nineteen more Lancasters and Halifaxes, half of them in the Berlin area, in the six months between September 1943 and February 1944. Werner comments:

> During early 1943, our units of NJG5 around Berlin didn't get the chances to claim the same amount of victories as the other units of NJG1

Pilots of II./NJG3, 1943. Left to right: Hptm. Szameitat; Hptm. Förster; Dr Straussenberg; Foster and Piper. Paul Szameitat, an ace with twenty-eight night victories, plus a B-24 in daylight, became Kommandeur of II./NJG3 in early December 1943. He transferred to command I./NJG3 on the 14th of the month. On 1/2 January 1944, he was critically injured by return fire, and whilst trying to crash-land his damaged Ju88C-6 in a clearing in the woods near Bückeburg in the Weser Mountains, the aircraft somersaulted, killing the whole crew. Szameitat was posthumously awarded the Ritterkreuz. Hptm. Josef Förster survived the war as an ace with twenty-one confirmed victories in NJG2 and NJG3. Coll. Peter Petrick.

Hptm. Hans Baer and crew of 4./NJG3, posing in front of their Do217 in 1942–43. Hptm. Baer was killed in action on 20 December 1943 whilst he served as Kommandeur of II./NJG5, when his Bf110G-4 crashed at Garwitz in Germany. At the time of his death, Baer had shot down twelve British bombers. Coll. Peter Petrick.

Bf110G-4s of II./NJG1 in late 1943, equipped with both the old Lichtenstein BC *and the* SN-2 *AI radars, and with auxiliary tanks fitted under the wings. These increased the range of the aircraft by around one hour, for* Tame Boar *operations.* Coll. Otto H. Fries.

and NJG2 which were based further forward in Holland. This situation changed once the *Tame Boar* night fighting was initiated after Hamburg and the attacks started against Berlin in the winter period. We operational crews, our Staffelkapitäne and Gruppenkommandeure, had already discussed this type of freelance night fighting as early as February 1943, as we felt we had to get into the bomber streams, fly along with them and shoot them down. Still, our wish was curbed by Kammhuber for the time being.

By the autumn of 1943, we were still very well guided by ground control, not by just one ground control officer like in the Himmelbett days, but by the Division HQs, who told us in a running commentary where the enemy aircraft were, what their course was, etc. When we took off from Stendal, the aircraft had already been reported flying in over the North Sea or Holland. We were then sent towards them, and one way or the other we were infiltrated into the bomber stream. From then on, it was often relatively easy to hunt the bombers, as the stream was usually marked by exploding aircraft and exchanges of fire.

The first time I was shot down happened over Berlin on the night of 20 January 1944. The flak was ordered to fire up to a height of 6,000m [19,500ft], and above that height, the nightfighters were allowed to play around. Of course, the British found out about this arrangement, and endeavoured if possible to cruise over Berlin at a height of between 5,000 and 6,000m [16,200 and 19,500ft]. When we saw that the flak was unable to shoot any bombers down at this height, we said to ourselves that surely, they would not hurt us either. Because we were ambitious and had 'Halsschmerzen' ['sore throat' – the Ritterkreuz was a neck decoration] we felt that we had no option but to bring the 'comrades of the other side' down at that height.

On this night, beneath us we saw Berlin brightly lit up with fires, flashes from exploding bombs, searchlights, etc., and like a real numbskull I attacked a bomber from underneath, just like the *Wild Boars* used to, and of course I was clearly visible to the tail gunner. Of course, he let off a burst at me, and shot my right engine on fire. The Bf110 with all its equipment like the *SN-2* could hardly be flown on one engine, and besides, we were under strict orders not to carry out a crash-landing at night, as we crews were deemed more valuable than our machines. Therefore, we had to bail out. I had never practiced bailing out, but I did at a height of some

Major Werner Hoffmann, Gruppen Kommandeur of I./NJG5 from July 1943. Hoffmann ended the war with fifty confirmed victories and was awarded the Ritterkreuz on 4 May 1944 after thirty-one Abschüsse. Coll. Werner Kock via Werner Hoffmann.

5,500m [18,000ft], and as I had been instructed, I counted 21...22...23, and then pulled the rip cord.

There I was, hanging under my parachute over the northern districts of Berlin at a height of some 5,000m [16,200ft]. All around me, both British and German aircraft flashed past, from above me bombs were falling down, from beneath me the flak was shooting. The air was rather 'ferrous' and uncomfortable and I was therefore very relieved to get out of this circus at a height of some 2,000m [6,500ft] and approach the earth. The roaring still continued, but I later found out that this was caused by a flak battery which had received a direct hit which blew its ammunition up.

Beneath me a large fire was raging and I had considerable fear of falling into the middle of it and being roasted, but fortunately the hot air pushed me up again and aside and away from the fires. The earth approached damn quick in the final seconds and I landed in a field. I was taken to a nearby flak battery and next morning I was transported to Döberitz airfield again.

It was the first time that I physically experienced the misery of the civil population, the small personal belongings they had been able to save were piled up in the streets. The fires were still raging and the air was filled with smoke. Having grown up in Berlin, it made a deep and lasting impression on me. I had never seen anything like this before, normally one flew high over the cities and saw the burning infernos deep down below. It was a distinctly depressing experience.

Sgt Jim Donnan was the WOp. in F/O. James 'Gil' Bryson's crew with 550 Squadron. They had joined the squadron on its formation at Waltham, Grimsby on 25 November 1943, having transferred from 12 Squadron at Wickenby. They were veterans, having flown on operations from 3 September that year. The last two trips had taken the crew to Berlin:

It was New Year's Day 1944. Following two days of rest, we were back on operations. Our crew was on the Order of Battle and for this particular trip we were to fly in Lancaster DV189 T2.

We had been engaged in routine pre-operational checks and testing of our equipment prior to the main briefing, which commenced in a tense atmosphere. When the curtain was drawn aside exposing the operational map, the target was Berlin for the third consecutive time, only this time our route to the 'Big City' was almost direct from the Dutch coast across an area which was becoming increasingly dangerous because of nightfighter activity.

Deteriorating weather conditions delayed our take-off for several hours. It was therefore difficult to relax during this period. As New Year's Day was drawing to a close, we were preparing for take-off and at fourteen minutes past midnight we were airborne and on our way at last. The sky was dark and overcast as we flew through layers of broken cloud, climbing to our operational height, heading east over the North Sea.

As we approached the Dutch coast, we could see that the anti-aircraft defences were very active and we became alert to the dangers ahead. Flying over Germany, occasional bursts of flak and flashes lit up the thick, unbroken cloud along the route. While searching the night-fighter waveband, I was aware of considerable activity by the German control; we found it necessary to keep a sharp look out even though our trip had been uneventful so far. Our navigator called for a slight change in course for the final leg to Berlin as we reached a position between Hanover and Bremen.

It was almost immediately afterwards that a series of thuds vibrated through the floor and the aircraft seemed to bank away to starboard. I leapt up from my seat to the astrodome where I could see the starboard engines were on fire. As I switched over from radio to intercom, I saw that a fire had started under the navigator's table on the floor just behind the pilot. It was soon burning fiercely.

The pilot gave the order to abandon the aircraft. I clipped on my parachute and as I moved forward it was found that the front escape hatch would not open. The engineer joined the bomb aimer in trying to release it. As I stood behind the navigator waiting to exit, the rear gunner said that he was having trouble with the rear turret. I then signalled that I would go to the rear exit. The navigator was standing beside the pilot ready to exit as I scrambled over the main spar and along the fuselage to the rear door, losing my shoes on the way.

F/O. James 'Gil' Bryson and crew, 550 Squadron, shot down 1/2 January 1944. Coll. Dick Breedijk, via Jim Donnan.

Lancaster EE129 MG–Y of 7 Squadron at RAF Oakington, December 1943. This aircraft was lost on the Berlin raid of 1/2 January 1944 (with F/Lt Kingsbury DFC and crew, all POW). Far left, back row: F/Sgt David McHaffie (AG. in Capt. Angus's crew, KIA 22 February 1944). Front row, (l–r): F/Sgt R.H. Martin (MUG.); F/Lt H.J. Smith (RG.); F/Sgt T.D.J. Morgan (Eng.); Alsatian dog 'Kim'; F/Lt John A. Hegman DSO DFC RNZAF (Skipper, as S/Ldr KIA with another crew on 15/16 February 1944 when 7 Squadron lost four aircraft and crews on a Berlin raid); F/Sgt F.R. Cox (WOp.); F/Lt R. Macilwaine (Nav.); W/O. P.J. Adams (BA.).
Coll. W/Cdr Frank Cox, via Robert Woodberry.

When I got there, the mid-upper gunner was ready to leave and the rear gunner was out of his turret and preparing to come forward. I then jettisoned the rear door as the flames from the starboard wing streamed past, licking the tail plane. Grasping the release handle on my parachute, I was preparing to jump, but I must have lost consciousness as I have no recollection of what happened next, nor how I left the plane.

When I regained consciousness, my parachute was already open and I was floating in pitch darkness, very cold, and my feet were freezing. I seemed to be a long time coming down but as I descended through the clouds, dark shadows appeared and I landed on soft ground in an open space. Gathering up my parachute, I dashed over to a clump of trees, where I sat on the ground shivering and wondering how I could avoid capture.

Jim Donnan stayed on the loose for the next twenty-four hours, but was taken into custody after having asked for some food and drink from German civilians. His Lancaster DV189 crashed between Holtrup and Schweringen and blew up

Lancaster Mk II DS831 QO–N and crew of 432 (RCAF) Squadron. This aircraft was intercepted at a height of 19,700ft (6,800m) and shot down by Oblt Heinz-Wolfgang Schnaufer (St.Kpt. 12./NJG1) on the night of 16 December 1943. It was his fourth kill on this night and his fortieth Abschuss. *The Lancaster flew over Leeuwarden town trailing a sheet of flames, and crashed at Wytgaard just to the south at 18.41 hours. It completely disintegrated on impact, followed by the explosion of the bomb load. The American Skipper, F/O. W. Charles Fischer and five of his crew were killed.* Coll. Douwe Drijver.

with its full bomb load, including a 'cookie', in a deafening explosion. The pilot F/O. 'Gil' Bryson, and navigator Sgt Thomas 'Rocky' Roxby, had been trapped in the cockpit and were killed in the crash. They were interred at Hassel and at Hoya, later re-buried in Hanover War Cemetery. F/Sgt Paul Evans, the bomb aimer, and Sgt Don Fadden, flight engineer, had a very lucky escape: they were also in the nose section when the aircraft suddenly dived, pinning them down with the centrifugal forces. They were released when an explosion blew off the front of the nose section, enabling them to escape by parachute just before the bomber crashed.

The Lancaster was most probably shot down by twenty-seven-year-old Major Heinrich Prinz zu Sayn-Wittgenstein, who had set the starboard wing and the incendiary bombs (in the front of the bomb bay) on fire by a surprise *Schräge Musik* attack. Zu Sayn-Wittgenstein, a brilliant pilot of aristocratic descent, had served with distinction in KG51 during 1940–41, completing some 150 bombing sorties against France, Britain and Russia. In August 1941 he transferred to Nachtjagd and rapidly became a legend in the arm. Within a year, he had claimed twenty-two RAF bombers destroyed, had been awarded the Ritterkreuz and was appointed Kommandeur of IV./NJG5. During 1943, he was the second-highest scoring Nachtjagd pilot (after Lent), and on the first day of 1944 Major Wittgenstein was appointed Kommodore of NJG2. Before he took off on the evening of 1 January, his tally stood at sixty-eight *Abschüsse*. In his Ju88C-6, state-of-the art with *SN-2* radar and *Schräge Musik*, he succeeded in penetrating the bomber stream bound for Berlin and claimed no less than six Lancasters shot down in quick succession, as his sixty-ninth to seventy-fourth victories. Most of these *Viermots* were Pathfinders flying at the front of the bomber stream.

Wittgenstein finally met his fate when he was probably shot down by return fire from a vigilant Lancaster gunner east of Magdeburg, on the night of 21/22 January 1944. His crew managed to bail out but Wittgenstein was killed when his Ju88C-6 crashed south of Lübars. In the hours before he was killed in action, he claimed five *Viermots* in the Magdeburg area, which brought his final tally to eighty-three in only 170 sorties. This made him the highest scoring nightfighter pilot ever. After his death, he would only be surpassed by Oberst Lent and Major Schnaufer.

Not only did General Schmid deploy his nightfighter crews in *Tame Boar* operations against the bomber streams, they were also used in Himmelbett Nachtjagd. Along the coastlines of Holland and north-west Germany, the Himmelbett GCI stations were still in full use against Bomber Command stragglers, RAF minelayers and anti-shipping aircraft, as P/O. Peter 'Smoky' Osborne experienced personally. Peter and his pilot Bob Hollands DFM served in Beaufighters with 236 Squadron in Coastal Command on anti-shipping operations:

F/O. William Charles Fischer, the Captain of Lancaster DS831 'N–Nan' of 432 (RCAF) Squadron and who was shot down by Schnaufer. After the war, he was re-buried at Neuville en Condroz in Belgium.
Coll. Douwe Drijver.

> On 26 January 1944, my pilot and I were briefed for a night operational sweep of a segment of the Frisian Islands from Ameland to Texel, looking for German convoys, the eastern part of the islands being undertaken by another Beaufighter (pilot F/Sgt Lowe). Both aircraft had to start the sweep from the eastern end of their patrol at the same time – 02.00 hours.
>
> We were flying at about 1,000 to 1,500ft [300 to 460m]. It was a dark night with no moon. After about ten minutes into the patrol we heard over the R/T 'I am being attacked by a nightfighter' this of course was Lowe in the other Beau. There was a deadly hush and our blood nearly froze! Several minutes later a further message from Lowe said 'I've been hit, I am going down' and then there was silence except for our heartbeats (perhaps louder than the engine noise). Where was this nightfighter? Would he be after us? Who knows? I said to Bob: 'I am swivelling my seat face aft and

> cocking the rear Browning machine gun, just in case the inevitable happens!' We, of course, were still on patrol. We waited; minutes flashed by which seemed like hours, but the well founded preparations paid off – tracers began to hurtle through the night towards us, at the same time I saw them coming I let out a burst from the rear gun in the general direction of the oncoming volley which was coming up from the rear but below us. Quite naturally Bob started weaving the aircraft. Could he see us? Where was he? Will he fire again? Darkness is a funny thing especially when you can only see tracers coming or going and the imagination can play havoc if you don't keep it under control. However he did not fire at us again, perhaps we frightened him off? This time we were lucky – our patrol finished we headed for home having found no ships or convoys. We believe that the night-fighter was an Me110.

F/Sgt Dennis Lowe and his navigator Sidney Wheatley both went missing in their aircraft, Beaufighter LX845 ND–Y of 236 Squadron, and are commemorated on the Runnymede Memorial.

The Nachtjagd crews were also deployed in *Wild Boar* target area night fighting against Mosquitos, and as an emergency measure against surprise RAF attacks. By responding with flexible tactics to individual raids, Schmid managed to make the most of the defensive means at his disposal. Nachtjagd had recuperated remarkably well from the crisis following the Battle of Hamburg, even though the arm had not been significantly strengthened after the reorganization in October 1943.

Twenty-six-year-old Tasmanian P/O. Geoffrey Breaden served as navigator with 83 Squadron PFF during 1943 and early 1944. Three Tasmanians served in his crew, including the Skipper F/O. Ken Hutton and twenty-one-year-old F/O. Ron Walker, the mid-upper gunner. Geoff tells of his crew's final sortie on 21/22 January 1944 to Magdeburg:

P/O. Peter 'Smoky' Osborne, navigator in 236 Squadron from August 1943 till May 1945. Coll. Peter Osborne.

> The previous night we had returned from a successful raid on Berlin. Our sixth on the 'Big City' as it was known to all of us. During the pre-flight briefing for the raid on the next night, 21 Jan, tension started to rise while we all awaited the unveiling of the target for tonight. We all felt that our luck was being stretched by so many consecutive sorties to this heavily defended spot. Imagine the almost audible sigh of relief when the target of Magdeburg was revealed to us. Our task this night was 'Primary Blind Marking' and our time on target was shown as zero minus five! I could hardly believe my eyes. Five minutes alone over a target in Germany before anyone else arrived. Suicide, I thought. As the navigator, I felt that I would be signing my own death warrant, as it were! In the event we contrived to time our arrival for zero hour, 23.00 hour Z.

The whole journey was a copy book exercise as far as I was concerned, navigationally perfect. My ETAs at turning points had been spot on and then, on our timed run into the aiming point all systems seemed GO! We were only minutes away from 'Bombs Away' when the mid-upper gunner screamed out 'Dive Port'. Too late, the Focke Wulf 190 had already blasted us with his first salvo of 20mm cannon fire. Despite our violent evasive action, he was able to destroy our port inner engine. The Lancaster, of course, can fly on only one engine. Not, however, with a persistent fighter glued to its tail. Surely this couldn't be happening to us! This was something we only read about happening to other poor unfortunates. Dreamtime was past. This was for real! Time seemed to stand still. The fighter came in again. This time, raking the fuselage, killing the two gunners, wounding my bombardier alongside me, and also as if for good measure, setting us on fire. The noise was unreal. A hollow sort of sepulchral echoing, rather like several tons of rocks dumped onto a tin roof. It was no tin roof. It was our aeroplane, Lancaster OL–G 365, 83 Squadron PFF, RAF.

The cordite fumes and the smoke gave the scene a theatrical touch. This was live theatre, sure enough. A third attack and we, that is, the survivors, were obeying the dreaded command 'Abandon Aircraft'. The flight engineer was first out through the nose escape hatch. The pilot Ken steadying so that we could exit safely. I tried to help Mac the bombardier but time forbade any first-aid measures, I was only able to guide him into the unknown, ready to follow myself. A scenario like this was, of course, what all of our 'Emergency Training Drills' had been about. My own thoughts were: one, to get down to earth quickly from the 20,000ft [6,100m] where we were; two, how to get down without floating slowly down, providing perhaps a very inviting target to the enemy; three, to do all that without passing out for lack of oxygen. The answer, rather obviously – a delayed parachute opening. It is difficult enough to make decisions at the best of times. Without our training it would have been well nigh impossible.

The overpowering feeling was that I was observing all this as an 'out of the body' experience, certainly, I believe that my subsequent actions were under Divine guidance. All of the other survivors followed the laid down procedures of jumping, counting ten and then pulling the ripcord. They all landed in the target area. One, F/O. Ken Hutton was shot, two were badly bashed-up and were being lynched by the angry populace, only being saved, in time, by the local police.

Following my free fall of about 15,000ft [4,600m] I then actuated the ripcord, falling the rest of the way at a more sedate pace than previously. Because of these actions, I was not carried by the airstream downwind as were the others. My landing was several miles away, in open country. Well away from immediate danger. The night was spent wrapped up in my 'chute. It was cold. The air temp at 20,000ft [6,100m] had been –40°C. Ground level would have been zero. I was not apprehended until the following day, Saturday, 22 Jan. 1944. The mood of my captors was, as could be expected, very hostile.

Geoffrey Breaden ended up in Stalag Luft 3, Sagan, from which six weeks later the famous Great Escape took place. His crew's Lancaster crashed south of Schartente, on the outskirts of Magdeburg. F/O. Ken Hutton, F/O. Ronald E. Walker the mid-upper gunner, and Sgt Ronald H. Easton, rear-gunner, found their final resting place in Berlin.

F/Sgt Bruce 'Doug' Bancroft and his crew had only just completed a short conversion course on the Halifax Mk II at 1663 HCU in mid-January 1944, before being posted to an operational squadron, when he was called upon to fly on his first op as second pilot in another crew. His story illustrates the diminishing bombing results gained by Bomber Command in this period, against mounting losses inflicted by Nachtjagd:

A good friend of mine, Flight Sergeant M. 'Mick' Cowan, and I were advised during the morning of 21 January that, following our midday meal at 1663 Heavy Conversion Unit at

Lancaster NG243 BQ–M2 of 550 Squadron at North Killingham.
Coll. Frank Pritchard.

Rufforth, we were to be transported to No. 10 Squadron at Melbourne, Yorkshire, to each act as 2nd pilots (2nd 'Dickies' as we were known) with two crews from that squadron on an operation to take place that night for our operational acclimatization. We were duly taken to Melbourne at about 14.00 hours and each of us reported to separate flight commanders for allocation to a crew. Passengers such as 2nd 'Dickies' were not really welcomed by the crews they were to join and I can well understand that kind of reasoning in the minds of a trained and experienced operational crew. The pilot with whom I was to fly just shook my hand and said that he would see me at the main briefing a little later in the afternoon. Mick Cowan was similarly greeted and, in fact, when having the 'flying meal' together we agreed that we would rather be attached to another squadron when we became operational ourselves as the whole atmosphere at Melbourne appeared on the 'damp' side.

For the take-off I took up a crash position at the main spar whilst the bomb aimer retained his usual position in the second pilot's seat; a situation that I could well understand. At about 1,000ft [300m] altitude, when the crew took up their usual positions in the aircraft, I sat in the second pilot's seat for the remainder of the flight. The crew acted most efficiently all through the flight with very little conversation between them except to pass essential information or instructions and I, of course, was not included in these matters other than to be told to keep my eyes searching for other aircraft in the vicinity. I did gather that the met. wind forecast was not reliable and that the course required correction several times as a result of this, but I was most interested in noticing how clear was the sky and how brightly shone the stars on this very cold night. It was brought to my attention, also, that enemy nightfighters were extremely active just after crossing the enemy coast as I had seen several of the bombing force going down in flames and blowing up, and some exchanges of tracer fire.

Our flight to the target was incident-free however, and a successful run-up was effected on a target which had been set burning well by the time that we arrived. There was not a great amount of anti-aircraft gun-fire but the enemy nightfighter force was very active and had many successes in the target area.

Looking down at Magdeburg at the time it seemed to me to be of quite an unusual lay-out, especially for an old city, as the fires were burning in a quite rectangular pattern seemingly about 8 miles [13km] long by 3 miles [5km] wide with fires in straight lines in two directions at right angles to each other as though along the length of straight roads. It did strike me as being rather odd.

Having disposed of our bomb load of mainly incendiaries we turned for the flight home which again was incident-free except for suddenly being caught by a radar-predicted searchlight near Wilhelmshaven but which was fortunately almost immediately lost by diving into a patch of cloud.

On returning to base and in the debriefing process I learnt that my friend, Mick Cowan, and the crew he was with were missing, and later all were posted as killed in action. Although we actually had a quite easy and uneventful flight to and from the target, losses were heavy for the Command and bombing appeared very scattered and inaccurate and the attack was somewhat ineffective as a result.

I returned to my unit at Rufforth during the morning of 22 January to a warm welcome from my crew and also to talk to Mick Cowan's crew members who were deeply saddened and shocked at the loss of their pilot, whilst I could not help but ponder on the fortunes of such operations as it was like a mere 'toss of a coin' as to whether it would be Mick or I who went with that missing crew.

The Nachtjagd's regained effectiveness in early 1944 culminated in a number of exceptional successes. *Tame Boar* pursuit night fighting scored high on the night of 19/20 February 1944, when Bomber Command dispatched 816 heavies and seven Mosquitos for Leipzig. The first turning point of the stream north of Terschelling Island was accurately identified by *H2S* bearings and I Jagdkorps successfully infiltrated a strong force into the stream. In a running battle, seventy-four heavy bombers were shot down, which represented a casualty rate of 9.5 per cent. Nachtjagd only lost seventeen aircraft on this night. Another severe blow was inflicted on Bomber Command during the night of 24/25 March, when Berlin was the target for 811 aircraft. Due to the wrongly predicted weather conditions on the 'night of the strong winds', the bomber stream became scattered. Over the target some fourteen heavies were destroyed by nightfighters, with dozens of other bombers falling victim to the flak and fighter defences on the way back. When the surviving bomber crews returned back home, the wrecks of seventy-two Lancasters and Halifaxes were left smouldering on the Continent. F/Lt R.J. Armstrong and his navigator F/O. Mold had taken off from West Raynham in Mosquito VI W4084 of 239 Squadron for a Bomber Support *Serrate* sortie on this Berlin raid, and noted in Sagan POW camp:

> Backing up the 'Bomber Boys' on Berlin, 24 March. Was almost two hours out from England (nearly there). Got a clue on a Hun nightfighter quite close. Stalked him through jinking orbits, finally came up line astern and below. Observer coped magnificently. Poor old Mick. Switched on guns and reflector sight having recognized Ju88 by exhausts and then by silhouette. Gave a three second burst from about 200yd [m] and saw a bright flash amidships. Like a fool I broke away to port and immediately something hammered in my leading edge inboard of engines. Rads broke up and glycol filled cockpit. Returned fire or wreckage? Observer bailed out. Couldn't see a thing. Ammo exploded below me. No glycol left. Couldn't see instrument panel. Bailed out. Banged head. Delayed drop. Damned cold. Ploughed field. Local 'Home Guard'. Local pub.

Halifax HX333 NP–J of 158 Squadron belly-landed in the early hours of 29 January 1944 near 't Zand in Groningen Province after sustaining heavy flak damage over Berlin. F/Sgt D.A. Robinson and his crew were all taken prisoner. HX333 completed only three operations before it was lost. Coll. Douwe Drijver.

> No beer. Month in cooler. Arrived Stalag Luft 3 on April 26th. Sordid ain't it?

Armstrong's Mosquito crashed nearly 1.5 miles (2km) east of Monceau-le-Wast in France. On this final raid against the Reichshauptstadt during the Battle of Berlin, ten *Serrate* and nineteen intruder Mosquitos were able only to claim one Ju88 and a Fw190 shot down.

Nachtjagd's absolute highpoint took place only a few nights later, during the infamous 30/31 March raid on Nuremberg. From the assembly of the force over England, the 795 strong bomber stream could be followed correctly by *H2S* bearings. German battle control was not fooled on this occasion by Mosquito spoof raids on Cologne, Frankfurt and Kassel as the 'Mossies' were apparently flying without *H2S*. The first switching-in into the bomber stream in the area south of Bonn succeeded well and from then onward the bomber stream was marked, in bright moonlight, by exploding and crashing aircraft. Additionally, single-engined units were employed over Nuremberg in target area night fighting. In all, 246 German nightfighter aircraft were involved in this biggest night air battle of the war, claiming 107 aircraft destroyed. In fact, ninety-seven Lancasters and Halifaxes were shot

One of the first Lancasters fitted with 'sharper teeth': a 550 Squadron machine in 1944 with .5in Browning machine guns in a Rose tail turret. Sgt 'Danny' Driscoll rear gunner RAF in his turret, with (l–r): P/O. 'Bill' Mann RAAF (Nav.); P/O. 'Frankie' Petch RAAF (WOp.); F/O. Gordon Markes (Pilot); P/O. Vernon 'Wilkie' Wilkes (BA.) (holding a practice bomb). Coll. Frank Petch.

down over the continent (seventy-nine by night-fighters), with another nine crashing on return in England. 545 British and Commonwealth air-crew were killed, with a further 159 men becoming prisoners of war. Nachtjagd's losses amounted to a mere five aircraft destroyed, with eleven crew members killed or missing.

Sgt Len Whitehead manned the twin Brownings in the mid-upper turret of one of the fourteen Lancasters of 61 Squadron dispatched from Coningsby on the raid:

> As regards the Nuremberg raid, that is the one most of us have tried to black out from our mind. Our crew had already taken part in the Leipzig raid, 19/2/44 with a loss of seventy-nine, and the Berlin, 24/3/44 with a loss of seventy-five. This was with cloud cover, so that when we had clear sky and moonlight we knew we were in for trouble. It was normal for the gunners to report to the navigator when we saw an aircraft go down and give such details as to whether we saw any bail out, if it was flak, or if a fighter etc. On this occasion there were so many going down that the skipper told us not to report, just concentrate on looking out for and avoiding attacks. It was difficult not to look at those going down but we knew we had to keep a careful watch. We would sometimes see some tracer fire and then a small flame which would quickly grow until it lit up the whole aircraft and then frequently would finish with a terrific

> explosion. Sometimes we were rather puzzled because we did not see any tracer fire and no flak, just the aircraft catching fire. I did not learn the answer to this for many years. It was of course *Schräge Musik*. When using this no tracer was present so that it did not give away the form of attack. When an aircraft went down, or jettisoned the bombs there would be a long line of incendiaries burning with a bright silver and further illuminating the aircraft above.
>
> I also remember some problem with the forecast winds not being at all accurate and that our navigator instructed the pilot to 'dog leg' (that is to leave the stream at an angle and after a few minutes return so as to lose time) on at least two occasions. However it was not as bad on this raid as it had been the week before on 24 March when we encountered a jet stream for the first time with winds far in excess of 100mph [160kph] which caused the stream to be spread over a vast area and was responsible for the heavy losses that night. There is little I can say about the Nuremberg raid itself, we were just sitting ducks.

The German defensive success on 30/31 March 1944 was one in the most literal sense of the word, as the Nachtjagd crews had managed to scatter the bomber stream and prevent a concentrated bombing raid on the city of Nuremberg. Most of the bombs that were dropped fell into open fields around the target area without causing any significant damage. On this night, the German arm succeeded, for the first and last time during the war, in actually preventing a heavy Bomber Command attack.

But the nights in which Nachtjagd succeeded in inflicting losses of 9 per cent and more on Bomber Command were too few and far between to force the RAF to halt its offensive. German nightfighter crews, always fighting the heavy bombers at a ratio of at least one to five, were too heavily outnumbered on most occasions to put up a truly devastating defence. Nachtjagd could hit Bomber Command hard at times, but was never able to affect the final outcome of the campaign. On each and every raid (from late 1942 onwards), the majority of the British heavies broke through the flak and fighter defences and managed to drop their bombs in the target area. In the autumn of 1943, Germany's war leaders had missed the last opportunity to stop the Allied bombing offensive by radically shifting their strategy in favour of air defence of the Reich. Their lack of interest in the problems faced by Nachtjagd had further worsened the situation. Now, it was too late.

CHAPTER 7

The Road to D-Day

After the Nuremberg debacle, Bomber Command temporarily stopped deep penetration raids into the Reich. Harris was forced to break off his Battle of Berlin, without having been able to achieve his main aims. It is true that the 'Big City' had suffered considerably from the attacks, with one-and-a-half million Berliners being bombed out, but it had not been completely razed to the ground. Moreover, the Third Reich had not been bombed into submission, as Harris had hoped. On the German side, Milch considered the British Nuremberg disaster to be the turning point in the strategic bombing offensive. He even went so far as to put the Nuremberg raid on a par with RAF Fighter Command's victory over the Luftwaffe in the Battle of Britain in 1940. Yet Nachtjagd had not won a decisive victory over Bomber Command, in that the German arm had not created a lasting and effective air defence of the Reich. And Bomber Command's shift in strategy from 1 April onwards was not dictated by Nachtjagd, but by the Combined Allied Chiefs of Staff, who had earlier ordered Harris to postpone his strategic bombing offensive against Germany from that date. From now on, he was to commit his heavy bombers to attack tactical targets, mainly in France, in preparation for D-Day. Directed by the 'Transportation Plan', Bomber Command was to disrupt German supply lines and transport links in the hinterland of the invasion coast by precision

Sgt 'Danny' Driscoll (Rear Gunner) spitting on tailplane of Lancaster 'B' of 550 Squadron for luck prior to an operation, 1944–45. Coll. Frank Petch.

raids. Harris had already known in early 1944 that he had until April to force Nazi-Germany to its knees by strategic bombing. That he did not achieve this goal may be considered as a *tactical* success for the German air defence, and especially for Nachtjagd. The *strategic* aim of the German air defence however, had not been achieved. German cities and industry had not been effectively shielded from the often devastating RAF raids. In spite of the dramatic losses Bomber Command had suffered on the Nuremberg raid, Harris strongly expressed a wish to continue the Battle of Berlin 'until the heart of Nazi-Germany ceases to beat'. However, much against his will, he now had to deploy his force in the preparations for D-Day.

Nachtjagd had grown considerably, both in quantity and quality, during the final phase of the Battle of Berlin. Whereas I Jagdkorps had reached rock bottom on 1 February 1944, with only 179 nightfighter aircraft available, by 15 March this number had already risen to 271, and grew further to 451 combat-ready aircraft by 1 May. And by March, the crews flying these aircraft were well-trained in the freelance *Tame Boar* tactics. At times, even complete Gruppen were infiltrated in close formation into the bomber streams, under the guidance of experienced Gruppen Kommandeure. This so-called 'Geschlossener Gruppeneinsatz' characterized Nachtjagd's regained strength. By the end of the Battle of Berlin, the arm had grown into the Luftwaffe's most powerful and effective branch. Deep penetration raids into the Reich had become hazardous ventures for British bomber crews.

Gottfried Hanneck was one of the pilots who joined Nachtjagd during this period. He had entered the Luftwaffe in July 1939 and was trained as a fighter pilot during the next year. Expecting a posting to an operational unit, he was selected to serve as an instructor instead. Throughout 1942 he then served in a liaison unit on the Eastern Front, but he got so bored with this work that he voluntarily applied for a posting to the nightfighter arm in spring 1943. The next full year was spent in passing through the various phases of night fighting training, and then as a fully qualified nightfighter pilot he was finally posted to 5./NJG1 in April 1944:

By this time I had already served almost five years as a pilot and had flown some forty different aircraft types. Thus I had been able to accumulate a wealth of flying experience and I am quite sure that this formed the basis for the fact that I was able to survive in the Nachtjagd.

I started my time in the Second Gruppe of NJG1 at Deelen (near Arnhem) on 1 May with flight testing combat aircraft for the next four days – just flying around the airfield. During the early hours of 5 May I did an overland flight in a triangle to St. Trond, Venlo and Deelen, followed by five night take-offs and landings. On 7 May I flew a night target finding exercise in the Himmelbett box 'Hase' (Hare) and on 9 May my first operational sortie followed. It was uneventful and on the same night I took off again for a Mosquito chase. During the following evening I flew my third mission.

II./NJG1 was stationed at Deelen airfield in May 1944, to combat the RAF night raiders flying into the Reich's territory. During this time of the year, with its relatively short and clear nights, the British restricted themselves to shallow penetration raids against targets on the western German border, mainly in the Ruhr area. The massing of nightfighter units in the forward defence area in Holland and Belgium was obviously known to the enemy and forced them to resort to these shallow penetration raids. Our leaders responded to these raids with the concentration of even more defensive forces in the areas where the bombers were expected to fly in.

And so it came to be that in the early morning of 11 May 1944 I and my crew were detached from Deelen to Düsseldorf. In the evening, we came on immediate readiness there at around 18.00 hours and one hour later, I was ordered to fly to the Belgian 'drome of Melsbroek, near Brussels and 'towards the enemy', as I was told. I touched down at Melsbroek at 20.42 hours and came on immediate readiness again. Our patience was really tested,

Oblt Gottfried Hanneck, pilot in 5./NJG1 claimed six Viermot Abschüsse *during May–July 1944.* Coll. Gottfried Hanneck.

as only just before 23.00 hours our nightfighter controllers reported aircraft flying in. After having been ordered to scramble at 23.20 hours, we flew in the direction of the Ruhr area in the hope of intercepting the *Viermots* during their outward flight. And we succeeded, we caught one on our *SN-2*! My radar operator gave me courses to steer to get a visual on the target. However, before we caught a first sight of our target, a steam of tracer appeared before me which smashed into a *Viermot*, put it on fire and it plunged down out of control. All of a sudden, the night sky was turned into daylight by the burning bomber and I had to break off and 'hide' into the darkness some distance away, fearing that the massed fire power of other *Viermots* would 'fry' me!

In the meantime, I had arrived over the edge of the Flak Zone, so I turned away and started searching for a new target in the withdrawal route of the British. We were successful in our search, as we flew several tracks to the west and north-west. Thus, we got a new contact on the *SN-2*, a four-engined aircraft that tried to get home and away at high speed, whilst slightly losing height. This time, no 'colleague' was chasing the same target. I slowly got closer, until I could make it out with my bare eyes. Approaching at the same altitude (of some 4,000m [13,000ft]), I gradually lost some height, and positioned myself 100 to 150m [yd] beneath my target. It now hung over us, as large as a barn door. I put my sights on the fuselage and with the *Schräge Musik* I fired through the whole length of it, by slowly pushing my aircraft down and away from the bomber. We watched how many hits registered in the whole fuselage, our target dived down steeply and crashed onto the ground in the area of the mouth of the River Scheldt. We saw how it exploded on impact, with a huge detonation and a sheet of flames. Time of our *Abschuss* was 00.48 hours.

Fifty minutes later we touched down on our aerodrome at Deelen, it was a good landing and we were unhurt. Later on, our weapons mechanics established that I had used ample ammunition. This was quite understandable, as I was only a novice who wanted to make sure of the kill. During my later *Abschüsse*, I was more economical!

Lancaster ME779 of 166 Squadron, with P/O. Geoffrey J.R. Clark at the controls, was probably Hanneck's first victim. Clark was killed together with three of his crew when their aircraft crashed at the hamlet of Elkerzee, to the north-east of Haamstede. The three survivors were all taken prisoner. Oblt Hanneck succeeded in shooting down another five Lancasters and Halifaxes, all in June and July, before he in turn became the victim of Mosquito XIX 'D' of 85 Squadron, flown by F/Lt House and his radar operator, F/Sgt McKinnon, on the night of 13/14 September 1944. Gottfried bailed out wounded, but his crew were killed when Bf110G-4 G9+EN crashed at Birresborn in the Eifel at 23.35 hours.

Lancaster 'M–Mike' 'Mickey the Moocher' of 61 Squadron, November 1944, with F/O. Frank Mouritz and crew.
Coll. Frank Mouritz.

Barely recovered from his wounds, Oblt Hanneck flew his next operational sortie on 1 February, 1945 with a new crew. They had only just started their patrol, when a Mosquito once again surprised them, although this time the whole crew survived. Gottfried comments: 'So, the long range nightfighters of the RAF revenged my six *Viermot*-kills, which made the final score 6 to 2!'

During April and May 1944, Bomber Command was fully committed to the pre-invasion bombing campaign. Usually, the short penetration by Bomber Command forces striking at French targets gave little time for the German nightfighters to find their prey. There were one or two exceptions to the rule, however, as Sgt Len Whitehead experienced. Len flew a tour of operations between 13 December 1943 and April 1944, flying as mid-upper gunner in 61 Lancaster Squadron in both Sgt Martin's and F/O. Fitch's crews:

> On 1 May 1944 I was flying as a third gunner. It was suspected that aircraft were being attacked from underneath so that some aircraft were fitted with a single .5in Browning on a swivel mounting through a hole approximately 3ft [1m] dia in the floor. This was where it had originally been the intention to fit a mid-under turret, and where later *H2S* was fitted. The gunner sat with his back to the rear of the bomb bay on a seat only an inch or two from the floor and of course the gun pointed to the rear of the aircraft. The gunner had two safety straps fastened to his back. As can be imagined the field of vision was very small and standing up did not increase it much, and to crouch doubled-over for hours on end was just not possible. However it was thought that the attacks were normal ones from the rear, well below, with the fighter climbing at a steep angle and therefore in view of the extra gunner. As we had no idea of the upward firing gun, *Schräge Musik*, until after the war, it was assumed that a .5in this position would solve the problem. Unfortunately this was not true, as we now know that the attacking aircraft positioned itself well below and gradually came up directly underneath, when the bomber would be silhouetted against the sky, and whereas they would be hidden against the earth's background.
>
> On this occasion we had a 'hang up' that is the bomb had not been released by the apparatus when the switch was operated. About half an hour after we had left the target, which was Toulouse, the BA. [Bomb Aimer] requested that the bomb doors be opened so that he could attempt to release the bomb, which was done. The next thing we heard was him shouting, 'Weave skipper!', which the pilot did. Although his warning was in time to save us being shot out of the sky it must have come just as the fighter fired. We never did know exactly what happened as the BA. was killed and the FE. [Flight Engineer] very badly wounded. In spite of his wounds the FE. refused to leave his controls and assisted the pilot to bring the

severely damaged aircraft back. After well over two hours we landed at the first aerodrome we came to.

When daylight came and we examined the aircraft we were amazed that it had kept flying as we had no hydraulics, there were massive holes in the wings and the fuselage, and even the control tubes were damaged. One of the tubes which operated the rudder was cut about three-quarters of the way round, how it held out I do not know. For this effort the pilot was awarded the DFC and the FE. the CGM. I did not fly with that crew again and I understand that the FE. never flew on operations again. The other five went on to complete their tour of operations.

1/2 May was a typical night during the Bomber Command pre-invasion campaign. In all, 801 sorties were despatched in fourteen separate operations, with forces of between forty-six and 137 bombers attacking railway yards, locomotive sheds, railway stores and a repair depot, motor works, an aircraft assembly and an explosives factory in six French towns. Most of these targets were hit with great accuracy and destroyed, with only nine aircraft being lost to flak and nightfighters.

Nachtjagd achieved its greatest success during the Bomber Command pre-invasion campaign just two nights later on 3/4 May 1944, when Bomber Command dispatched 346 Lancasters and fourteen Mosquitos of 1 and 5 Group, aided by two Pathfinder 'Mossies', to bomb a German

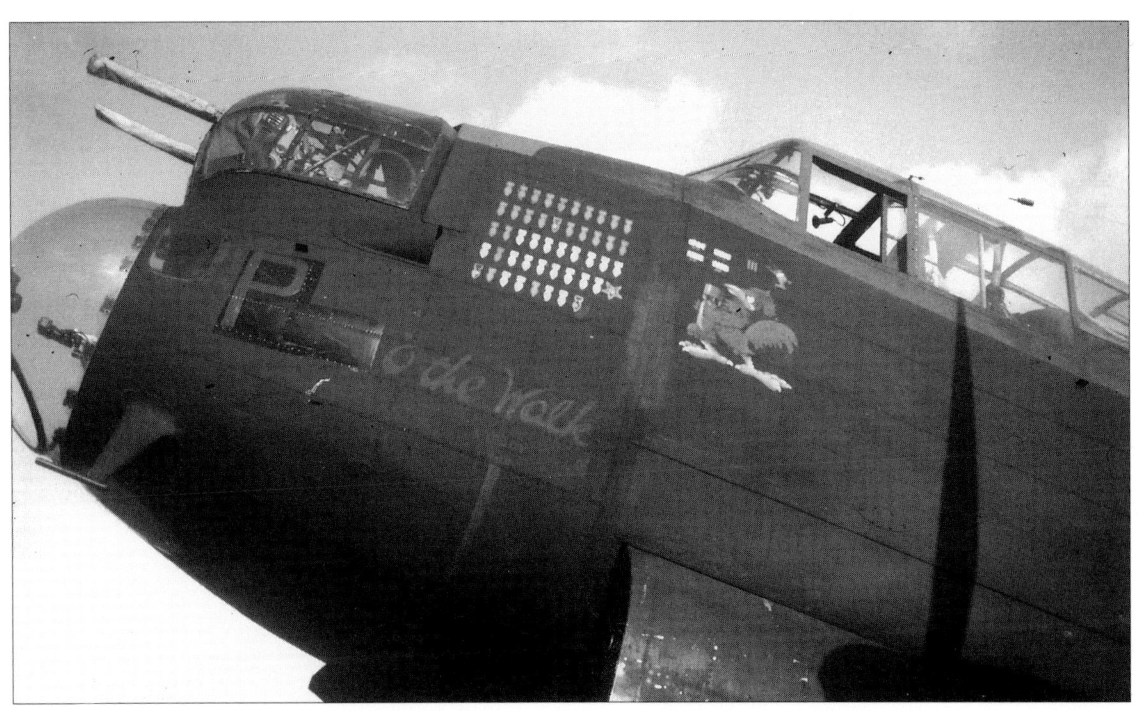

Nose art. Lancasters of 463 and 467 Squadrons at Waddington in 1944. These two Australian units formed part of Bomber Command's main force during the second half of the war. Together, they lost 173 Lancasters on operations. Depicted here and on the following pages are: (A) 'Cock 'o the walk' (showing forty-eight completed raids); (B) LM130 JO–N 'Nick the Nazi Neutraliser' of 463 Squadron (with forty-eight trips); (C) PO–N of 467 Squadron with eighty-five trips; (D) a Lancaster with forty-one completed raids; (E) a brand new Lancaster with pin up. Coll. Jack Hamilton.

(A)

(B)

(C)

(D)

(E)

military camp at Mailly-Le-Camp in central France. The bombing was delayed and while the majority of the force was waiting near the target for the order to bomb, German fighters arrived on the scene in force. Aided by perfect visibility and an almost full moon, the nightfighters had a field day. Twenty-three-year-old Hauptmann Helmut Bergmann, St.Kpt. of 8./NJG4 claimed six Lancasters as his twenty-ninth to thirty-fourth victories. Some eight crews of III./NJG1 were infiltrated into the bomber stream, and destroyed twelve Lancasters. Hptm. Martin Drewes, who by this time had risen to Kommandeur of III./NJG1, was the most successful marksman of his Gruppe, with five confirmed Lancaster *Abschüsse.* Ofw. Erich Handke, Martin Drewes' *Bordfunker*, comments on his 113th operational sortie:

> On 3 May, we took off before midnight for our most successful sortie so far. As we were told later, an ammunition depot was attacked in central France (south of Epernay). In the area of Chamäleon (south of Compiegne) we were directed into the bomber stream, and at a height of 2,500–3,000m [8,100–9,700ft] I immediately had contacts on my radar on a reciprocal course, but by the time we had turned, they were out of our radar range.
>
> We flew on and finally saw the target burning in front of us. We proceeded in the direction of the target, course 140 degrees, until we re-entered the bomber stream. I led my pilot to the nearest aircraft, which we could already see at a range of 600m [660yd], to the left and over us. The weather was brilliant, almost a full moon. The flak was putting up a barrage over the target. We decided not to follow the Lancasters over the target, for fear of being hit by their bombs. Some 20km [12 miles] to the south we again headed after the bombers, descending all the time as the Lancasters had in the mean time lost height to some 2,300m [7,500ft]. We caught a Lancaster in our sights and fired from below into one of its wings, which immediately burst into flames. Shortly after, the machine plunged down in flames and crashed. It was our forty-first *Abschuss.*
>
> I already had the next target on my screen at 270 degrees, which meant it was a home-bound aircraft. It flew at a height of 2,000m [6,500ft], and at a distance of 500m [550yd] we spotted it, it was another Lancaster. We positioned ourselves some 500m [550yd] beneath the aircraft, then pulled up until we hung 70m [yd] under the cockpit area and fired into the middle of the fuselage. It erupted into a bright fire and immediately crashed, ten minutes after our first victim.
>
> Then I again caught a machine on my radar while we were already overtaking it; it flew just in front and underneath us, we dived down fast, and we spotted it 500m [550yd] to our left and over us. Again we positioned ourselves quite far underneath it, pulled up slowly and fired into the middle of it: a bright fire, and immediately the Lancaster plunged down. It exploded into several parts and crashed eight minutes after our second, and just like our forty-second, it came down on the banks of the river Seine near Romilly. This was our forty-third kill.
>
> Then Schorsch, our gunner, suddenly saw one passing diagonally over us. We immediately banked towards it; as visibility was so splendid, we could keep our eyes on it easily. Again we dived down to position ourselves low underneath it, as of course we didn't want to be seen, slowly pulled up, but the Lancaster also ascended all the time, so that only at a height of 3,000m [9,700ft] did we get into effective firing range. After a long burst of fire, again aimed upwards into the middle of the bomber, the whole tail unit broke off completely, and engulfed in bright flames it plunged down, six minutes after our third *Abschuss.*
>
> Schorsch immediately spotted another one, which however weaved quite violently, whilst climbing all the time. We adapted to its weaving pattern, and flew along, some 500m [550yd] underneath it. After some ten minutes, when we had reached a height of 4,300m [14,000ft], Schorsch saw another one closing in from behind, but this one flew on a steady course. Then I spotted two more to the right and over us, of which we picked out the aircraft that

Twenty-five-year-old Major Martin Drewes, Gruppen Kommandeur of III./NJG1 (left) talks with his Funker *Ofw. Petz (right) in front of their Bf110G-4 in the late summer of 1944. Forty-seven victories are chalked up on the tail unit of Drewes' aircraft.* Coll. Martin Drewes via Rob de Visser.

> cruised on most steadily. The others were only some 600m [660yd] away, when we shot up this one from below, from a distance of 80m [yd]. At the same instant, it plunged down in flames and my pilot had to pull away sharply. This caused us to lose contact with the others and unfortunately, we didn't succeed in finding them again. All our kills were Lancasters. Our final victim crashed some 50km [32 miles] south-west of Paris near Dreux.

Martin Drewes' and Erich Handke's fifth kill on the Mailly-le-Camp raid was possibly Lancaster EE185 KM–A of 44 Squadron, which crashed at Dreux with the loss of the Australian skipper P/O. Allen W. Nolan and his crew. The seven men were all buried at Dreux, where they still rest. In all, forty-two Lancasters were lost on this raid, 11.6 per cent of the force dispatched. The aircraft of 1 Group, which formed the second wave of the attack, suffered the most casualties, with twenty-three of the 173 aircraft dispatched failing to return. 460 (RAAF) Squadron suffered no less than five out of seventeen Lancasters shot down on the raid. Although this was a heavy blow for Bomber Command, the attack on Mailly-Le-Camp was carried out with great accuracy; some 1,500 tons of bombs were dropped and 114 barrack buildings, forty-seven transport sheds and some ammunition buildings in the camp were hit; 102 vehicles, including thirty-seven tanks, were destroyed. 218 German soldiers were killed and 156 injured. The only French civilian casualties in the nearby village of Mailly occurred when a Lancaster crashed into a house. Among the aircraft shot down was that of S/Ldr Sparks, the Deputy Master Bomber, who had taken over command from W/Cdr Deane, the Master Bomber, and who had stayed over the target until the end. Sparks evaded capture and soon returned to England. Hptm. Bergmann, the most successful fighter pilot on 3/4 May, went missing in action on 6/7 August 1944 during a sortie in the Invasion area of Avranches–Mortain. He and his crew probably fell victim to a Mosquito. Two months previously, Helmut Bergmann had been awarded the Ritterkreuz after his thirty-fourth *Abschuss.* No trace was ever found of his Bf110G-4, nor of the crew.

Another occasion when the German nightfighter crews managed to put up a good fight took place on 2/3 June 1944, only three nights before D-Day. During this night, Bomber Command sent out three separate forces to attack coastal batteries in the Pas de Calais, a radar jamming station at Berneval and, finally, to bomb the railway yards at Trappes. Australian P/O. Bruce 'Doug' Bancroft served as a pilot with 158 Squadron between 28 February and 1 September 1944, when he was grounded from operational flying. However, his tour might just as well have been violently cut short on 2/3 June 1944:

> As the Allied 'D-Day' invasion of occupied Europe drew near, Bomber Command was required to strike consistently at targets such as railway marshalling yards, road centres, canals, etc. in order to deny supplies of men and materials to the coastal areas of Normandy and regions nearby. Towards this end, on the night of 2/3 June 1944, the Command despatched 128 heavy bombers to attack the large railway marshalling yards at Trappes, approximately fifteen miles south-west of the centre of Paris. For the attack, 158 Squadron contributed twenty-three aircraft and my crew was one of those detailed for this action using our regular squadron aircraft, Halifax III, LV792 NP–E ('E–Easy').
>
> Zero hour on the target was 00.50 hours and we were logged airborne at 22.16 hours into a clear, cloudless sky lighted by an almost full moon. A trouble-free flight was made to the target and we released our load of high explosive bombs from 7,500ft [2,300m] and were able visually to see the bombs hitting right in the middle of the railway yards and to witness the destruction of the tracks and rolling stock.
>
> As the bomber stream left the target area, which was only lightly defended by anti-aircraft gun-fire, attacks began by enemy nightfighter aircraft in substantial numbers and there were many combats in the bright moonlight. Some twenty-five miles to the south of Rouen and near Evreux at a position logged by the navigator, P/O. Alwyn Fripp, as 49°00′N 01°02′E at 01.17 hours and on the way to the French coast, our aircraft was attacked from below by a Ju88 nightfighter apparently using the recently German devised form of attack known as *Schräge Musik*. The attacking aircraft flew at a lower altitude and directly beneath our bomber and was therefore unseen against the darker background below. Our 'fishpond' warning system at our tail did not operate anywhere near ninety degrees downwards.
>
> The enemy's cannon and machine gun fire ripped into our aircraft from tail to nose of the fuselage and also into the wings and started fierce fires in the bomb bay, inside the fuselage

One that got away. Cannon fire from a German nightfighter raked the wing of this Lancaster, 1944. Coll. Bill Pearce.

Halifax Mk III LV792 NP–E of 158 Squadron, shown here at Lissett, Yorkshire in April 1944. As a result of a devastating Ju88 attack on 2/3 June 1944, the aircraft was written off on return to the UK. 158 Squadron lost five Halifaxes to nightfighters on the Trappes raid of 2/3 June, plus LV792 written off, from twenty-three aircraft despatched. Coll. Doug Bancroft.

forward of the rear bulkhead, and oil from fractured hydraulic lines also caught fire. A fire also started in the starboard inner engine. A hole about three feet wide was made across the width of the fuselage forward of the rear bulkhead where the radar dome and scanner had been blasted away and another hole some eighteen inches in diameter was blown in the port side of the fuselage alongside the wireless operator's position above the port wing root. Both wings and flaps and ailerons were severely damaged and a fuel tank in the port wing was holed and fuel from that tank left a white vapour trail as it was blown backwards.

Shells and bullets punctured many holes in the aircraft, including the cockpit where the instrument panel was pitted by shrapnel and I saw several tracer missiles as shells came up between my legs and close to the front edge of my seat and blew out the perspex of the cockpit covering immediately above my head. The radio set and intercommunication system were completely destroyed as were the navigational aids of *H2S* and *Gee*, and several oxygen bottles were hit and exploded. As the hydraulic system had been severely damaged and broken in several places, both the mid-upper and rear gun turrets were inoperable, the wing flaps dropped to about forty-five degrees and the bomb bay doors partly opened. Much of the turret gun ammunition exploded in the transporter racks on the port side and the bullets pierced the starboard side of the fuselage.

I feathered the propeller and switched off the starboard inner engine and pressed the switch to activate the fire extinguisher in that engine and saw the Ju88 on the starboard bow breaking away from the engagement at a distance of about 30 yd and immediately put our aircraft into a steep diving turn to starboard. I could clearly see the face of the enemy pilot as he looked back at us from his cockpit. Evidently seeing the fires burning and the aircraft in a diving turn he must have been quite satisfied with his work and, fortunately for us, he did not return.

The engine fire was extinguished and the navigator, P/O. Alwyn Fripp, and the bomb aimer, F/O. Eric Tansley, came up from their forward positions in the nose with their parachutes attached and I handed them the nearest fire extinguisher (which was by my seat) and told them to immediately begin to fight the fires within the aircraft with all available extinguishers and fire axes as I had the aircraft fairly well under control and that, as the wings were not on fire, the fuel tanks were safe for the present time other than the one which had been holed and showed signs of sealing off (being self sealing tanks).

F/O. Tansley advised me that the wireless operator, Sgt Leonard Dwan, evidently had been very seriously wounded and suffering great pain had somehow managed to bail out through the forward escape hatch, and it was quickly found that the flight engineer, Sgt Leonard Cottrell, and the mid-upper gunner, Sgt Kenneth Leheup, were also missing. It was later accepted that Sgt Dwan did not survive and his body has never been found.

The rear gunner, Sgt David Arundel, forced his way out of the rear gun turret with the aid of a fire axe and came forward along the starboard side by holding onto the 'stringers' of the fuselage framework in order to cross the hole in the fuselage flooring and to pass the fire which was burning in that area. He said that he came part of the way forward and saw my back and considered that I was in control of the aircraft and he then went back to attack the rear fire with an extinguisher, a fire axe and even his gloved hands whilst F/O. Tansley and P/O. Fripp were tackling the fires in the bomb bay.

I had kept the aircraft in the diving turn to starboard and levelled out at about 3,000ft [900m] and as the P4 magnet compass had been damaged and the D/R compass had tumbled, I turned to a north-westerly course using the North Star (Polaris) as a visual guide and headed for the English Channel and the English coast. As the aircraft was losing height, I decided to re-start the inner engine and was able to do so successfully without any further outbreak of fire and increased all engine revolutions and boost to maximum cruising output in an endeavour to maintain altitude. The aircraft was a bit 'sloppy' on the controls and still slowly continued to descend because of the partly down position of the flaps, the partly opened bomb bay doors and the holes in various parts which all created a great deal of drag, and we finally crossed the French coast over Le Havre at about 2,000ft [600m]. In the moonlight the streets and buildings of Le Havre were clearly visible but, although this city was notorious for its heavy concentration of anti-aircraft defences, not a light was seen or a shot fired at us.

Having crossed the enemy coast and out over the English Channel, I gave some consideration to the likelihood of having to ditch the aircraft in the Channel and decided to keep airborne as long as possible in order to get nearer to the English coast as we did not have a radio with which to send a position signal or 'mayday' call for assistance. There was a radio for use in the aircraft's dinghy but it seemed obvious that the dinghy, stored in the port wing, would have been badly holed in the attack and we would be solely dependent on our 'Mae West' life jackets for survival.

By the time that we were about half way across the Channel, by my approximate calculation, the three crew members had virtually extinguished the fires within the aircraft except for some still smouldering patches in the bomb bay which needed watching.

Eventually we crossed the English coast at 700ft [200m] and I switched on the navigational lights and instructed the navigator to fire a double red Very signal in case the coastal defences might think that we were 'intruders'. Not far away, on the starboard bow, I saw an airfield lit up for night flying and turned towards it and increased the

Crew of Halifax LV792 NP–E of 158 Squadron, standing under their aircraft in April 1944. Left to right: Sgt Leonard Dwan (WOp., MIA 2/3 June 1944); Sgt Kenneth Leheup (MUG., POW 11 June 1944); Sgt David Arundel (RG.); Sgt Leonard Cottrell (FE., picked up by Maquis on 3 June 1944 and returned to UK safely in autumn 1944); F/O. Eric Tansley (BA.); P/O. Bruce 'Doug' Bancroft (Pilot); F/Sgt Alwyn Fripp (Nav.). Coll. Doug Bancroft.

engine power in order to try to maintain our existing height as we were getting down somewhat low. As we approached the circuit, I had the navigator fire another red Very signal followed by another as we turned onto the down-wind leg of the circuit at under 600ft [180m] as indicated on the altimeter. I instructed the bomb aimer, F/O. Tansley, to withdraw the undercarriage uplocks and to take up a crash position with the rear gunner, Sgt Arundel. As I had expected, the undercarriage dropped into landing position and locked under its own weight and then I was required to apply full climbing power to the engines in order to overcome the extra drag caused by the undercarriage. I had the navigator stand by with the Very pistol which I told him to fire once more on the downwind leg of the circuit and again on the crosswind leg and finally as we turned to the approach to the runway and then he took up his crash position. On turning onto the runway approach, we thankfully received the green light to make our landing to which we were totally committed in any case either on the runway or on the grass beside it as there was definitely no hope of making another circuit.

The landing was completed satisfactorily at 02.51 hours on 3 June and as the aircraft settled on the runway I realized that we had a blown out starboard tyre and that there appeared to be some problem with the tail wheel but I was able to maintain control along the runway until the landing run was almost completed and the aircraft swung gently to port and was stopped clear of the runway. It had blown out starboard and tail wheel tyres. The three crew members left the aircraft through the hole in the rear of the fuselage whilst I switched off the engines and turned off the fuel cocks and left through the missing section of the top of the cockpit and slid down over the port wing. An ambulance and fire tenders were in attendance at the scene but the ambulance was not needed and the fire crews doused a couple of still smouldering spots in the fuselage and bomb bay and we discovered that we had landed at Hurn airfield, near Bournemouth, Hampshire.

Whilst on the downwind leg of the circuit, the airfield lights on the port side disappeared completely from my view for several seconds and I saw a red beacon light some 30ft [10m] higher up at an angle of about forty-five degrees on the port side which had me puzzled for some time as I thought a tall hangar or some other structure had blocked my line of vision. In the morning, on investigation, I realized that we had narrowly missed hitting St. Catherine's Hill, approximately 400ft [120m] high, which was in the circuit area and had not been visible in the faded moonlight. The navigator could not have advised me as to our exact position as his maps etc. had been blown away through the open front hatch and other items were scattered throughout the aircraft by the incoming airstream.

The Command report on the operation was that ours was probably the most seriously damaged aircraft to have ever been flown back to the United Kingdom. Of the twenty-three aircraft despatched from 158 Squadron for this attack, five failed to return and our aircraft LV792 NP-E was categorized B/FB (beyond economical repair due to operational damage) and finally written off the charge of the squadron. Of the total of 128 aircraft of Bomber Command despatched for this operation fifteen Halifaxes and one Lancaster failed to return, 12.5 per cent of the force. Sgt David Arundel was awarded an immediate Distinguished Flying Medal and F/O. Eric Tansley, F/O. Alwyn Fripp and I were awarded an immediate Distinguished Flying Cross each for our parts in the action.

Leonard Cottrell has since told me that he mistakenly took my action of feathering the starboard inner propeller by raising my right arm with my thumb extended to press the feathering switch as a signal to evacuate the aircraft. He went back accordingly and advised the mid-upper gunner, Kenneth Leheup, to bail out and both of them, finding that the rear escape hatch was jammed, then went through the flames and out through the hole left by the missing radar dome and scanner. Both of them landed safely but Sgt Kenneth Leheup was captured eight days later and became a prisoner-of-war whilst Sgt Leonard Cottrell was picked up within a few hours by a group of 'Maquis' who hid him safely for over three months until the area was secured by Allied troops and he was then moved back to the United Kingdom.

Sgt Leonard Stanley Dwan, the twenty-three-year-old WOp. in Doug Bancroft's crew is commemorated on panel 228 of the Runnymede Memorial. He is one of the 20,456 RAF aircrew declared missing during W.W.II.

On the few times when deep penetration raids on German cities were carried out during the period between the Nuremberg raid and D-Day, RAF Bomber Command got a pasting. During the nights of 22/23 and 26/27 April for example, when Bomber Command raided Düsseldorf and Schweinfurt, the Luftwaffe mounted successful *Tame Boar* operations: thirty-three and thirty-seven bombers respectively were destroyed during these raids. The German defences never really succeeded in deflecting Bomber Command from its purpose, however, no matter how hazardous they made the operations. Despite the successful *Tame Boar* operations in late April, the large majority of British heavies reached their target cities on each of these raids and usually caused significant damage.

The only regular bombing raids on Germany during this period were carried out by the Light Night Striking Force (LNSF). Equipped with fast Mosquito bombers, this force flew to targets deep in the Reich virtually every night, two-thirds of them when the heavies were grounded. Nachtjagd tried to ward off the Mosquito plague with specially prepared day and nightfighter aircraft like the He219, Ta154, Ju88S, Me410, and the single-engined Fw190A-6 and Bf109H, but it was to no avail. Virtually all attempts proved fruitless: the Mosquitos simply flew too high and too fast and remained an elusive thorn in the German flesh. During 1944, Oblt. Fritz Krause served as a pilot with the experimental 1./NJGr.10 under Hptm. Friedrich Karl Müller. With *Neptun* AI equipped Fw190A-5s and A-6s and Bf109Gs the unit flew *Wild Boar* missions against the LNSF Mosquitos over Berlin, but its pilots enjoyed few successes. Hptm. Müller brought his score to twenty-three kills with four *Abschüsse* whilst commanding 1./NJGr.10. Oblt Krause destroyed Mosquito MM147 of 692 Squadron over Berlin on the night of 8 July as his only kill in 1./NJGr.10. F/Lt Burley DFC, the pilot was killed but his navigator F/Lt Saunders DFC was taken prisoner. Krause, a Fw190 pilot, recalls one typically frustrating night over Berlin three nights later:

> I took off from Werneuchen at 01.20 hours on 11 July 1944. On this night, with good weather conditions for the searchlights which were now effective up to great heights, once again five single-engined nightfighter aircraft were ordered to take up their waiting positions to the NW, NE, SW, SE and also over the middle of the city

at a height of over 10,000m [32,000ft] and from there to try and intercept the Mosquitos. The effective range of the heavy flak batteries was restricted to a height of 8,000m [26,000ft] by adjusting the detonator on the shells.

This experimental scheme, which had been introduced a few weeks previously, seemed to promise positive results against the very fast formations of between thirty and fifty Mosquitos which attacked Berlin at a height of between 7,000 and 9,000m [22,800 and 29,200ft]. There was no doubt however, that under the prevailing ratio of power, these regular nightly raids could not be prevented.

Our fighter aircraft were normally ordered to scramble some twenty-five minutes before the enemy formations were due to arrive over the city. By the time we had reached our waiting positions above the effective range of the Flak, the latter received the order 'Free to fire', and then the first Mosquitos flew in over the outskirts of the city in the Potsdam area.

On this particular night, I had been ordered to take up the position over the middle of the city. My marker searchlight, which in our fighter pilot's slang we had dubbed 'the curtain', was positioned near the railway station at the Friedrichstrasse.

After having taxied to my take off position at Werneuchen airfield, I suddenly experienced mechanical trouble. One of the two brakes on my undercarriage didn't function. As a result, I had to taxi in several full circles, despite applying full rudder and power on the engine, before I could line up for take off with only one brake functioning. Consequently, I had lost so much time that I was climbing some 2,000 to 3,000m [6,500 to 9,700ft] below the four other fighter aircraft.

Before I had been able to reach the relatively safe height above the ceiling of the flak fire, evidently the unrestricted order 'Free to fire' had been issued automatically on approach of the formation of bombers. Although by this time only the five friendly fighter aircraft circling over the city could have been identified on the radar screens of the Flak ground control organization, and especially my single and lonely aircraft which had only reached an altitude of 6,500m [20,100ft], a barrage was sent up from all the flak barrels. Unfortunately, at this instant I was in the immediate range of the strongest heavy Flak battery, the 12.8cm cannons of the large Flak bunker in Oranienburg.

One of the shells that exploded all around me tore off a large part of my right wing, including the elevator. Yet, my aircraft still remained controllable. Although I immediately fired off the colours of the day with the flare pistol which had been built into the cockpit, and shouted out a mayday call over the R/T, nothing happened. So, I had no option left but to bail out of my machine, which I announced over the R/T. Shortly before I jettisoned the cockpit canopy, in my headphones I heard one of my comrades who was flying over the flak fire crying out to me: 'Herr Oberleutnant, don't forget your briefcase!'

However, I was not the only one to overhear this. The call also resounded from all the loudspeakers in the Battle HQs of the ground control organization which had switched onto the fighter frequency. This violation of the 'holy' radio discipline came from Ofw. Günter Migge, a *Wild Boar* pilot who had shot down five *Viermots* and had bailed out once himself. Despite the general constrained grimness that ruled amongst our superiors, Migge's offence was taken in with a sense of humour and had no disciplinary consequences for him. The only effect it had, was that for some time afterwards, I was asked with a knowing smile by officers completely unknown to me about the whereabouts of my briefcase. Actually, I have never possessed one during my military career!

Before I hung safely under my parachute, I was struck by a terrible fright. After having catapulted myself obliquely upwards from my seat by applying violent elevator, something broke away from my back, hit the upper part of my thigh and then my calf. I froze under the assumption that I had not only unlatched my straps, but also inadvertently the girdles of my parachute pack – and now it had taken leave of me with a few unfriendly thrusts. Fortunately, this was not the case. As I later found out, the removable, but normally firmly locked seat of my Fw190 had got stuck to me, and only by the hurricane-like air current after bailing out it had been torn off.

Luckily, when I came down in the pitch darkness of the night, no obstacles hindered my fall of 5m per second. I came down safely in the rushes on the soft edge of the Gran Lake to the north of Berlin.

Oblt Fritz Krause kept flying *Neptun*-equipped Fw190s in 1./NJGr.10 until September 1944, when he changed to specially-modified Bf109Hs in 1./NJG11. He claimed a Lancaster shot down during a heavy Bomber Command attack on Bochum on 4/5 November 1944 and survived the war unscathed, despite three parachute jumps.

As a direct result of the Allied pre-invasion air campaigns, Nachtjagd had to put up with an increasing number of bombing raids and surprise strafing attacks on its airfields, both by day and by night. The increasing weight of these attacks forced Schmid to withdraw many Nachtjagd units from bases in the Low Countries and northern France and to deploy these Gruppen to airfields deep into the Reich. These were the first signs of Nachtjagd's final struggle with a vastly superior adversary, in which the arm would soon become entangled.

The DB605 of this highly-polished and light blue Bf109H 'White 3' of 1./NJGr10 was fitted with a high-performance compressor and flown by Oblt Fritz Krause as a specially prepared high-level Mosquito hunting aircraft during the summer of 1944. Whilst chasing a Mosquito which he had detected through its vapour trail at a height of 32,500ft (10,000m) on the night of 8 September 1944, the compressor disintegrated, and Fritz had to bail out over Frankfurt at 01.45 hours. Coll. Fritz Krause.

CHAPTER 8

The Fall: Jammers, Hitler's Oil and Mosquitos

The crushing Allied bombing offensive in early 1944 finally resulted in a more positive attitude amongst some of Germany's war leaders towards the needs of an adequate air defence system. On 1 March 1944, Luftzeugmeister Milch and Albert Speer, the Minister of War Production, set up the 'Jägerstab'. As its primary goal, this 'Fighter Staff' aimed to mobilize as many industrial resources as possible for the mass production of fighter aircraft. The initiators, Milch and Speer, with the support of Adolf Galland, fully realized that the survival of German cities and the war industry depended on a drastic strengthening of Germany's air defences.

Jägerstab's efforts had an immediate effect on fighter aircraft production figures, which in April increased considerably despite relentless Allied bombing raids. Nachtjagd received hundreds of the latest Ju88G-series nightfighter aircraft to replace the largely obsolete Bf110. The Ju88G became Nachtjagd's standard nightfighter aircraft during 1944. After the absolute low of early February 1944, when I Jagdkorps had only 179 aircraft and crews at its disposal, the arm now gradually expanded once more. By 20 May, Schmid had 480 operational aircraft under his command.

In spite of all the Jägerstab's efforts, both Hitler and Göring were not convinced of the need of giving such a priority to defensive fighter aircraft. Influenced by the new Luftwaffe Chief of Staff, General Korten, and others in his inner circle, Hitler remained convinced that his offensive strategy was still the right one. During a conference with Speer and Milch on 23 May 1944, both Hitler and Göring rejected the Jägerstab plans: instead, there would be an increase in the production of bombers for the Luftwaffe! It is true that the two leaders of the Third Reich had come to recognize the necessity of an 'air umbrella' over Germany, but should this be done at the expense of bomber aircraft production? Hitler once again expressed on this occasion his completely unreal and outmoded view that the Reich could better be defended by flak instead of the fighter arm. Consequently, a considerable part of Germany's remaining industrial capacity was reserved for the production of anti-aircraft guns, ammunition and related equipment, instead of being used to produce fighter aircraft.

Six weeks later, when the situation in the west had become critical for Germany after the successful Allied invasion in Normandy, and due to the massive bombing raids on Germany's oil industry, the Führer finally approved plans for the mass production of fighters at the expense of the bombers. It was a historic moment. At last, for the first time in the war, Hitler acknowledged the primary need for defence – although by now it was too late.

Nachtjagd grew considerably during the second half of 1944 due to the efforts of Jägerstab. From 685 machines on 1 July, the arm had 830 nightfighter aircraft at its disposal by early October. However, the hitting power of Nachtjagd did not grow proportionally. Whereas during June, its crews still managed to shoot down 2.9 per cent of the British raiders, in December this figure had declined to a mere 0.7 per cent.

The final decline of Nachtjagd as an effective fighting force commenced about a month after D-Day. In the early hours of 13 July, Ju88G-1 no. 712273 R4+UR of 7./NJG2 took off from Volkel airfield in the Netherlands for a North Sea patrol. The aircraft was fully state-of the-art with the still unjammable *SN-2* AI radar, *Naxos* and *Flensburg* devices. Over the expanses of the North Sea, its inexperienced pilot inadvertently steered a reciprocal compass course and arrived over England without realizing it. The Ju88 touched down at RAF Woodbridge in Suffolk at 04.30 hours with almost dry tanks, and the crew got out of their aircraft assuming they had landed in the vicinity of Berlin. It only took the British boffins a few days to unravel the secrets of the hitherto unknown *SN-2* radar and also of the *Naxos* and *Flensburg*. From 23 July onwards, Bomber Command was able to effectively jam the *SN-2* with *Window* cut to a new length (*'Long' Window*). The *Monica* tail warning radar sets which the heavies had carried to warn them of approaching German nightfighters were also removed, and the use of *H2S* was restricted, thus rendering the *Flensburg* and *Naxos* virtually useless. Lt Arnold Döring, another pilot with 7./NJG2 recalls:

> A few of our crews are employed in combating the British flying jamming stations. These are Short Stirlings, which patrol over the North Sea with new jamming equipment and jam our long range radars covering the forward defence zone. One Stirling is shot down during these sorties. Ogfr. Mäckle lands in England during one of these operations and thus divulges the secret of the wavelength of our *SN-2*, as a British long range nightfighter pilot who was shot down declares later on. From this time onwards, the *SN-2* is virtually useless, the Tommy counters it with *Düppel* which has been cut exactly to our wavelength. Nothing else but 'snow' shows on our cathode-ray tubes, and tracking a *Viermot* in the bomber stream has become a matter of sheer luck. Nachtjagd 'walks with a stick' and nights like Nuremberg are now merely a legend!

Hence, from August 1944 onwards, the nightfighter crews were left with virtually no means of tracking RAF bombers. The *SN-2* could not be replaced by a new AI radar set working on a different wavelength, as no such device had yet been developed for operational service. Matters were further complicated as 100 Group RAF increasingly jammed the German ground control radars and radio communications with a wide range of electronic countermeasures. Thus, it had become virtually impossible for Nachtjagd's ground control organizations to set up the running commentary, and the Luftwaffe nightfighter crews were largely unable to find the bomber streams. Nachtjagd had been rendered 'blind' once more. F/Lt 'Dutchy' Holland did his second tour with 199 (Radar Countermeasures) Squadron in Halifaxes and Stirlings after D-Day, as a Radar Countermeasures Operator:

> I spent my time in the windowless fuselage operating a variety of RCM [Radar Countermeasures] transmitters whilst glued to a four-inch cathode ray tube, trying to identify German radar pulse recurrence frequencies so that I could then tune a transmitter to that frequency in order to jam it. On most operations we carried up to two tons of *Window*, which for centre-of-gravity purposes at take-off had to be stored in the centre section of the wing mainplane, and as soon as we were airborne, had to be 'humped' down the fuselage to the flare chute, ready for dropping. We tried to get this done before we reached 8,000–10,000ft [2,400–3,000m], as we could not use oxygen whilst running up and down the fuselage, and on quite a number of occasions some fault would occur in the Stirling's many

A crew from 199 Squadron posing in front of their Special Duties Stirling. Left to right: Sgt Stearman (AG.); Sgt Moverly (BA.); Sgt Melhuish (FE.); Sgt Finnimore (Pilot); F/Lt 'Dutchy' Holland (RCM Op.); Sgt Hunt (AG.); Sgt Fowler (W/Op.); Sgt Scapa (Nav.).
Coll. Dutchy Holland.

electrical systems and a return to base would be needed, and we then had to shift the bundles of *Window* back to the centre section. Sometimes the faults would be in the electric raise and lower system of the undercarriage, which would then have to be lowered by handwinding – taking over 700 turns of the manual gear per wheel!

199 Squadron briefings were always interesting, because the routes and targets of all the main force and diversionary forces were shown, as well as any 'jamming' screens through which bomber streams would emerge. It was like seeing the strategy for a chess match.

In 1944–45 I believe that 100 Group losses were less than the main force losses from fighter activity in 1943, which rather surprised me as we often put up a racecourse of aircraft as a screen which I thought would be obvious to the Germans as a sitting target.

P/O. Leslie Boot, Special Operator with 223 Squadron from September 1944 further comments on 100 Group's secret RCM activities:

There were two squadrons on the station; we flew B-24 Liberators and the other squadron American Fortresses (with British RAF crews). One of each squadron, flying in pairs, were spaced ahead and along the main bomber force flying approximately 1,000ft [300m] above the main stream when over the target and patrolling for twenty minutes around the target. The Special Operator worked his set some fifteen to thirty minutes before and after the target and, of course when over it. Our worry was that we were very aware that we were making long transmissions endeavouring to jam German radar but, could be in turn similarly 'picked up' by another German receiver.

Rightly or wrongly we thought we were effective as, through a very small porthole nearby, I could see searchlights apparently out of control – as to the guns, who could tell, just hope we were having some effect!! As an SO. [Special Operator] I had very little idea of what was happening, particularly over the target, as we were not in communication with the crew when working the radar. The ordinary Wireless Operator was within touching distance so that if anything drastic happened it was hoped he would let us know.

One of the young men on the receiving end of 100 Group's unwelcome attentions was Fw. Eberhard Scheve. He served as *Bordfunker* in the

Leslie Boot, depicted here on a Hampden of 61 Squadron during his first tour. Coll. Leslie Boot.

Fw. Eberhard Scheve, Bordfunker. *During 1944, Scheve served as* Bordfunker *in the crew of Oblt Hermann Leube, Staffel Kapitän of 4./NJG3. Leube claimed twenty-two bombers destroyed, before he was killed in action on 27/28 December 1944. On that night, 4./NJG3 not only lost its St.Kpt., but also two other crews and their Ju88Gs.* Coll. Ad van Lingen.

crew of Oblt. Hermann Leube, St.Kpt. of 4./NJG3. On one of their sorties, the crew took off at 23.03 hr on 24 May 1944 in Ju88G-1 D5+KM from Plantlünne, a satellite airfield between Rheine and Lingen/Emsland. Air gunner Stfw. Druschke was the third man in the crew. Bomber Command's main target on this night was Aachen, with 264 Lancasters, 162 Halifaxes and sixteen Mosquitos dispatched. Bomber Support was supplied by six RCM heavies and a few dozen *Serrate* and intruder Mosquitos. Oblt Leube went in pursuit of the bomber stream, as Fw. Scheve recalls:

> Until this day our night fighting radar *SN-2* was only jammed by *Düppel*, the silvery foil, which showed up on the radar screen as aircraft targets. On this night however, our equipment was jammed by a flying transmitter, which caused a flickering of the waves over the full width of the picture tube and which completely prevented the blips from appearing normally. I tried a few tricks, switched off the transmitter of my *SN-2* set, then dimmed the amplifier on the receiver and then had two different flickering bands to the left and to the right of the middle line. I told my pilot to alter his course and established that

the flickering bands changed accordingly. I therefore decided that I could use this jamming transmitter as a flying beacon to home on to. As the jamming transmitter probably flew inside a bomber stream to give protection to the formation, we decided to investigate this.

It took us a long time before we spotted the bomber, and we attacked it no less than six times before we were able to shoot it down. At once when the bomber exploded the jamming of the *SN-2* ended. The vanishing of the jamming at this instant was confirmed by our Staffel comrades, who had also flown around aimlessly for several hours. At debriefing we told of our observations, but we were then told that no such thing existed as a jamming transmitter for the *SN-2*, and that we had experienced jamming by the overlapping of other *SN-2* sets.

Oblt Leube's victim was B-17 SR384 BU–A of 214 (SD) Squadron, one of three Fortresses despatched from the squadron on Bomber Support patrols for the Aachen main force. F/O. Allan J.N. Hockley, the skipper, and his mid-upper gunner Sgt Raymond G.V. Simpson were killed, but the seven other men in the crew escaped alive. Oblt Leube first shot the fuselage of SR384 on fire, then the wings, and finally the Fortress exploded over the Oosterschelde near Antwerp at 00.57 hours. The victorious Ju88G-1 crew safely returned to base at 02.20 hr. Oblt Hermann Leube met his end on 27/28 December 1944. At the time of his death he had scored 22 victories.

The Allied armies forced their way out of their bridgehead in Normandy and liberated France during the late summer of 1944. Almost all the German early warning radar sites and Y-stations in

Fortress SR384 BU–A of 214 (SD) Squadron at Oulton, photographed on 24 May 1944 before taking off on a Bomber Support sortie to Aachen. The aircraft failed to return: it was intercepted and shot down by Oblt Leube of 4./NJG3 over the Oosterschelde near Antwerp. Coll. Gerhard Heilig.

this forward area were captured, driving a large hole into the German Y-organization, from the Eiffel mountains to the Swiss border. This meant that Bomber Command raids could no longer be tracked early in their flight, which was an essential precondition for organizing a successful *Tame Boar* operation. Nachtjagd's tools with which the arm had successfully fought Bomber Command during the Battle of Berlin, were being lost one by one, without anything substantial to replace them.

To add to Nachtjagd's woes, the British stepped up their long range night intruder offensive. From late 1940, Fighter and Bomber Command had despatched a handful of intruder sorties to Luftwaffe 'dromes during bombing raids, to suppress the nightfighters. But the few Hurricanes, Blenheims, Havocs and Bostons were insufficient in numbers, range and striking power to pose a real threat to Nachtjagd until mid-1943. This situation changed in June of that year when 141 Squadron's Beaufighters, equipped with *Serrate* homers and AI Mk IV radar began regular bomber support operations. *Serrate* could pick up the emissions of the *Lichtenstein* AI radar from a range of up to 50 miles (80km), and Nachtjagd crews soon began to fall victim to this new threat. A few months later 141 Squadron's Beaufighters were backed up by the first Mosquito intruder sorties. With the creation of 100 Group in November 1943, a number of Mosquito nightfighter squadrons were incorporated into the Group to hunt down the Nachtjagd crews over the Reich. From January 1944, these Mosquito crews exacted a mounting toll on their German adversaries.

As a direct result of the Nuremberg debacle, Arthur Harris requested that a minimum of ten Mosquito squadrons should be made available to combat Nachtjagd. Within a matter of a few months, each Bomber Command raid was now accompanied by dozens of 100 Group Mosquitos. With their 2nd Tactical Air Force colleagues also roaming the night skies over the Reich, they became a growing menace to Nachtjagd. The Mosquitos were fitted with a most efficient AI radar, supplemented by *Serrate* and *Perfectos*, this latter a device which homed onto the German IFF (Identification Friend or Foe). The roles were gradually reversed; the German hunters became the hunted. There was nowhere left to hide. At any stage during their sorties they ran the risk of being shot down in a surprise attack from a dreaded Mosquito: during take off; over their airfields; whilst circling a radio beacon before being infiltrated into a bomber stream; inside the stream of heavies; on their way back to base and during landing. Between December 1943 and April 1945, Mosquitos of 100 Group accounted for 257 German aircraft destroyed, most of them nightfighter aircraft, for a loss of only sixty-nine Mosquitos. Additionally, 2nd TAF and ADGB (Air Defence of Great Britain) Mosquitos claimed around 230 German planes shot down on offensive operations between early June 1944 and late April 1945.

Moreover, it is quite obvious that the Mosquitos, by undermining the morale of the German crews, played an important part in limiting their success against the bombers. As a result, during the autumn of 1944, the Nachtjagd was forced to change its tactics, seriously reducing efficiency. Crews switched off all radio and radar equipment on board their aircraft, for fear of being homed onto by the Mosquitos. Many also reverted to flying at very low level in order to prevent sudden Mosquito attacks. This low-flying tactic was referred to by the German crews as 'Ritterkreuzhöhe', or 'Knight's Cross height'; if the Nachtjagd pilot decided to climb to the level of where the bombers could be found, he would surely be intercepted and probably killed in a Mosquito attack, and thus would never get the chance to gain the coveted Ritterkreuz. The other side of the coin of course was that this low flying caused many fatal accidents, and crews often arrived too late at the height where the bombers streams were reported.

The Mosquitos of 100 Group and 2nd TAF wreaked havoc amongst their Nachtjagd adversaries during the months of November and December of 1944, and created 'Mosquito panic'. The ageing Bf110 proved an especially easy prey for the British 'wooden wonder', as it lacked both the speed and manoeuvrability to

In late 1944, a Czech 68 Squadron (ADGB) crew prepares for a North Sea patrol in Mosquito NF Mk XIX WM–Z, equipped with the superior AI Mk VIII radar. ADGB, 2nd TAF and 100 Group 'Mossies' accounted for at least 487 German aircraft, mainly nightfighters, destroyed during 1944–45. Coll. Ted Cox.

escape once it was engaged. German crews who were interrogated after the end of the war spoke with bated breath about the Mosquito. One Staffel Kapitän said: 'If only we'd had Mosquitos with your AI radar', and another Nachtjagd pilot declared that the German nightfighter prayer was 'Dear Hermann [Göring], give me a Mosquito'.

The events of 4/5 November 1944 illustrate the impossible situation into which the German air defences were being manoeuvred by the RAF. On this night Bomber Command dispatched 174 Lancasters and two Mosquitos of 5 Group to breach the Dortmund-Ems Canal. For the loss of only three Lancasters the canal was left unusable. The bombing of the canal prevented smelting coke from the Ruhr mines reaching three important steelworks near Brunswick and Osnabrück, which was a severe loss to the German war industry.

The Main Force on 4/5 November however, went to Bochum for a standard area bombing raid. The force comprised 720 bombers, a mixed force of Halifaxes and Lancasters, plus twenty-nine Mosquitos, and carried out a most successful raid which caused severe damage to the centre of Bochum. More than 4,000 buildings were destroyed or seriously damaged, including the city's important steelworks. Some 980 Germans, plus fourteen foreign workers were killed. 100 Group Mosquitos also operated in force, claiming four Ju88s and two Bf110s destroyed, plus two more damaged. Although the raid on Bochum was a success, German nightfighter controllers managed to infiltrate twelve He219s, ten Bf110s and a handful of Ju88s into the bomber stream. Twenty-three Halifaxes and five Lancasters were lost, most of them falling victim to these nightfighters. Alfred F. Weinke, twenty-one-year-old *Bordfunker* in Lt. Rolf Ramsauer's crew with 4./NJG1, took off in Bf110G G9+LM to intercept the Bochum force:

> We were one of the so-called 'green crews'; older crews were hardly around any more, except for the Staffelkapitäne. Enemy bomber formations had been reported in the area of Düsseldorf–Cologne. After take off from Paderborn at 18.45 hr we headed in the appropriate direction. At a height of some 5,000m [16,200ft], I got the echo of a bomber in my *Lichtenstein SN-2* radar set and led our Bf110 towards this aircraft, until we came into visual range. A few bursts of fire from our cannons, and we observed the crash of the four-engined bomber.
>
> A few minutes later, I found another bomber on my radar screen. We approached it fast – as soon as we were within firing range my pilot opened fire. Only a couple of seconds later, in the midst of the air combat, our air gunner shouted excitedly into the intercom: 'Fighter on our tail!' A de Havilland Mosquito had us in its sights. In the same draw of breath shells smashed from behind into our machine and tracer ammo flew around our ears. Our aircraft dived down steeply. At the same moment, my pilot's head disappeared from my sight. The two of us were

Fw. Alfred F. Weinke, Bordfunker, *(left) and his pilot Lt Rolf Ramsauer siting on the tail unit of their Bf110G '13' with NJG102, Wormditt, in eastern Prussia, August 1944.* Coll. Alfred F. Weinke.

separated by an unbridgeable wall which formed our radar, radio and navigation equipment. The *Bordfunker* was only able to see 10 to 15cm [4 to 6in] of the upper part of his pilot's head. I received no reply to my desperate cries into the intercom. It must have gone u/s. We plunged down at raging speed. Rolf must have been hit and wounded during the attack. The machine was out of control.

I ripped open my escape hatch in the canopy, after having signalled to the air gunner to get out. I was able to push myself out up to my hips. The lower part of my body however was stuck in the diving machine as if it were immured. The air pressure and centrifugal forces, at a diving speed of some 600 to 700kph [370 to 430mph], were stronger than my bodily strength, and I was in mortal fear.

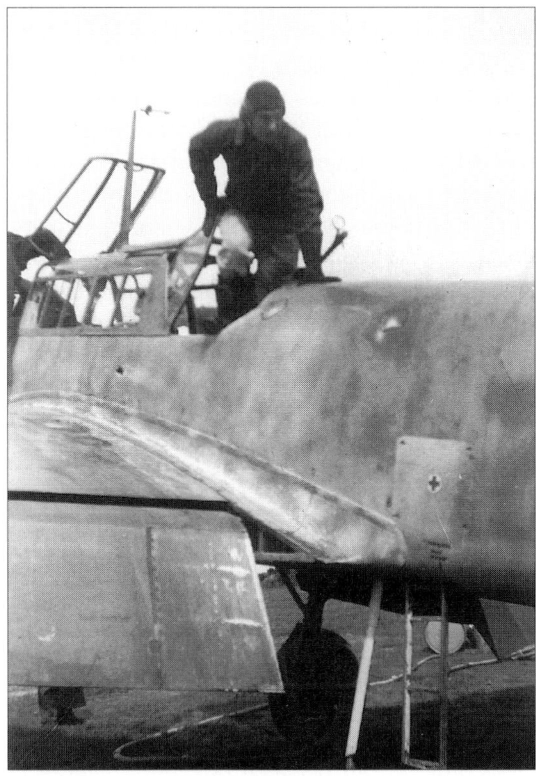

Fw. Alfred F. Weinke, Bordfunker *with 4./NJG1, climbing out of his Bf110G, 1944–45.* Coll. Alfred F. Weinke.

After a seemingly endless descent into hell, a sudden and unexpected jerk and I was out of my prison. I immediately pulled the rip-cord and the canopy opened at once and without delay. After around one second under my opened parachute, the earth took re-possession of me. I had come loose at a height of under 200m [yd]. My first reaction was a little prayer that I spoke out loud in the middle of a glade in the woods where I had landed. Praying was something we had rather unlearned in the course of the past years.

I got through the woods somehow or other until I came across a signalman, where a car from the State Police collected me. My Gruppen Kommandeur of the Second Gruppe of NJG1, Major August Huchel, was stationed at Kaiserswerth near Düsseldorf, not far away from where I had come down (I had landed between Langenfeld and Cologne). As I wished to be brought to him, they took me to Major Huchel. On arrival, he received me and started a de-briefing. His first question was: 'What happened to the other two men in your crew?'. I expressed my sad misgivings and told him that both could not possibly have survived. The fact that I myself had got away alive bordered on a miracle, and I dared not think of another miracle. No-one could possibly have escaped after me and fully have opened his parachute.

After an endless and sleepless night, I was lost in thought, reflecting on my time together with Rolf Ramsauer. The two of us had formed an Austrian crew in late 1943 during training at the Night Fighting School. We soon made a good team. Our gunner Alfred Gilke had accompanied us since August 1944 on all our operational sorties with NJG1. He had been trained as a *Bordfunker*, and from the first time we met we became good friends and confidants.

Early in the morning, Major Huchel came looking for me, he was radiating with joy. At first I thought he had gone mad. His first words were: 'Your crew is alive!' This could only be a sick joke or a case of mistaken identity. What had happened?

The air gunner gave a picture of what had happened. Like me, he had but one wish: get out of the doomed machine. He struggled with the emergency handle to jettison his canopy, but it wouldn't budge. Then he saw how I was stuck in the emergency hatch; he got hold of my legs and pushed me out, whilst holding on to me, so I dragged him with me. One of the straps from his breast-type parachute then got stuck to the oblique cannons behind the canopy. He kept hanging to the side of the fuselage. When almost at ground level, Rolf managed at the last moment to pull back the stick and attained level flight. He was not wounded. After a wandering flight (he had neither radio-navigational equipment nor R/T communication with the ground), he finally touched down at Bonn-Hangelar at 21.00 hours. As a coincidence, the flare path had not been switched off yet. As Rolf got out, he saw the air gunner hanging against the side of the fuselage. My seat was empty.

Air Gunner Gilke had been exposed to a temperature of some –30 degrees Celsius as he dangled against the side of the Bf110. Hardly able to breath in the gale, he had pulled his head down into his fur coat as far as he could, in order to get at least some air. After the landing, when freed from his predicament, he lost consciousness. His head was smeared with blood, caused by a small wound in his mouth. After one or two days in hospital, Gilke came to again.

Alfred Gilke, air gunner in the crew of Lt Rolf Ramsauer with 4./NJG1, 1944–45. Coll. Alfred Gilke, via Alfred F. Weinke.

A few weeks later, Rolf Ramsauer's crew (with a new air gunner) had another close call. In the early hours of 17 December, they had a combat with a four-engined bomber in the area of Mülheim (Ruhr). Return fire from the vigilant tail gunner set the Bf110's right engine on fire and Rolf Ramsauer ordered his crew to bail out. Alfred Weinke was the first to jump, at a height of some 16,200ft (5,000m), and on pulling the rip-cord found to his bewilderment that his parachute failed to open. He fell down at least 9,700ft (3,000m) before in death-struggle he finally managed to literally rip open the parachute pack and float down safely. The crew, re-joined by gunner Gilke in January 1945, kept flying on operations until March 1945. On landing one night that month at Dortmund with no instruments and in extremely bad weather, they crashed, which was the end of their war. In all, the crew had scored two confirmed victories, plus a probable, in NJG1.

The severe losses amongst the Nachtjagd aircrew in the last year of the war are clearly illustrated by those of Alfred Weinke's Gruppe, II./NJG1. During May 1944 – April 1945, this unit lost thirty-nine aircraft and fifty-four aircrew killed, eighteen missing and sixteen wounded in action. A further seventeen groundcrew were killed by bomb blast in an air raid. Whereas a Gruppe should normally consist of some thirty to thirty-five operational crews, II./NJG1 could only muster between fifteen and eighteen crews over the last nine months of the war.

By now, Nachtjagd had to operate in any weather conditions, which often proved fatal for poorly-trained green crews. Hptm. Fritz Lau, Staffelkapitän of 4./NJG1 recalls an operation on the night of 9 November 1944, when German fighter controllers reported a strong force of bombers heading for Cologne. In fact, these were twenty-two aircraft of 100 Group which penetrated the Reich on a *Window* faint to draw up German fighters. This time the ruse worked:

> It was a night on readiness as on so many nights. For a change, and to avoid falling asleep, I had started a game of cards with Hptm. Schmidt and Oblt Stephan.
>
> The complete Staffel at Paderborn was ordered on immediate readiness. Because of the bad weather conditions I phoned the Division HQ. I expressed my objections to having the complete Staffel taking off in this weather. In these adverse weather conditions, at the most Hptm. Schmidt and I should start, as we were both experienced in flying in bad weather. HQ took note of this in a general sense, however with the addition that Oblt Stephan should also fly on this mission as he had flown on the operation to Bremen a few days before, during which bad weather had also prevailed. I objected that during the Bremen mission bad weather conditions did prevail, but that the overall situation had been more favourable in regards to icing up and the ceiling of the clouds. Yet, HQ rejected my objections.
>
> The order to scramble came for the three crews. We laid down our cards, and Oblt Stephan remarked: 'We'll finish the game when we get back'. I had agreed with Oblt Stephan that he should keep in radio contact with me. We then received the order to head towards a radio beacon to the west of the Rhine. On approaching this radio beacon I saw a mighty towering cumulus cloud, which rose high above the upper ceiling of the cloud layer. I tried to get into contact with Stephan and his crew over R/T, but couldn't establish contact. Still, I transmitted a message blindly over the R/T: 'Do not enter the cumulus cloud!' Despite all my warnings it ended in catastrophe. Stephan's final words to his crew, whom he had ordered to bail out, were: 'Greet my family for me'. The game of cards had come to an end.

Oblt Karl-Frank Stephan was killed when his iced up Bf110G-4 440355 G9+KM crashed in a field near Grevenbroich. His *Bordfunker* Uffz. Walter Seeger and gunner Uffz. Heinz Schulze were slightly injured when bailing out.

On the whole, more Nachtjagd aircraft and crews were lost during the war due to non-operational causes than to Allied action. II./NJG2, later renamed to IV./NJG1 for example, was in the thick of the action from the early pioneering days until the bitter end. This Gruppe lost seventy-two aircraft during the war, of which thirty-seven (or some 56 per cent) were lost due to flying accidents, bad weather, engine failures, own flak, and such like. Of the thirty-five aircraft lost due to enemy action, fourteen were shot down by return fire from RAF heavies. Thirteen were destroyed by Beaufighter and Mosquito intruders. Three fell victim to Allied fighter aircraft in daylight and three more were claimed by return fire from American bombers during daylight raids. Finally, two aircraft were lost when the bombers they attacked exploded at close quarters.

Not only the young and inexperienced Nachtjagd crews fell victim to roaming Mosquitos and bad weather during the winter months of 1944/45. Amongst the 114 German nightfighter crews lost during December were a number of top-scoring pilots. Hptm. Heinz Strüning, St.Kpt. of 9./NJG1 died on Christmas Eve at the hands of a Mosquito of 2nd TAF when his tally stood at fifty-six kills. Others, like Hptm. Kamp of NJG4 (twenty-three *Abschüsse*) and Hptm. Leube of NJG3 with twenty-two victories were also killed in action. Another Nachtjagd ace who died in a Mosquito attack was Hptm. Hans-Heinz Augenstein. At twenty-one years of age, he had joined 7./NJG1 at the end of 1942 with his radar operator, Fw. Günter Steins. It took him almost six months before he finally claimed his first victory on 13/14 May 1943. Two weeks later, on 27/28 May, he destroyed four bombers in a row. This was the start of a meteoric rise in Nachtjagd, and Augenstein became one of the most successful of those pilots who joined the arm

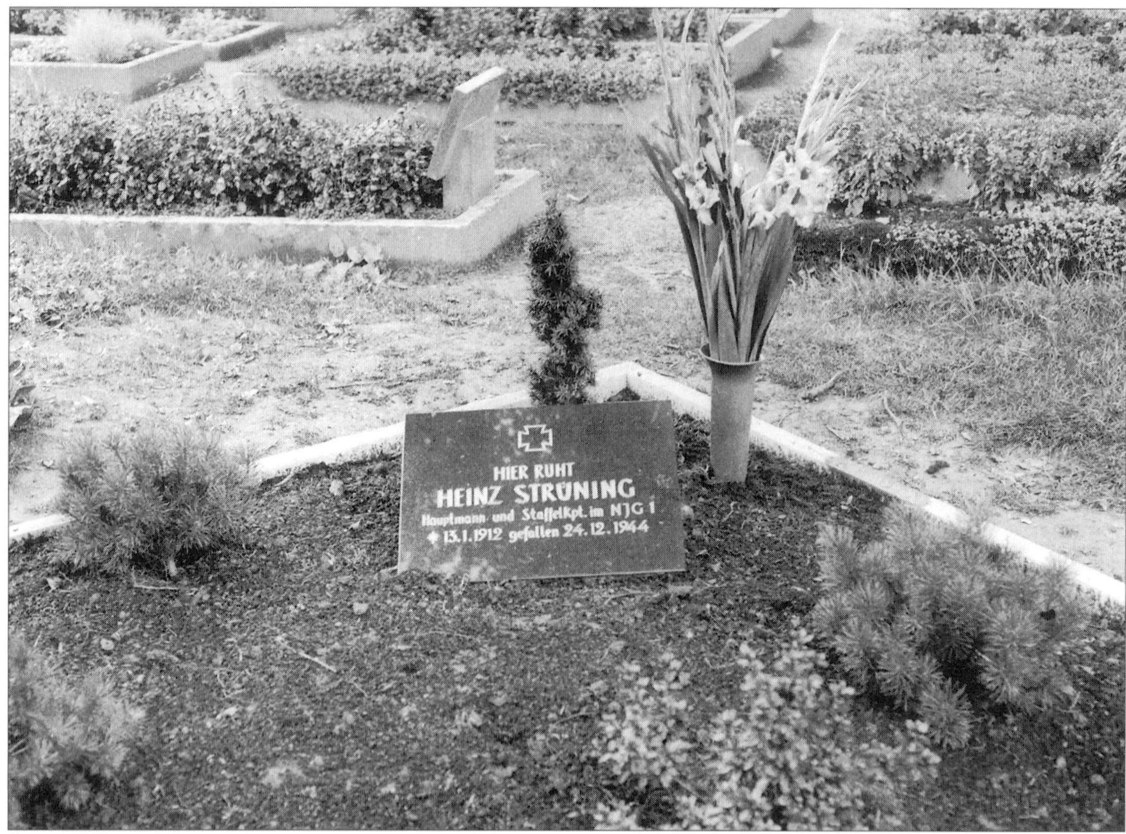

Grave of Hptm. Heinz Strüning, St.Kpt. of 9./NJG1, Oak Leaves holder with fifty-six night kills. He was shot down on the evening of 24 December 1944 at 22.00 hours, probably by a Mosquito of the 2nd TAF. On bailing out, he struck the tail unit of his Bf110G-4 and was killed at the age of thirty-two. Coll. Hans-Jakob Schmitz.

after the pioneering years. From 31 January 1944, he led 7./NJG1 as Staffelkapitän; 12./NJG1 came under his command one month later. When he was awarded the Ritterkreuz on 9 June 1944, he had shot down forty-two British bombers within a year. Over this period, he was shot down and severely injured twice. On the night of 4/5 November 1944, he claimed three *Viermots*, which brought his total score to forty-six night kills, forty-five of which were *Viermots*.

Uffz. Kurt Schmidt joined Augenstein's crew as rear gunner in September 1943, as a precaution when the British night intruders started exacting an increasing toll on the German night-fighters. Kurt took part in the destruction of twenty-seven 'Dicke Autos' ('Fat Cars') with Augenstein, and tells of the crew's final sortie:

> On 6 December 1944 the Fourth Gruppe of NJG1 was based at Dortmund. Shortly after the weather briefing the first incoming aircraft are reported. We come into immediate readiness at 18.30 hours, which shortly after was called off. Around 19.00 hours we come to immediate readiness again, and the first long range night intruders arrive over the airfield – they are a real plague of late. A few minutes later we are

Uffz. Kurt Schmidt, Bordschütze *(AG.) of Hptm. Augenstein, St.Kpt. 12./NJG1, 1944.* Coll. Kurt Schmidt.

ordered to take off. Our left engine refuses to start. I unstrap and assist Hptm. Augenstein with the engine. In the meantime, the light flak is firing to drive away the intruders. Suddenly, the engine comes to life and I am almost swept off the wing. Hptm. Augenstein is in a bad mood, as he now isn't the first one to take off. He doesn't say a word. We taxi to the take off point. The 'drome is enveloped in complete darkness, just one mechanic walks in front of our machine and shows us the way with his dimmed electric torch. We are the last one to take off. The only light is a lamp at the end of the runway, in which direction we take off.

Over the R/T we now hear: 'Watch out for small Indians in your immediate vicinity'. We peer into the darkness until our eye balls almost come out of their sockets, but we take off unscathed and immediately disappear into a layer of cloud at some 1,000m [3,250ft] and set course for a radio beacon near Münster. The weather conditions are ideal for us. We arrive over the beacon and wait there at a height of some 7,000m [22,700ft]. Hptm. Augenstein doesn't fly in a corkscrew as he normally does. Radar operator Steins and I make objections to this, as we had already been shot down once by a long range intruder over the invasion front in June. Hptm. Augenstein replies: 'There are no small Indians at this height'. The main force of 'Dicke Autos' are over Osnabrück now and fly straight at us, their probable target is Berlin. We discuss where we should land when we fly with the bomber stream.

Then, all of a sudden, our machine is rocked, tracer bullets fly all around me. We plunge down, I believe Hptm. Augenstein is trying to shake off our attacker and ask him what is going on. The cockpit is full of smoke and the engines are screaming at full power. We still dive down. Augenstein shouts 'Get out, I can't hold her anymore!' The control cables are probably shot through. Radar operator Steins, who is not yet fully recovered from the last time we were shot down, has slumped forward. I jolt him and shout 'Get out!' He doesn't move, he has probably been hit. The intercom is dead and smashed. The cockpit canopy won't budge. Only when Hptm. Augenstein jettisons his cockpit roof, mine also flies away. I am pushed against the cannons of the *Schräge Musik* and whilst exerting all my strength, I can only get my upper body out of the machine. The straps of my parachute are jammed somewhere. Without being able to move, I am glued to the fuselage, with my legs still inside the cabin. I almost lose my senses from the noise and the air pressure. I give in!

Suddenly, whilst spinning down, the machine assumes another attitude and the air current changes. Without doing a thing, I am hurled away. I immediately come to my senses again and free fall down, until the somersaulting slows down. I pull the rip cord, thank God my 'chute opens immediately. Now a swinging and turning starts, I don't know any more where the top and where the bottom is. Some of the cords have snapped and all I do is swing. I move my arms and legs to check if everything is still OK. I see our machine crash in flames. I get a fright, as during the fumbling, I suddenly have the lock of my parachute harness in my hand. I find out that I have pulled loose the cover of the harness lock, and carefully I grab some cords in order to hold on to them in case of emergency. Yet, with the vicious swinging I can't hold on to them.

I have come loose from the machine at a height of some 3,000m [9,700ft]. Near to me, I hear the noise of an aircraft. Then, with a deafening noise flak shells start exploding over me, and with every salvo I count on being hit. I fire off the colours of the day, and everything is quiet. I float through a thin layer of clouds, then it turns completely black and I fire off a couple of flares. I discover that I am still a few hundred metres off the ground, I spot a farmer's house and a silvery line, towards which I am floating. It looks like a canal (in fact, it was an asphalt road which had become wet in the rain), so I see if the pressurized air bottle in my Mae West is still functioning, and it does. Just before I come down to land I intend to fire off another couple of flares, but I have no time left to execute this.

I awake as from a narcosis executed with a sledge-hammer, I'm unable to take off the harness, as the lock is broken. Fortunately, I have a hunting knife on me. I can't get up on my feet, the inside of my head resembles a combination of a steam-hammer and a saw-mill. Still, I'm alive! I laboriously creep towards a house some 100m [yd] away, knock on the door; a woman answers the door and looks at me appalled. A small girl asks: 'Mummy, is that St. Nicholas?'

Our radar operator Steins was found the same night. He was hurled from the aircraft in the crash. During the next few days, not a trace was found of Hptm. Augenstein. Only after three days, a farmer found his body in a ditch on his land, with unopened parachute. Both my comrades were buried at the military cemetery in Münster. After the end of the war, Hptm. Augenstein's mortal remains were re-buried in his home town at Pforzheim.

Hptm. Augenstein's Bf110 G-4 no. 140078 G9+HZ was probably shot down by an 85 Squadron crew of F/Lt E.R. Hedgecoe DFC and his radar operator F/Sgt J.R. Whitham, and crashed some 6 miles (10km) north-west of Münster-Handorf.

Besides the dreaded Mosquito nightfighters, the Mosquito bombers of the Light Night Striking

Hptm. Augenstein (on the left) and crew of 7./NJG1 in the 'Ops' Room at Twenthe, summer 1943. Coll. Kurt Schmidt.

Force remained a thorn in the side of Nachtjagd. The German arm remained virtually powerless against the elusive 'wooden wonder'. Following the fall of France, when the bulk of the Nachtjagd units had been withdrawn to Germany, Mosquito raids were not intercepted any more by piston-engined aircraft as they could hardly be caught in any event.

Numerically, the Luftwaffe day and nightfighter arms increased steadily as a result of Jägerstab's efforts, and also through the strategic reorientation of early July 1944. The Luftwaffe High Command was determined to set up a concentrated air defence system in a last desperate effort to save German cities and industry from imminent ruin. However, this final attempt was frustrated by the Führer himself. Throughout the war, Hitler had taken the position that wherever his armies fought, the German troops had to hold their positions until the last man. He now applied this principle to the Luftwaffe. Whereas Speer, Milch and Galland primarily intended to bring the day and nightfighters into action in the air defence of Germany, Hitler ordered them to deploy the fighter aircraft over the front lines for direct support of the ground troops. During August 1944 some thirty to forty nightfighter crews made their debut in the ground attack role in France, in a desperate effort to slow down the Allied advance. During the Battle of Arnhem the following month, these 'Nachtschlachteinsätze' (ground attack sorties) were also flown, but to precious little use.

During December 1944, 140 Ju88s and Bf110s were withdrawn from the Reichsverteidigung to give direct support to the advancing troops in the Battle of the Bulge. As these sorties were very risky, the large majority of the Nachtjagd crews employed were expendable, green crews. The seasoned aces remained held back for intercepting night raids. The ground support missions produced little result with heavy casualties: one Gruppe in NJG5 lost twelve out of thirty crews in just three weeks. By the end of the Ardennes offensive, one-third of the German fighter force in the west had been employed in the ground attack role, without even having succeeded in delaying the Allied advance.

Hitler's decision to divert such a large part of the fighter force had a disastrous effect on the fighting power of both the day and nightfighter arms. His air force bled to death over the battle front in France and the Low Countries without being able to gain even local air superiority, and prevented any chance of an effective and powerful air defence of Germany. The German people paid heavily for this during the remaining months of the war.

But the final and most important factor which undermined Nachtjagd's fighting power was the chronic fuel shortage during the last year of the war. After the loss of Rumania's oil fields to the Russians in the autumn of 1943, the German armed forces had come to rely completely on synthetically produced oil. So from 12 May 1944, the Allied air forces started a strategic bombing campaign to destroy oil production. The combined offensive had an immediate and devastating effect. Within five weeks 90 per cent of Germany's synthetic oil production facilities and reserves had been destroyed, and of the original reserves of 195,000 tons of oil, only 20,000 tons remained. During the following months, oil production declined even more dramatically, and by September, only 7,000 tons were left. The Luftwaffe had become incapable of protecting its own lifeblood, and both the USAAF and the RAF could carry out these raids almost with impunity. As a result, the OKL was forced to drastically cut back the number of operational sorties flown by the Luftwaffe by mid-summer 1944. Nachtjagd was hit particularly hard by this measure as the Luftwaffe day fighter units took priority in the allocation of fuel. At the same time, nightfighter pilot and *Bordfunker* training was cut back due to the fuel shortage.

Nachtjagd may have expanded considerably thanks to the efforts of the Jägerstab, but this was undone by the acute fuel shortage. This situation went from bad to worse: from November 1944 onwards, complete nightfighter units were grounded as there was simply no fuel left. Generalleutnant Adolf Galland, General of the Luftwaffe fighter arm during 1942–1944, declared

Although the Bf110G was largely phased out of operational service in Nachtjagd after the summer of 1944, some units kept operating the aircraft. Here a Bf110G of 4./NJG1 is prepared for a mission at Paderborn in October 1944. Note the flame-dampers on the engine exhausts and the large aerial array of the SN-2 *radar.* Coll. Alfred F. Weinke.

after the war: 'The attacks of the Allied bomber forces against the German production of fuel were the main factor that led to the German collapse'. Due to the acute fuel shortage, only the most experienced crews were usually scrambled during the remaining months of the war – to send out green crews would just be a waste of fuel, and often meant certain death as the task proved beyond most of these poorly-trained men.

Bomber Command had grown stronger than ever before. During the spring and summer of 1944 it had expanded into a mighty force of some 1,300 Lancasters and Halifaxes, supported by a wide range of aircraft and scientific devices to make life impossible for Nachtjagd. This air armada was released by the Allied Chiefs of Staff on 25 September, now that the Allied arms were on solid ground in France. Harris was allowed to resume his strategic bombing offensive against German industrial cities. He still believed in the theory that a crushing bombing offensive would suffice to force a surrender, so from late September 1944, German cities were once more subjected to relentless heavy area bombing.

Nachtjagd, on the other hand, had become almost impotent. The loss of the early warning stations in France, the almost complete jamming of both their radio and radar by 100 Group's electronic countermeasures campaign, the lack of fuel, the constant bombing and strafing of their

Destroying the Luftwaffe's life blood. Target photograph of Pölitz oil plant near Stettin being bombed from 17,500ft (5,300m) by F/O. Ovens and crew in Lancaster 'Z' of 630 Squadron, 13/14 January 1945. After the attack by 218 Lancasters and seven Mosquitos of 5 Group, this oil plant was reduced to a shambles. Coll. Geo Mather.

airfields, and the Mosquito intruders all had an effect. Nachtjagd reacted to the British night raids as an unsteady boxer, trying to hit his adversary with blind uncontrolled punches. During August 1944, Nachtjagd still managed to destroy 164 night bombers, but this represented a loss of only 1.6 per cent of all sorties dispatched by Bomber Command. On the debit side, thirty-eight German nightfighters were lost during this month, a casualty rate of 2.5 per cent. The German crews still tried to infiltrate the bomber streams in *Tame Boar* fashion, but most of the time they could not even find the streams at all. The time-honoured Himmelbett GCI system was also still in use, as was *Wild Boar* target area night fighting, but it had become a fight against overwhelming odds. Bomber Command had come to rule the nocturnal skies over the Third Reich.

Experienced Nachtjagd aces did what they could to save the German cities from destruction, but could achieve little. During October 1944, the force claimed a mere 0.5 per cent of all British bomber sorties, 0.9 per cent in November and 0.7 per cent during December. At the same time, their own losses increased to an alarming rate, with an all time high of 114 aircraft and crews lost during December 1944, some 10 per cent of all sorties dispatched. Most of these Nachtjagd aircraft were destroyed by Mosquitos; these were the months of the 'Mosquito panic'. Lt Arnold Döring, pilot with 7./NJG2 flying the Ju88G-6 from Volkel aerodrome in Holland sums up the situation for Nachtjagd in the second half of 1944:

> In France, Belgium and Holland, many of our airfields are subjected to air raids and are rendered useless by these bombing attacks. When Volkel also gets its share of bombs, the Staffeln move to alternative fields at the break of dawn, which are large pastures, and there the aircraft are dispersed and camouflaged. By the evening, the crews return to the operational airfield again.
>
> Our 'drome is mobbed almost every night by Mosquitos, they intrude on our operational take off and landing pattern and one has to take diabolic care so as not to be caught. During take off we only use a white light at the starting point, a red one indicates the end of the runway. These lights are shielded by a large sheet and can only be seen from the ground. The illumination of

FK

buildings and other obstacles on the field are switched off most of the time, and looking at it from above, the 'drome is enveloped in darkness during take off. On final approach to land, on request the flare path is switched on for a short time and is switched off immediately again after touch down. Taxying is done in darkness. Whilst in the circuit and awaiting permission to land, we only fly in very tight turns, as one who flies on a straight course for a longer period of time is shot at by Mosquitos. They really are a true plague, these Mosquitos!

On 3 September, Volkel aerodrome is thoroughly bombed out during a daylight attack by British night bombers. The RAF treats us with a raid as they normally carry out at night. First, the Pathfinders turn up, which drop cascades and other markers, upon which hundreds of Lancasters unload their bombs. Among these, in the dust and muck, more and more marker flares are thrown in. Dust is blown up in large amounts and hangs in such a large cloud over the airfield that our airfield defences can't see much. When the attack is finally over and we take a first look at our 'drome, we see a moonscape, in which delayed action bombs go off. The taxi-tracks and runways are completely gutted and unusable, and several buildings and hangars are razed to the ground. Despite all this, a lot of our aircraft are still serviceable. The dispersal area of my 7th Staffel has suffered the most in the attack. Immediately in front of my machine a dud has fallen, I can see its tail still sticking out a few centimetres above the ground. A hangar nearby is on fire and has buried the Ju88 of our Staffel Technical Officer under its remains. I carefully roll my Ju88 away from the hangar and over the unexploded bomb and put my kite aside. It has been hit by a few bomb splinters, but nevertheless it can still fly!

Aided by the air traffic controllers, in between the bomb craters we mark a 600m [660yd] long runway in a field as best we can, although it is rather winding. We clear the path from splinters, fill in a few small craters and stamp the earth in them, and in the late afternoon the Gruppe takes off with twenty-eight aircraft from this moonscape, in which some 3,000 bombs of a larger calibre have left deep craters and whilst a few delayed action bombs are still going off!

We touch down at Wahn, are diverted to Hangelar in the evening and fly an operation over Stettin, but we have arrived too late to catch the bombers. A few days later our Gruppe is then diverted to Langendiebach where we will stay until mid-October.

Our machines are thoroughly overhauled in the maintenance hangar. By day, large American combat formations penetrate the Reich, but at night, the Tommy almost exclusively shows up in Mosquitos. In the meantime, juice has become very scarce, so that only expert crews still appear on the battle orders. Amongst these crews are the aces and those who can fly in any weather conditions. Nevertheless, we hardly fly on operations any more.

In *Tame Boar* night fighting the *SN-2* is jammed and hardly usable. During these months, a layer of dust is formed at greater heights in which the Tommy can hardly be traced. In all NJGs the number of kills drops dramatically, our leadership is filled with impotent anger, the Tommy laughs up his sleeve. The only thing that can bring relief is a new airborne radar. At last, we receive an *SN-2* with a wavelength of 7, the aerials of this device have been mounted at an angle. At first, we are able to gain mounting successes with this set, but the device

(Opposite) Junkers Ju88G-1s of NJG4 in late 1944 and early 1945. Through the Jägerstab's efforts, Ju88 nightfighter production reached a peak during 1944 and early 1945, with 2,873 aircraft built. Powered by two air-cooled 14-cylinder 1,700hp BMW 801 D radial engines, the G-1 reached a top speed of 520kph (320mph) at 6,000m (19,700ft). It packed a hard punch with two upward-firing MG151 20mm Schräge Musik *cannons and four forward firing MG151s mounted in an underbelly gunpack. The aircraft was equipped with the FuG 220* Lichenstein SN-2 *AI radar and the FuG 227* Flensburg *as standard. By early 1945, the majority of the Nachtjagd Gruppen operated the Ju88G-series against Bomber Command.* Coll. Charles F. Kern.

is soon jammed by *Düppel*. All we are left with now is target area night fighting.

Because of the continuing strafing and bombing attacks by Thunderbolts, Mustangs and Lightnings by day, and the Mosquitos by night, the Gruppe is split up and our Staffeln are dispersed over several 'dromes in mid-October. The Stab and 7th Staffel is now based at Gütersloh, the 8th in Bad Lippspringe and the 9th at Werl. Our operational region is the Ruhr area, where at last I get into a firing position once more on 10 October and I destroy a Lancaster over Duisburg. It is my twentieth aerial victory, including my *Abschüsse* in Russia whilst flying the He111. During this operation Lt Hoevermann and Stfw. Piewartz are shot down by Mosquitos on return over Gütersloh airfield, Hptm. Schneider belly-lands his burning aircraft on the 'drome and the crew is rescued. Yet, only little later, on 6/7 November, Hptm. Schneider is shot down and killed by a Mosquito, his crew save their skins by bailing out. A few days later, on 11/12 November the crew of Uffz. Wuttke crashes in bad weather, and only the *Bordfunker* escapes alive. Over Holland, on 1/2 January 1945, Fw. Werthner is shot down by a Mosquito and he is the only one who can escape by bailing out. His crew were killed in the attack.

From mid-November, following an order from the powers that be, we fly with a crew of four in the narrow cockpit and can hardly move any more. Eight eyes can see more than six and the *Bordfunker* should cover our backs because of the increasing Mosquito threat. From being the hunter we have become the hunted!

Despite all these adverse circumstances, Nachtjagd grew considerably during the last months of 1944, which was a remarkable achievement. Since the German aviation industry now largely concentrated on fighter aircraft production, and the Jägerstab at the same time did all it could to keep the training of crews up to a reasonable level, the arm expanded from 614 to 982 operational aircraft and crews between July and December 1944. Many Nachtjagd Gruppen even converted from the ageing Bf110G to the modern Ju88G-6 during the closing months of the war.

CHAPTER 9

Into the Jet Age: The Final Months

Although Nachtjagd expanded considerably in quantity during the second half of 1944, its aircraft were not re-equipped with new radio and radar equipment. German scientists and technicians worked hard on a new range of often revolutionary gadgets, but nothing became available in numbers. Nightfighter aircraft remained equipped with the *SN-2* radar, which could be heavily jammed, and *Naxos*, which was negated by new Bomber Command tactics. In practice, the German crews had to rely on the 'Mk I Eyeball', just as in the old pioneering days. Likewise, Nachtjagd's ground control organization struggled with the almost complete jamming of all its equipment, though there were experiments with searchlights, parachute flares, signalling in Morse code, etc. in an attempt to track the bomber streams and guide the nightfighters. However, there was no time left for Nachtjagd to introduce these new inventions and tactics on a large scale before the complete breakdown and eventual surrender in May 1945.

Fw. Fritz 'Pitt' Habicht served as *Bordfunker* in a He219 Uhu from the autumn of 1943. With his pilot Oblt Josef Nabrich, Staffelkapitän of 3./NJG1 he claimed fourteen bombers shot down, including two Mosquitos of the Light Night Striking Force. Nabrich was killed during a strafing attack on Münster-Handorf on 27 November 1944, after which Fritz crewed up with Hptm. Alexander Graf Rességuier de Miremont. Fritz tells of the difficult conditions under which Nachtjagd operated by the winter of 1944–45:

> For us nightfighter crews, the situation in the air war had become all but hopeless during the autumn and winter of 1944–45. Our adversary jammed our radio communications to a considerable degree and had effectively rendered our *SN-2* AI useless. The bombers, on the other hand, could detect us with their warning devices and fiercely defended themselves with their ten to twelve machine guns and unfortunately often with success. The British long range nightfighters, the Mosquitos, were faster than we were and tracked us with AI radar with an effective all-round range of 16km [10miles] and were equipped with IFF. Thus we, the former successful hunters, had been turned into the hunted. Consequently, our losses in crews and aircraft rose considerably.
>
> Due to the shortage of fuel, of the twenty to thirty operational crews in our Gruppe, only some five were normally scrambled to intercept the incoming bomber stream. This meant that of our NJG1 with its four Gruppen, only some twenty to thirty aircraft and just as few from our

neighbour Geschwader (NJG2) were thrown in to counter the between 300 and 600 heavy four-engined bombers and the over fifty British long range nightfighters on each raid. This led to grievous losses amongst us on every raid, and everyone of the flying personnel could count on the fingers of one hand when it would be his turn to die.

For all of these reasons, the growth of Nachtjagd over this period was one of quantity, not quality. Ironically, at the peak of its strength, hundreds of its aircraft could not be brought to bear against Bomber Command. By this time, nothing could save Germany from ruin save a quick and unconditional surrender – unlikely after the failure of the airborne landings at Arnhem in Holland. The Allied ground offensive from east and west had ground to a temporary halt, and only by the early spring of 1945 would the advance into Germany be resumed.

But the roof over Germany, which had never been made absolutely watertight, now completely caved in. Between August 1944 and March 1945, Harris's bombers resumed their strategic offensive against major German cities. Braunschweig, Nuremberg, Hanau, Würzburg, Pforzheim, Wiesbaden, Chemnitz, Dresden, Dessau, Potsdam and several cities in the Ruhr valley were largely transformed into rubble. Smaller cities, and towns, like Darmstadt, Bremerhaven, Bonn, Freiburg and Heilbronn, were also attacked, simply because Bomber Command ran out of major industrial cities to destroy. Purely military targets such as synthetic oil plants, traffic junctions, war factories, bridges etc. also featured on Harris's target lists during the final months of the war.

The overwhelming power of Bomber Command and the almost completely impotent Luftwaffe fighter arm during the closing stages of the war are underlined by two remarkable facts. In the first place, of the total tonnage of bombs dropped by Bomber Command during the five year offensive, almost half was dropped during the final nine months of the war. Secondly, over a third of all sorties flown by the British heavies during this period were made in daylight.

One remarkable development did take place in Nachtjagd during this period: the introduction of the Me262 twin-engined jet aircraft as a nightfighter. Oblt Kurt Welter, one of the top-scoring *Wild Boar* pilots during the Battle of Berlin had been ordered in the late summer of 1944 to find a solution to the LNSF Mosquito scourge. He soon found that the Me262 was the only German aircraft capable of ending the air supremacy of the 'wooden wonder'. From early

Two-seater Me262B-1a/U1 of 10./NJG11 at Berlin-Werneuchen, June 1945. This jet nightfighter was equipped with Neptun *radar and* Naxos Z. *Armed with four forward-firing nose-mounted 30mm MK108 cannons, it reached a top speed of 500mph (810kph) at a height of 20,000ft (6,100m).* Coll. Hans-Peter Dabrowski.

December 1944, he led 10./NJG11 or 'Einsatzkommando Welter'; and with only a handful of Me262s and some ten volunteer pilots, they tried to stem the almost nightly LNSF onslaught on Berlin. No less than 3,900 Mosquito bombing sorties were mounted by 8 Group against the 'Big City' during January–April 1945, dropping about 4,470 tons of bombs. Forty-eight Mosquitos, mainly aircraft of the Light Night Striking Force, were claimed destroyed by the jet pilots of Kommando Welter, although the LNSF only actually lost fourteen aircraft on these Berlin raids. Welter himself became a legend for claiming twenty-five Mosquitos shot down at night with the 262, although his claims are subject to some controversy (he is officially credited with only three whilst flying the jet).

Feldwebel Karl-Heinz Becker was trained as a fighter pilot during 1944 and was about to travel to Rheine at the end of the year where he was posted to JG26. This was not to be, as he recalls:

> The first attempts to employ the Me262 as a nightfighter must have taken place around November 1944. By this time, Oblt Kurt Welter had experimentally flown a single-seat 262 from Rechlin-Lärz airfield on operational sorties over Berlin. After these sorties, he usually landed on one of the 'dromes around Berlin and returned to Rechlin-Lärz the next day. He claimed a number of kills during these sorties. This led to the idea of using the Me262 on freelance night fighting missions over Berlin with the special purpose of combating the Mosquito. The Mosquito was fitted with Rolls-Royce Merlin engines and was simply too fast at height for our Bf109 and Fw190. A successful interception of these aircraft was only possible by diving on them from a greater height. This however led to little success and one was forced to look for a way out of this problem. The solution at this point in time had in fact been successfully tried out by Welter.
>
> In December 1944 he received the green light from the Reich Air Ministry to draw up a Special Command for the combating of the Mosquito with the Me262 in the Berlin area.
>
> On 15 December 1944 Welter gave me a ring and he asked me to travel to Rechlin-Lärz. Here, the Staffel 10./NJG11 was formed with the available materials. On strength were ten single-seaters with two additional reserve aircraft. Moreover, four crews were equipped with two-seaters. In January 1945, we moved to Burg, near Magdeburg, which became our regular operational base. Soon, we carried out our first

Close up of the nose of an Me262A-1 single-seater jet nightfighter of the Kommando Welter, with the nose-mounted FuG 218 Neptun *radar and armament of four 30mm MK108 cannons. The single-seater Me262 reached a top speed of 530mph (860kph) at 20,000ft (6,100m).*
Coll. Hans-Peter Dabrowski.

flights around the 'drome, followed by the first experimental sorties over Berlin. From mid-February, the first operational sorties were flown over Berlin, with good results. We mainly flew freelance night fighting sorties over Berlin against Mosquitos, often with the aid of searchlights. We also made good use of the vapour trails of enemy aircraft to detect them, and at times we were guided in the well known Himmelbett GCI. Central guidance was provided by the fighter controllers at Döberitz–Berlin, and our operations were co-ordinated by Oberst Wittmer under the code-name Silber (Silver), later altered to Ahorn (Maple). We also flew in daylight against reconnaissance aircraft.

The Arado 234 jet aircraft was also tried out by Oblt Welter, but he only flew this aircraft once! His judgement of the Ar234 as a nightfighter aircraft was completely negative, since at night the reflections on the honeycomb-like canopy had a great blinding effect on him. Each glass panel reflected both the outside sky and the radiation from the instruments. After some time in the air, he didn't know which side was up and which one down, he was completely at his wits end and ready to bail out.

I personally flew only the single-seater Me262, but I was originally scheduled to fly the two-seater with a radar operator. My *Funker* was already a member of the Staffel.

On take off, we very carefully had to shove the throttle forward whilst constantly checking the temperature, which should not exceed the 750 degree Celsius mark. Otherwise the blades in the turbines were deformed, which usually led to a crash immediately after taking off! When one throttled back at great height, the turbines could break down due to lack of oxygen necessary for the combustion process; the rotation velocity of the turbine blades became too small. Yet, in-flight re-starting of the turbines was possible.

Radio contact was over the FuG 16. In addition, we had an efficient IFF; on the ground radar a control lamp lit up after which we had to say over the R/T to our fighter controller 'Habe grosse Freude' ('Having jolly good time'). On receiving this message, we had established contact with the GCI station. Each one of our aircraft had it's own fighter ground controller officer. When we experienced jamming attempts by the enemy's RCM, our instructions were transmitted over the radio transmitter Brocken, which by means of its high kilowatt power could overcome the jamming attempts.

One tried to infiltrate the two-seaters into the bomber stream in the early stage of a raid. The problem however was our high overtaking speed; our Me262 was not equipped with speed brakes. Adapting to the speed of the enemy aircraft was only possible whilst climbing. This we did by entering our operational area some 1,000 to 1,500m [3,200 to 4,900ft] lower than the enemy, then slowly pulled up which gave us the same speed as our adversary. This automatically led to our attacks almost always taking place from below and behind ('von hinten unten'). Normally we had an overtaking speed of some 250kph [150mph]. The chance of actually shooting down an aircraft was small due to the very short time we had to aim accurately.

Due to these operational conditions, we only used two MK108 30mm cannons. Their rate of fire was not very high and the muzzle-velocity rather low in comparison to other gun systems, which always forced me to approach the adversary to very close range. A second approach on the same target at night was all but senseless, because we had to shoot them down whilst they were illuminated by searchlights and by the time I would have completed a second approach the target would have disappeared into the dark night.

For all these reasons, I always opened fire on the target at the last possible moment! I approached the target until I had both engines of the Mosquito filling the outer circle of my sights, distance some 180m [yd] or less, only then I opened fire, and under these conditions I always hit it. By only using the MK108 cannons with their very low rate of fire, this in turn led only in a small number of instances to the explosion of the adversary. Therefore, we hardly ever suffered damage to our own aircraft from parts of the adversary, which would have been the case if we had used other types of cannons. At the high speed we were flying, it was impossible to abruptly alter course in our Me262, due to the force of inertia! And moreover, Welter and I had a bit of a silent contest going, to see who succeeded in shooting an enemy aircraft out of the sky with the smallest quantity of ammunition.

Every fifth cannon shell was a glowing shell – tracers were too bright and therefore very irritating. Moreover, tracers were spotted quickly by the enemy. Between the glowing shells, we had armour piercing and 'mine' ammunition. The mine-ammo was most effective as on the slightest contact, this type of ammunition blew an enormous hole, or even tore off a complete wing. The MK108 guns had one distinct disadvantage: they were unheated. At great height, this caused stoppages, one flashed past the enemy and had no option left but to turn back to base. Therefore we started with putting oblique cannons into the Me262. The MG131 was used in these experiments, and it was installed behind the pilot's seat in a reinforced carriage. One had access to these guns through the large aperture leading to the radio equipment. The two MK108s were removed and the exits were sealed.

Strangely, we lost no aircrew through air combat. Five pilots in our Staffel were killed in crashes, with a sixth missing. Oblt Kurt Welter was killed in a car accident after the war.

Although Karl-Heinz Becker claims that probably no Me262 nightfighters were lost in air combat with Bomber Command aircraft, the following combat report suggests that at least one jet was lost due to return fire. On the night of 23 February 1945, Pforzheim in the south-west of Germany was the target for 367 Lancasters and thirteen Mosquitos. In a very concentrated and accurate area bombing attack, a hurricane of fire developed in which 17,600 people perished and 83 per cent of the town's built-up area was destroyed. Twelve Lancasters were lost, all falling victim to six ace crews of I. and II./NJG6, who claimed thirteen Lancasters destroyed in the target area between 20.00 and 20.30 hours. Jets were also active on this night. Lancaster III PB155 'K–Kripes' of 460 (RAAF) Squadron with F/O. Sam Cox at the controls fought off an Me262 at 20.14 hours whilst flying at a height of 7,500ft [2,400m] in the target area:

The Rear Gunner (F/O. Bert Curren) sighted two glows, light orange in colour, and evenly spaced approaching the bomber at a high speed, from the

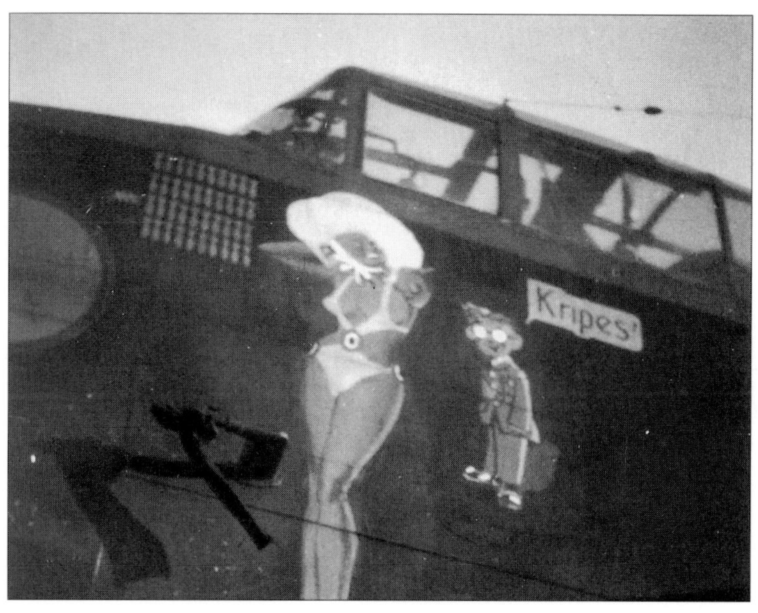

Lancaster III PB155 'K–Kripes' of F/O. Sam Cox and crew of 460 (RAAF) Squadron, January 1945. The little man to the right, looking at the 'luscious sort' with his eyes bulging out is exclaiming 'Kripes!' Coll. Alex Tod.

F/O. Sam Cox (third from left) and his Australian crew from 460 (RAAF) Squadron posing on the wing of Lancaster 'K–Kripes' in early 1945. P/O. Don Crosby (2nd from right, mid-upper gunner) and F/O. Bert Curren (2nd from left, rear gunner) claimed an Me262 jet nightfighter shot down from this aircraft on the night of 23 February 1945 during a raid on Pforzheim.
Coll. Alex Tod.

Port Quarter (nearly Port Beam) at an approximate range of 1,200yd [1,100m]. The glows banked round to the Port Quarter and at 800yd [700m] (approximately) the RG. [Rear Gunner] ordered a corkscrew port, and both AG.s [Air Gunners] opened fire. The fighter followed the bomber in the corkscrew and closed to 400yd [350m]. At this stage the fighter broke away fine Port Quarter down, and both gunners saw a small fire in the starboard wing. The fire was seen to grow larger as the fighter went down, and the silhouette of the aircraft could be seen. The MU. [Mid-Upper] (P/O. Don Crosby) recognized the wing as that of an Me262. Both AG.s followed the burning a/c to the ground, where it exploded on impact. The explosion was also seen by the bomber's pilot and WOp. (P/O. Alex Tod). Throughout the attack, both gunners fired continuously, the RG. using the GCS and the MU. the Reflector sight for sighting purposes and claim the fighter as destroyed.

Another pilot flying the Me262 jet in 10./NJG11 was Lt Kurt Lamm. After having served in 5./JG301 as a *Wild Boar* pilot during the autumn and winter of 1943–44, he went on to fly daylight sorties against the American combat boxes during the summer of 1944. Although he managed to destroy a B-24 Liberator, he was shot down by return fire and severely wounded.

Only in February 1945 was Lamm fit for flying duties again. Oblt Welter then asked him to join his 'Kommando Welter':

Lt Kurt Lamm, who flew the single-seater Me262 with 10./NJG11, combating the Light Night Striking Force Mosquito raids against Berlin during the final months of the war. Coll. Kurt Lamm.

> Many people might wonder why we took up the challenge of flying on operations in the Me262 jet at night by this stage of the war, which was obviously all but lost. There were two decisive factors which made us decide to continue flying and fighting. We were passionate pilots, and the challenge of mastering the then fastest jet fighter aircraft at night and gain successes with it incited us, moreover since we had taken severe losses by an adversary much superior in strength. We also hoped in a small way to lighten the sufferings of the population of Berlin with our high-performance jets. This latter motive however bordered on sanctimonious self-deception. After all, what's the use of shielding the roof of a house, of which the foundations have already been bombed away?
>
> Our Staffelkapitän Kurt Welter, who had some months of flying experience in the Me262, briefed me on the flying techniques. His detailed practical instructions struck a note of warning to proceed cautiously. He literally told me: 'This fast deer will have a few surprises in store for you too'. Since we had no two-seater training aircraft at our disposal, I mounted a single-seater and did a few circuits and bumps. Two longer flights by day in the area of our 'drome and two at night followed, and then I was ordered to collect a Me262A–1a from Zerbst. Without any red tape, I now was a nightfighter pilot in 'Kommando Welter'.
>
> I flew my first operational mission on 27/28 March 1945. With four aircraft we took off for a sortie over Berlin, as Mosquitos were reported approaching the Reich's capital. Kurt Welter instructed me: 'You will be the last one to take off, as this will enable you to see the illuminated flare path in time on your return. The vertical flak-searchlights positioned to the left and right of our path of final approach are our "gate" through which we must fly'. Soon after taking off, whilst still at low level, the undercarriage of my aircraft dropped all of a sudden. This was the first surprise. My vast flying experience and fast reactions came to my rescue. I immediately put the aircraft's nose down, went over into horizontal flight, pressed the button for 'undercarriage up' and I was lucky. The undercarriage stayed locked up. I proceeded on my way towards Berlin whilst climbing with some 20m/s. The thought crossed my mind that most other, less experienced, pilots would have crashed in similar circumstances.
>
> Over Berlin, concentrations of searchlights attempted to catch the enemy bombers in their cones. Then we got into range of our adversary. The first one I heard over the R/T was Welter, he exclaimed 'Pauke' and 'Horrido' to announce his first success of the night. Subsequently, each one of us shot a Mosquito down in flames to crash into the ruins of Berlin. Then once more, Welter shouted 'Horrido'. Two successful interceptions in one sortie, he was the only one who could pull that off. He had an exceptional feeling for the game of night fighting. 'Bonzo', his cloth dog talisman, accompanied him on every sortie.

Ofw. Karl-Heinz Becker flew one of the other three Me262s on this night:

> As an example of my victories, my sixth *Abschuss*, which was the 27th of our Staffel, took place on 27.3.1945. I took off at 20.58 hours for a night sortie over Berlin. The visibility over the area was bad, and I did not succeed in getting a target aircraft that was caught in the beam of a searchlight. Therefore, I flew back into the area over the city. Above and on a reciprocal course, I then spotted a Mosquito that gave itself away with a long vapour trail. Shortly before I saw the aircraft, I observed how it dropped cascades. I curved towards it and slowly got closer to the target. Flying at a height of 8,500m [27,600ft], I clearly saw the target at 21.38 hours and opened fire from a distance of some 150m [yd] whilst pulling up the nose of my aircraft. I hit it squarely. On pulling my aircraft away to the left, I observed large burning parts of the Mosquito falling down and hitting the ground scattered in sector FF5 near Nauen. On landing, I found that a part of the Mosquito had left a dent in the right turbine cowling of my Me262. I had used 20 mine-shells of 30mm ammunition.

Ofw. Becker's sixth and final Mosquito victim in 10./NJG11 was MM131 XD–J of 139 Squadron, which had taken off from Upwood at 19.12 hr for a sortie against Berlin. S/Ldr H.A. Forbes DFC, the navigator/bomb aimer escaped alive to be taken prisoner, but not a trace has ever been found of his pilot. Journey's end came over Berlin for F/Lt. André A.J. van Amsterdam, a Dutch escapee who was decorated with the DFC and the Dutch Air Force Cross. He is commemorated on panel 266 of the Runnymede Memorial. Lt Kurt Lamm continues:

> During our flight back to base at Burg, we received the warning of Mosquito intruders lurking in the vicinity. It was their tactic to try and pick us off from behind on final approach. After having passed through the 'gate', the two searchlights immediately formed a cone and the light flak defences hosed up their ammunition into the cross of light. This saved my skin. When I had touched down and taxied into the dispersal area, I was informed that one Mosquito which had actually followed me in had been shot down.
>
> Whilst my machine was being towed into the hangar, the mechanic groundcrews observed: 'You have brought home the confirmation of your kill, look at the dents in the leading edge of the wing'. I had rushed towards the fast bomber aircraft with a speed of some 850kph [530mph] and was so fascinated by the action that I had opened fire a bit on the late side. The burst of fire from my four 30mm cannons had torn up the Mosquito and I had to pull away steeply to avoid getting hit by the debris flying around. Kurt Welter was not pleased when he saw the dents in my machine and warned me to keep a better eye on the difference in speed during the coming missions.

The Light Night Striking Force lost three aircraft from eighty-two sorties despatched for Berlin on the evening of the 27 March, an unusually high loss percentage, as the average losses usually only amounted to 0.99 per cent of the fast Berlin raiders. Two of the three aircraft are believed to have fallen victim to the jets of 10./NJG11.

Not only were Mosquitos engaged by the Me262s of Kommando Welter, as P/O. Ron James, air gunner with 214 (SD) Squadron in 100 Group recalls. His crew went to Leipzig on 8/9 April 1945 in support of a Main Force raid on the oil plant in nearby Lützkendorf:

> This operation was the first time that I saw a jet fighter in action. Looking below our aircraft I saw what appeared to be a rocket coming towards us, but on reaching our level it straightened out and I recognized it as an Me262. The speed that it was travelling at was unbelievable. Fortunately for us it had a Lancaster in its sights, only a few hundred feet away, and in a matter of seconds it had fired and turned away leaving the Lanc. in flames. I was very glad that we were not the chosen target.

At last, the Me262 proved to be an effective solution to the Mosquito, but it was a case of too little, too late. The war would be over before a truly decisive jet nightfighter force could be created.

Although Nachtjagd failed to intercept Bomber Command on most nights during the final months of the war, it remained a force to be reckoned with right to the end. During January, 1945, German nightfighters claimed 117 of the 134 heavies that failed to return from night raids on the Reich. F/Sgt Doug 'Ben' Benbow from Adelaide, Australia, personally experienced this final sting of Nachtjagd. 'Ben' was the WOp. in F/O. Peter Birt's (who hailed from Perth) veteran crew in 460 (RAAF) Squadron. F/Sgts Spen Symes (navigator) and Ern Truman (bomb aimer) both came from Melbourne, and F/Sgt Gordon Wilson (tail gunner) of Nowra and F/Sgt Doug 'Scarlett' O'Hara (mid-upper) from Glen Innes completed the Aussie part of the crew. Sgt Alf Fields (the flight engineer) came from Halifax in the UK. 'Ben' Benbow recounts his crew's final operation:

> We arrived back at 460 Squadron, Binbrook, after leave to find that our kite 'A–Able' had been taken up by a new crew on a training flight and who, on their return to base had landed in the bomb dump, not doing much good to the bomb dump nor 'A–Able'. Next day, 28 January 1945 we were on standby and that night we took off for Stuttgart in 'S–Sugar'. No sooner were we airborne than Alf said to Pete: 'This isn't "S–Sugar", its "S–Shit", bloody Packard-Merlins instead of Merlins, we'll never keep up!' How true, we were twenty minutes late over target and a Junkers 88 came down on us from seven o'clock high at about 23.43 hours. It was either at or near full moon and it was possible to clearly see every detail of the Ju88. Gordon to Pete: 'Dive port Pete, dive port!' Down we went but as we sheered off the 88 hit us with cannon shells in the port inner motor and wing, both of which burst into flames.
>
> The thing that stands out in my memory is the flashes of the cannons – who could forget that? Pete to Alf: 'Feather port inner Alf'. Alf to Pete: 'She won't Pete'. The fire extinguishers had no effect. The port wing was extensively damaged and cannon shells were lacing through the fuselage.
>
> A second 88 joined in the attack. Gordon to Pete: 'I got one Pete'. His last words. I was at the astrodome and saw it going down. Then a long burst of cannon shells took off the rear turret and Gordon with it. I stepped down from the astrodome and sent an SOS to Group with our call sign. Not, of course, for help but just to let them know the time of the attack. By now we were in a very steep dive from 18,000ft [5,500m]. Pete: 'Bail out, bail out'. Cannon shells were still hitting the aircraft. Alf, Ern and Spen went out the front hatch, I went to the rear and found the rear door shot to pieces and the broken hydraulic lines to the rear turret spraying burning oil across the open rear end.
>
> Scarlett was wandering about in shock, perhaps wounded, so I grabbed his arm and signalled forward. I scrambled over the main beam, gave Pete who was still at the controls, the thumbs up and then found the forward hatch cover had somehow blown diagonally across the hatch and jammed, so there was much kicking and pulling before forcing an exit. I was partially concussed by a cannon shell exploding nearby just as I exited. I was the last man out of the last bomber shot down in the last raid on Stuttgart in W.W.II.
>
> The aircraft with full bomb load, 10,000lb [4,500kg] of mixed high explosives and incendiaries, hit the deck and exploded at about 23.49 hours. I later learned that the remains of Pete and Scarlett lay nearby, the remains of the tail turret and some bits and pieces of Gordon were found some distance away. Spen, Ern and Alf landed in and about Stuttgart, whilst I landed in the top of a very tall pine tree many miles from Stuttgart. My chute had only just opened. I thought I had suffered a bit of damage, as it turned out later, it was quite a bit. It will never be known if Scarlett had been wounded, he may have got out of the aircraft but too late. There hadn't been any panic but I still remember the fear and the way Pete stuck to the controls and that Gordon had shot down an 88.
>
> Our crew which, because of overall ability, had been considered the one most likely to survive

Australian Lancaster crew of 460 (RAAF) Squadron, (l–r): F/Sgt Doug 'Ben' Benbow (WOp.); F/Sgt Spen Symes (Nav.); F/Sgt Doug 'Scarlett' O'Hara (MUG.); F/Sgt Gordon Wilson (RG.). Ben and Spen were taken prisoner on 29 January 1945, whilst Scarlett and Gordon were killed.
Coll. Doug Benbow.

had been taken out by two 88s because of those bloody Packard-Merlins.

During February 1945, Nachtjagd flew 772 sorties resulting in 181 *Abschüsse* for the loss of forty-seven fighters. During this period of sharp decline, the old Nachtjagd foxes remained successful even though the odds were stacked high against them, as *SN-2* radar operator Uffizier Walter Schneider, *Bordfunker* in Hptm. Hager's (St.Kpt. in II./NJG1) crew, recalls:

On 21/22 June 1944, the *Bordfunker* of our Staffelkapitän, Fw. von Bergen, was killed in air combat during a mission in He219 G9+LP. After we had been posted to Düsseldorf in September 1944, I finally became the *Bordfunker* of Staffelkapitän Hptm. Hager and his gunner, Ogfr. Bärwald. I was very lucky to acquire such an experienced and successful 'driver', the more as our adversary by now had gained complete air superiority. Especially in daytime, we had become the hunted.

Hager preferred the Me110 over the He219, which he had already flown in June 1944. I also preferred to fly in the Me110. I feared that in the event of the He219 crashing on a cratered runway, it would easily stand on its nose or even somersault once the nose wheel had collapsed. Besides, there were rumours of the ejection seats dislodging easily. These were necessary as the crew in the He219 sat in front of the propellers.

At 18.15 hours on 31 December 1944 we took off for a mission in the Essen area. Our machine was a Bf110G with registration G9+AP. By this time, the night fighting tactic was always of the *Wild Boar* type. Our *SN-2* airborne radar was once again heavily jammed, but nevertheless usable. I kept two *Viermots* on my screen, which Hptm. Hager shot down in flames near Essen at 19.00 and 19.05 hours. We landed again at 19.30 hours.

On 21 February 1945 we took off at 00.24 hours. I soon spotted a *Viermot*, which our pilot shot down after a short chase at 01.12 hours. On the outbound flight from Düsseldorf, I managed to get hold of another one on my radar and this one was made to crash at 01.23 hours. Later on the same day, at 22.48 hours, we again received orders to take off, this time we had to fly in the direction of Duisburg. Soon, we encountered

Uffz. Rolf Michelsen, who served as Bordfunker *with 5./NJG2 in Ju88s from mid-1943 till the end of the war. In all, he contributed towards the destruction of nineteen British bombers, mainly Lancasters, but at a price. On 20/21 December 1943, his first pilot, Lt Heinz Schrode, shot at a Lancaster on its bombing run near Frankfurt/Main from a distance of 50yd (m). Possibly due to nervousness, as it was the crew's first interception, Heinz Schrode hit the bomb load, whereupon the 'Lanc' exploded, taking the Ju88 down. Michelsen and his pilot, although injured, managed to bail out, but FE. Gefr. Sepp Wolf was killed. When Michelsen got back to his unit after three months in hospital, his old pilot was dead, killed in a crash near Wesel on 21 January 1944. He now crewed up with Major Max Eckhoff of the Gruppenstab II./NJG2 and scored a further eighteen* Abschüsse *in the Reichsverteidigung. On 16/17 March, 1945, the crew flew their last sortie: 'Take off from Seligenstadt/Main during bombing raid on Nürnberg, we shot down four bombers, Ju88G-6 received hits from return fire in starboard engine, tried to reach Stuttgart/Echterdingen on one engine, by 23.30 hours port engine on fire. Bail out at low level, come down safely, Max Eckhoff dead, didn't get out any more.'*
Coll. Rolf Michelsen.

the formation of bombers, from which we succeeded to shoot down in all six *Viermots* between 23.09 and 23.21 hours. By skilful use of the oblique cannons, my pilot was able to set the bombers on fire with short bursts into the fuel tanks which were situated between the engines. The crews thus had more time to safely bail out. After this exploit I was commissioned.

On 21 March 1945 we took off from Werl at 02.30 hours for our final successful mission against the enemy. It was to become our hardest battle. A large-scale raid was reported over Kassel. After a prolonged search I at last was able to trace three *Viermots* on my radar screen. Whilst we gave chase on the first one, which we shot down at 03.01 hours, the second and third one had moved away a considerable distance. After an intensive search I managed to get hold of one of them again. Only moments later, our pilot was in position and shot it on fire at 03.04 hours. I needed some time longer to find the third one again. I hardly had finished telling my pilot the position of and distance from the target, when I yelled: 'We're on top of it already!' I glanced out of my cockpit and to my horror I watched its tail unit approaching quick as lightning. I was prepared to bail out, but my pilot managed to get in a burst from point blank range at 03.11 hours and with a brilliant swerving manoeuvre avoided a collision. The rear gunner had no opportunity at all to return fire. Undoubtedly, the aircraft's pilot had lowered the flaps to rob us of the time necessary to aim and shoot accurately. By now, it was time to return to base. Up to this time, our 'drome at Düsseldorf had been reported to be still in action, but often we had experienced enemy nightfighters shooting up the airfield at the last moment and leaving it u/s. Fortunately, luck didn't leave us on this night and we finally touched down at Werl at 04.02 hours. On this sortie, we had caught and destroyed three RCM aircraft which tried to delude our fighter controllers into believing they formed a major bomber force. These were Hptm. Hager's forty-sixth to forty-eighth aerial victories. I personally contributed to his last thirteen kills (all Lancasters and Halifaxes).

Since our air gunner, Ogfr. Bärwald had flown with Hptm. Hager for a longer period than me, he had personally experienced more kills than me. Whereas the great series of combat victories had to be attributed mainly to the personal skills of the pilot, I have to give credit to our air gunner for the fact that we were never shot down ourselves.

After the capitulation we were interned by the RAF at Silberstedt in Schleswig-Husum. We were treated correctly. In July 1945, I was released.

In fact, Hager's final three *Viermot* kills were probably Lancasters from a force of 224 aircraft that accurately bombed the synthetic oil plant at Böhlen on 20/21 March, for the loss of nine machines. One RCM Liberator and an RCM Fortress were also lost on this night.

Many experienced Nachtjagd crews met a violent end during these final months of the war, as Fw. Fritz Habicht recalls:

From around 19.00 hours on the evening of 3 February we were sitting in cockpit readiness in our machines on the edge of the runway. We had received reports of strong formations of British bombers flying in. Despite the desperate overall war situation we had to and wanted to continue chasing the enemy, in an effort to shelter the people in our cities as best we still could!

Soon, we were ordered to take off, with the instruction to head for radio beacon 'Rheine', in order to intervene from there into a suspected heavy bombing raid on the Ruhr area. We sneaked away from our 'drome at low level to evade any lurking British long range nightfighters and when we arrived on the northern edge of the Ruhr we climbed to our operational combat altitude. Meanwhile, we both kept a sharp look out – I also used the flickering and heavily jammed *SN-2* to watch the airspace – and shortly we spotted the first flares being dropped by the raiders over the industrial area, as well as searchlight and flak activity. It could burst out any moment now.

All of a sudden, in front of us the green marker flares (or Christmas trees as we called them) were positioned by the British Pathfinders to mark the target. In my opinion it was the Dortmund–Essen area, over which the bombing inferno now broke from the clear winter skies. Innumerable flashes of bomb strikes, the muzzle fire of the flak, many ghostly arms of the searchlights, enemy flashlight-bombs exploding in the sky to blind us, and bombers going down like flaming torches produced a horrifyingly impressive picture of the night bombing raid, which had an even more terrible effect by the ever more expanding fires raging below.

There – a few hundred metres overhead, in the cone of a number of searchlights is a *Viermot* bomber! We're going to catch that one! He turns in a wild corkscrew, in an effort to vanish into the darkness again and finally jettisons his bombs. For a few seconds we watch how they tumble down. At once, we have reached the height at which the bomber flies, at 6,000m [19,500ft]. Hopefully it will remain in the cone of light, as my radar set just indicates muddled and vague echoes. The bomber has turned onto a westerly course and makes a desperate effort to escape the flak and searchlights. As we chase him we also have to fly through the bursting flak, and we are shaken up uncomfortably by the shock waves of the exploding shells. We are now flying some 200m [yd] behind the aircraft which we have identified as a Lancaster and are in attacking position. I inform our operations HQ of our position and with the cry of 'Pauke Pauke' I announce the start of our attack. My pilot manoeuvres us to some 60 to 80m [yd] behind and a few metres below and opens fire. And then it happens what one has so far only experienced in one's worst nightmare, in all its dangerous reality! Two searchlights have swung backwards

He219A-5 DV+DL being serviced. This aircraft was equipped with both the old FuG 212 Lichtenstein C1 *and the FuG 220* SN-2 *(with the larger radar antennae).* Coll. Hans-Peter Dabrowski.

and catch our machine, we are sitting in a glaring and blinding light.

The events now tumble over each other! At the same instant when our six cannons blaze away, the return fire from the four machine guns in the tail turret of our adversary flashes up. It rattles violently in our machine, only seconds ago I heard the victory cry of my comrade and I saw the burning bomber plunging down, and now our 219 is also burning over the whole right wing, including the engine. I get the impression that we are also exposed to gun fire from an enemy aircraft flying behind us, as from behind, flames are also bursting out of our fuselage. I feel blood trickling down from the left side of my breast – obviously the result of a blow I received during the exchange of fire. My headphone is deaf, all my radio equipment is smashed to pieces. The cockpit is full of a stinging thick smoke and tongues of flames. We must get out as quickly as we can, must jettison the canopy, I pull the lever and the next moment raging whirlwinds of fresh air tear at us. Our burning machine plunges down in a shallow power dive with a speed of over 500kph [300mph]. I turn around and see my mate Axel as a shadow in the dark, desperately trying to control the dive somehow or other.

He now signals with his hand to get out! Bail out! I sit in the prescribed position, reach for the ejection lever, but in vain – it has disappeared! Because we sit in the forward area of the cockpit, we need ejection seats to get out safely as without these, we would either be cut to pieces by the propellers or smash ourselves up against the tail unit.

A terrible fright shoots through me. So far, no one has escaped alive without the ejection seat! I bend over to the back, grope and search, but the lever has been shot away. Just now, my pilot ejects himself, he must have assumed that I have already gone overboard.

Sitting with my back to the direction of flight, I try and pull myself over the edge of the back of the cockpit with all my strength. As soon as I have made some progress, the whirling air drags me back with frightful violence. The 100m [yd] needle of the altimeter in front of me rotates much too fast for my liking. Still 3,000m [9,700ft] left, but how many seconds or minutes before I crash to my death? Almighty God, come to my aid, let me live!!! I struggle upwards again and again, but all the time the swirling air sucks me down again. 'In these seconds, one's life flashes in front of one's eyes', as the saying amongst the airmen goes, but this time, it is a dramatic, deadly earnestness! There, the altimeter indicates less than 1,000m [3,200ft], soon the end will come. I cry out loud to give myself courage, I pray … and make a final desperate effort to get out. I brace myself against the side of my cockpit, am still stuck fluttering in the blowing gale, extricate myself and then I somersault backwards over the fuselage and away.

Suddenly, my reason works quite clear and sharp. I cannot wait for the usual three seconds to pass before pulling the ripcord, as any second now I can thud down. I therefore pull the metal handle rapidly, but still I plunge down – doesn't the canopy unfold?!? Yes, it does! I almost lose consciousness due to the sudden and violent jerk, but immediately after an excruciating pain tears through my body and I find myself crashing into some tall trees in a wood –then the light goes out!

Cramps of pain, exploding ammunition and the glaring flames of our machine burning in the neighbourhood jerk me from my unconsciousness. I cry out for help, call for my Ruth and try to fire off an emergency flare, but to no avail. I then again lose consciousness.

Fritz Habicht remained unconscious for four days before he woke up in hospital. He had lost his memory, but when he was shown a picture of a lover of his youth, everything came flooding back. 'Pitt' remained in hospital for a long time with all his ribs broken or bruised, a broken pelvis, severe concussion, internal injuries and scores of other, less serious injuries. He had been very lucky to escape alive, as the collar of his Mae West was riddled with bullet holes to the left and right of his neck – he had got away with only a graze on his shoulder. His pilot Hptm. de Miremont was also admitted to hospital with a graze on his skull. In all, Bomber Command lost

Fw. Fritz 'Pitt' Habicht, Bordfunker *in 3./NJG1 during 1943–45. In the crew of St.Kpt. Oblt. Josef Nabrich, Fritz contributed to the destruction of twelve* Viermots *at night, plus four unconfirmed. The crew also claimed two Mosquitos of the Light Night Strike Force. 'Pitt' was severely injured during his last sortie on the night of 3/4 February 1945, when his He219 was shot down by return fire from a Lancaster over Roermond.* Coll. Fritz Habicht.

twelve Lancasters of two forces attacking benzon plants at Bottrop and Dortmund; two fell victim to I./NJG1.

On the night of 13/14 February 1945 Bomber Command attacked Dresden, a Gothic city on the River Elbe. Close on 800 Lancasters dropped 2,660 tons of bombs in a standard area bombing raid on the city. In the course of the raid, a firestorm developed, as had happened in Hamburg some eighteen months earlier. In the sea of fire, an estimated 50,000 Germans perished. Some fifteen hours after the British raid, the US 8th Army Air Force attacked the burning city with 311 B-17 Flying Fortresses, causing the death toll to rise to at least 80,000. Nachtjagd had to watch, impotent, as the tragedy of Dresden unfolded. Only some twenty-seven aircraft were scrambled, despite the bad weather, but they were sent from beacon to beacon and most crews could not get at the bomber stream. Six Lancasters were lost, two crashing in France. Just one bomber fell victim to a nightfighter.

Ritterkreuzträger Major Werner Hoffmann, Gruppenkommandeur of I./NJG5 with forty-five confirmed victories took off from Parchim at 01.01 hours to try and intercept the Dresden force:

> Another distinctly depressing experience for me happened on the night of the Dresden raid. The enormous mass of Britons flew over the city, whilst all our equipment was heavily jammed. I did not succeed in shooting any of these huge bombers down, one only saw them lit up for a fraction of a second when bombs exploded down below, the next moment they were swallowed up by the darkness again, and thus it was completely impossible to catch one. By this time, early 1945, the British completely jammed our radio and radar etc. We were practically dependent on our eyes, for all practical purposes we were blind again.

Werner Hoffmann claimed two *Viermots* destroyed on the next night, and three more on the evening of 16 March 1945, surviving the war with fifty confirmed *Abschüsse.* Ofw. Helmut Bunje of 4./NJG6 also recalls the raid on Dresden and on the nearby Chemnitz on 14/15 February:

> Our leadership, obviously through inadequate information, did not let us take off to intercept the Dresden force on the night of 13/14 February, and on the next night, we were scrambled too late and moreover were sent on a wrong heading. The situation in the air was confused. We spotted some lights in the Darmstadt area, and then strong formations were reported to the north,

Ofw. Helmut Bunje, pilot with 4./NJG6, who shot down twelve night bombers between March 1944 and March 1945. Coll. Helmut Bunje.

heading towards Magdeburg... After receiving further instructions, we flew towards radio beacon 12 which was positioned on a mountain, when all of a sudden, far away to the south-east, the target for the bombers was lighted. Already from a distance of some 200km [124miles] the enormous glow of fire was visible: Dresden!

Only a successful infiltration into the stream of bombers flying homewards could bring us success. From my position over the Harz, I headed on a course of 170 degrees. Some time passed – the burning target was in the meantime at an angle to our aircraft, when our *Naxos* indicated a target aircraft. We concluded that not far away, a Briton was using his navigation radar. Almost simultaneously, I saw a bomber silhouetted against the clear sky, it was on my left side on a diagonal course. The Lancaster was diving at high speed towards the layer of cotton wool-like clouds, which stretched out at a height of some 3,500m [11,400ft]. We couldn't get into a shooting position any more in our Junkers. Our adversary had already dived into the clouds and had disappeared! Still, from our unjammed *SN-2* radar, we established that it flew just under the upper ceiling of clouds. We adjusted our speed to that of the bomber and then very slowly entered the blue-grey clouds. The distance was closed to 400 ... 300 ... 200m [yd], and that was the limit of the range of our *SN-2*! For every 100m [yd], we used ten seconds. We now had to be very precise in our calculations: count to twenty, slowly lose a little height, left thumb on the course-steering switch, right forefinger on the cover of the gun tit – eye fixed to the reflector sight ... 15 ... 16 ... 17 ... There! Two giant tail fins, only a few metres in front! In between them and almost over us the gun turret of the tail gunner! ... Thumb and forefinger reacted correctly – whilst slowly pulling away, the Lancaster was covered in my gunfire. It started to burn! I immediately dived away to the right. Over our left wing, a man flashed past in a fraction of a second – there was a gaping hole now where the glass tail turret had been only seconds ago. The yellow glow of fire became fainter in the hazy clouds whilst the bomber plunged earthwards.

It was not without a feeling of pride when I reported on this unusual interception to my Kommandeur immediately after landing, when Peter Spoden came storming in: 'Now listen to what happened to me: I have one on my *SN-2*, it flies somewhat below me in the clouds. Well, I think, get at it slowly and shoot it down! I'm only 300m [yd] away, when I see a glow of fire, and all of a sudden there are two blips on my screen, one goes down and one stays up! Some damn asshole just shot the chunk out of the sky in front of my face – in the clouds!

Ofw. Helmut Bunje's victim crashed to the west of Saalfeld at 21.50 hours, as his sixth victory, one of thirteen heavies lost on the Chemnitz raid on 14/15 February 1945. Bunje went on to claim another six Lancasters in the course of the next four weeks, ending the war with twelve confirmed night victories.

One week after Dresden, Nachtjagd scored its final, albeit marginal, success of the war. In the early hours of 21 February, Bomber Command mounted a major raid on Dortmund, with other smaller forces attacking Düsseldorf, Monheim and the Mittelland canal. Of the 1,283 RAF sorties despatched, twenty-two aircraft were lost when a handful of *Experten* managed to infiltrate the bomber streams bound for Dortmund and Düsseldorf. Major Schnaufer, Kommodore of NJG4, claimed two bombers shot down as his 108–109th victories. Hptm. Hager, St.Kpt. of 6./NJG1 also claimed two bombers destroyed. Hptm. Breves of IV./NJG1 took off from Düsseldorf airfield at 02.13 hours and went on to claim his fourteenth to sixteenth victories, all three *Viermots* in the Ruhr area in a sortie lasting 110 minutes. One of these aces' victims may well have been Lancaster PB701 GT–Q of 156 (PFF) Squadron, flown by F/Lt Andy Pelly. Australian W/O. Bill Pearce was the WOp./AG. in this crew:

> On 20 February 1945, F/Lt Pelly's crew were listed on the battle order, to fly in 'Queenie'; so we were off to do it again. This was my forty-second operational flight. Our target for the night was to be the Rhenania Ossag Oil Refinery at Reisholz, about 20 miles [32km] south east of the centre of Dusseldorf. This was to be a diversionary raid of 173 aircraft, the main target was to involve 528 aircraft in a raid on Dortmund. This was another 'Happy Valley' target for us, but I didn't think we let the Ruhr 'hoodoo' worry us too much, it was another 'op', so, get on and do it!! Our duty was to back up visually, other TIs on the ground, at the direction of the Master Bomber. It was to be a six-minute attack.
>
> We took off at 22.30 hours, and the trip was going well, until about three hours later, in the morning of 21 February, when we were approaching the target area. We had just started on our bombing run, when what all Bomber Command aircrews feared might happen, did happen to us. There was a loud, rendering, explosive 'whoomp', (I can't really describe the sound), it came from not very far from me, and I knew instantly what it was, we had been hit by either flak or gunfire from a nightfighter. I was latter to find out that we had been hit by a burst of 20mm cannon shells, fired by a German Ju88 nightfighter. The Ju88 was fitted with *Schräge Musik*, which, translated to English means 'slanting music', but I can assure you, there is nothing musical in the sound of a burst of 20mm cannon shells, when they blast into an aeroplane.
>
> The burst of cannon fire hit the tail and rear turret, killing my rear gunner, and then went into the starboard inner engine, elevators, and petrol tanks. The engine immediately exploded and caught fire. I felt bloody awful, I remember I went cold all over, I felt this sensation surge through my body, my world just shattered to pieces around me. This was emphasized by the feeling in the pit of my stomach, which felt like it had dropped down into my boots.
>
> We had not yet reached the target, we were still carrying our full bomb load, the 4,000lb [1,800kg] 'block buster', other high explosive bombs and target indicating flares. We also still had about half of our fuel load on board. With fire in the starboard inner engine, and with the adjacent petrol tanks, this made our position rather untenable, and the Skipper came up on the intercom and ordered us to 'bail out'. I immediately acknowledged this order, with, 'WOp. bailing out'. I didn't have to be told twice.
>
> All this took only a fleeting period of time to happen, and while I fully realized that I was in real trouble, I did not freeze with fright, I knew that I had to move, and move I did. We had practised the 'abandon aircraft' procedure on many occasions, and now the time had come to put this training into practice. I discarded my flying helmet and oxygen mask, we were hit at about 18,000ft [5,500m] and were using oxygen. The oxygen point is a fixed position on the side of the aircraft, and the mask is attached to the helmet, so, to move in a hurry, the helmet and mask have to be removed. Therefore, I was immediately feeling the effects of lack of oxygen.

The lack of oxygen certainly took a lot of the terror out of what happened to me next, which was probably just as well. I was in a rather dangerous situation, but I went about the business of bailing out of the aircraft in a rather carefree manner. After I had discarded my helmet and oxygen mask, I picked up my parachute pack from the floor beside me and started to make my way to the exit point, which was the rear door of the aircraft on the starboard side, just a few feet forward of the tail plane. I had to climb over the main wing strut, which runs across the fuselage, just to the rear of the cabin. I sat on the strut, fumbling to attach the parachute pack to the clips on the front of the harness. This was where the lack of oxygen was starting to have its effect. I was feeling very light headed, and I remember thinking that I had better get moving, and not being greatly concerned about my predicament!

I eventually reached the rear door, and I was lucky in so far as the aircraft was still flying pretty well straight and level, making it easier to get to it. My mid-upper gunner was there before me, his turret being closer to the door than my position in the cabin. He had opened the door and was standing in the doorway. I was just able to tap him on the shoulder as he went out. However, he had made a fatal mistake, maybe he had panicked, he had picked up his parachute pack by the shiny handle, the 'D' handle of the ripcord, and the pilot 'chute had exploded in the aircraft. He had, however, clipped the 'chute pack to his harness, and gathered the canopy in his arms in front of him, and I remember seeing the folds of white silk as he stood in the doorway. His body was found later on the ground, still attached to his parachute and harness. I think his death was caused when he left the aircraft. Even in my light headed lack-of-oxygen condition, I saw his body go below the tailplane, and the open 'chute canopy go over the top. He was then pulled back to, and around and over, the tail plane, and was probably killed by the impact.

Now it was my turn to leave the aircraft, with Germany about 18,000ft [5,500m] in darkness below me. I was crouched over the doorsill, still rather light headed. I remember looking at the fire in the wing, around the engine nacelle, and thinking, 'Gee, that sure is burning well'. The next moment, I must have leaned a bit further out, I was torn out of the aircraft by the slipstream, and falling head over heels through space.

After tumbling for what seemed an age, I can still remember I had another thought, and that was, 'Well, I'd better pull it now'. I found the ripcord handle and pulled it, the 'chute opened, my descent was halted, and I was left suspended, I felt at the time, almost on nothing, in the middle of a black void, I could barely see the 'chute canopy above me. As I hung there, with the dark

W/O. Bill Pearce, WOp./AG. 156 (PFF) Squadron, shot down on his forty-second 'op' on 20/21 February 1945, by a Ju88 fitted with Schräge Musik *cannons.* Coll. Bill Pearce.

night around me, I was overcome by a feeling of absolute loneliness. The cold, and the lower altitude, brought me back to my proper senses, but then I could hear other aircraft 'swishing' past me. I could not see them, they must have been above me, but I had the frightening thought of what would happen if one of them hit me! These aircraft soon passed on, and I was left hanging there in complete silence, in the darkness and absolute loneliness.

As I drifted down, I could make out a bank of cloud below me, and moving around on the underside of this cloud, was the end of a searchlight beam. This gave me another frightening thought, of breaking through the cloud, being picked up by the searchlight, and then becoming target practice for an anti-aircraft battery. (This was a very real fear. I had heard some terrible stories of 'things' that had been done to parachuting aircrew, and by both sides!!). Again my feelings were groundless, the searchlight was switched off before I entered the cloud bank. I drifted down through the cloud bank, and below it, the darkness was even more complete, I couldn't see the ground. I realized at this time, that I was drifting slightly backwards, and trying to remember my parachute drill, I started trying to spin myself around, to approach the ground frontwards. I wasn't very successful in my attempts to achieve this, and then I hit the ground and crashed in an ungainly heap.

My parachute collapsed gently on to the ground beside me, there was very little wind blowing. This was fortunate for me, as I had injured my left shoulder in my badly directed landing, and my left arm was already practically useless. However, I had been fortunate enough to land in the middle of an open paddock, and did not have any trouble, using only my right hand, in releasing the parachute harness buckle. I gathered up the parachute and harness and stood there listening, there was nothing to hear, I was expecting the German Army to jump on me at any moment. I groped my way to the edge of the field, and buried my parachute, harness and Mae West jacket under fallen leaves and branches from nearby trees.

So, I had arrived in Germany, quite unexpectedly, a real case of, 'well fed and in a warm cosy bunk in England one night, in the middle of the Ruhr Valley, cold, injured, miserable and bewildered, the next night'. What do I do now?

Bill Pearce was on the loose for six days and nights, before he was taken prisoner and spent the remaining months of the war in a POW camp. Apart from the rear and mid-upper gunner, Bill's navigator also was killed by a mishap when he bailed out.

The following night, 21/22 February, 1945, Bomber Command mounted raids on Duisburg, Worms and the Mittelland canal, despatching a total of 1,110 sorties. German ground control identified the course and height of the bomber stream heading for Worms and before the bombers reached their target, succeeded in perfectly infiltrating fifteen 'Spitzenbesatzungen' of NJG6 into the bomber stream in the area of Mannheim–Worms. For a change, the crews experienced no jamming of their *SN-2* sets and encountered no Mosquitos either. They did not let this opportunity go to waste, and within twenty-nine minutes, between 20.30 and 20.58 hours, eight crews claimed twenty-one bombers destroyed in the target area. Ofw. Günther Bahr of 1./NJG6, flying Bf110 2Z+IH with Fw. Rehmer as *Bordfunker* and Uffz. Riediger as gunner was the most successful; he shot down seven Lancasters of the Worms force in quick succession between 20.30 and 20.50 hours, before the heavies had dropped their bombs on target. Bahr was awarded the Ritterkreuz a month later and survived the war with thirty-seven *Abschüsse.*

A few *Experten* from other units were also guided into the bomber streams and, helped by the bright moonlight, wrought havoc among the heavies. Hptm. Breves of IV./NJG1, who had already destroyed three *Viermots* on the previous night, was scrambled from Düsseldorf again at 23.44 hours. In a fifty-minute sortie he claimed two more *Viermots* in the Ruhr area as his seventeenth and eighteenth and final victims of the war. Hptm. Johannes Hager, St.Kpt. of 6./NJG1 claimed six as his fortieth to forty-fifth victories: he

Armourers loading 50 Squadron Lancasters, 1944–45. Coll. Roy Day.

was consequently awarded the Ritterkreuz. Hptm. Heinz Rökker, Ritterkreuzträger and St.Kpt. of 2./NJG2 also destroyed six as his fifty-sixth to sixty-first kills between 20.46 and 21.19 hours. Finally, Hptm. Heinz-Wolfgang Schnaufer, Kommodore of NJG4 claimed seven Lancasters in a record nineteen minutes between 20.44 and 21.03 hours, as his 110th to 116th *Abschüsse*! One of his victims was probably Lancaster III NE165 'Y' of 83 Squadron, piloted by G/Capt. A.C. Evans-Evans DFC, Station Commander of Coningsby. NE165 crashed near Eindhoven with the loss of six of the crew. One of the gunners, P/O. E.H. Hansen, an Australian, was the only survivor. No Nachtjagd aircraft were lost on this night. Bomber Command lost a total of thirty-four aircraft, or 3.1 per cent, an unexpectedly heavy loss, probably all of them shot down by nightfighters. However, this represented merely a pin-prick to the mighty Bomber Command, and did not stop the heavies carrying out devastatingly successful raids on three major targets that night.

F/Lt Roy Day was Captain of Lancaster SW261 'H–How' in 50 Squadron. His aircraft formed part of the force of 165 Lancasters and twelve Mosquitos of 5 Group that headed to the Mittelland Canal at Gravenhorst. Their 'Lanc' was to contribute to the breaching of the canal with fourteen 1,000lb [500kg] bombs, with half hour delay fuses. The raid was a complete success and the canal rendered completely unusable, but on the way back, German nightfighters mingled with the bomber stream, as Roy Day recalls:

Roy Day's crew in 50 Squadron, posing in front of Lancaster PB821 with 'clear vision' rear turret, 1945. Coll. Roy Day.

The initial sighting was by the mid-upper gunner, Peter Macdonald, who reported a Mosquito passing overhead! As soon as the Bomb Aimer/Front Gunner, Roy Skinner, identified it correctly as a Ju88 I initiated a corkscrew down and to port. When we realized the Ju88 was not giving chase I turned the tables and went in pursuit of him, saying over the intercom something like 'Shoot the bastard'. Roy Skinner opened up as soon as he got his sights to bear, but to no effect. The Ju88 passed under us, which brought the mid-upper turret into action and Peter opened up. I could now see the aircraft and shortly after Peter opened fire I saw a flash amidships and, it must have been at this stage that he realized he was under attack and dived to port, and we lost him.

Fighter flares were seen along our track and as we continued on our flight home we saw many aircraft shot down by fighters. Thirteen Lancasters were lost, two were from our squadron. The percentage loss of just under 8 per cent was almost the highest I experienced out of twenty-three sorties flown.

We reported the incident as best as we could recall on return to base, Skellingthorpe, and some time later we were credited with 'Ju88 damaged confirmed' – I proudly entered this remark in my log book. The day after the incident the aircraft, SW261, was taken to the butts and on test firing the front turret guns they were found to be grossly misaligned; which explained Roy's lack of success.

One of Nachtjagd's final victims. This 49 Squadron Commonwealth crew was shot down by a Ju88 on their seventeenth 'op', during a raid on the Harburg oil refinery on 7/8 March 1945. Left to right: F/O. Roussell Stark RAAF (Pilot, KIA); Joe Dixon (RG., POW); Fred Brennan (Eng., POW); Ralph Bairnsfather RAAF (BA., KIA); Gus Lovett (WOp., KIA); Paddy Gilbert (MUG., KIA); Johnny Yeoman RAAF (Nav., POW). Coll. Martin B. Stark.

Nachtjagd's success on 20/21 and 21/22 February was one of the last for an arm rendered almost completely impotent. During February 1945, the organization began to break up, as Germany and her armed forces continued their collapse into chaos. Firstly, Schmid's I Jagdkorps was dismantled. All nightfighting units now came under command of IX Fliegerkorps, led by Major Peltz, the former 'Angriffsführer England' or 'Attack Leader England'. During March, seventeen nightfighter Gruppen were disbanded, their redundant personnel being transferred to the infantry and flak arms. Apart from 'Operation Gisela' on 3/4 March, (described in Chapter Two), there were very few occasions when Nachtjagd crews took off in force to hunt Bomber Command. On one or two nights however, single units were still successfully led into the bomber streams. On 14/15 March and 16/17 March, a handful of experienced crews of NJG6 claimed respectively sixteen and twenty *Viermots* shot down for the loss of only six aircraft and ten crew members.

Twenty-two-year-old and 6ft 3in (1.9m) tall F/O. Roussel Stark (RAAF) was one of Nachtjagd's final victims. 'Russ' lifted Lancaster

'M–Mother' of 49 Squadron from Fulbeck's runway on the evening of 7 March 1945 for his crew's seventeenth operation. The Lancaster formed part of a 234 strong Lancaster force of 5 Group, supported by seven 'Mossies', which set out to bomb the oil refinery at Harburg. Sgt Joe 'Dixie' Dixon from Liverpool, England, manned the four Brownings in 'M–Mother's' rear turret:

> On the night of 7 March we bombed the oil refinery at Harburg. We watched our bombs drop right in the middle of the fire, everybody was laughing and joking about the state of the fire when Russ spotted a Fw190, there were a few planes going down in flames. We ran into a lane of flares which were lighting the sky up and Russ and Paddy Gilbert, the mid-upper gunner, saw a Ju88 pass underneath us. When I spotted it I opened fire and got it. We did some manoeuvres then flew level, Russ and Paddy watched the Ju88 going down in flames. I was temporarily blinded by my own gun fire when something hit my turret and set it on fire. I told Russ and started getting ready in case we had to get out. A few seconds later Russ gave orders to jump out immediately. I tried to get out and had a bit of a fight to do it as my turret was now well alight, Russ kept control of the plane to give us a chance to get out. I believe Paddy and Gus Lovett, the wireless operator, were killed outright. When I did finally get out and I was floating down, seconds later I saw our plane hit the ground in flames. Russ and Ralph Bairnsfather, the bomb aimer, must have died at once.
>
> After I got down I found somewhere to stay the night. The following day I set out walking at about 6am. After going 25 miles [40km] Fred Brennan, the engineer caught up with me, he had slept in the same wood as I did but neither of us had known it. Fred told me that the last he saw was Ralph fastening his straps ready to jump. He must have lost his life by only a second or two. Later on in a Stalag (I was taken POW on 8 March) I met Johnnie Yeoman, the navigator. He was badly scratched because he fell in an awkward place near some barbed wire. He had been unable to see what was going on from his place in the plane.
>
> I honestly believe Russ could have saved his own life at the risk of the others, but he thought of his crew first. He gave his life to try and save the rest of the crew. Three other mothers gave their sons in the cause of Freedom so we can only hope that Russ, Ralph, Gus and Paddy lie peacefully together at rest.

F/O. Russ Stark and his three crew members were laid to rest at Becklingen War Cemetery, not far from Hamburg. In all, the Harburg force lost fourteen Lancasters. 189 Squadron, also operating from RAF Fulbeck, was hit especially hard; it lost four out of sixteen aircraft dispatched on the raid. From other raids on Dessau and Hemmingstedt, plus minor operations, a further twenty-seven aircraft were lost this night.

The disbanding of the majority of the Nachtjagd Gruppen during March was a sad end for a once mighty arm. The end of the war found eager aircrews grounded, fighting with *Panzerfaust* and *Panzerschreck* as anti-tank detachments in the climax of the land battle. There were still some 200 combat-ready nightfighter aircraft and crews available for the air defence of the Reich, but fuel had all but completely run out and the remainder of the ground control organization was overrun by the Allied armies. Early April saw the end of IX Fliegerkorps: the majority of Peltz's nightfighter aircraft and crews came under the command of Luftwaffe Command North-East in Schleswig-Holstein. Only a few experienced crews, both in conventional and in Me262 jet aircraft, ventured into the night skies any more, as Lt Kurt Lamm of 10./NJG11 recalls:

> On 12 April, our operational flying from Burg came to an end. Our presence at Burg had not remained a secret for long. Besides our unit, a number of 'Mistel' composite aircraft – Ju88s loaded with explosives and with Me109s mounted on their backs – as well as jet reconnaissance Arado 234s were stationed at our 'drome. The Allied bomber formations treated us to a thorough bombing raid and reduced

everything to ashes. It was easy for them, as there were hardly any airfield defences.

A few Me262s which had been dispersed in blast pens in the woods had remained unscathed. 10./NJG11 was moved to Lübeck. After a corduroy road had been constructed, our machines were towed to the highway. Low bushes had grown up in the centre strip, and we had to cut some of them. We took off from the right side of the highway and flew to Lübeck at low level.

My final operational sortie from Lübeck, which took place during the second half of April 1945, was decisive for my attitude towards the war until the end of the hostilities. Two Me262A-1a aircraft were prepared for the mission. Oberleutnant Peter Erhardt (an experienced *Tame Boar* night-fighting ace with twenty-two victories in NJG5) and I were on immediate readiness. Formations of Mosquitos were reported heading for Berlin. The flare path at Lübeck was not switched on and we took off into the darkness under a new moon. We were not yet at our operational height when we arrived over Berlin, and the Mosquitos had already discarded their loads and turned back home. Oberleutnant Erhardt and I both successfully engaged and destroyed a Mosquito.

We were the only aircraft left in the sky over Berlin, which was lit up by the fires raging below, and the Flak searchlights were therefore switched off. We had received orders to land at Staaken near Berlin, as this was the only airfield left in the area with night-landing facilities still in operation. In order to save petrol I throttled back to economical cruising speed and flew on at a height of some 8,000m [26,000ft]. Enormous clouds of thick smoke billowed up over Berlin. After several requests for a course to steer and a despairing cry for 'fireworks', I finally spotted flares in the boiling sky over Staaken. Oberleutnant Erhardt had probably flown somewhat lower and in a more advantageous position, for he had already touched down. With one eye, I regularly glanced at my fuel gauge and at my watch. Normally, we should have landed after sixty minutes at most. Suddenly, the memories of bailing out of my burning Me109 to the south of Wiener–Neustadt came flooding back. The last thing I wanted was to bail out over the burning ruins of Berlin. I once more called: 'Am very thirsty, please ignite fireworks!'

The airfield was somewhere in front of me. My eyes were straining to look through the layer of smoke and dust. A stroke of flyer's luck: in front of me there was the chain of lights marking the runway. Immediately after touching down, one turbine started to cough. The fuel tanks ran dry after having taxied only halfway to the airfield hangars. With a flight duration of one hour and twenty-three minutes, I had set a new record for an operational flight in the Me262 at night. However, that was not a hero's act.

I was completely worn out and kept sitting in my 'fast deer' until a tractor arrived to pull me away. I wondered if I had already left my power of reason behind at Burg, or only after having moved to Lübeck, and when would I come to my senses again. I confronted myself with the pressing question if these missions made sense any more. My feelings told me that I had changed since taking off from Lübeck for this mission. Actually, for some time already we were not the same enthusiastic young men, who had gone to war for 'People and Fatherland', and with the song 'Germany, you sacred word, full of endlessness, through the ages you will be blessed' on our lips. Our youthful ideals for a 'national-socialistic' Germany had been shaken a long time ago, if not buried completely. In my mind, I desperately searched for a light at the end of the tunnel. It dawned on me that in the future, I would only permit myself to be submitted to my own will. I strongly felt that I should quit the errors and flaws of my young life immediately.

At Lübeck, we were again subjected to an area bombing raid and we moved to the highway at Reinfeld near Hamburg. I received orders to fetch the last remaining Me262 from Rechlin, where the Red Army already had advanced to within a few kilometres, and fly the aircraft to Schleswig. Welter reluctantly accepted my decision not to board an aircraft any more after this final flight. For example, I should have ferried

> another machine to Prague. It was all madness. The end then came in Schleswig, where we were interned by the British. Royal Air Force experts took over our aircraft. There was a lot of interest in our Me262s. Allied test pilots flew them everywhere, including in Farnborough.

On the night of 25/26 April, *Experte* Oblt Herbert Koch of NJG3 claimed a Lancaster destroyed as his twenty-third, and Nachtjagd's final, victim of World War II. Two weeks later, the curtain fell for the Third Reich. Manfred Eidner concludes:

> Many people often wonder how it was possible that Hitler was able to win over a large part of the German people for his terrible aims, from the moment of seizing power in 1933 until war broke out in 1939. With hindsight, I would comment that he attracted the young generation by means of a purposeful propaganda. The best example is myself.
>
> In 1935, I became a member of the 'Young People' (an organization of the Hitler Youth for ten- to fourteen-year-old children). Here the principles of a military training and the claims for power of the German people were explained to us. The Hitler Youth Flyer organization took me over in 1939. We constructed gliders and learned how to fly. The organization was perfect. We flew our gliders during the week-ends and were an inspired bunch. In the so-called flyer camps lasting some four weeks, our dreams of flying came true. Aged sixteen, I qualified as a glider pilot and was mentally ready to sign up with the Luftwaffe for a twelve-year commitment. Having completed my training as a fitter, I was posted to the Aircrew Training School

Broken Wings. Ju88 B3+KK of KG54 with broken back at Ingolstadt airfield in May 1945. Coll. Bill Pearce.

A/B61 at Oschatz in 1942. Here I attended a technical course for flying personnel and finally I was posted to the 11th Staffel of IV./NJG1 at Leeuwarden in 1943.

By this time, the war had been decided for a long time but we youngsters of eighteen still believed in Hitler's wonder weapons. Every day and night, I witnessed the Allied bomber formations flying in and how they destroyed the German cities, arms industry and chemical factories. I experienced my first bombing attack at Leeuwarden, when between 400 and 500 heavy bombers knocked out our 'drome within forty minutes on an extraordinarily beautiful summer's day.

Around the clock on every day, we performed our servicing duties on the aircraft, as it was our first priority to keep the aircraft serviceable. Still, by this time already we experienced problems with the supply of spare parts and fuel.

Since I was still with the technical servicing personnel, but had also volunteered for flying duties, I was soon called up to fly on operations. In my case, I was the NCO fitter of the aircraft and flew on operations as gunner. The night fighting tactic was to fly with the incoming or outward bound bomber streams and try and shoot aircraft down in the process. After landing on an airfield somewhere in the Reich, I then serviced the aircraft. One night, we took off for a mission from Bergen airfield in northern Holland in our Me110, fitted with two auxiliary tanks and an extra gun pack with two MG151s under the fuselage. Guided by a ground station, we were led into an enemy formation and we succeeded in shooting down a Lancaster. We completely surprised the bomber crew with a burst from below and behind. We hit the aircraft between the inner engine and fuselage, it burst into flames and only moments later it plunged down.

The strategic round-the-clock bombing campaigns of the RAF and USAAF left most German cities in ruin by May 1945. Depicted here is Cologne; clearly recognizable are the famous cathedral, which miraculously escaped major damage, and the city's main railway station. Coll. Ted Baumfield.

When I reflect on my experiences today, I often feel bad. Millions of people lost their lives in this war, caused by the mad ideas of a small group of men who wanted to rule the whole of Europe. Now, the nations of this world have the obligation to make sure that such dreadful events never happen again.

Glossary

ADGB: Air Defence of Great Britain.
AG: Air Gunner.
AI: Airborne Interception Radar.
BA: Bomb Aimer.
Bordfunker: German radar/radio operator.
Dunkle Nachtjagd (*DuNaJa*): Dark Night Fighting. Radar-directed night fighting without the aid of searchlights.
Düppel: German code name for *Window*.
EK: Eisernes Kreuz or Iron Cross.
ELINT: ELectronic INTelligence. The gathering of information on the operation and performance of electronic equipment by electronic means.
Experte: Ace.
FE: Flight Engineer.
Fernnachtjagd: Long range night fighting (intruding).
Flensburg: German device to enable Luftwaffe nightfighters to home onto *Monica*.
Gardening: RAF mine-laying.
GCI: Ground Controlled Interception.
Gee: British navigational device.
Helle Nachtjagd (*HeNaJa*): Illuminated night fighting.
Himmelbett Nachtjagd: Close range and radar ground-controlled night fighting (roughly equivalent to Allied GCI tactics).
IFF: Identification Friend or Foe.
(Kleine) Indianer: (Small) Red Indians, i.e. Mosquito night intruders.
Kombinierte Nachtjagd (*KoNaJa*): Combined Night Fighting, the co-ordination of Flak, searchlights and nightfighters over the bombers' target.
Kurier: Luftwaffe codeword for heavy bomber.
Lange Kerle: Long range German nightfighter pursuit of British bomber aircraft over the North Sea.
Lichtenstein: German airborne interception radar.
LNSF: Light Night Striking Force.
Marie: Luftwaffe code for distance to target (in kilometres).
Monica: Tail warning radar device in British bombers.
MUG: Mid-upper Gunner.
Nachtjagd: Night Fighting Arm.
Nachtschlachteinsatz: Ground attack sortie.
Nav: Navigator
Ober Kommando der Luftwaffe (OKL): Luftwaffe High Command.
Objektnachtjagd: Target area night fighting.
OCU: Operational Conversion Unit.
OTU: Operational Training Unit.
Pauke! Pauke!: 'Kettledrum! Kettledrum!' (going in to attack!).
RCM: Radio Counter Measures.
Reichsverteidigung: Air Defence of the Third Reich.
RG: Rear Gunner.
R/T: Radio Telephony.
Schräge Musik: 'Slanting Music'; oblique/upward firing guns in German nightfighter aircraft.
Seeburg: Plotting table or screen used by fighter controllers in Himmelbett control rooms.
Serrate: British equipment designed to home in on *Lichtenstein* AI.
Spitzenbesatzung: Ace crew.
2nd TAF: Allied Second Tactical Air Force.
Viermot: Four-engined bomber.
Wilde Sau (Wild Boar): Tactic of using mainly single-engined night fighters over Bomber Command's targets, relying on freelance interceptions whilst aided by the light from fires and searchlights.
Window: Metal foil strips dropped from aircraft to produce many false targets on enemy radar.
WOp: Wireless Operator
Y-Verfahren: Y-Service, or ground-controlled navigation by means of VHF.
Zahme Sau (Tame Boar): Tactic of feeding twin-engined nightfighters into the bomber stream with the aid of a running commentary over R/T and then letting the fighters 'swim' with the stream whilst shooting down as many bombers as possible.
Zerstörer: 'Destroyer', Bf110 twin-engined fighter aircraft.

Appendix I. Luftwaffe Operational Chain of Command 1939–45

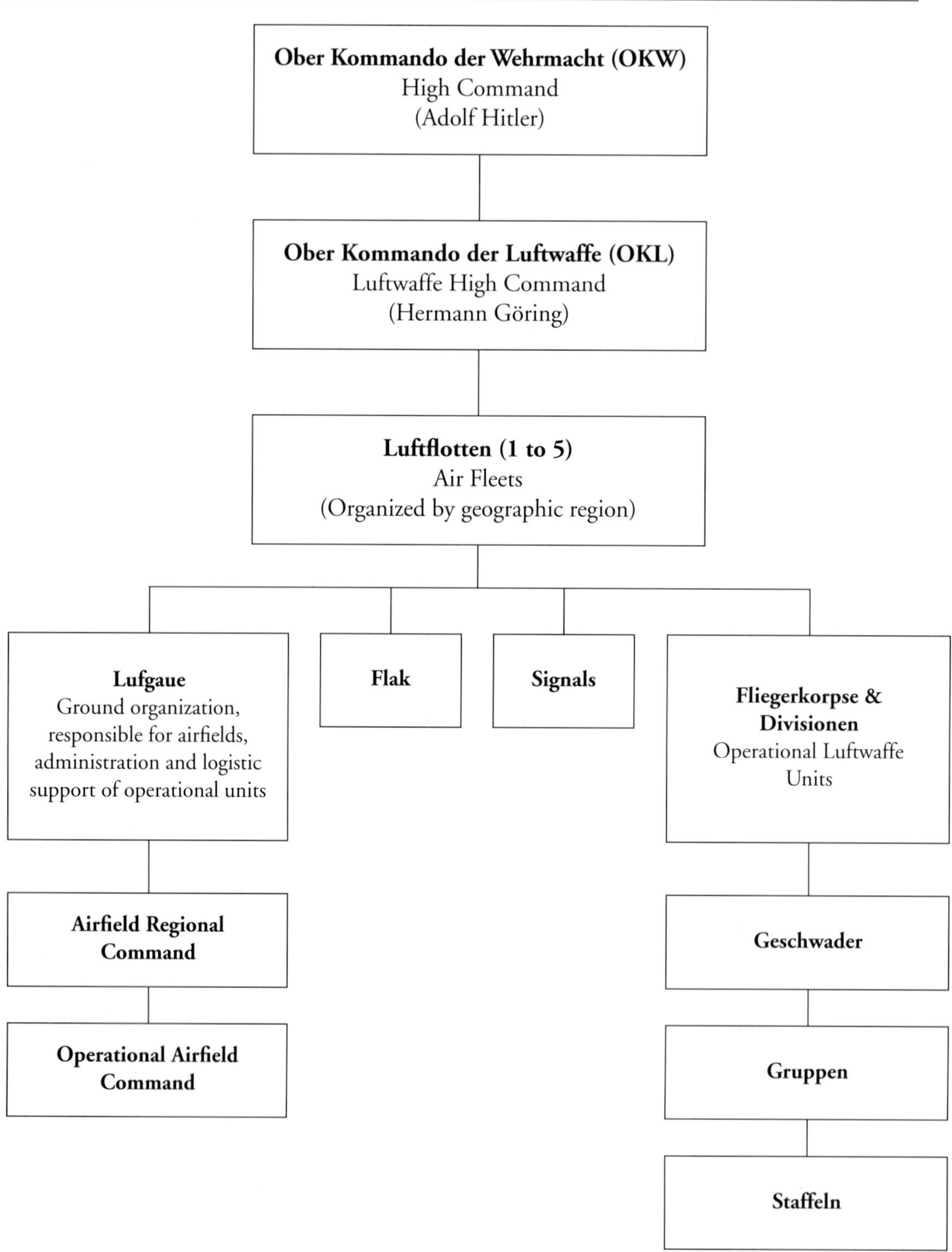

Appendix II. Organization of Luftwaffe Operational Units

Operational Luftwaffe units were sub-divided as follows:

Geschwader (Wing)
Gruppe (Squadron)
Staffel (Flight)
Kette (four-aircraft unit)
Rotte (two-aircraft unit)

Each Geschwader nominally consisted of between 100 and 120 aircraft. These aircraft were divided between a Geschwader Stab (Wing Staff Flight) and three Gruppen. A Gruppe consisted of between thirty and thirty-five aircraft. Each Gruppe was sub-divided into a Gruppen Stab (Squadron Staff Flight) and three Staffeln of some ten aircraft each. A Staffel consisted of between two to three Ketten of three or four aircraft each. The smallest fighting unit was the Rotte of two aircraft; a leader and his wingman.

The operational task of a Geschwader was recognized by its prefix. Thus, a Night Fighter Wing (Nacht Jagd Geschwader) was abbreviated to NJG. Day Fighter Wings were merely abbreviated to JG (Jagd Geschwader). Gruppen were indicated with Roman characters. For example, the third Gruppe of the First Night Fighter Wing was abbreviated to III./NJG1. As already stated; each Gruppe was sub-divided into three Staffeln, which were indicated with Arabic numerals. Thus, the eighth Flight of the First Night Fighter Wing was abbreviated to 8./NJG1 which in turn belonged to the III./NJG1.

Appendix III. Battle Strength of Nachtjagd in W.W.II., and Battle Strength of I Fliegerkorps during the Battle of Berlin

Battle Strength of Nachtjagd in W.W.II.

	Intended battle strength	*First line strength*	*Serviceable aircraft*
1 Jan 1941	197	164	106
9 Sept 1941	254	263	174
2 Feb 1942	367	265	159
30 Jun 1942	406	255	167
1 Aug 1942	465	322	214
10 Dec 1942	548	375	282
10 Feb 1943	653	477	330
9 Aug 1943	831	577	376
26 Dec 1943	966	627	421
7 Feb 1944	966	557	350
1 Jul 1944	?	830	500
27 Jul 1944	1,059	849	614
17 Sept 1944	1,086	959	792
17 Nov 1944	1,170	?	905
1 Dec 1944	1,319	1,355	982

Battle Strength I Fliegerkorps, 15 September 1943 till 15 May 1944

15 Sept 1943	339
1 Oct 1943	285
15 Oct 1943	221
1 Nov 1943	241
15 Nov 1943	272
1 Dec 1943	259
15 Dec 1943	260
1 Jan 1944	258
15 Jan 1944	224
1 Feb 1944	179
15 Feb 1944	259
1 Mar 1944	273
15 Mar 1944	271
1 Apr 1944	233
15 Apr 1944	372
1 May 1944	451
15 May 1944	419

Over the same period, roughly covering the Battle of Berlin, I Fliegerkorps lost 349 nightfighter aircraft, or more than its complete frontline strength on 15 September 1943.

Appendix IV. Fernnachtjagd Claims and Losses

Abschüsse claimed by I./NJG2, 1940 and 1941:
1940: 18 claims.
1941: 125 claims.

Admitted RAF losses caused by Fernnachtjäger:
1940: 5 aircraft.
1941: 86 aircraft.
1942: No aircraft.
1943: 4 aircraft.
1944: 40 aircraft.
1945: 38 aircraft.

Losses I./NJG2, 1940–1941:
1940: 21 aircraft (3 Bf110s, 15 Ju88s and 3 Do17).
1941: 55 aircraft (52 Ju88s and 3 Do17s).

Losses I./NJG2 in flying personnel, 1940–1941:
1940: 32 aircrew.
1941: 74 aircrew.

Appendix V. Total Nachtjagd Victories and Losses during W.W.II

NGJ1: 2,173 confirmed night and 145 day victories.
NJG2: 800 confirmed night and day victories.
NJG3: 820 confirmed night and day victories.
NJG4: 579 confirmed night and day victories.
NJG5: 850 confirmed night and day victories.
NJG6: 400 confirmed night and day victories.
NJG101: 200 confirmed night and day victories.
NJG102: 50 confirmed night and day victories.
NJG100, 200
and independent Gruppen and Staffeln: 1,070 confirmed night and day victories.
Wild Boar JG300/301/302: 330 confirmed night and day victories.

Total Luftwaffe Nachtjagd: 7,308 confirmed night and day victories.

Nachtjagd victories, split up into years and theatres of operations:

Year	*Reich Air Defence and Occupied Western Europe*		*Mediterranean*	*Eastern Front*	*Totals*
	Day	*Night*			
1939	0	0	0	0	0
1940	42	0	0	0	42
1941	421	1	5	0	427
1942	687	4	51	38	780
1943	1,820	110	45	425	2,400
1944	2,335	100	2	545	2,982
1945	528	0	0	33	561

Total Nachtjagd losses in W.W.II:

Aircraft (including *Zerstörer* losses): 6,700 aircraft destroyed, plus 4,300 10–60% damaged. Of these losses, 4,800 aircraft were destroyed or damaged in action. 6,200 were lost due to non-operational causes.

Flying personnel (excluding *Zerstörer* losses): 3,800 KIA/MIA, plus 1,400 WIA.

Appendix VI. Luftwaffe Ranks and their RAF Equivalents

Luftwaffe:	*Royal Air Force:*
Flieger (Flg.)	Aircraftsman 2 (AC2)
Gefreiter (Gefr.)	Aircraftsman 1 (AC1)
Obergefreiter (Ogefr.)	Leading Aircraftsman (LAC.)
Hauptgefreiter	
Unteroffizier (Uffz.)	Corporal (Cpl)
Unterfeldwebel (Fw.)	
Feldwebel (Fw.)	Sergeant (Sgt)
Oberfeldwebel (Ofw.)	Flight Sergeant (F/Sgt)
Stabsfeldwebel	Warrant Officer (W/O.)
Leutnant (Lt)	Pilot Officer (P/O.)
Oberleutnant (Oblt)	Flying Officer (F/O.)
Hauptmann (Hptm.)	Flight Lieutenant (F/Lt)
Major (Maj.)	Squadron Leader (S/Ldr)
Oberstleutnant (Obstlt)	Wing Commander (W/Cdr)
Oberst	Group Captain (G/Cpt.)

Bibliography: Published and Unpublished Works

Aders G., *Die Geschichte der deutschen Nachtjagd* (Stuttgart 1978)

Der Adler, 1939–1945. Eine kommentierte Auswahl abgeschlossener, völlig unveränderter Beiträge aus der Propaganda-Zeitschrift der Deutschen Luftwaffe (Hamburg 1977)

Air Ministry, *The Rise and Fall of the German Air Force 1933–1945* (London 1948)

Barker R, *The thousand plan* (London 1966)

Bartz, K., *Swastika in the air* (London 1956)

Bekker, C., *The Luftwaffe war diaries* (London 1964)

Bekker, C., *Augen durch Nacht und Nebel* (Hertford 1980)

Bishop, E., *Mosquito: The Wooden Wonder* (Shrewsbury 1990)

Boiten, T., *Intruders: Het Britse nachtjager-offensief 1941–1945* (unpublished university thesis, Groningen 1991)

Boiten, T., *The Luftwaffe Nachtjagd, 1933–1945: History of a strategic failure* (unpublished university graduate thesis, Groningen 1992)

Bowman, M.W. & Cushing, T., *Confounding the Reich* (Sparkford 1996)

Bowyer, Ch., *Mosquito at War* (London 1973)

Bowyer, Ch., *The Wellington Bomber* (London 1986)

Braham, B., *Scramble!* (London 1961)

Brandon, L., *Night Flyer: RAF night fighters in action* (London 1969)

de Bruin, R., et.al., *Illusies en incidenten: De militaire luchtvaart en de neutraliteitshandhaving tot 10 mei 1940* (Den Haag 1989)

Brunswig, H., *Feuersturm über Hamburg* (Stuttgart 1978)

Chorley, W.R., *RAF Bomber Command Losses of the Second World War, Vol.I (1939–1940); VolII (1941); Vol.III (1942); Vol.IV (1943)* (Earl Shilton 1992–96)

Constable, T.J. & Toliver, R.F., *Das waren die deutschen Jagdfliegerasse 1939–1945* (Stuttgart 1972)

Cooke, R.C. & Conyers Nesbit, R., *Target: Hitler's oil. Allied attacks on German oil supplies 1939–45* (London 1985)

Cooper, A., *Bombers over Berlin: The RAF offensive, November 1943 – March 1944* (Wellingborough 1989)

Cooper, M., *The German Air Force 1933–1945. An Anatomy of Failure* (London 1981)

Deboeck, M., *De Duitse Nachtjacht 1941–1944: Studie van de basis Sint-Truiden in het kader van de luchtoperaties in het Westen* (unpublished graduate thesis at KMS. Brussels 1984)

Derix, J., *Vliegveld Venlo: Met een kroniek van de luchtoorlog in Zuid-Nederland 1941–1944* (Leeuwarden 1990) 2 Vols

Dierich, W., *Kampfgeschwader 'Edelweiss'* (London 1975)

Dierich, W., *Die Verbände der Luftwaffe 1935–1945. Gliederungen und Kurzchroniken* (Stuttgart 1976)

Döring, A., *Mit Re-Vi am nächtligen Himmel. Meine Nachtjagderlebnisse* (unpublished private diary)

Engau, F., *Nachtjäger, Bomber, Wolken und Sterne* (Graz 1993)

Faber, H., (ed.), *Luftwaffe: An analysis by former Luftwaffe Generals* (London 1979)

Foreman, J., *1941: The Turning Point, Parts 1 & 2* (Walton-on-Thames 1993–94)

Frankland, N., *The Bombing Offensive against Germany. Outlines & Perspectives* (1964)

Franks, N.L.R., 'Schnaufer, the Night Ghost of St.Trond', *Aircraft Illustrated* (March 1975)

Freeman, R.A., *Mighty Eighth War Diary* (London 1981)

Galland, A., *Die Ersten und die Letzten* (München 1953)

Girbig, W., *Im Anflug auf die Reichshauptstadt* (Stuttgart 1970)

Girbig, W., *Start im Morgengrauen: Ein Chronik vom Untergang der deutschen Jagdwaffe im Westen 1944–1945* (Stuttgart 1973)

Girbig, W., *...Mit Kurs auf Leuna: Die Luftoffensive gegen die Treibstoffindustrie und der deutsche Abwehreinsatz 1944–1945* (Stuttgart 1980)

Gould, A.H., *Tales from the Sagan Woods* (Bundanoon NSW 1994)

Goulding, J. & Moyes, P., *RAF Bomber Command and its aircraft 1936–1940* (Shepperton 1975)

Green W. & Swanborough, G., 'Heinkel's noctural predator... the He219', *Air Enthusiast 40* (Bromley 1989)

Griehl, M., *Deutsche Nachtjäger im 2. Weltkrieg* (Friedberg 1986)

Griehl, M., *German jets in World War Two* (London 1988)

Gunston, B., *Night Fighters: a Development and Combat History* (Cambridge 1976)

Hadeball, H.M., *Nachtjagd* (München 1968)

Handke, E., *War Diary of time as Bordfunker in NJG1, 1942–45* (unpublished)

Harris, A., *Bomber Offensive* (London 1947)

Hastings, M., *Bomber Command* (London 1987)

Hermann, *The rise and fall of the Luftwaffe* (London 1943)

Held, W. & Nauroth, H., *Die deutsche Nachtjagd: Bildchronik der deutschen Nachtjäger bis 1945* (Stuttgart 1982)

Hentschel, G., *Die Geheimen Konferenzen des General-Luftzeigmeisters. Ausgewählte und Kommentierte Dokumente zur Geschichte der Deutschen Luftrüstung und des Luftkrieges 1942–1944* (Koblenz 1989)

Herrmann, H.J., *Bewegtes Leben* (Stuttgart 1984)

Hinchliffe, P., *The Other Battle: Luftwaffe night aces versus Bomber Command* (Shrewsbury 1996)

Howard Williams, J., *Night Intruder: A personal account of the radar war between the Luftwaffe and the RAF night fighter forces* (London 1976)

Huhn, H., *Private diary on night fighting in II./NJG2 & IV./NJG1* (unpublished)

Irving, D., *Poel van Vuur* (Hoorn 1963)

Irving, D., *The Rise and Fall of the Luftwaffe: The life of Luftwaffe Marshal Erhard Milch* (London 1973)

van Ishoven, A., *Messerschmitt Bf110 At War* (London 1985)

Jablonski, E., *Airwar. An illustrated history of air power in the Second World War* (New York 1979)

Various issues of *Jägerblatt: Offizielles Organ der Gemeinschaft der Jagdflieger e.V*

Jansen, A.A., *Wespennest Leeuwarden* (Baarn 1976–78) 3 Vols

Johnen, W., *Duell unter den Sternen* (Düsseldorf 1956)

Kennett, L., *A history of strategic bombing* (New York 1982)

Kock, W., *Das Kriegstagebuch des Nachtjagdgeschwaders 6* (Wittmund 1996)

Kube, A., *Pour le merité und Hakenkreuz: Hermann Göring im Dritten Reich* (München 1986)

Kurowski, F., *Der Luftkrieg über Deutschland* (Herrsching 1984)

Lee, A., *The German Air Force* (London 1946)

Mason, F.K., *Battle over Britain* (London 1969)

Mason, H.M., *The Luftwaffe 1918–1945* (Wien 1973)

Messenger, C., *Cologne: The First 1000-Bomber Raid* (London 1982)

Middlebrook, M., *The Nuremberg Raid* (London 1973)

Middlebrook, M., *The Battle of Hamburg* (New York 1981)

Middlebrook, M., *The Peenemünde Raid* (London 1982)

Middlebrook, M., *The Bomber Command War Diaries* (Harmondsworth 1985)
Middlebrook, M., *The Berlin Raids* (Harmondsworth 1988)
Kit & Aders, G., *Chasseurs de la nuit Allemands de la derniere guerre* (Paris 1979)
Mitcham, S.W., *Eagles of the Third Reich: Hitlers Luftwaffe* (Shrewsbury 1989)
Möhlenbeck, O. & Leihse, M., *Ferne Nachtjagd* (Stuttgart 1975)
Mosley, L., *The Reich Marshal: A biography of Hermann Goering* (London 1974)
Murray, W., *Luftwaffe: Strategy for defeat* (London 1985)
Niehaus, W., *Die Radarschlacht 1939–1945* (Stuttgart 1977)
Nowarra, H., *Die Ju88 und ihre Folgemuster* (Stuttgart 1978)
Nowarra, H., *'Uhu' – He219 – Best Night Fighter of World War II* (Pennsylvania 1989)
Obermaier, E., *Die Ritterkreuzträger der Luftwaffe 1939–1945. Band I: Jagdflieger* (Mainz 1989)
Overy, R.J., *Goering. The 'Iron Man'* (London 1984)
Palmer, R.R. & Colton, J., *A History of the Modern World* (New York 1983)
Parry, S.W., *Intruders over Britain* (Surbiton 1987)
Pearce, W.G., *The Wing Is Clipped* (unpublished manuscript, Camp Hill 1994)
Petsch, K., *Nachtjagdgleitschiff Togo* (Reutlingen 1988)
Philpott, B., *Fighters defending the Reich* (Bar Hill 1978)
Philpott, B., *Famous Fighter Aces* (Wellingborough 1989)
Piekalkiewicz, J., *The Air War 1939–1945* (New York 1985)
Price, A., *Messerschmitt Bf110 Night Fighters* (Windsor 1967)
Price, A., *Instruments of Darkness: The History of Electronic Warfare* (Los Altos, California 1987)
Pütz, R., *Duel in de Wolken* (Amsterdam 1994)
Rawnsley C.F. & Wright, R., *Night Fighter* (London 1968)
Ries, K., *Luftwaffe photo-report 1919–1945* (Stuttgart 1984)
Robinson, A., *Night Fighter: a History of Night Fighting since 1914* (London 1988)
Roell, W.P., *Laurels for Prinz Wittgenstein* (Keston 1994)
Rumpf, H., *Das war der Bombenkrieg* (Oldenburg 1961)
Scutts, J., *Luftwaffe Night Fighter Units* (London 1978)
Sharp, C.M. & Bowyer, M.J.F., *Mosquito* (London 1971)
Steinhoff, J., *Die Strasse von Messina: Tagebuch des Kommodore* (Bergisch-Gladbach 1979)
Strawson, J., *Hitler as Military Commander* (London 1971)
Streetly, M., *Confound and Destroy* (London 1985)
Taylor, E., *Operation Millennium: 'Bomber' Harris's Raid on Cologne, May 1942* (London 1987)
Terraine, J., *The Right of the Line: The Royal Air Force in the European War 1939–1945* (London 1985)
West, K.S., *The Captive Luftwaffe* (London 1978)
Wood T. & Gunston, B., *Hitler's Luftwaffe* (London 1979)
Wynn H.,& Young, S., *Prelude to Overlord* (Shrewsbury 1983)

National Archives, Washington D.C., U.S.A.
ADIK Report No. 16/1944, Untitled, Interrogation of Jagdführer Holland/Ruhr Area
ADIK Report No. 252(A)/1943, Controlled Night Fighters in the Denmark Area
ADIK Report No. 283/1944, Wilde Sau: Night Defence of Germany by Single-Engined Fighters
ADIK Report No. 337/1945, The German Night Fighter and the RAF Night Bomber
ADIK Report No. 508/1944, German Night Fighter Tactics with Airborne Interception and Homing Equipment
ADIK Report No. 599/1944, German Air Force Night Fighters: RAF Bomber Command Countermeasures and their Influence on German Night Fighter Tactics
ADIK Report No. 620/1944, Upward Firing Armament in German Aircraft
ADIK Report No. 700/1944, German Air Force Night Fighters
ADIK Report No. 338/1945, German Aircraft Reporting Service and Night Fighter Commentary
ADIK Report No. 369/1945, Radio and Radar Equipment in the Luftwaffe VI: Target Homing Aids for Night Fighters
ADIK Report No. 416/1945, The History of German Night Fighting
APWIU (9th Air Force) 21/1945, New Messerschmitt Twin Engined Night Fighter: the German Mosquito
APWIU (2nd TAF) 70/1945, Untitled

Public Record Office, Kew/London, UK
Air 40 126, Junkers aircraft; photographs
Air 40 184, Ju88 C,G,D,H,R,S,T (1942 Jan – 1945 Sept)
Air 40 195, Messerschmitt 110 aircraft (1939 Apr – 1945 Mar)
Air 40 1139, Chain of command in the G.A.F. 1939–1945 (1946)
Air 40 1164, Procedure of German Night Fighter Units in relation to Bomber Command operations since the introduction of Operation Corona: report (1944)
Air 40 1178, ADI(K) periodical progress reports 1–5: interrogation of German Air Force prisoners of war with ADI(K) and of civil scientists and technicians at 'Inkpot' (Wimbledon camp)
Air 40 1207, The German Air Force: first line strength at three-monthly intervals during the European war 1939–1945 (1945 Oct)
Air 40 1386, Germany: report on G.A.F. night fighter system; a post mortem (1946)
Air 40 1395, Germany: G.A.F. night fighters; developments in night fighting and organization and control on the Western front (1945 Jan – Mar)
Air 40 1397, Germany: German night fighter defence interrogation reports (1943 June – 1945 June)
Air 40 1474, G.A.F. interrogations of high ranking officers (1945 July – Sept)
Air 40 1511, Remarks on present day aerial warfare and prospects for the future: translation of German paper dated 16-5-'44 (1945 Aug)
Air 40 1724, The threat of the German Air Force to our planned strategic air operations (1944 Oct)
Air 40 2022, Enemy aircraft: visit to Germany to collect German aircraft for R.A.E.; photographs (1945 May – 1947 May)
Air 40 2047, German Night Fighters: report on establishment and equipment, performance and armament, attacks over Great Britain and North Sea, etc. (1941 Aug)
APWIU 93/1944, Untitled. Report on employment of German night fighters during the Ardennes Offensive

Index

German Personnel

Commonwealth Personnel

Places

Luftwaffe Units

Royal Air Force Units